THE DEADLIEST DECADE

THE DEADLIEST DECADE

How **speed**, **money**, and **technology** transformed **auto racing**

PRESTON LERNER

OCTANE PRESS

Octane Press, Edition 1.0, July 2026
Copyright © 2026 by Preston Lerner

On the cover: Henri Pescarolo threads past the fiery wreck that destroyed Jacky Ickx's Ferrari and Jackie Oliver's BRM during the Spanish Grand Prix in 1970. *Bernard Cahier*
On the front endpapers: Jo Bonnier *barely* avoided disaster at Spa-Francorchamps during the sodden Belgian Grand Prix in 1966. *Revs Institute / Eric della Faille Photograph Collection*
On the rear endpapers: Old meets new as Arturo Merzario drives his Ferrari 312 PB to victory in the Targa Florio in 1972. *Pete Lyons*

All rights reserved. With the exception of quoting brief passages for the purposes of review, no part of this publication may be reproduced without prior written permission from the publisher.

Library of Congress Cataloging-in-Publication Data

Names: Lerner, Preston, 1956- author
Title: The deadliest decade : how speed, money, and technology transformed auto racing / Preston Lerner.
Other titles: How speed, money, and technology transformed auto racing
Description: Edition 1.0. | Austin, Texas : Octane Press, 2026. | Includes bibliographical references and index.
Identifiers: LCCN 2026003987 | ISBN 9781642341843 hardcover | ISBN 9781642342024 epub
Subjects: LCSH: Automobile racing--History--20th century | Automobile racing--Accidents--History--20th century | Automobiles, Racing--Safety measures
Classification: LCC GV1029.15 .L48 2026
LC record available at https://lccn.loc.gov/2026003987

Project Edited by Faith Garcia
Cover Design by Linsey Dodaro
Interior Design by Tom Heffron
Copyedited by Christine Florie

OCTANE PRESS
octanepress.com

Octane Press is based in Austin, Texas.

Printed in China

To Emily. My sun, my moon, my everything.

CONTENTS

Bobby Unser manhandles his ten-year-old Watson-Offy dirt Champ Car like a rodeo cowboy riding a bucking bronco before finishing third in the Hoosier Hundred in 1969. The mile-long dirt track at the Indiana State Fairgrounds was built for horse racing. (The building in the background is a horse barn.) Cable fencing was added to prevent wayward cars from being launched over the low guardrail. *John Mahoney*

INTRODUCTION

Today, professional racing is a commercial enterprise employing thousands of people and generating billions of dollars in revenue. Well, *of course* it is. A professional operation is, by definition, a business valued on the basis of profits versus losses. The curious paradox about racing is that even the avowedly professional variant wasn't always a moneymaking proposition. In fact, from the dawn of the automobile in the late nineteenth century to well into the 1960s, motorsports were just that—sport rather than business. Oh, race promoters got paid. Car builders got paid. The vendors they commissioned got paid. The mechanics they employed got paid—not very much, but more than nothing. Drivers? Well, some of them got paid. Car owners? If they were lucky, they broke even. And, generally speaking, they were fine with that.

Two of the most prominent Indy car entrants of the 1950s and '60s were Al Dean and Lindsey Hopkins Jr. In those less cynical days, they were known approvingly as sportsmen—guys who'd made (or inherited) enough money that they could afford to dabble in racing or big game hunting or competitive yachting. Dean owned Dean Van Lines, one of the biggest moving companies in the country, and as he put it, "I make money moving furniture, and I lose money moving race cars."[1] Hopkins was even wealthier than Dean. In addition to lucrative real estate and banking interests, he was on the board of directors of Coca-Cola. Here was Hopkins's take on racing: "I do this for fun and relaxation. I don't want another business. I've got other places where I make my money. The reason I have race cars is because I don't like horses."[2]

During the 1970s, sportsmen like Dean and Hopkins were squeezed into irrelevance. With the arrival of television coverage and major-league sponsorship, money—serious money—began flowing into the sport, and as it did, racing was transformed from a sport into a business. The effects could be seen in a wide variety of obvious ways—larger teams, slicker liveries, heftier paydays, drivers and owners climbing into ever more stratospheric tax brackets. The injection of capital into motorsports also helped fund groundbreaking advances in aerodynamics, engine design, and tire construction. Speeds skyrocketed even as racetracks remained unchanged. The result, inevitably, was a soaring death toll. It's no coincidence that more people were killed from 1964 to 1973 than during any other ten-year stretch in racing history—nearly 1,400 fatalities across all forms of racing. This includes hundreds of accidents in small, otherwise forgettable and largely forgotten events, many of them run on a grassroots basis. But even at the uppermost levels of motorsports, death was a constant companion.

The Deadliest Decade is an account of this harrowing era. Despite the sensationalistic title, it isn't a chronicle of grisly accidents. Safety is the overarching theme—how and why attitudes changed, and the gradual emergence of an industry devoted to making the sport safer. But it's also a book about how the transition of a sport into a business compelled a radical rethinking of the existential foundation of racing. Yes, designers, drivers, and fans wanted to see cars going faster. But at the same time, sponsors didn't want to watch the drivers they promoted crashing fatally into trees or burning to death on television. The tension between these two contradictory visions redefined the sport in the 1960s and '70s. Ten drivers were killed during Formula 1 race weekends between 1964 and 1973, and each death was considered business as usual. One driver has been killed in F1 races since 1994, and that's widely considered to be one too many. To modern viewers who've grown up with an expectation of almost perfect safety, racing circa 1968 isn't merely ancient history; it's a fundamentally different version of the sport.

Hundreds of books about auto racing in the 1960s and '70s have been published, among them dozens of memoirs written by actual participants. And there are thousands—tens of thousands—of articles that ran in magazines and newspapers back in the day, when racing was covered far more assiduously by the print media precisely because television broadcasts were so spotty and timely information was so hard to come by. Which begs the question: Is there anything new left to say about the subject? In my defense, I interviewed more than one hundred of the survivors from this period, and I reviewed the existing literature from a new perspective. In the course of my research, I unearthed several fresh nuggets while recovering others that had been lost or forgotten.

But offering revelations was never my sole objective. From the beginning, my goal has been to come up with what Einstein called (in a completely different context) a unified field theory to comprehensively explain the revolution that occurred in the motorsports world from the mid-1960s to the mid-1970s. Full disclosure: Einstein never proved his theory, and I might be just as misguided as he was. But I'm convinced that it's impossible to understand how and why safety changed from an afterthought into a guiding principle without also understanding the technological, political, and cultural forces that were at play during this critical era. In this book, I've taken a holistic approach by examining everything from the rise in tobacco sponsorship to the controversy over roll cages, from the invention of fire-retardant uniforms to the development of wings, from adventures in racetrack design to the role played by television. In other words, just about everything you want to know about racing during this uniquely consequential decade.

A few caveats. First, and most important, I suffer from a common American affliction—the inability to speak any language other than English. So I limited my research to English language sources. For better or worse, this means that I focused on American motorsports. But I also covered Formula 1 and endurance racing because their global reach meant that ignoring them would be simply perverse. Second, I didn't include any material about grassroots racing. Yes, the vast majority of racers in the world are amateurs, and they deserve a book of their own. But most of the developments that affected club racing trickled down from the professional ranks, so that's where I concentrated my attention. Third and last, a ton of people generously shared their memories and insights with me, and I'm grateful for all their help. Sometimes, unfortunately, nuances get lost in translation. Any errors that appear in the following pages are entirely my responsibility, and I apologize for them in advance.

During its first decade, before the construction of superspeedways, NASCAR staged most of its stock car races on dirt, and the annual event at Daytona Beach was run on the sand, not the paved high banks of Daytona International Speedway. Here, Joe Weatherly leads teammate—and fellow master of mayhem—Curtis Turner in the convertible division race in 1957. *Revs Institute / Tom Burnside Photograph Collection*

CHAPTER ONE

DEATH OF A CLOWN

They called Joe Weatherly the Clown Prince of Stock Car Racing. He was a stubby imp from Roanoke, Virginia, with a moon-shaped, ever-smiling face marred by a long, angry scar that made him look like a cherub who'd lost a bar fight. "Little Joe" wore his chestnut hair in a curly pompadour, and he was partial to wild print shirts and saddle shoes. His face turned red when he laughed, which was often because he thought just about everything was funny, including his many crashes. (The only exceptions were snakes, which terrified him, and traditional racing superstitions such as avoiding peanuts and the color green.) He was sometimes called "Bebop" because he spoke even faster than he drove. When he got excited, he couldn't spit the sentences out fast enough, and the words piled up like crashed race cars stuffed in the sandy gulley marking the perimeter of the South Turn of the old Daytona Beach and Road Course. On occasion, his syntax was so mangled and his Tidewater patois so inscrutable that close friends had to be called over to translate postrace interviews for out-of-town reporters.

Weatherly adored practical jokes. Not just plastic snakes and joy buzzers but elaborate pranks, like sauntering through the garage and pilfering keys from the ignitions of race cars so they couldn't be started when the race was supposed to begin. His favorite prop was a small wooden box that was painted black and topped with wire mesh. Inside, he claimed, was an African—sometimes Chinese—mongoose. "It's the fastest goddamn thing on earth," he would say. "It'll eat your damn flesh so fast, your face'll be picked clean before you even know your skin is gone."[1] He'd poke inside the box with a stick to agitate the mongoose, while his victims peered in for a closer look. Then, suddenly, he'd press a button, the top would swing open, and a long, spring-loaded foxtail would pop out. Women would shriek, men would run, and Weatherly would cackle gleefully while his face turned crimson.

Weatherly's most notorious escapades unfolded while he was playing Robin to Curtis Turner's Batman. Turner was NASCAR's first superstar—a rugged, charismatic, larger-than-life character who abided by no rules other than the ones he wrote himself. Tall and honey-voiced, Turner was a matinee idol whom women wanted to bed and men wanted to be. He'd been born in the Blue Ridge Mountains of southwestern Virginia, the son of a bootlegger, and he made his first moonshine run when he was ten. Many years later, he demonstrated a bootlegger's turn—a high-speed one-eighty—for a journalist on a freeway in Los Angeles. Not unexpectedly, this captured the attention of a California Highway Patrol trooper. To prove that the maneuver was perfectly safe, Turner demonstrated it again—with the trooper riding shotgun.

Turner and Weatherly met in 1951 at a modified race at Victory Stadium, a makeshift quarter-mile oval stuffed between football grandstands near Roanoke. NASCAR had been sanctioning stock car races for only three years, but Turner was already a legend on the red clay of the Southern Piedmont. Weatherly, though new to race cars, had ridden Harley-Davidsons to three American Motorcycle Association nationals over the previous three years, and those races were won only by the toughest of the tough. The two of them were a happily mismatched set with an insatiable appetite for mayhem and hilarity. "You could go to a race with Curtis Turner and Joe Weatherly, and you never knew what the Christ was gonna happen," Jacque Passino, who had the sometimes-dubious pleasure of employing them while he was running Ford Motor Company's stock car operation, complained later.[2]

Turner was known as "Pops" because that's what he called every man he met, whether he knew his name or not. Women, meanwhile, were "doll babies," and as far as he was concerned, they were all fair game.[3] Although Weatherly had a petite girlfriend he called "Short Track," he was Turner's equal on the hound dog front. Pops and Little Joe maintained a "party pad"[4]—a green wood-frame house behind Robinson's Bar in Daytona Beach—where they entertained as many doll babies as possible. Between conquests, they liked to stay "tuned" with a bottomless supply of Canadian Club and Coke.[5] To keep the guests lubricated, Weatherly premixed cocktails in a fire extinguisher and served them in giant cups "so you don't have to make as many pit stops."[6] Engineering sorcerer Smokey Yunick remembered a series of epic bacchanals at the party pad. "The Romans had a word for it: orgy," he wrote. "It was an unhurried drinking party that started at 9:00 pm, and usually ended at 5:00 am, each wilder than the last."[7] Often as not, the festivities ground to a reluctant halt only when the cops arrived to shut things down. "Don't worry about nothing," Turner would announce. "Another party's starting in about fifteen minutes."[8]

Weatherly and Turner were perfect emblems of NASCAR's formative years during the 1940s and '50s, when stock car racing had more in common with a traveling carnival than the well-polished marketing powerhouse it's become. No family was more emblematic of the sport's roots than the Fabulous Flocks, where even the women were daredevils. (One sister raced while another was a wing walker.) The eldest son, Carl, went into the moonshine business in Atlanta with his uncle, Peachtree Williams. His brother Bob parlayed what he learned "trippin' whiskey"—transporting illegal liquor in high-performance street cars—into a career as one of NASCAR's first stars. Next came Fonty Flock, a flamboyant showman with an Errol Flynn–style mustache who won the Southern 500 at Darlington in 1952 while wearing argyle socks and what he referred to as "Bamooda shorts." After taking the checkered flag, he parked his car on the front straight, clambered onto the hood, and led the crowd in a rousing rendition of "Dixie." His youngest brother, Tim, not to be outdone, won a one-hundred-mile Grand National race at Hickory while a monkey named Jocko Flocko—who wore a bespoke driving suit with his name embroidered on the chest and a hole for his tail—rode in the passenger seat of his Hudson Hornet.

"Stock car racing was a format whereby everyone started even, next to no education and no money," Yunick wrote in *Best Damn Garage in Town*, his wonderfully profane and scandalously honest memoir of his efforts to transform cheating from a sordid misdemeanor into an esoteric science. "A racer was a social outcast, no chance for credit, no insurance, not wanted in hotels, social status just a little better than an ex-con or a 'mon-backer.' In spite of all the drawbacks, to me, it was still a thrill on race day morning to walk into the pits, pull up my pants, look around and say, All right, you sons-of-bitches . . . let's have a race."[9]

Today, NASCAR is the eight-hundred-pound gorilla of American motorsports—the biggest, baddest, most popular, and most profitable form of racing in the country by such a huge margin that no other series is even visible in its rearview mirror. But back in 1964, stock car racing was still derided as a glorified thrill show staged for liquored-up good ol' boys waving Confederate flags. In those days, single-seat open-wheel thoroughbreds were the royalty of American motorsports, and the Indianapolis 500 was the crown jewel. While Indy cars had been racing at the internationally renowned Brickyard since 1909, NASCAR dated back only to 1947, when a moderately successful race-car-driver-turned-enterprising-promoter named Bill France convened a meeting at the Streamline Hotel in Daytona Beach that's now remembered as the Constitutional Convention of stock car racing. "I believe stock car racing can become a nationally recognized sport," he declared.[10] And thanks largely to his own tireless efforts, he turned out to be correct.

According to conventional wisdom circa 2025, France was the Moses who led stock car racing out of the motorsports wilderness to a promised land larded with milk and honey—and rivers flowing with billions of dollars in sponsorship money. Before he founded NASCAR, so the story goes, stock cars were raced for table scraps by moonlighting moonshine runners at makeshift racetracks run by promoters who were just as likely to skip town with the purse as they were to pay out a few paltry dollars in prize money. It was France, his hagiographers say, who created order out of chaos, and without his leadership, stock car racing never would have been anything more than a sideshow attraction.

Bill France at Dover Speedway, a long-defunct half-mile dirt oval in New Jersey, not to be confused with the modern Dover Motor Speedway in Delaware. This photo was probably shot in 1948, barely three months after France spearheaded the creation of NASCAR. Thanks to his six-foot, five-inch stature and commanding presence, France was known fondly—and not so fondly—as "Big Bill." *Revs Institute / Bruce R. Craig Photograph Collection*

Looking back on the sport from a vantage point in the 1970s, Tim Flock told author Sylvia Wilkinson, "In the mid-'30s, in a cow pasture in Georgia, that's where racing began. We didn't have no tickets, no safety equipment, no fences, no nothing. Just a bunch of these bootleggers who'd been arguing all week about who had the fastest car would get together to prove it. True story. This happened long before organized stock car racing begun. Thirty or forty of these bootleggers showed up in this cow pasture at Stockbridge, which was about fifteen miles outside Atlanta. They made a track by running around and digging their wheels in the ground in about a half-mile circle. These guys would run and bet against their own cars, betting who had the fastest car. That night they'd be hauling liquor in the same car. About fifty people saw this dust cloud and came up trying to see what was causing it. Next time, a hundred would show up. Then three or four hundred would show up. And they was all free. Then the guys—not me, this was a little early for me, I was too young to be driving—they got these old football helmets, and they would go around the fences and people would put nickels and dimes and quarters in the helmet, and that was all they would charge then. And they took this and put it in the purse along with the bets. Pretty soon, they raced every Sunday. Five and six thousand people started showing up. Then Bill France came along and he started putting up fences, the whole bit. He made stock car racing what it is today."[11]

Like most enduring creation myths, this one works on several levels. It's easy to understand, and it's so breezy and engaging that it seems churlish to question the implausible details. Also, Flock's tale dramatizes some essential elements of what actually happened in the 1930s and '40s, so it's useful as a sort of grade school primer. But as is all too often the case, the truth is a lot more complicated than the fable.

Barely a decade after the automobile was popularized, there was a split between cars designed for the road and those built specifically for racing. The first events open only to the former while barring the latter were the aptly named Savannah Stock Car Races of 1908. Still, the modern conception of stock car racing—competition between modified versions of the prosaic machines owned by Mr. and Mrs. John Q. Public—presupposed the existence of automobiles that were mass-market commodities. So it's fair to say that stock car racing really didn't take shape until the Model T Ford started rolling off an assembly line in Dearborn in 1908. By the time production ceased in 1927, more than fifteen million Tin Lizzies had been built, and a vibrant aftermarket industry offering go-fast parts had sprung up to cater to devotees of high performance.

In 1932, Ford solidified its place as the foundation of the do-it-yourself racing industry by introducing the flathead V-8. At the time, elegant straight-8 engines were customary in luxury automobiles such as Duesenbergs and Auburns, and a handful of models from Lincoln and Packard featured V-12s. Cadillac even offered a V-16 through the entirety of the Depression. But the flathead Ford was the first eight-cylinder engine to be sold in a high-volume vehicle, and it jump-started what's now known as the hot rod movement. When the first major-league stock car race was staged in 1933 in Elgin, Illinois, Ford V-8s swept the first seven places, and the fastest one was timed at 100.3 miles per hour on the front straight, which was pretty impressive motoring for an economy car driven straight off the showroom floor. But the Elgin National Road Races were a one-and-done affair. The history of professional stock car racing really began three years later at Daytona Beach. This was only fitting since, other than Indianapolis, Daytona Beach was the closest thing the United States had to a motorsports capital.

At low tide, the level, hard-packed white sand of the eastern shore of Florida provided an optimal surface for high-speed blasts alongside the Atlantic Ocean. In 1903, a three-mile stretch was marked off between Ormond Beach and Daytona Beach for a pioneering match race between the Winton Bullet and the Olds Pirate. Three years later, a Stanley Steamer earned the first land-speed record, at 127.659 mph, set in the United States. Starting in 1927, Daytona Beach became an annual destination for aspirants to the title of Fastest Man on Earth. In 1936, with no land-speed-record attempts scheduled, the city of Daytona Beach decided to drum up tourism by promoting a race. Local racer Sig Haugdahl laid out a rectangular 3.2-mile course near the ocean. Atlantic Avenue, which doubled as State Highway A1A, served as the front straight and a parallel stretch of the beach as the backstraight. Arcing parabolas cut through the sand dunes formed the North and South Turns. Entries were limited to street-legal cars built in 1935 and 1936. Indy 500 winner Wild Bill Cummings was fastest in a supercharged Auburn, and Milton Marion won the race—which ended early when the tide rolled in—in a flathead-powered Ford. But the most important name in the results was the man who finished fifth.

William Henry Getty France had been born in Washington, DC, in 1909, the son of a bank clerk with an optimistic streak. (His father bestowed the name "Getty" on his son in the hope that it would bring him a financial windfall.) As a teenager, France worked on Model Ts and watched exotic Millers and Duesenbergs scream around the high-banked board track in Laurel, Maryland. As an adult, he found work as a mechanic and raced when he could. By this time, he was known as "Big Bill" in honor of his imposing six-foot, five-inch frame and equally commanding presence. In 1934, he decided to move to Florida. "I just started thinking that if I was going to have to work all the time fixing automobiles, I might as well fix them where it wasn't snowing," he said.[12] He loaded his tools and other belongings in a trailer, hooked it to his Hupmobile, and headed south with his wife, young son, and twenty-five dollars in cash. When they reached Daytona Beach, France stopped for a swim in the Atlantic. It felt so good that he decided to stay put.

After working as a mechanic, France opened a gas station on Main Street near Halifax Avenue that became a go-to spot for out-of-town racers. By 1936, he was so well established that he was entrusted with preparing what turned out to be the race-winning Ford for the inaugural beach race. The next year, he copromoted the beach race with Haugdahl, but nonpaying, walk-in spectators sucked up all the profits. After Haugdahl bailed, France partnered with Charlie Reese, the owner of Charlie's Grill and Hi-Hat Club on Seabreeze Boulevard, where cocktails flowed to the accompaniment of big band jazz. Together, they promoted a race over Labor Day weekend. By doubling ticket prices and adding "Careful – Rattlesnake"[13] signs to discourage freeloaders from sneaking in through the palmetto trees, France managed to clear $2,000. The future of racing at Daytona Beach was assured, and France had found his life's work.

Here's where it's worth hitting pause to emphasize a crucial point: Bill France didn't invent stock car racing. Nor did he singularly popularize stock car racing. Nor was he the first promoter to recognize the possibilities of stock car racing. At bullrings and fairgrounds tracks all over the country, promoters staged races featuring American cars of various vintages, some events governed by detailed rules and others organized on a more or less run-what-you-brung basis. These races were popular with entrants because the cars were cheap and with fans because they drove coupes like the Fords, Chevys, Hudsons, and whatnot they saw beating and banging on the track. But it was in the South—at least, a very specific part of it—that stock car racing put down roots strong enough to survive the Great Depression and thrive into the twenty-first century.

The key was red clay, a magical surface that's slippery enough to allow cars to slide while providing enough grip so they can hook up in the corners. Closer to the Appalachians, the soil is too rocky for dirt track racing. Closer to the ocean, it's too sandy and porous. Farther south, there's mostly white clay, which dries hard and breaks up into potholes the size of lunar craters. But stock car racing found fertile soil in a sharply delineated and surprisingly compact area known as the Southern Piedmont. A plateau nestled between the Appalachian Mountains to the west and the Atlantic lowlands to the east, the Piedmont cuts a narrow swath from Virginia, through the Carolinas and Georgia, and ends in Alabama. Even as tracks popped up in big cities like Richmond in the northeast, Atlanta in the southwest, and Charlotte in the center, ramshackle ovals spread like kudzu near small towns such as Rocky Mount, Easley, and Thomaston.

The other factor the region had going for it was moonshine—untaxed liquor brewed by bootleggers in illegal stills hidden in hollows and foothills. To get white lightning to market, bootleggers hired hot shoes driving pedestrian-looking sedans with heavy-duty springs and hopped-up engines to outrun the dreaded federal agents known as "revenooers." Thunder Road turned out to be an ideal training ground for would-be racers. The moonshine industry also created a class of bootleggers wealthy enough to commission race cars and sponsor race teams. The most audacious liquor tycoons even built their own racetracks.

France had spent the war years meditating on his future—and the future of stock car racing. Barely two months after Japan surrendered, he rented the track at the Southern States Fairgrounds in Charlotte to promote an event of his own. After staging a beach race at Daytona Beach the next spring, he formed the National Championship Stock Car Circuit and promoted several events that drew huge crowds. He wrote his own rules, lined up cars and drivers, and ran ads in the trade papers billing himself as the "Largest Operator of Stock Car Racing Throughout the Country."[14] This was what might charitably be called hyperbole; in fact, there were several bigger and better-established promoters plying the same territory. When he sought the sanction of the American Automobile Association (AAA)—then the gold standard in American motorsports—the old-boy network shined him on. "We're only interested in big races," he was told.[15] Translation: Take a hike, small fry.

As it turned out, France didn't need the AAA. By 1947, his burgeoning empire had expanded to the point that he flew from race to race in a sleek Ryan Navion. Two weeks before Christmas, he invited a group of promoters, track owners, car owners, drivers, and mechanics to join him at the Streamline Hotel, near the Daytona Beach and Road Course. The goal, he said, was "to set up a complete organization which will act as a guide to stock car racing throughout the United States."[16] Thirty-five men attended at least one of the three sessions in the Ebony Lounge, on the roof of the white-with-lime-green-trim Art Deco landmark overlooking Highway A1A. But France spoke with the loudest and clearest voice. "We don't know how big this can be if it's handled properly," he said, "and neither does anybody else here."[17]

On February 21, 1948, the charter establishing the National Association for Stock Car Racing was signed. Ace mechanic Red Vogt came up with the name, but France retained most of the shares himself and became NASCAR's de facto dictator. The first race under NASCAR sanction was run on February 15, 1948, even before the charter had been signed, on a new 2.2-mile beach course at Daytona Beach. The event drew a record sixty-two entries competing for a $3,000 purse. Official attendance was fourteen thousand. Fonty Flock led early before losing a wheel and crashing into a patch of palmettos. Red Byron, who raced with his left foot braced to the clutch because his leg had been shredded by shrapnel while serving as a flight engineer in a B-24 during World War II, won the race—his third Daytona Beach victory in a row. Every one of the top ten finishers was in a 1939 Ford. And that was a problem.

Because automobile production had stopped during the war, there weren't many new cars available in the early postwar era, which is why most of the race cars were modified versions of prewar models. But from the beginning, France understood that the key to making stock car racing a success was featuring actual stock cars. "I think it was important that we chose the American car to be our race car. In stock car racing the spectators have to have a rooting interest," he explained later. "One of the strongest factors in stock car racing's success has been the way that plain, ordinary working people can associate with them. People in the stands would give drivers parts right off their own cars if they needed them."[18]

On June 19, 1949, NASCAR sanctioned its first Strictly Stock race at Charlotte Speedway. Entries were limited to cars built from 1946 onward, "without any modification." Attendance—thirteen thousand paid—was so strong that fans shut down Wilkinson Boulevard, and at least one thousand of them didn't make it into the track. The thirty-three starters included nine makes: Ford, Lincoln, Hudson, Oldsmobile, Mercury, Buick, Kaiser, Chrysler, and Cadillac. Less than a month later, France promoted a second Strictly Stock event at Daytona Beach, and a month after that, he replaced a scheduled modified field with Strictly Stock cars that drew seventeen thousand "screaming"[19] fans to Occoneechee Speedway in Hillsborough. About twenty thousand fans attended the next Strictly Stock event, at Langhorne, and a non-NASCAR Strictly Stock race at Lakewood Speedway attracted 33,452 spectators. France got the message. In 1950, Strictly Stock was renamed Grand National and repositioned as NASCAR's premier division.

France pushed the win-on-Sunday, sell-on-Monday business model to entice automakers to NASCAR. Hudson was the first automaker to sponsor a factory team, and the step-down Hornet became the sport's first champion. Other manufacturers soon followed, and when the Detroit horsepower wars erupted in the early 1960s, NASCAR became its biggest and bloodiest battleground. In racing, money begets speed, and with automakers spending money at a Homeric clip, speeds took off. By this time, France had built Daytona International Speedway with high banks to humble the Indianapolis Motor Speedway. Here, the pole speed climbed from 140.121 mph at the first race in 1959 to 174.91 mph in 1964. The year after Daytona debuted, 1.5-mile speedways opened in Charlotte and Atlanta. By 1964, twice as many races were run on pavement as on the dirt tracks that had nurtured NASCAR's development. Suddenly, drivers had to deal with the consequences of ramming into concrete barriers at 120-plus mph instead of rolling lazily on red clay at half that speed, and safety standards hadn't kept pace with the progress in performance. "A lot of people died about that time," car builder Banjo Matthews said darkly, a decade after the fact. "It was the transition time I was talking about, going from homemade things to the cars we have today."[20]

NASCAR regulations demanded the use of the stock frame, so stock cars were saddled with willowy chassis designed to be used on streets and highways rather than superspeedways. There were no fire-suppression systems. Fuel cells were illegal. Although a roll cage surrounded the cockpit, the drivers themselves were largely unprotected. Seat belts were required, but shoulder harnesses were optional. Window nets were unheard of. Driver gear was totally unregulated. (Richard Petty raced in work boots until he retired in 1992, and Dale Earnhardt was wearing

In 1959, NASCAR's premier race moved to Daytona International Speedway. During the Daytona 500 in 1961, Junior Johnson, later anointed "The Last American Hero" by Tom Wolfe in a celebrated article in *Esquire*, leads Paul Goldsmith and the rest of the field. Unlike modern stock cars, these machines look recognizably like the Pontiacs, Fords, and Chevys that spawned them. *Revs Institute / Bruce R. Craig Photograph Collection*

an open-face helmet when he was killed in 2001.) An increasingly bitter war between Firestone and Goodyear stressed tires to the point that drivers started calling them "maypops."

There was a sense of impending disaster going into the 1964 season. "I could see what was coming," Jack Smith said.[21] Despite winning five Grand National races in 1962, he ran only half the schedule the next year and quit after four races in 1964. "I had said three months before my contract runs out, 'Next year will be the roughest year that's ever been in racing history.' My wife says, 'Why?' And I explained to her why, that everybody's going to be running on the ragged edges. . . . Real ragged edges." Or as Buck Baker put it, "It's reached the point at the superspeedways where it's a relief when a race ends and you're okay, no matter how you finished. Other drivers I've talked to say they feel the same way. It's become a pretty jumpy game."[22]

The first big race of 1964 was at Riverside International Raceway, way the hell out in Southern California. Although France was eager to extend NASCAR's sphere of influence to the West Coast, most of the teams weren't thrilled about making the grueling tow to the Los Angeles area. The other knock on Riverside was that it was a road course rather than an oval like the ones the stock car drivers were accustomed to. This meant that they had to turn right as well as left, plus deal with upshifting, downshifting, and working the brakes. Overweight, undertired, and saddled with woeful drum brakes, the cars that looked so purposeful on superspeedways were ludicrously unsuited to Riverside. The front ends plowed, and the rear ends danced drunkenly. Once the tail started to wag, it usually led to a tank slapper, and the car would swing like a pendulum until swapping ends. The Esses, a series of fast, linked bends forcing cars to transition quickly from side to side, were a particular challenge, and cars spun on them early and often. Sports car ace Ken Miles, who probably had more laps at Riverside than anybody, rolled his car in the Esses and said sayonara to stock car racing. Another local driver crashed so violently in Turn One that he was knocked out.

One driver who wasn't at Riverside was Curtis Turner, who'd gone broke building Charlotte Motor Speedway. Even more problematic, he'd gotten crossways with France over his quixotic efforts to unionize stock car drivers under the Teamsters banner. France banned Turner, and Pops was reduced to running on outlaw tracks and a handful of races on lesser circuits. But even as the sun was setting on Turner's career, his old running mate, Joe Weatherly, was enjoying an improbable Indian summer. In 1962, driving a Pontiac for decorated D-Day veteran Bud Moore, Weatherly won nine races en route to his first Grand National championship. The next year, Moore couldn't commit to the full schedule because he was short on money. Weatherly ended up running fifty-five races for nine different owners. But the results were the same as in 1962, and he wrapped up his second consecutive title.

Weatherly was at Riverside in a new 1964 Mercury Marauder owned by Moore and prepped by West Coast racing stalwart Bill Stroppe. As usual, the car was painted scarlet red, with a black hood, hardtop, and rear deck, and carrying his customary No. 8. "That way fans can't tell if I'm on my wheels or on my top," Weatherly joked.[23] Unlike the purpose-built cars that race in the modern Cup series, Grand National machines looked remarkably similar to street cars—which, in fact, they were, with their chrome bumpers, tape-covered headlights, and exposed door handles. None of them carried the garish sponsorship signage that's now typical not only in NASCAR but in virtually every other form of racing. Aside from small decals from oil companies and parts manufacturers, the only obvious sponsors were local car dealers like English Motors, Lafayette Ford, and Bristol Lincoln-Mercury, in Weatherly's case.

Although Weatherly had no interest in Indy cars, which he dismissed as "big cucumbers with hay-raking wheels," he insisted that he was as comfortable at Riverside as he was at Winston-Salem. "'Tain't a bit different than driving on the country roads back home," he said. "I like bouncing over all kinds of roads. I don't mind turning left and right."[24] He qualified a lowly sixteenth, second-slowest of the drivers who posted lap times. (After rain curtailed qualifying, the remaining twenty-seven drivers were gridded on the basis of when they'd posted their entry fees.) Nevertheless, he was relaxed enough before the race to conduct an interview with Chris Economaki, editor of *National Speed Sport News*. Economaki wanted to know why Weatherly preferred to "flap around"—Weatherly's words—in the cockpit rather than use the shoulder harnesses worn by most of the other drivers. "I don't use a shoulder harness because it would snap your neck in a quick stop," Weatherly said. "My way of thinking is that I move around so much that I feel it's a hazard."[25] Prophetic words.

Strong promotion by *Motor Trend* and aggressive coverage by local newspapers, radio outlets, and television stations pumped up interest in the race. Fans started arriving the night before the race despite damp weather, and there was a line of people waiting to get in when the gates opened at 7 a.m. Sunday. Official attendance was close to sixty thousand. Because the track was still slick, the race started under caution, and pole-sitter Fred Lorenzen was credited with leading the first seven laps. But as soon as the green flag flew, Richard Petty muscled past in his blue Plymouth. Before long, a raucous, multicolored conga line of stock cars was snaking around the circuit, many of them sideways or dirt-tracking through dusty runoff areas.

Back in mid-pack, Weatherly lost second gear almost immediately, and his transmission started to disintegrate. On lap fifteen, there was another long caution to clean up the mess caused when a local driver barrel-rolled into a berm. Weatherly ducked into the pits, where Moore expected him to park the car. "Let's change the transmission," Weatherly said. When Moore objected, Weatherly snapped, "Put a transmission in it."[26] By the time Moore and the crew had swapped in a new gearbox, Weatherly was twenty laps behind the leader.

By two-thirds distance, road-race ringer Dan Gurney had grabbed the lead and disappeared from the field. But even though he was way behind, Weatherly was still pushing hard. Flat-out in fourth gear, he rumbled across the start-finish line to begin his eighty-seventh lap. He crested a mild rise and whistled through the left-hander at the end of the front straight. Then there was a sweeping right before he bent his car into the Esses, a fast series of switchbacks that gradually tightened up, forcing the driver to bleed off speed even as he maintained momentum. Weatherly drifted to the left, then right, then left again, the graceful attitude of his Ford belying all the work he was doing inside the cockpit, constantly feathering the throttle and sawing at the steering wheel to keep the car barely under control. It all went wrong as he approached Turn Six, the slowest corner on the track.

When Weatherly stomped on the brakes, the pedal went to the floor and smoke belched out from underneath the chassis. Carrying far too much speed to make the right-hander, he drove his Ford up on the dirt-and-grass berm and tried to straight-line the corner. The Ford bounded over the apex and crashed at a forty-five-degree angle into the steel boiler plate sheathing the three-strand guardrail. The hit was hard enough to pop the windshield out of its frame and shower the fans sitting in the nearby bleachers with broken glass. After the initial impact, the car pivoted on the left-front fender and smacked the barrier broadside. The collision left a macabre outline of the Ford on the boiler plate. While the race continued, Weatherly was laid out on a stretcher with his saddle shoes visible and his left arm dangling casually off the gurney, as if he'd fallen asleep while lounging on a hammock. "I don't know why that struck me as so pathetic, but it did," Stroppe said. "There was Joe, dying, wearing them damn shoes. It really got to me. He looked like a little boy."[27]

Moore blamed brake failure for the accident. Although the first news reports said that Weatherly's head had struck the wall and smashed his skull, an autopsy found that he died of massive internal and head injuries. In photos of the wreck, Weatherly's body can be seen bending sharply at the waist and leaning far forward and to the left. While it's possible that his head struck the roll cage or another solid object inside the cockpit, it seems likely that he died from a basal skull fracture caused when his head snapped forward after the abrupt stop.

Weatherly was the first driver to be killed in a Grand National race since Bobby Myers died in the Southern 500 in 1957. His fatal accident at Riverside was the first act in what turned out to be a horror show worthy of a Wes Craven production. Two more NASCAR drivers lost their lives before the 1964 season was over, and three were killed in 1965. Four more would die by 1973, by which time Grand National had been superseded by Winston Cup, and stock car racing was poised to ascend onto the national stage.

Carnage wasn't unique to NASCAR. Similar tragedies were unfolding in every form of racing, from Indy cars to drag racing, Formula 1 to sprint cars, exotic endurance prototypes to humdrum Sports Car Club of America (SCCA) sports cars. Nearly 1,400 people would be killed at racetracks across the world during the next ten years, mostly drivers but also mechanics, race officials, spectators, and supremely unlucky passersby. The causes of death were easy to identify, but understanding *why* these accidents were suddenly occurring with increasing regularity was a trickier proposition. It's only now, looking back with the benefit of a half-century of retrospection, that we can clearly see the interplay of the powerful structural forces that were at play.

Money was the biggest factor. Tens of millions of dollars began flooding into a sport that had always been a commercial backwater. This was the era when mainstream automobile manufacturers started pumping vast amounts of capital and engineering resources into

Like Eddie Sachs in the Indy car world, Joe Weatherly fashioned himself as the clown prince of NASCAR. But he was deadly serious behind the wheel of his race cars, which helped him win back-to-back Grand National championships in 1962 and 1963. Shortly before the ill-fated Motor Trend 500 at Riverside International Raceway in 1964, he looks back from the cockpit of his Bud Moore–owned, Bill Stroppe–prepared Mercury. *Ford Motor Company*

racing. It was also the period when the tire wars prompted Goodyear and Firestone to spend ungodly sums sponsoring teams and drivers as well as developing new rubber compounds and tire architecture. Most important of all was the explosive growth of sponsorship, which burst out of the automotive ghetto to embrace Fortune 500 companies. By the early 1970s, tobacco giants such as Marlboro, Winston, L&M, and John Player were sponsoring not only individual teams and drivers but entire series.

All of this money led to an unprecedented investment in R&D, and what followed was the most rapid development of technology seen during any ten-year period since the formative years in the life of the automobile. Wings became a thing, and "downforce" entered the motorsports lexicon. Tires grew bigger and fatter and wider and stickier until treads were eliminated altogether, creating the racing slick that's now ubiquitous. Cornering speeds rose to levels unimaginable even a decade earlier, ratcheting up the pressure on chassis, suspension components, and, most critical of all, the drivers charged with keeping the shiny side up.

More money meant more professionalism, which meant stiffer competition and greater pressure to produce the results necessary to win the prize money and secure the sponsorships that kept the machine humming. Money also translated into power—horsepower, that is, scads of it. Engines grew and grew, from five liters to six and seven liters and then to more than eight liters. Turbochargers allowed old-school Offys and exotic Porsche flat-12s to make more than 1,000 horsepower. The pole speed at the Indianapolis 500 jumped by 26 mph in two years. At Le Mans, terminal velocity on the Mulsanne Straight went from 180 or so mph in 1963 to nearly 240 mph in 1971. In 1973, at Spa-Francorchamps, Jacky Ickx drove a lap in a Ferrari prototype at a mind-boggling average speed of 163.68 mph. That's an *average* speed of 163.68 mph, despite a first-gear hairpin, and it was faster than the *top* speed Graham Hill had seen a decade earlier in the Belgian Grand Prix.

Speeds were skyrocketing while the race circuits remained essentially unchanged. The results weren't predictable so much as they were inevitable: There were more crashes than ever, more serious injuries, more fatalities. Making matters even worse, the accidents were being seen by more people, thanks to television. Up until the 1960s, races were watched only by spectators who attended the events in person. With the emergence of television, the audience now numbered in the millions. But broadening the reach of the sport was something of a double-edged sword. On one hand, it attracted sponsors who were eager to showcase their products to as many potential consumers as possible. On the other hand, footage of drivers being crushed to death wasn't the type of advertising they had in mind.

By the late 1960s, thanks to a variety of factors and a handful of true believers, concerns about safety finally, belatedly, prompted serious action to make cars and racetracks less dangerous. Although the movement gained strength during the '70s and '80s, a generation would pass before the fatal accidents of Ayrton Senna in 1994 and Dale Earnhardt seven years later sparked a stem-to-stern reappraisal of what would and would not be tolerated on the racetrack. Today, thanks to the metamorphosis triggered by the high-profile deaths of those two transcendent superstars, there is a zero-tolerance attitude toward death in racing.

This outlook would have been incomprehensible in 1964. Fatalities were an inescapable fact of auto racing, even when the wrecks didn't seem especially bad. "He wasn't doing but about 60 mph when he got killed," Turner said plaintively after hearing the news about Weatherly. "I was at Indy listening to the race, and I couldn't hardly believe it. He'd crashed before at 160 and nothing had happened. But when the car hit, it threw his head out the window, and his head hit the wall. Car wasn't tore up much. Ol' Joe was just about getting ready to quit racing. He told me he planned to quit pretty soon." Turner paused. "Damn. There's 40 ways that little bastard could have made a living, but I don't guess he'd of been happy doing anything else."[28]

An overflow crowd attended Weatherly's funeral while hundreds of mourners stood outside, listening to the service on a public-address system erected for the occasion. Weatherly was buried in Forest Lawn Cemetery in Norfolk, Virginia. Engraved on his gravestone was a stone course map of the Riverside circuit, with an X marking the spot where he crashed.

The date was January 24, 1964. Racing's deadliest decade had just begun.

It's business as usual after Chet Gardner rolled his Miller at Legion Ascot Speedway in 1932. Dubbed "King of the Money Drivers," Gardner survived this wreck only to be killed in another one six years later. During its thirteen-year reign of terror, Legion Ascot was the site of accidents that claimed the lives of twenty drivers, one riding mechanic, two spectators, and a policeman. *Revs Institute / Bruce R. Craig Photograph Collection*

CHAPTER TWO

LIVE AND LET DIE

"There are three sports. Bullfighting, motor racing, mountain climbing. All the rest are recreations."

What a great quote, right? The idea is simple and compelling. If you drop a pass in football or strike out in baseball, it might cost you the game and maybe even your career. But making a big mistake in racing might put you into a wall and maybe even into a morgue. Ergo, motorsports are *by their very nature* more riveting than stick-and-ball games. The stakes are higher; the pot is always no limit. We're not talking about the difference between merely winning and losing. In the world of racing, we're talking about life and death.

The quote sounds like something Ernest Hemingway might have said or written, which is why dozens of articles have attributed it to him. Alas, one of racing's favorite aphorisms was actually coined by automotive journalist Ken Purdy in 1957 in a long-forgotten piece of short fiction in *The Saturday Evening Post*. And from our vantage point in 2026, these words no longer make any sense. Thanks to a half-century of advances—better driver gear, stronger cars, safer tracks, more responsive medical teams—fatal accidents have largely been eliminated from racing. Even when a car explodes after cannoning into a SAFER Barrier at 175 miles per hour, we expect the driver to hop out of the cockpit with his thumbs up. On those unthinkable occasions when somebody is killed, a period of soul-searching and finger-pointing usually leads to radical changes on the ground—revamped racetrack design after Ayrton Senna died at Imola in 1994, mandatory HANS devices after Dale Earnhardt's fatal wreck at Daytona in 2001, the IndyCar aeroscreen after debris pierced Justin Wilson's helmet at Pocono is 2015. These days, racing seems closer to video games than bullfighting and mountain climbing.

It wasn't always so. For three-quarters of a century after its birth, racing was a blood sport. Death wasn't a rare anomaly, like a four-leaf clover or a triple bogey. It was par for the course, and anybody who regularly attended races back then can remember the mournful scenes that were once commonplace from coast to coast and continent to continent—race engines suddenly stilled, the wail of sirens, emergency lights flashing, then the racetrack enveloped in ominous silence as everybody waited anxiously for an announcement over the PA system. In those days, the specter of death hung over the sport like a dark cloud always poised to blot out the sun.

Looking through the blemish-free lens of hindsight, it seems like a miracle that there were no fatal accidents during the world's first automotive competition, staged on public thoroughfares between Paris and Rouen in 1894. At the time, nobody understood just how dangerous these newfangled horseless carriages could be—not the spectators camped out on the edges of the road, not the pedestrians wandering blithely across it, not the dogs mindlessly chasing the madly spinning automobile wheels, not even the drivers themselves, who were too ignorant to realize how foolhardy they were to trust their lives to crude, hastily built, largely untested vehicles that could barely stop or turn. Two years later, in another town-to-town race between Paris and Marseille, French engineer Émile Levassor, an automotive pioneer who'd finished fifth in the Paris–Rouen race in 1894, swerved to avoid a dog. His tall, short-wheelbase Panhard et Levassor flipped, and his chest was crushed by the tiller. (Steering wheels hadn't been invented yet.) Six months later, he would die from injuries suffered in the crash.

Others would follow—a driver here, a riding mechanic there, spectators pretty much everywhere, not to mention poor, hapless dogs by the dozens. But the open-road era of racing thrived until 1903, when the Paris–Madrid event ended it with a cataclysmic finality. By this point, the public had become so fascinated by motorsports that an estimated three hundred thousand spectators thronged to French roadways to witness the action for themselves. Roughly two hundred vehicles left the starting line. Nearly half of them crashed. At least seven people were killed—two drivers, three riding mechanics, a policeman, and a spectator—and about fifteen more were injured. The race was halted and then canceled at Bordeaux, less than halfway to Madrid. News reports dubbed the event as "The Race to Death."[1]

British entrant Charles Jarrott, a heralded driver of the day, reflected later on what he'd seen: "I went back over the road after the race and I marveled, not that several had been killed but that so many had escaped. Cars in fragments, cars in fields, some upside down, others with no wheels. The sufferers were not all inexperienced and two of the old brigade, Marcel Renault and [Claude] Lorraine Barrow, handled the steering wheel for the last time, drove their last race and paid the extreme penalty," he wrote. "Road racing was dead. Never again would it be possible to suggest a speed event over the open roads and the sport—which, while it was sport, was in my opinion the best of all sports—was finished. The peculiar thing about it all was that the outside world had not appreciated up to that moment that there was an element of danger in motor racing. One or two drivers had certainly been injured, but accidents were very rare; and then, suddenly, by one of those compensations which occur with all things in life, the toll was paid in one event, and so heavy was it that with a shudder and a gasp the world at large realized that motor racing might be really deadly."[2]

And it was about to get deadlier. Much, much deadlier. If you focus your attention on the accidents, browsing through race reports from the formative years of the sport through the early 1970s makes for painfully disheartening reading. It's not so much the breadth and extent of the accidents, which extended to every corner of the world and spanned every form of racing. No, what's really heart-wrenching about the accounts is that the same seemingly preventable causes of death occur over and over and over again: Hit a tree. Ejected from the cockpit. Skull crushed. Trapped in a burning car. Struck by an errant wheel. The initial reaction is horror. *Was racing really this deadly?* Then horror gives way to bewilderment. *Why weren't seat belts and helmets required? Why weren't trees cut down and ditches filled in? Why weren't guardrails and catch fences erected?* But after a while, the truth becomes apparent. Nothing was done because nobody thought there was a problem. *A driver/flagger/spectator was killed? Jeez, that's too bad. How'd the Yankees do today?* Well into the 1960s, death on the track wasn't merely tolerated. It was the tariff that motor racing levied on not only its participants but also its fans.

Certain race circuits, especially ones lauded as "classics," pop up with mind-numbing regularity: The Nordschleife, or North Loop, of the Nürburgring, described by Jackie Stewart as "The Green Hell";[3] Langhorne, the one-mile oval so treacherous that hard-bitten pros like Rodger Ward flatly refused to race there; Monza, where a driver and twenty-two spectators were killed when he crashed into a grandstand in the Italian Grand Prix in 1928. Five years later, three more drivers were killed in a pair of separate accidents that left a column of smoke rising over the circuit. But races at Monza were a drive in a city park—literally—compared with the havoc at the Indianapolis Motor Speedway.

Built in 1909 as a showcase for the nascent automobile industry, Indy was a high-speed 2.5-mile rectangle that was, from the beginning, a laboratory for catastrophe. One driver, two riding mechanics, and two spectators were killed during the inaugural events. To "improve" the track, brick paving and concrete retaining walls were added before the first Indy 500 was staged in 1911, but this didn't prevent yet another riding mechanic from being killed during the race, nor did it do much to promote safety in the coming decades. From 1929 to 1939, no fewer than twenty-four fatalities were recorded during practice, qualifying, and the race—drivers, riding mechanics, pit workers, spectators, and an eleven-year-old boy who was hit by a flying tire while he was playing in his front yard, across the street from the track. During this stretch, there was only one year when somebody *wasn't* killed. Think about that for a few seconds and try to process the ramifications. Would you take your children to a sporting event if you knew there was a reasonable chance that they'd see someone lose their life? Would you go yourself?

By twenty-first-century standards, would this even qualify as recreation? Or was it the twentieth-century version of gladiators fighting to the death? *Are you not entertained?*

Nor was road racing exempt from the tragedies endemic to Indianapolis. Consider this catalog of black-letter days: June 11, 1955, when a Mercedes-Benz 300 SLR vaulted over an embankment at Le Mans and scythed through the crowd, killing the driver, Pierre Levegh, and at least eighty spectators. May 12, 1957, when a Ferrari 335 S sliced through a telephone pole during the Mille Miglia and careened into a group of onlookers, killing Alfonso de Portago, his codriver, and nine bystanders. September 10, 1961, when Wolfgang von Trips and Jim Clark touched wheels on the second lap of the Italian Grand Prix. Von Trips died when he was flung out of his shark-nose Ferrari, and the driverless car killed fifteen spectators who were standing behind a flimsy fence. The accident was replayed so incessantly on Italian television that Pope John XXIII felt compelled to weigh in. "It would be criminal to allow absurd performances of death like this to repeat themselves," he declared, much to the annoyance of racing enthusiasts all over the world.[4]

It wasn't merely that they wanted the pope to stay in his lane, so to speak. The larger peeve, for motorsports fans, was that the general public and what we now call the mainstream media paid attention to racing only when a tragedy occurred. Smokey Yunick described this as the "YHTBKTBWA" convention—you have to be killed to be written about.[5] As far as most daily newspapers were concerned, racing was the tattooed lady of the sports world, and if it was covered at all, the stories were assigned to newbies who didn't know anything or old-timers who couldn't have cared less. "It's just below wrestling and a shade above billiards," is how one editor characterized racing's status in the sports hierarchy.[6]

To be fair, not all newspapers ignored racing. A handful of big-city dailies, whether out of moral indignation or crass sensationalism, crusaded regularly against the sport. The *Los Angeles Examiner* waged a long-running campaign against Legion Ascot Speedway, the short oval known for good reason as the "Killer Track" because twenty-four men died there during its twelve-year run. When fire destroyed the grandstand in 1936, the *Examiner* editorialized mordantly, "Legion Ascot

Speedway burned down today, with a great saving of life."[7] For the *Chicago Tribune*, the Indy 500 was a favorite whipping boy. "We believe that the alleged benefits of this dangerous spectacle are not worth the costs in human life," the paper wrote. "The same appetite for blood that caused the Romans to flock to see Christian martyrs thrown to the lions may help to keep the race profitable. The same hope for money and a kind of fame that has caused countless men to take foolish risks may keep the contestants coming. But for our part we would like to see an end to the spectacle."[8] Still, it was Jim Murray, the *Los Angeles Times* columnist renowned for his one-liners, who penned the ultimate slam on the 500: "Gentlemen, start your coffins."[9]

This sort of coverage sparked indignation among the enthusiast press. But in their own stories, the racing magazines were oddly reticent about the risks drivers ran, much less the price they sometimes paid. Injuries were mentioned only in passing, and even fatalities rarely received more than cursory treatment. In its detailed report on the 1964 Indy 500, in which Eddie Sachs and Dave MacDonald were killed, *Sports Car Graphic* didn't mention the accident until eleven pages into a twelve-page story. Three months later, the death of jovial privateer Carel Godin de Beaufort in the German Grand Prix merited a single sentence buried deep in *Road & Track*'s race coverage. "Also, tragic to relate, poor de Beaufort went off at Bergwerk, suffering injuries that were to prove fatal a few days later," Henry N. Manney III wrote before hurrying on to more important matters.[10]

It was almost as if race fans and motorsports journalists had made a conscious decision to downplay the more gruesome aspects of the sport they loved to serve as a counterweight to the overblown hysteria of the mainstream media. "When a driver was maimed or killed, you hardly heard or spoke his name again," said John Mecom Jr., whose Texas-based team won Indy in 1966.[11] This might have been understandable at the time, when racing was an outlier that resided on the fringe of pop culture, obscure and vaguely exotic. But to modern readers, this attitude seems weirdly indifferent, if not overtly callous. We now live in a culture with an almost pathological aversion to risk, formalized through mandatory helmet laws and smoking bans to public health campaigns against sodas served in volumes deemed to be repugnant to civilized society. In a country where there's a serious movement to outlaw youth football, can you imagine the furor that would flame up if a prominent athlete was incinerated on live network TV?

The world was a very different place in the 1950s and into the '60s. Most of the racers were members of the generation that had survived World War II, which claimed the lives of roughly twenty million combatants and fifty million civilians. Since then, the United States had been through the Korean War, and the country was now embroiled in another bloody conflict in Southeast Asia. When Denny Hulme, the blunt, burly Formula 1 world champion nicknamed "the Bear," was asked if he thought the live television coverage of Lorenzo Bandini's immolation at the Monaco Grand Prix in 1967 was in bad taste, he snapped, "Well, it happened, didn't it? There's no use trying to hide that. It's certainly no worse than some of the things about Vietnam, and they're showing that, aren't they?"[12] With young men being shipped home in body bags in ever-increasing numbers, it was hard to work up righteous indignation over somebody who'd died while doing something millions of fans wished they could do themselves. The accepted bromide of the times was "he died doing what he loved." A fatal accident sparked sadness and sympathy, not outrage and demands for accountability. "But it must be remembered that they chose to be racing drivers," a letter writer declared in the British magazine *Motor Sport*. "No one forced them into it. And the great road circuits of Europe were there before they came on the scene. What arrogance, to seek to alter circuits that were raced on by drivers who were far better than they will ever be."[13]

Drivers were supposed to maintain a stiff upper lip, and most of them did. But they weren't idiots, so they understood the risks they ran. "At one point, I had a one-in-three chance of dying," said Emerson Fittipaldi, who won Indy twice after earning a pair of F1 world championships.[14] One in three? Seriously? That's got to be an exaggeration, right? No, actually, it wasn't. At the Italian Grand Prix at Monza in 1970, Fittipaldi's fourth F1 race, twenty-seven drivers clocked laps during practice. Nine of them—exactly one-third—later died in race cars. One of them was his Lotus team leader, Jochen Rindt. "I had breakfast with him that morning, and two hours later he was dead," Fittipaldi recalled. "It was a big trauma to me and to my family because that was the reality of racing at that time, and we didn't always want to live in reality."[15]

The risks could be ignored, but they couldn't be escaped. As three-time Indy 500 winner Johnny Rutherford put it, "The unfortunate part of that period of racing was that most drivers didn't live past 30, if they stayed in the game. If you ran hard enough to win some races, sooner or later your number might come up. It was the nature of the business."[16] The danger was, if anything, even clearer to the guys who worked on the cars rather than driving them. "I still believe that every race car is a lethal weapon, and to my mind a driver *should* be scared of his race car," said longtime crew chief Clint Brawner, who gave Mario Andretti his break in Indy cars. "Hell, if racing was ever made entirely safe, I'd be a race driver myself."[17]

Bob Riley, America's greatest postwar race car designer, began his career as a driver, and he remained ambivalent about the dangers associated with racing even after he transitioned to building cars for other people. "I have to tell you the truth: I was scared at most of the races," he said. "I often asked myself, especially during those early days of the 500, 'What am I doing here in this business where so many people get hurt?' When a yellow flag came out, everyone would stop and see who was missing. It was just accepted that something bad could happen to your driver. And the drivers were willing to take the chance. They were very, very, very brave people. I remember one guy telling me, 'Buy a used car from George Bignotti and you get a good engine, and you get a good chassis, and there's still enough money left over at the end of the year for a funeral.' That's how bad it was."[18]

David Hobbs, who enjoyed a charmed thirty-year career as a front-liner racer before a successful second act as a television broadcaster, did his open-wheel apprenticeship in a Formula 3 Lola that looked as spindly as a mosquito and was just about as fragile. "Because I was a bit taller than most guys, there was no room for the seat on top of the fuel tank," he says, "so they took the seat out, and I sat *on* the tank. And in those days, the tank was just a piece of aluminum—no rubber bag inside it—with a bit of plastic tubing that you'd get from [a store like] Walmart connecting it to the engine, and that pipe would come off in a heartbeat in any sort of shunt. I must've been stark-raving fucking mad! Every time I drove away from home, I'd look in the rearview mirror and see my wife and my two little boys, and I'd think, 'This could be it—the last time I see them.' And when I finished a race, I'd think, 'That's another one I got away with.'"[19]

Many of his fellow drivers weren't so lucky. The incomparable Jim Clark was killed after hitting a tree in a modestly attended Formula 2 race at Hockenheim in 1968. At Clark's funeral in Scotland, Hobbs wished fellow driver Mike Spence luck at Indy, where he was scheduled to drive a Lotus turbine. Four weeks later, Hobbs attended Spence's funeral. Four weeks after that, F1 winner Ludovico Scarfiotti was thrown out of his car and died in a German hill climb. And four weeks after that, Jo Schlesser perished in a fireball at the French Grand Prix. Veronica Attwood, the wife of Richard Attwood, another survivor of this era, once told Brian Redman, "During our first years of marriage, I went to more funerals than weddings."[20]

Like Hobbs, Redman enjoyed a racing career at the pointy end of the grid for the better part of four decades. He was driving for Porsche in 1969 when his teammate, Gerhard Mitter, was killed at the Nürburgring in a Formula 2 car. Redman got a call from the factory. "You will attend the funeral in Stuttgart," he was told. "Please wear your driver uniform."[21] In a scene that could have been scripted by a hack Hollywood screenwriter, seven uniformed drivers carried the casket into the cathedral on their shoulders. Mitter's widow was sobbing. Next to her were two children, roughly the same age as Redman's kids. Redman felt his eyes well up, and tears streamed down his cheeks. Afterward, another teammate, Udo Schütz, spoke to him.

"Brian, I see you're very upset," he said. "I never knew you cared so much for Gerhard."

"I didn't care for him at all!" Redman admitted. "I didn't even like him! I was thinking that it's going to be me next."[22]

If you wanted to be a race car driver, death and dismemberment were part of the bargain, and accepting this harsh reality was a nonnegotiable job requirement whether you were pursuing a career as a professional or simply running your puny Crosley Hotshot in SCCA club races.

After Gerhard Mitter was killed in a Formula 2 car before the German Grand Prix in 1969, Porsche ordered seven of its drivers to serve as pallbearers at his funeral—dressed in their driving suits, no less. On the left were Udo Schütz, followed by Dick Attwood and Brian Redman (not visible). On the right were Jo Siffert, followed by Rolf Stommelen, Kurt Ahrens, and Hans Herrmann. Siffert and Stommelen later died in racing accidents. *Corporate Archives Porsche AG*

Drivers dealt with this reality in different ways. Some of them banished thoughts about worst-case scenarios from their mind. "Let's face it, I lost some of my closest buddies in racing," said Mario Andretti, the only American to win the Indy 500 and a Formula 1 championship. "But if I'd dwelled on that side of it, I would have never stepped in a race car."[23] Some drivers were exuberantly cavalier about the risks. Phil Hill, America's first F1 world champion, climbed the racing ladder during what he described as the "eat, drink, and be merry"[24] era of Grand Prix racing. "When I was younger," he said, "I was constantly annoyed by people who were cautious about their lives. I felt they should be like us and live a little—or die a little."[25] Not that most drivers thought that they—they, personally, that is—were going to buy it on the track. "What are you talking about?" longtime Indy car and Silver Crown driver Steve Chassey asked, in a mock incredulous tone. "We were invincible. If something happened, it was going to happen to the other guy."[26] Patrick Bedard, the longtime *Car and Driver* writer-editor who was nearly killed in a hellacious wreck at Indy in 1984, best summed up the prevailing belief system: "You have to buy into an essential delusion if you're going to be a race car driver. And that is that nothing bad will happen to me."[27]

In their defense, drivers weren't statisticians or engineers. They were in the business of winning races, not designing cars and tracks, and they assumed—naively, perhaps—that the people who were in charge of these things had made racing as safe as it could possibly be. "I never realized that not having trees around tracks was an option," said Skip Barber, who raced briefly in Formula 1 before becoming a race-driving school mogul. "I didn't know that guardrails existed. I never thought, 'Gee, why don't we use something like what John Fitch has done with his barrels [to mitigate crash impacts]?'"[28] And why didn't that thought occur to him? Because drivers could no more imagine racing without risk than fish could imagine a world without water.

The paragon of the age was open-wheel oval track ace Duane Carter, who set the standard for fortitude during an AAA sprint car show at Winchester in the summer of 1951. Winchester was a fast and nasty high-banked paved oval that demanded courage as well as car-control skills. During qualifying, Cecil Green spun in Turn One and died after rocketing through a guardrail. There was a somber delay before qualifying could resume. When it did, Bill Mackey was killed after crashing in exactly the same spot where Green had gone out of the ballpark. The mood was positively lugubrious while that wreck was cleaned up. Carter was next in line. Not only did he qualify on the pole, but he also set a world record for half-mile ovals. "That's my definition of a race car driver," said Wally Pankratz, a member of the National Midget Auto Racing Hall of Fame.[29]

Pankratz started racing in 1970, and he didn't retire until 2022, so he benefitted from a host of changes that eliminated much of the danger from the sport. Looking back on his early days, he said, "I reckon that if you talked about safety, certain people would have thought that you weren't worthy of being a race driver. It was just a macho deal. I mean, there were a lot of drivers who didn't want roll cages [in midgets and sprint cars] because that would let anybody drive a race car."[30] Fear was the third rail of racing, a subject that drivers wouldn't—and couldn't—discuss in public. "No driver confessed to being afraid, and we never discussed the possibility of death," Redman said. "Admitting fear would have been worse than unmanly; it would have been unprofessional."[31] That's why the racing world was shocked when the debonair French playboy Johnny Servoz-Gavin retired in 1970, only two years after leading the Monaco Grand Prix—stunned not because he quit in the middle of the season but because he stated the usually unspoken out loud: "Fear has won me over."[32]

Partly because drivers have always deflected talk about it, fear is a subject that fascinates nonracers. The first question people invariably ask drivers is, "How fast do you go?" The second is almost as predictable: "Do you ever get scared?' In interviews, journalists who would never have dreamed of asking Pelé why he played soccer or Jean-Claude Killy why he skied, asked drivers why they raced. The subtext was obvious: *Why do you engage in a sport that can kill you?* While the enthusiast press promoted images of drivers as comic book heroes with superpowers that allowed them to speed around corners faster than mere mortals, armchair psychiatrists invested racers with a variety of more complicated qualities. They were said to be everything from brainless hedonists on a machismo high to philosopher kings seeking eternal truth, from muddled misfits OD'ing on testosterone and self-doubt to masochistic head cases afflicted with that old Freudian fave, the death wish. Exhibit A: the film *Grand Prix*, which managed to stuff all of these clichés into one 176-minute, widescreen Metrocolor motion picture.

Or for TL;DR types, here's a paragraph from a book written by journalist Phil Shirley: "Men who drive racing cars fear failure, but not half as much as they fear fear itself. Fear is more powerful than power and money and death. Fear fuels motor racing and it impacts upon men more than any other emotion. Fear of losing, fear of being vulnerable, fear of not being powerful enough, fear of not being in control, fear of not being a real man. And often most powerful of all, fear of being seen as afraid. Male identity is bound up with fear and so is motor racing, even though most racing car drivers won't admit to it. Despite its pervasive presence, fear is an emotion rarely talked about openly by us as men, least of all within the tough, masculine sport of motor racing. One of the beliefs of traditional masculinity is that a man must not show he is afraid. Riddled with fear he may be, but if he wishes to be seen as a man—a champion and a warrior of men—he must hide his fear behind a mask of fearlessness. A racing car driver hides his face behind a mask of protection and his true emotion behind a mask of bravado. Many drivers are afraid and many drivers pray but few admit to it. It takes a brave man to admit he is afraid or that he prays to ease his fear, especially if failure and fear can mean the difference between life and death."[33]

Whatever.

The human impetus to race, whether on foot or in airplanes or on crazily souped-up lawn mowers, must be encoded in our genetic material. When the first Olympic Games were held in 776 BC, foot races were one of the events. The invention of the automobile added a new wrinkle to man's eternal quest to make it from point A to point B faster than his peers. Driving a car at the limit of its performance capabilities is a challenging, thrilling, and exceedingly rewarding exercise. When you add the factor of competition, it becomes an intoxicating and genuinely addictive experience, hence the perennial popularity of Steve McQueen "Racing is Life" T-shirts. This was as true in 1926 as it is in 2026, and if cars are still being driven a century from now, it will be equally true in 2126.

But what separated motorsports circa 1964 from the hundred-meter dash or the marathon—or baseball or football, for that matter—was the real risk of a potentially fatal injury. Almost from the dawn of the automobile, it was an article of faith that danger was an essential element of the sport. This was the facile go-to rationalization motorsports journalists deployed whenever they were confronted with the ugly reality of death on the racetrack. "I must accept—and in consequence profess—that in spite of the revulsion it arouses in me, car racing, with all its attendant dangers, is good because it is necessary," Belgian journalist Jacques Ickx wrote in summing up a 1958 season during which drivers were killed in four of the eleven races on the world championship schedule. "Necessary, not for any immediate, illusory profit, but because it represents the generous and eternal exercise of one of the most precious faculties man has been endowed with—that of daring," he wrote. "It is even more than a question of freedom: it is a right. Young people have the right to take risks."[34] In the Ain't It Ironic? Department, Ickx's son, Jacky, would be involved in five fatal racing accidents during a career punctuated by six Le Mans victories.

Ken Purdy, the doyen of American automotive journalism during the postwar era, resorted to variations on this hoary theme while writing about racing for a nonracing audience in magazines like *Esquire* and *The Saturday Evening Post.* "It has long been held gospel that racegoers hope to see drivers killed," he wrote. "I do not believe this. I do believe that they want to see drivers go to the very edge of the precipice, to the rim of death, but they want them to come back. It is important that they come back, because the spectator so tightly identifies himself with the driver. He does not want to die; therefore he does not want the driver to die. But he does want the driver, as his alter ego, to demonstrate his bravery by hazarding death."[35]

The most emphatic and influential champion of racing existentialism was Denis Jenkinson, the proudly idiosyncratic and opinionated correspondent for *Motor Sport.* "I am sure that had motor racing been invented with no element of risk or danger it would have never got off the ground, for it is the very challenge of cheating death in motor racing that attracts the human being," he wrote. "I can never see a 'maestro' driving between nine-and-a-half tenths and ten tenths without having to catch my breath and feel a bit sick in the stomach, for I become acutely aware that I am watching a truly brave man playing with one of the most dangerous situations that the human being has devised in his uncontrollable quest in search of mechanical development and perfection. In these days of apparent safety and security all around us, with 'civilization' blinding us into a state of almost lethargic torpor, where we have no need to indulge in anything the slightest bit risky, it is a wonderful sight to see a man, by his own choosing, do something that is really stretching the safety factor to the limit; deliberately flirting with danger for no real gain other than his own personal satisfaction."[36]

Members of one genotype of drivers accepted this worldview as one of racing's natural laws, immutable and unavoidable. "If I die tomorrow, still I have had 28 wonderful years," Alfonso de Portago declared only weeks before he was, in fact, killed in the Mille Miglia.[37] Or Eddie Sachs, a few years before he died at Indy: "If I knew I'd get killed in racing, I wouldn't regret having raced; I love racing. But I'd regret not having won the 500."[38] Or Masten Gregory, the American best known for his penchant for bailing out of race cars the instant before they crashed: "Frankly, if I couldn't go motor racing, I'd have to do something else involving hazard because it is the moment of risk that makes the rest of life bearable, valuable or delightful."[39] And the beloved Juan Manuel Fangio, five times a world champion and a friend even to his foes: "To race is to live. But those who died while racing knew, perhaps, how to live more than all the others."[40]

Of Fangio's contemporaries, Stirling Moss came closest to channeling the Jenkinson ideal—no surprise considering that they won the Mille Miglia together in 1955, with Moss driving and Jenks navigating. "Danger *is* an important and integral part of motor racing to me," Moss said. "I don't mean it's important because I want to get hurt, I don't want to get hurt. I'm *petrified* of dying. I hate it. The thought of dying is terrible. I love life too much—particularly when I was racing. It was a fabulous life, the greatest life a man can have. But I feel that you've got to have high stakes to make the thing worthwhile. And the highest stake a man can pay is his life. Therefore, if you are going to gamble and you say, 'My life on this' when you go into a corner, and 'I'm going to take first,' you can't go higher than that. You can't be higher than that, boy. I mean, that's a royal straight flush, isn't it, when you haven't even looked at your cards? To me, this is a very important part of what motor racing is all about."[41]

Although most drivers rejected the dicing-with-death metaphor as media blather, Moss and Jenkinson perpetuated the myth of the driver as warrior, bravely confronting the grim reaper like a medieval knight or a World War II fighter pilot. It's impossible to imagine these archetypes being applied to Max Verstappen or Lando Norris, much less Scott Dixon or Alex Palou. But this credo had a devastating effect on racing for previous generations because it established an unwritten code that not only ignored safety but also actively fought changes that would have made the sport less dangerous. "Father, you had the war. I didn't,"[42] Piers Courage, who would be killed in the Dutch Grand Prix in 1970, once told his father. To contemporary readers, actions like requiring seat belts and chopping down trees in runoff areas seem like no-brainers. But not if you believed in an ethos that winning races didn't mean anything unless you were also running the risk of being killed. As an irate reader wrote to *Motor Sport*, "Life is bad enough with 'recommended speed limits' for prams in this country without chicken-hearted Grand Prix drivers, too."[43] Racers weren't seen as athletes. They were worshipped as avatars courageous enough to confront death one lap at a time.

Before Doug Nye became one of the world's premier motorsports historians, he was a young fan who attended races on his own dime—well, pence. "You'd hang on the fence and think, *Crikey, I'd love to do that. I think I'm good enough. But I'm nowhere near brave enough*," he said. "Tony Brooks—who was far too intelligent to be a racing driver—told me that on every race morning, he would pause in the doorway and look at the bed and think, *By this time tonight, am I going to be in a bed, or am I going to be in a box?* But he still went out and did it. And that was the difference. His generation and a lot of mine were brought up on the basis that life is dangerous—not cheap but dangerous. And if you wanted to live on the edge, and if you wanted to prove yourself to be the best in the world at something that other people wouldn't dare to do, then racing is what you did."[44]

Although Brooks was one of the premier British Grand Prix drivers of the 1950s, he retired in 1961. The rest of the decade was a time of upheaval—in domestic politics, in foreign affairs, in music and literature, in business, and, yes, even in racing. But the impetus for a change in the perception of risk came not from within. On the contrary, new attitudes slowly permeated the sport, as if by osmosis, thanks mostly to events that were compelling the pooh-bahs of the automobile industry to change the way they thought about safety on roads and highways.

For as long as anybody could remember, "safety" had been a dirty word in Detroit. Master promoter Preston Tucker had championed a so-called safety cell and several other safety features as major selling points of his much-ballyhooed four-door sedan in 1948. What happened? He went broke after a production run of fifty-one cars. In 1956, Ford marketed more crashworthy passenger cars with a so-called Lifeguard option package that included seat belts for nine dollars. Sales were anemic, supposedly prompting a dyspeptic Henry Ford II to quip, "[General Manager Robert] McNamara is selling safety; Chevrolet is selling cars."[45] Volvo made safety the linchpin of its brand image after its chief safety engineer, Nils Bohlin, patented the three-point seat belt in 1959, but the marque remained a bit player in the American market, appealing mostly to pipe smokers who quoted Kierkegaard and wore elbow patches on their tweed jackets.

Still, a paradigm shift was on the way, and like the line about bankruptcy properly attributed to Hemingway, it came gradually, then suddenly. If you had to pick the moment when the transformation commenced, it might be February 2, 1966. A Senate subcommittee was holding a hearing on the federal role in traffic safety, and the star witness was a tall, young, Harvard-trained attorney whose black eyes shone with the intensity of a monastic religious zealot. His name, then obscure, was Ralph Nader, and he would quickly emerge as one of the country's best-known soldiers for social justice. In 1959, he'd written an article for *The Nation* titled "The Safe Car You Can't Buy."[46] This brought him to the attention of Labor Department assistant secretary (and US Senator-to-be) Daniel Patrick Moynihan, who was establishing himself as a leading public intellectual. Moynihan hired Nader as a part-time consultant for the princely sum of fifty dollars a day. In 1963, Nader wrote in another magazine article, "Slaughter on the highways has been a perennial phenomenon for nearly half a century, and still an industry is permitted to produce, unhindered, vehicles full of accidents and tragedies waiting to happen."[47] Two years later, he expanded his takedown of the American automobile industry into a book that endures as an extraordinary piece of muckraking in the grand progressive tradition of Lincoln Steffens, Ida Tarbell, and Upton Sinclair.

No activist did more to raise public consciousness—and mold public opinion—about automotive safety than progressive muckraker Ralph Nader. His book *Unsafe at Any Speed* became a bestseller in 1965, and his testimony before the US Senate the next year made him a household name. Eventually, his attitudes about safety trickled down to the racing world and helped launch a revolution. *State Archives of Florida*

Unsafe at Any Speed was more polemic than journalism, and it was suspect as a technical document. But Nader's larger point was spot-on. He targeted corporate greed, and he scored a bull's-eye by detailing how the automakers in Detroit had prioritized profits over safety, seducing American consumers with pretty baubles while cutting corners on features that would have made cars more crashworthy. When the book was published in November 1965, it ignited blistering denunciations from executives who were accustomed to more flattering coverage. But hardly anybody outside the automobile industry had heard of Nader until the US Senate subcommittee hearing gave him a national forum, and he used it to skewer car manufacturers. "A civilized society should want to protect even the nut behind the wheel from paying the ultimate penalty for a moment's carelessness, not to mention protecting the innocent people who get in his way," he testified.[48]

Automakers were enraged by Nader's critique. At the same time, they were also afraid that car buyers might take it seriously if they didn't crank up the damage-control apparatus. Besides denouncing Nader in the court of public opinion, General Motors hired private detectives to investigate him. According to a lawsuit that was eventually settled out of court for $425,000, Nader was followed, wiretapped, and propositioned in an effort to dig up material that would discredit him. The plan backfired spectacularly when the dirty-tricks campaign became the subject of another US Senate hearing, and GM Chairman James Roche was forced to issue a humiliating public apology. In the fall of 1966, the National Traffic and Motor Vehicle Safety Act was passed, requiring front and rear seat belts, padded dashboards, and backup lights. Two years later, the more comprehensive Federal Motor Vehicle Safety Standards took effect.

Obviously, race cars couldn't be subject to the same safety standards as road vehicles. Nor was anybody suggesting that racing ought to be as risk-free as driving on the street. But Nader's most salient point—that making a mistake shouldn't condemn a driver to getting killed on the way to the grocery store—resonated with more enlightened members of the motorsports fraternity. Bruce Wennerstrom wrote in a guest editorial in *Sports Car Graphic*: "However, it is not part of the code of racing that if a driver exceeds his limits he must pay for his error with his life. The myth that racing is inherently dangerous and nothing much can be done about it has been repeated so often that it has come to be accepted as fact. No responsible person connected with the sport has ever suggested that automobile racing was without risk; but the fact is, that while racing is inherently dangerous, much can be done to eliminate or minimize these risks."[49]

Paradoxically, the push for safety didn't come from racers themselves but from the journalists who wrote about them. Not so much the beat writers who went from race to race and were indoctrinated into the cultural norms of the sport but the columnists and editors whose distance from the day-to-day operations gave them the perspective and freedom to speak the unspeakable. As the acerbic Brock Yates wrote after the death of Joe Weatherly: "Every step forward for safety since they told the drivers to stow the booze and keep both hands on the wheel has been met with opposition. Each time somebody suggests a way to reduce the risk, the chest-beaters cry and gnash their teeth about the sport turning into a pastime for pansies."[50]

While conservative magazines such as *Road & Track* and *Motor Sport* continued to soft-pedal the endless tragedies and lobby for maintaining the status quo, upstarts like *Car and Driver* launched a movement to bring some sanity to the sport. Yates was the principal mouthpiece for this campaign. An amateur racer and the chief agitator behind the outlaw Cannonball Run cross-country road race, he was a live-free-or-die type who railed against federal seat belt laws and other promulgations of the nanny state. But he could hardly contain his frustration—or scorn—when self-described racing traditionalists opposed even the most sensible safety regulations. "Year in and year out," he wrote, "our beloved sport can be counted on to supply more violence and bloodshed than any endeavor this side of a Chicago peace demonstration, and what do we do about it? Nothing, except to stand around like dolts and drool inanities like, 'Death and injury are part of racing, and without it, the sport would have no meaning.'"

Then he paused before delivering the haymaker: "I will tell you one thing. Until the stench of death can be removed from auto racing, it will remain a 'bush' sport."[51]

DOCTORS IN THE HOUSE

With headlights blazing and exhausts blaring, Mario Andretti bombed out of the pits at Le Mans in his Ford GT Mark IV. It was 3:30 in the morning during the summer of 1967, and he was amped up after an unscheduled pit stop to change brake pads. Andretti was honking along at 150 mph when he reached the Esses. When he tapped the brakes for the first time after leaving the pits, the car slewed so sharply to the right that it ripped the steering wheel out of his hands. The Mark IV plowed into a dirt embankment, then pinballed back across the track and into a concrete abutment. The hit was hard enough to break his watchband in two places, shatter several ribs, and leave his chest and shoulder crisscrossed with welts where the seat belts had dug into his body.

The demolished car slid to a stop on the racing line. Wincing from the pain, Andretti crawled out of the cockpit and onto a dirt hill on the side of the track. While he lay there gasping, Roger McCluskey purposely spun his Ford GT Mark II—because he thought Andretti was in the wreckage—and crashed into a barrier. A few seconds later, a third Ford GT driven by Jo Schlesser clipped McCluskey's car. Andretti was the only one who was hurt, and he was alive largely because the Mark IV was the safest race car ever built, thanks to a four-point harness, a heavy-duty NASCAR-style roll cage, and an automatic fire suppression system. "Safety was foremost in Ford's mind," Andretti said. Which is why Ford officials had given the drivers strict instructions for what to do if someone was injured: "Absolutely do not go to their [Le Mans's] hospitals," Andretti added.[52]

Ford was convinced that the substandard medical facilities at Le Mans would do more harm than good, so the team had brought its own doctors with them. French marshals kept trying to shepherd Andretti into an ambulance, while Andretti and McCluskey kept shouting at them—in English—to cease and desist. When the language barrier proved to be impossible to navigate, McCluskey reached into the cab of the ambulance, grabbed the keys, and tossed them into the bushes. "Then he put me in the trunk of one of the corner worker's cars and took me back to the Ford compound to be treated there," Andretti recalled.[53]

To be fair, the racetrack medical situation wasn't any better in the United States. At a lot of small tracks, in fact, you would have been lucky to find a doctor at all. In the summer of 1962, a few months after finishing fourth at Indy, Donnie Davis crashed at the end of a United States Auto Club (USAC) sprint car show at New Bremen Speedway, a mildly banked half-mile dirt oval in rural Ohio, and he was critically injured when his car flipped twice. Clint Brawner happened to be at the track. He climbed into the ambulance to accompany Davis to the hospital. When he asked the attendant for a prognosis, he was told, "I'm no orderly. I'm the local florist."[54] Davis died three days later of massive brain injuries.

If you'd been told to rate the general quality of medical care at racetracks in the early 1960s you'd have asked, "Is there any letter grade worse than an 'F'?" Insurance policies often required promoters to provide emergency vehicles, but this was long before the paramedic specialty had been created, so medical expertise typically ranged from slim to none. If there were physicians on site, it was usually because they were racing fans and/or friends of the promoter. There were no infield care centers, so doctors worked with whatever instruments they brought with them in their little black bags, and most injuries, especially concussions, went untreated. Fatalities were common, and fatalism was the prevalent philosophy. "The drivers I knew loved the sport and would do it come hell or high water," said Dr. Steve Olvey, a neurosurgeon who would become a linchpin of the medical staff serving the Indy car circuit. "If they got killed, *boom boom*, that was it."[55]

Olvey was a native Hoosier who'd first attended the Indy 500 when he was eleven years old. From his seat in the grandstands, he saw the smoke billowing over the backstraight after the fatal accident that killed his hero, Bill Vukovich, in 1955. He began volunteering at the Speedway in 1966, joining a small staff headed by local general practitioner Dr. Thomas Hanna. By the time Olvey graduated from medical school in 1969, he lived near Turn Four of the track and had befriended several of the drivers. That fall, he attended an open test for sprint cars at Winchester. When Bruce Walkup wrecked, Olvey stabilized his neck with a greasy towel and drove him to the nearest hospital. The place was empty, and it was only after Olvey yelled for assistance that a nurse came out. When he requested an X-ray and a neurosurgeon, she told them to stop bothering her. "The surgeon's on the golf course, and I'm not about to call him for any stupid race driver!"[56]

Olvey was part of a small coterie of doctors around the world who worked tirelessly over the next few decades to change attitudes about safety and establish protocols for treating injured drivers. His counterpart in Canada was Dr. Hugh Scully, a surgeon based in Ontario. In 1968, Scully visited nearby Mosport Park for the first time, and he was appalled by what he found. "The rules said you had to have a physician if you were going to have a competition, but all they had were a family physician, a psychiatrist and a gynecologist," he recalled. "There was no medical center. There was no medical equipment. There was no vehicle to transport an injured driver or pedestrian or track worker to the hospital."[57]

Scully was instrumental in creating Ontario Race Physicians to provide teams of doctors and nurses with emergency room and intensive-care experience. The organization worked with the Canadian Automobile Sport Club—the sanctioning body for motorsports in Canada—to implement nationwide medical standards. Scully also persuaded Mosport's hard-headed owner, Harvey Hudes, to upgrade the track's medical facilities. "We took one of the rooms with an attached bathroom and made that a medical center, and we begged or borrowed stretchers and medical equipment that was being rejected by Toronto General Hospital," he said. "Then we converted a couple of former race vehicles to intervention vehicles that could be called from Race Control to go to an accident. Then we realized that we needed something to transport people, so we got a couple of vans and equipped them as very rudimentary road ambulances."[58] Helicopters came later, along with many of the practices that are still routine.

Meanwhile, British neurosurgeon Dr. Sid Watkins was embarking on a career as, arguably, the most important physician in racing history, thanks to his groundbreaking work in Formula 1 during the 1980s and '90s. Known as "the Professor," Watkins was teaching medicine at Syracuse when he began assisting Dr. Francis Ward, the medical director of the US Grand Prix at nearby Watkins Glen, in 1962. Watkins returned to the United Kingdom in 1970 and joined the Royal Automobile Club's Motor Racing Medical Panel. Notwithstanding the panel's impressive title, he quickly discovered that race officials didn't have much use for doctors. "The RAC surgical team in those days was not always welcome," he said, "and I remember being told at Silverstone in 1973 that for major events like the British Grand Prix we would rarely be needed but should come to the Club events where driver inexperience led to more accidents."[59] Truth sometimes being harder to believe than fiction, there was an almighty wreck in the saloon car race at Silverstone even as this conversation was occurring. Three cars were destroyed, and two drivers were critically injured. Before they were transported to the hospital, Watkins treated them in the mobile medical center known as the "Stanley Passion Wagon."

As the nickname implied, the self-contained hospital on wheels was the pet project of Louis Stanley, who managed the British Racing

Motors (BRM) portfolio. Dubbed "Big Lou" by Dan Gurney, Stanley was one of the most polarizing and heartily mocked figures on the F1 scene. His wife was the sister of Sir Alfred Owen, the immensely wealthy industrial magnate who owned the team. Owen was a devout Anglican whose religious beliefs prevented him from attending races on Sundays, so Stanley was deputized to run BRM on a daily basis. Stanley was a ponderous figure who would emerge from his chauffeur-driven Rolls-Royce in a blue blazer and flannel slacks and issue pronouncements with an upper-class lisp. He fancied himself an English version of Enzo Ferrari, and like Il Commendatore, he relished theatrical gestures, holding meetings in a plush suite in the swanky Dorchester Hotel rather than a dreary office in the BRM factory in Bourne. Each year, he produced an annual Grand Prix yearbook featuring his quirky behind-the-scenes commentary and candid black-and-white photos. His many critics derided him as a pompous dilettante—the Colonel Blimp of the F1 scene and hapless overseer of BRM's sad, slow retreat to the tail end of the grid. But admirers were impressed by his aristocratic presence, and some of them addressed him as Lord Stanley, a mistake he made no effort to correct.

Although detractors claimed that he embodied the worst qualities of the British upper crust, Stanley broke with his fellow gentry in one remarkable way. Unlike virtually all of the other grandees who ran the sport, he believed that there was a moral case to be made for driver safety. When a driver was hurt, especially in a foreign country where medical care was questionable, Stanley took it upon himself to find qualified doctors and arrange for flights back to the UK. But this, he knew, was merely a form of triage, making the best out of a bad situation. So in 1966, he decided to address the root cause of the problem by building a well-equipped mobile hospital unit that could be transported from track to track. The International Grand Prix Medical Service debuted the following year. Funded by $28,000 in donations and lots of free labor, Stanley started with a Ford D1000 tractor powered by a Cummings diesel pulling a forty-two-foot-long trailer filled with state-of-the-art equipment, including a portable X-ray machine, blood banks, air-lock doors, and burn-treatment facilities. It was first used at the International Spring Cup meeting at Oulton Park in 1967 and then on fifty-five additional occasions over the course of that first year. One of the beneficiaries was Mike Parkes, who skidded on oil at Blanchimont during the Belgian Grand Prix at Spa in 1967 and was thrown from his Ferrari 312 when it rolled. (No seat belts in Formula 1 in those days.) Parkes was x-rayed and transfused in the mobile medical unit before being transported to a hospital in Liege, and he credited his recovery in part to the prompt treatment he received in the Stanley Passion Wagon.

And yet the International Grand Prix Medical Service wasn't universally welcomed. In many respects, in fact, it was as polarizing as Stanley himself. All Grand Prix circuits had on-site medical facilities of some sort, so turf wars were often fought over who ought to do what. In cases where the facilities were marginal, the mobile hospital was sometimes perceived by local physicians as an implicit slap in the face. There were also complicated legal issues to be considered. But most puzzling and troubling of all was that many members of the ruling hierarchy of motorsports flatly refused to take any sort of action that would upgrade safety. At the British Grand Prix at Silverstone in 1967, for example, the unit was moved from the ideal location where it had been situated all weekend to an unsuitable one on the day of the race. When Stanley complained, he was told by a race official, "If a man gets injured, he'll just have to take his chances like anybody else. I don't believe in mollycoddling any driver."[60]

Parkes, like many drivers, was incensed by this irrational resistance. As he wrote from his hospital bed in a letter to *Autosport*, "It is deplorable to think that such a valuable piece of equipment, especially in the absence of a helicopter, should have been the subject of political arguments by some race organizers who regarded it only as an insult and snub to the existing medical facilities. Any sensible person should realize that it is a valuable complement to existing facilities, offered *gratis*, which could make the difference between life and death, and that it should not be grudgingly given a site, often inaccessible, where best use cannot be made of it."

As the years passed, and as circuits upgraded their medical facilities, the mobile hospital became even less popular. A letter to the editor of *Motoring News* from Grand Prix Drivers' Association (GPDA) president Jo Bonnier requesting that injured drivers automatically be taken to the

Although an infield care center was built at the Indianapolis Motor Speedway in 1947, the track had no dedicated ambulances, so several nearby funeral homes provided emergency vehicles for the race. The most prominent was the red-and-white Cadillac leviathan owned by Conkle Funeral Home in Speedway, Indiana, ready for action on the front edge of Pit Lane. *Indianapolis Motor Speedway*

Medical Service unit sparked a firestorm. Dr. D.G. Nancekievill, who served as a medical officer at dozens of British races, both amateur and professional, wrote in response, "Unfortunately, as things stand, [the mobile hospital] falls far short of its obvious potential to the point where, in my opinion, it is unnecessary in this country for the treatment of seriously injured drivers, though for the treatment of less serious injuries it has proved useful."

Despite Stanley's patronage, his passion wagon never really caught on, and as BRM's performance declined in the 1970s, so, it seemed, did the mobile hospital unit's. Howden Ganley paid a visit the day after suffering a painful practice wreck at the Nürburgring in 1973. "The X-ray machine was not operational," he recalled, "and the attendants felt that as I was still walking and talking (and presumably not bleeding) I would probably survive, so they advised me to go back to England and see my GP. Along with all of the other drivers, I had made a financial contribution to the unit, so I was particularly unhappy about this lack of action. On reflection, I suppose that the unit was there largely as a symbol to make the locals lift their game and prove that they could provide adequate medical care."[61]

Surprisingly, the first sanctioning body to adopt the concept of a roving doctor was the youngest one—the National Hot Rod Association (NHRA). The project was entrusted to a newly minted physician, Dr. Leroy Hales, known universally as "Doc." Unlike Olvey, Scully, and Watkins, he was himself a racer. In fact, he'd made ends meet while attending medical school by driving a series of nitro-burning, big-block beasts known as Funny Cars. In 1972, his Dodge Demon burst into flames at 220 mph. "The seal came off the front of the crankcase," he remembered. "When I lifted off the accelerator, the car nosed down, and all the oil came back on the headers, and *boom*! Ball of flames as big as these three rooms. It just so happened that the fire was coming in right where I was holding the brake handle, and I burned my right hand significantly. No permanent problems. But for six, eight weeks, I couldn't use my right hand. And I'm in medical school. And I thought, 'This is not good.'"[62]

What made Hales the perfect candidate for the job of NHRA medical director wasn't the fact that he was a drag racer—well, a recently retired drag racer. It was that he was in the vanguard of a new generation of doctors who realized that emergency room medicine ought to be entrusted to specialists. "The ER was a mess back then because it used to be covered by residents in training," he explained. "The problem is, you might have a steering wheel stuck in your chest, and you've got a third-year dermatology resident trying to save your life. And my friend and I said, 'Something's wrong with this picture. We've got to change it.' And we did."[63]

A self-professed adrenaline junkie, Hales was one of the first physicians in California to specialize in emergency medicine. He and his friend, Dr. Jeffrey MacDonald, who was later convicted of killing his wife and two daughters in the "Fatal Vision" murder case, also put together one of the state's first programs to train paramedics. "Until then," Hales said, "paramedics didn't exist. I mean firemen had a little bit of training about how to cut somebody out of a wreck. But it was basically scooping them out, putting them on a gurney, and getting them to the ER so the dermatologists could save their lives."[64]

Hales joined the NHRA staff shortly after hanging up his gloves and hanging out his shingle. Technically, he was a volunteer whose travel expenses were reimbursed, and he was paid fifteen dollars per diem. He didn't work divisional events, only the big national weekends. During his first year, 1973, this meant a total of eight races.

It was a start.

Bob Burman, one of the titans of early automobile racing, wears what passed for safety gear at the 1911 Indianapolis 500. In 1916, Eddie Rickenbacker showed up at Indy with a steel helmet. Although that particular style didn't catch on, helmets were required at the Speedway starting in 1935. Hard-shell versions became the norm in the 1950s, and full-face lids were standard equipment by the early 1970s. *Indianapolis Motor Speedway*

CHAPTER THREE

RISKY BUSINESS

Speed can be quantified in many different ways, from 0–60 to terminal velocity. But on a racetrack, the only metric that really matters is lap time, which can be converted into average lap speed. The history of racing can be plotted as a graph of ever-increasing lap speeds. Most of the improvements have been incremental—a mile per hour here, a half-mile per hour there. Occasionally, there were spikes representing groundbreaking advances: the straight-8 Millers in the 1920s, for example, or the Silver Arrows in the 1930s. But never did speeds jump as quickly and as greatly as they did during the decade straddling the mid-1960s and early '70s. Consider these pole speeds:

1963 Indy 500, Parnelli Jones, Watson-Offy, 151.153 mph
1972 Indy 500, Bobby Unser, Eagle-Offy, 195.940 mph

1963 Daytona 500, Fireball Roberts, 1963 Pontiac, 160.944 mph
1970 Daytona 500, Cale Yarborough, 1969 Mercury, 194.016 mph

1965 Spa 500K, Mike Parkes, Ferrari 330 P, 131.771 mph
1973 Spa 1000K, Jacky Ickx, Ferrari 312 PB, 163.678 mph

1965 British GP, Silverstone, Jim Clark, Lotus 33, 116.048 mph
1973 British GP, Silverstone, Ronnie Peterson, Lotus 72E, 138.102 mph

In 1964, with wings, turbocharging, and ultra-wide low-profile tires on the immediate horizon, racing was poised to hurtle into a brave new world even as attitudes about safety remained stuck in the past. You didn't have to be a fortune teller to read the tea leaves. Consider the death toll during a single weekend in the summer of 1967. On Saturday, one driver was killed when he flipped his sprint car near Phoenix, another when his Formula Vee hit a wall at Spa, and a third when his AA gas dragster took out four light poles in Pennsylvania. The next day, three drivers died after accidents in a shambolic Italian Formula 3 race on a street circuit encircled by stone walls. Elsewhere in Italy a spectator was killed (and at least a dozen more injured) by a crash during a round of the Italian Hillclimb Championship and two more drag racers lost their lives in Wisconsin and South Dakota. That's nine fatalities in four wildly different types of racing in two days. (Well, technically, only eight, since the ninth died in the hospital a week later.)

Nearly sixty years later, this accident spree inspires horror—horror and mystification. How could such a thing happen? And more to the point, how could the powers that be *let* it happen? To be clear, people weren't any more ghoulish back then than they are now, and there wasn't a cabal of *pro*-death advocates out there who were pushing proposals that would kill more drivers. Attitudes aside, the fundamental problem was a dearth of technology. Items that we take for granted today, from fire-retardant garments and HANS devices to SAFER Barriers and gravel traps, hadn't yet been invented. Also, there was something of a chicken-or-egg issue at play here, which is to say, for example, that Armco guardrails weren't installed because track owners didn't consider them necessary. (Plus, they were prohibitively expensive.) Fire continued to be a nightmare even after rubber fuel bladders were introduced in the mid-1960s, and the modern fuel cell, with puncture-proof liners and dry-break valves, didn't arrive until the 1970s. "It wasn't like everybody had their head in the sand," said Mike Devin, a longtime Indy car crew chief who later became USAC's technical director and director of competition. "In the 1960s, there just wasn't the information or the equipment or the science behind it to build crashworthy stuff. The idea back then was, don't crash and you won't get hurt."[1]

So what was the state of racing safety technology at the start of the 1960s? The best description would be largely nonexistent. Crash survivability is a four-legged chair built on a foundation of driver safety, car

Although races were held at the Indianapolis Motor Speedway in 1909 and 1910, the inaugural Indy 500 wasn't staged until 1911. At the start of that historic event, the forty-car field was already shrouded in smoke, thanks in part to the total-loss oiling systems of the day. Twelve laps later, riding mechanic Sam Dickson was killed when his car lost a wheel and rolled over, hurling him into a fence. *Indianapolis Motor Speedway*

safety, track safety, and emergency response. If any single leg is broken, the chair will teeter precariously. If two are broken, the whole thing will tumble to the ground. In the 1960s, all four legs were compromised.

Driver gear hadn't changed radically for decades. Coveralls dated back to the 1920s, and more formal uniforms debuted shortly thereafter. But the only protection they provided was from dirt and grease. As late as 1960, the goateed Grand Prix veteran Joakim Bonnier, who looked like the art connoisseur he was, wore an elegant black polo shirt made in France, thin blue trousers imported from Argentina, and leather shoes cobbled in Italy, while journalist-racer Denise McCluggage ran at least one race in a Porsche 550 in shorts and a tank top, accessorized with red Keds to color-coordinate with her polka-dotted helmet. In the States, T-shirts and white duck pants or aviation-style jumpsuits were standard fare in circle track competition. Drag racing developed its own signature look. When he started racing nitro-powered Top Fuel cars, Don "The Snake" Prudhomme remembered, "I was wearing a helmet, of course, a leather jacket, leather gloves, a leather Tony Nancy mask, World War II goggles, shoes, not boots, and, oh my God, that was it."[2]

By the 1960s, uniforms hyped as fireproof were on the market. The most common, and least effective, garments were cotton suits dipped in a solution of boric acid. This was a DIY practice, and it left uniforms so stiff that they could almost stand up on their own. "At Daytona," stock car driver Dave Marcis said, "they had a solution that they kept warm in a big kettle. We had to dip our uniforms in it and hang them on the fence and let them dry."[3] Fabrics impregnated with fiberglass or other flame-retardant materials were also sold. But other than the bulky, heavy-duty aluminized asbestos suits used by firefighters, none of them were truly effective in a fire. It wasn't until a space-age polymer trademarked as Nomex became commercially available in 1965 that uniforms offered drivers any legitimate protection if they were engulfed in flames.

The first pair of dedicated race-driving shoes were custom-made by Sicilian cobbler Francesco "Ciccio" Liberto for Autodelta drivers Ignazio Giunti, Nanni Galli, and Geki Russo to use in the Targa Florio in 1966. Although highly praised for their comfort and quality, they were leather shoes with no fire-retardant qualities. Loafers and sneakers were widespread at the time, while lace-up boxing shoes represented the height of professionalism. In one of the last races of his career, a Can-Am event at Watkins Glen in 1970, Dan Gurney was informed by scrutineers that he couldn't race in his customary canvas-top, rubber-soled deck shoes—only leather would do. Leather was also popular in stock car country, not for safety but because the exhaust headers ran right behind the floorboard and a lot of drivers got deep blisters on their heels. Before a race at North Wilkesboro in the late 1960s, Marcis, who was just starting a career as one of NASCAR's most successful independents, spotted Bobby Allison limping badly on Pit Road and surmised that he'd burned his feet. "I don't have no trouble with that," said David Pearson, who wore penny loafers. "The leather helps insulate your feet. Don't you have any good leather shoes?" Marcis allowed that he had some Dexter wingtips in the trunk of his car. "Well, go get the damn things and wear them today," Pearson told him.[4] Marcis raced in wingtips until he retired in 2002.

Gloves were worn primarily to protect hands from the elements and kickback from the steering wheel, which could be severe enough to cause bleeding. The stylish stringback gloves popularized by Stirling Moss were de rigueur with the sporty-car set while black mechanic's gloves were typical in the oval track world. That said, Jack Brabham drove barehanded until 1962, which was after he'd won two of his three world championships. Richard Childress, who raced into the 1980s before transitioning to NASCAR ownership, did it longer than that. "I had to feel the car when I was driving," he explained.[5] By the 1960s, leather gloves were worn almost universally. This was a mixed blessing. Leather is great at preventing abrasions, but in a fire, it shrinks as it burns and melts and bonds to the skin, with regrettable results.

The one area where significant progress had been made was in helmets. As with so many safety advances, this one was spawned by a tragedy. The Snell Foundation was formed in 1957 after an SCCA club racer died of head injuries despite wearing a helmet. Although helmets carrying Snell certification provided reasonable protection, the SCCA was the only organization to require them. Many drivers continued to wear so-called pudding-bowl or polo-style helmets because they were cheap, light, and stylish, but if you hit your head in an accident, good luck. Not for nothing did Phil Hill refer to his helmet as "a cardboard hat."[6]

Things weren't much better inside the cars. Seat belts were used routinely in most forms of American racing by the 1950s, sometimes augmented by shoulder harnesses. But no belts of any sort were required in Formula 1 until 1972. Although it was generally believed that Joe Weatherly's head had hit the wall at Riverside in 1964—which probably wasn't true—NASCAR didn't mandate window nets until 1970, after Richard Petty nearly knocked down the inside wall at Darlington and came to rest on his roof, with his arm hanging limply out of the cockpit. "Mama Petty sewed the first one together, and I made the hookups to attach it to the car," longtime NASCAR crewman Richie Barsz recalled.[7] And while it was well-known that open-wheel drivers couldn't always keep their arms inside the cockpit in the event of a rollover, arm restraints weren't adopted for another decade.

Fuel cells didn't arrive until after the terrible wreck that claimed the lives of Eddie Sachs and Dave McDonald at Indianapolis in 1964, and those early examples weren't very effective. Roll bars appeared in the 1950s, but they usually weren't tall or robust enough to help in a rollover, and that's assuming that they'd been welded and braced properly, which wasn't always the case. "My first sports car race was driving a Ferrari for Luigi Chinetti at Bridgehampton in 1965," Mario Andretti said. "To comply with the rules, they had seat belts that were just sewed to the seat, and the roll bar was a small piece of tubing pop-riveted to the fiberglass behind my head. If a bird had landed on it, it would have fallen over."[8]

The notion of crush or crumple zones hadn't yet occurred to anybody. Ditto for cockpits designed as safety cells that would remain intact in case of a crash. On the contrary, 1960s-era formula cars were essentially bathtubs that surrounded the driver with fuel tanks. "Of course, I was very aware that the cars were mobile bombs with no protection for the driver," said Max Mosley, who topped out in Formula 2 before transitioning to Formula 1 team ownership and eventually becoming president of the Fédération Internationale de l'Automobile (FIA).[9] NASCAR deserves credit for developing the roll cage during this period, but its practices weren't widely copied. Behold, for example, the chassis of a Porsche 917. The frame consisted of an intricate latticework of thin, gas-pressurized aluminum tubing that looked like it had been welded by a beefy Bavarian dude during a break from Oktoberfest. The whole thing weighed 103 pounds. The driver's feet extended beyond the front axle, and the only cockpit protection was an unbraced roll hoop over his head. "It's 1,200 horsepower in a bunch of lawn-chair tubes," joked Rob Kauffman, who owns and vintage-races—cautiously—a 917/30 Can-Am turbopanzer.[10]

Philosophically, constructors had nothing against safety. Many of them were former drivers themselves, and guys like Brabham and Bruce McLaren were still racing the cars they built and sold to customers. But in most cases, adding safety gear took time and cost money. Even more damning, making cars safer also tended to make them slower, and in a sport that prioritized speed above everything else, that wasn't a tradeoff that car builders were willing to make. As Andretti put it, "There's no way to enforce safety unless it's in the rulebook. Any safety feature in a race car comes with a performance penalty, whether it's weight or aerodynamic or whatever. And so it has to be part of the rules."[11]

Even though their lives were on the line, most drivers were just as unwilling as constructors to sacrifice speed for safety. Emptying fire bottles to save weight was a well-known cheat, and there's a story told about a guy who supposedly tried to make it through Tech with a roll bar fashioned out of garden hose. In 1973, Benny Parsons raced a lightweight stock car whose roll cage had been built mostly with .029-inch and .060-inch tubing rather than the required .090. He famously won the Winston Cup championship at Rockingham, the last race of the season, after the right-side door bars were ripped off his Chevelle in an early crash. His crew cut the door bars out of a Monte Carlo that had failed to qualify, welded them into the wrecked car while the suspension was being repaired, and Parsons turned just enough laps in the Frankenstein-mobile to narrowly beat Petty for the title. But what Barsz remembered most vividly about that race was making sure that he didn't get busted by NASCAR inspectors. As he recalled, "The minute Benny crashed, I told my brother, 'Go down there in the corner and find them door bars because if NASCAR ever sees them, they'll lock us all up.'"[12]

Or consider the curious case of Jochen Rindt, the hard-nosed Austrian who was Jackie Stewart's great rival and second only to the Scotsman in his demands for more stringent safety regulations. Thanks to his tail-out driving style, he was admired for his bravery. "If a corner could be taken flat, he was often the first one to try it," said Helmut Marko, who attended boarding school with Rindt and followed him into F1.[13] In 1969, Rindt joined Team Lotus, whose owner and founder, Colin Chapman, had a reputation for building cars that were fast but fragile. The mechanical weakness of Lotuses was one of several reasons Parnelli Jones turned down Chapman's offer for a seat in F1 and declined to drive the Lotus turbine at Indy in 1968. (Mike Spence died in one during practice.) Sure enough, Rindt suffered two big wrecks early in the season and then a huge shunt when a rear wing failed at the Spanish Grand Prix, leaving him with a broken nose and a serious concussion. Shortly after being released from the hospital, he dashed off a letter to Chapman. "Honestly, your cars are so quick that we would still be competitive with a few extra pounds used to make the weakest parts stronger," Rindt wrote. "I can only drive a car in which I have some confidence and I feel the point of no confidence is quite near."[14]

Despite the implicit threat, Rindt stayed on with Lotus, not because the cars got any safer but because they were the fastest ones he could get his hands on. His faith in Chapman's ingenuity carried him to the top of the championship standings in 1970 after winning four consecutive races in the groundbreaking Lotus 72. Even so, he wasn't happy with the situation. "Jochen was scared like never before," Marko said.[15] As he was on the verge of clinching the title, Rindt was killed when his car suffered a mechanical failure and crashed at Monza. Later that year, he would become the first—and last—driver to be crowned world champion posthumously.

But even if cars had been fitted with every modern safety system, drivers still would have died by the dozens. The root problem in those days was racetrack design. It wasn't simply that the circuits were unsafe. It was that safety hadn't even been a consideration when they were put together. In 1966, after a spate of accidents, wheel-to-wheel racing was banned at Goodwood (though the track continued to be used privately until Bruce McLaren was killed while testing his new Can-Am car in 1970). The editors at *Autosport* were perplexed by this decision. "Apparently," they wrote, "it is felt that the high speeds of which these cars are capable could be dangerous to spectators. In other words, the circuit owners believe that their safety precautions are insufficient to deal with the latest vehicles. Other circuits have no intention of restricting types of cars, so the Goodwood decision is all the more inexplicable."[16]

Inexplicable? To modern readers, any other choice would have seemed criminal. Yet *Autosport*'s managing editor, Gregor Grant,

Briggs Cunningham, left, in a C4-R, leads a Cadillac-powered Allard J2 and the rest of the field down Franklin Street on the pace lap of the star-crossed Watkins Glen Grand Prix in 1952. On the second lap of the race, another Allard-Cad, driven by Fred Wacker, clipped a curb near this spot and sideswiped the crowd lining the unprotected straight. A seven-year-old boy was killed and at least a dozen spectators were injured. *International Motor Racing Research Center / Smalley Family Collection*

doubled down on the say-no-to-safety philosophy a few months later after Paddock Hill Bend, the notorious off-camber, downhill sweeper at Brands Hatch, claimed the lives of three drivers and nearly killed a fourth. "While there is a tendency to blame the circuit owners for not providing sufficient 'run-off' area, AUTOSPORT feels that this is not a solution," he wrote. "It would be like removing all the banks and trees around Nürburgring, or demolishing several walls and houses at Spa-Francorchamps. No, the answer surely lies in many of the drivers and cars permitted to race at Brands Hatch."[17] In other words, Grant was saying that the problem wasn't the design of the circuit. It was incompetent drivers who had only themselves to blame for causing fatal accidents. Or to paraphrase progun lobbyists: Tracks don't kill drivers; drivers kill drivers.

These days, racetracks feature all sorts of barriers and runoff areas designed specifically with safety in mind. There's also a large, well-ordered panoply of race officials and course workers with formal safety training and strictly delineated responsibilities. During the 1960s and into the '70s, the approach was much more laissez-faire. On long tracks like Spa and the Nürburgring, there weren't enough marshals to observe the entire track, and it was possible for wrecks—hellacious wrecks—to occur without a single official witnessing them. As Niki Lauda recalled, "In 1970, at my one-off Formula 3 event with McNamara, I had the famous, fundamental Nürburgring experience: hedge opens, Lauda disappears, hedge closes. I had always feared that one day I'd be lying there on the grass thinking, 'There's no way anyone will find me here.'"[18]

This was before television cameras, helicopters, and drones blanketed racetracks. Many corner stations weren't equipped with radios, so the officials in Race Control were often clueless about conditions on the circuit. As a result, there were countless races that should have been red-flagged, but weren't, after a massive accident. David Hobbs remembers racing a Lola T70 at Mosport in 1965. "Augie Pabst had a brand-new McLaren," he said. "It caught fire. And he's only three feet off the track. They showed the yellow flag for about two laps. Then when we all knew it was there, we carried on racing. Poor Augie was standing by his car, watching it burn to the ground, and we all just raced by without even thinking twice about it."[19]

Dedicated firefighters were the exception, not the rule, so fire-suppression duties were usually handled by flag marshals. Equipment was typically limited to handheld fire extinguishers, and because most corner workers were dressed in civvies, they usually couldn't get close enough to serious conflagrations to do much more than spectate. When drivers were trapped inside burning cars, it was often fellow racers, wearing fire-retardant Nomex uniforms, who braved the flames to yank them out of their cockpits. Course workers received minimal training, and meager on-the-job experience meant that competence was hit-or-miss, especially at circuits that were used only sporadically. The Nassau Speed Week, for instance, was a nonchampionship, year-end rave where nobody took the racing too seriously—an attitude that applied equally well to safety protocols. During one of his first practice laps at Oakes Field in 1966, twenty-one-year-old Rodrigo Borges Zingg rolled his newly delivered Ferrari 365 P2, which erupted after landing upside down. He managed to escape with his overalls blazing. While he rolled on the ground, trying to put out the flames, the circuit's lone fire truck was trapped in the paddock by a low bridge in front of it and rows of cars parked behind. By the time firefighters finally reached Zingg, he was unconscious. He died four weeks later, and the Nassau races died with him.

This isn't to suggest that all race workers were incompetent or unconscientious. On the contrary, plenty of volunteers went far beyond the call of duty, and there ought to be an honor roll for marshals who were burned while fighting fires. But it was unrealistic—and, frankly, unfair—to expect them to behave like heroes in life-threatening situations. "Why do the organisers, who coin the money, fight the idea of having fully trained, international marshals instead of half-trained amateurs?" two-time world champion Graham Hill complained. "For years, the idea has been running around that maybe it's not a good idea to have a vast multi-million-pound industry resting on the shoulders of unpaid enthusiasts who are as much interested in getting a front seat at the race as anything else. And who can blame them? They know the organizer is getting a lot of cash. The press tell them all the time about the millionaire racing drivers. Everywhere the marshal looks he sees everyone have a great time while he is expected to rush into danger for a bottle of Coke, a pork pie and his bus fare home."[20]

Very few tracks had on-site medical facilities, and heaven help the poor soul who had to be transported to the hospital. Station wagons and—irony alert—hearses often doubled as ambulances, and even when they were available, they weren't always ready for action. One of the worst crashes in sprint car history claimed the lives of dirt ace Don Branson and star-in-the-making Dick Atkins at Ascot in 1966. Inexplicably, it took nearly ten minutes for the ambulance to arrive at the scene on the half-mile oval. When Chris Amon was injured while testing a Group 7 McLaren at Brands Hatch in 1965, he was packed into an ambulance with commendable haste. Unfortunately, it wouldn't start, so the ambulance—with him in it—had to be towed to the hospital. And after Gordon Johncock broke his leg in an Indy car race at Milwaukee in 1974, he somehow slid backward out of the ambulance on the way to the hospital. He then refused to get back in. "I'm better off in my race car than I am in that fucking thing," he snarled.[21]

Still, in the grand scheme of things, overmatched track personnel and inadequate medical facilities were trivial issues. What made racetracks so dangerous was, well, the racetracks themselves. In the States, ovals were the default, all of them defined by barriers that served as a line of demarcation between the racers and the spectators, and, in many cases, between life and death. These barriers came in many forms. Low concrete walls were common. So were guardrails with one or two parallel strands, typically metal but sometimes wood—the legacy of the horse racing heritage that preceded the arrival of horseless carriages. Childress got dinged at Dover when he clobbered a fence made of battleship boiler plate. Trenton featured the material used as landing strips for the island-hopping campaign in the South Pacific during World War II. At Continental Divide, the pit wall was fashioned out of fifty-five-gallon oil drums filled with water and lashed together with steel cable. During a Formula A race in 1969, Jim Mulhall spun on a wet track. When he hit the retaining wall, the cable snapped like a bullwhip, scattering oil drums like bowling pins through the pits. Mulhall and mechanic Mike Des Jardins were killed, while two other crewmen were injured. That was the last big-time race held at the track.

Walls tended to be low—too low—and there were countless episodes of cars catapulting over them, with suboptimal results. In fact,

Tom "The Mongoose" McEwen, better known for his later exploits in Funny Cars, pops the chute of his front-engine Top Gas dragster at the Half Moon Bay Drag Strip circa 1962. Parachutes were among the first safety innovations to be developed specifically for drag racing. They were absolutely necessary accessories on the faster cars at Half Moon Bay because the short shutdown area ended in a gulley. *Tony Thacker Collection*

this happened so often on ovals that circle track racers coined a bleakly humorous phrase to describe it: flying out of the park. Erecting catch fencing was a partial solution. But the basic problem with walls was that they were immovable objects, and bad things happened when cars crashed into them. This prompted a remarkable letter to the editor of *Autoweek* in 1972. "I am amazed drivers accept the high degree of risk at Indy," Howard Bissell wrote. "The only solution would seem to be a semi-collapsible barrier about two feet thick in front of the wall. If this isn't done, how many drivers will be killed in the next 20 years?"[22] As it happened, thirty years passed before Steel and Foam Reduction Barriers, aka SAFER Barriers, or soft walls, were installed at Indy. Only one driver, Tony Renna, has been killed at the Speedway since then, and he died after he went over the wall and into the catch fencing above it.

The safety czars of the FIA now consider walls in impact zones the devil incarnate, and hard barriers have been exorcised from the sport wherever possible. But back when European road racers started making their annual summer pilgrimage to the Indy 500 in the mid-1960s, they considered walls to be a heavenly addition to the sport. "The retaining walls here—they let you go a bit harder," no less an authority than Jim Clark explained. "If these blokes drove this way on our tree-lined circuits, they'd all be bloody dead in a week."[23] Clark would demonstrate the cruel accuracy of his prediction at Hockenheim in 1968.

Aside from guardrails here and there, most road-racing circuits were what you might call free-range. Even when the runoff areas were expansive, they were never benign. In fact, they were best thought of as minefields liberally seeded with wicked antipersonnel devices—trees, telephone poles, fire hydrants, houses, boulders, power poles, culverts, and a host of other obstacles. Some runoff areas ended in thin air—that is, with a cliff—while others streamed through town and country. A torrential downpour sent Jim Hall hydroplaning helplessly off the track during the Belgian Grand Prix at Spa in 1963. "I went into a farmer's yard, between two fifty-five-gallon drums, right through where he had stacked his firewood," he recalled. "For some reason, none of it hit me, but it took all four wheels off of my Lotus. When the accident was over, I was sitting on the ground, straight up, kind of feeling around to see where I was hurt, when this guy taps me on the shoulder and says, 'Hey, you want a beer?'" Hall laughed as he told the story. "That was safety back in those days, I guess."[24]

Hay bales were widely deployed in front of self-evidently lethal obstructions such as lampposts and cast-iron bollards. It's not clear how effective hay bales were back in, say, 1924, when cars struggled to reach 100 miles per hour, but they were pointless at the speeds race cars were going in 1964. The next most popular option was encircling circuits with berms or sandbanks. These tended to be worse than nothing at all since they acted more like launch pads than barriers. Catch fences were first employed in 1962 at Zandvoort. Track manager Hans Hugenholz was the Hermann Tilke of his day, credited with designing Suzuka, Zolder, Jarama, the stadium section at Hockenheim, and the road course at Ontario. He was also his era's leading proponent of circuit safety. In the 1950s, he began experimenting with using a series of fences to corral and then stop a car that had left the racing surface. From the beginning, catch fencing was controversial. John Surtees was a passionate advocate of it because his experience racing motorcycles had taught him that sliding into an unforgiving barrier, whether a concrete wall or a metal guardrail, led to unhappy consequences. But critics worried about getting trapped in the fencing material, which was a terrifying prospect during an era when cars routinely caught fire. So Hugenholtz's efforts to bake safety into racetrack design were largely ignored and rarely replicated.

Since there was virtually no regulation of circuit safety beyond what little was required by insurance policies, the motorsports landscape was a crazy quilt of tracks built to widely diverging standards. Statistically speaking, Indianapolis Motor Speedway was the most dangerous oval in America, but it was also the holy grail for open-wheel drivers, and if it turned out to be their resting place, so be it. There were other tracks, though, that risk-averse drivers crossed off their to-do lists. The most fearsome ovals in the Midwest were the high banks at Salem, Winchester, and Dayton, known collectively as "the hills," which was short for "hills of death." Parnelli Jones was a little-known West Coast sprint car jockey running a small-block Chevy instead of a thoroughbred Offy until he outran Branson and A.J. Foyt at a USAC date at Salem. When Jones climbed out of his car, his hands were shaking so badly that he couldn't light a cigarette. "I never want to race that hard again," he said.[25] In 1964, a year after winning the Indy 500, he raced at Salem one last time, taking the pole and going flag to flag in a car owned by Foyt. He never raced on "the hills" again. Neither, by the way, did Foyt.

Langhorne was another track that inspired a lot of absenteeism. Drivers usually speak fondly about the tracks where they enjoyed success over the years. But even though Bobby Unser won the last USAC race run at Langhorne, he was thrilled when the track was dropped from the Indy car schedule in 1971. "Langhorne was the kind of place where, the bigger your huevos, the faster you went," he said. "I raced all over the world, and that was the most dangerous, most treacherous, most murderous track there ever was. Nobody liked it, and the ones who said they did were lying."[26]

Built in 1926 in the southeastern corner of Pennsylvania, "the 'Horne" was a one-mile dirt track shaped in a perfect circle. Known as the "Big Left Turn," Langhorne was for many years the world's fastest track of its size despite being unpaved. The unique layout meant that drivers drifted around virtually the entire circuit, with perilously limited vision. To go fast there, you needed deft car control, immense reserves of strength and endurance, and, it should go without saying, a set of huge huevos. And Langhorne was at least as tough on equipment as it was on drivers, according to Paul Goldsmith, who won there on a motorcycle (1953) and in stock cars (1956, 1963, and 1965). "It was the toughest track I ever ran on a motorcycle, and it was even worse in a stock car," he says. "I drove a car for the Wood Brothers one time, and I was leading the race, but it was so rough through Puke Hollow that the gas tank shook right out of the car."[27]

Ah, yes, Puke Hollow—the most infamous stretch of track in North America. Most of the nearly two dozen drivers and motorcyclists who were killed at Langhorne died after crashing in the scary-fast downhill stretch of rudely rutted purgatory between Turns One and Two. "Puke Hollow was, by far, the worst corner I ever drove," Jones said. "You'd bicycle through there—*fast*. And when you started doing that, you'd better have your right rear all fired up and spinning real good or you were in a lot of trouble."[28] The worst-case scenario was hooking a rut and spiraling into the air, which was how 1958 Indy winner Jimmy Bryan checked out during a one-off return from retirement in 1960.

In 1963, Andretti was an undersized Italian refugee who could only dream about racing in the USAC sprint car show at Langhorne. He was standing in Puke Hollow, on the outside looking in, when Bobby Marvin clouted the guardrail, went end over end, and burned to death in front of him. A year later, Andretti was scheduled to run the Indy car race at Langhorne in an old Wally Meskowski roadster. "That was the only race in my career that I was really worried about," he said. "I hardly slept the night before the race. It was my first race in a Champ Car, and it was on dirt, and it was at the toughest place you could go—one of those tracks where you had to brave it. I felt like I was going into battle."[29]

Some drivers—Len Sutton and two-time Indy 500 winner Rodger Ward, to name a couple—refused to race at Langhorne. But others, like Johnny Rutherford and Wally Dallenbach, insisted that they relished the opportunity to pound through Puke Hollow. "That was a track that separated the men from the boys," Foyt said. "On the list of toughest tracks to run, you'd have to put it at Number One. But I liked Langhorne because you could run fast there. To do well, you had to want to run fast, and you had to want to race."[30] Which raises an interesting point.

It's superficial and overly simplistic to say that drivers had a love-hate relationship with tracks like Langhorne. But there's no escaping the paradox that the very features that made one circuit more hazardous than another were the same ones that attracted racers to racing in the first place. Yes, negotiating a hairpin at the maximum possible speed is a serious technical challenge, and some race engineers will look at car data traces and tell drivers that there is more time to be gained or lost in the slow sections simply because more time is spent there. But drivers will tell you that the ultimate test in racing is balancing a car on the knife's edge of adhesion when the throttle is flat or nearly flat, with the right foot trembling, and the knowledge that it's really going to hurt if they get it wrong makes the challenge even more daunting. "At the end of the race, there's no feeling like it," said Brian Redman, who survived not one, not two, but three life-threatening crashes. "The grass is greener and the sun is brighter because you've reached the limit of what you can do."[31]

The European road-racing analogs of Langhorne and Salem were Spa-Francorchamps and the Nürburgring. Spa was carved out of the Ardennes Forest in southeastern Belgium, but old-growth trees weren't the only hazards drivers had to worry about. Before his first race there, the 1000 Kilometers in 1966, Redman was too apprehensive to sleep. The next year, while racing a 200 mph Ford GT40, he unexpectedly hit rain at the gut-check right-hander at Stavelot. He was instantly reminded of the sage advice he'd gotten from Denny Hulme. "Spa? In the rain?" Hulme told him. "Shit. Park it."[32] While Redman prudently slowed down, Belgian wild man Willi Mairesse kept his foot in it, and his Ferrari 412 P was demolished after he clipped a telephone pole and smacked the side of a building. Then a Porsche 906 passed Redman and flipped. The year after that, back at Spa, Jochen Neerpasch spun in front of Redman in a Porsche 908 and destroyed a bus shelter. Neerpasch was knocked out by a steel tube, and the car was demoed. Although he fulfilled his Porsche factory commitment by doing three more races in a 908, Neerpasch retired at the end of the year. "Brian," he said, "you can only play Russian roulette for so long."[33] Two weeks after Neerpasch's crash, Redman had his own Spa misadventure when the front suspension of his Cooper-BRM broke during the Belgian Grand Prix. Redman was lucky to survive with a badly broken arm and minor burns caused by a corner marshal who had a lit cigarette clamped between his lips while he tried to unbuckle Redman's seat belts. Honestly, you can't make this stuff up.

The Nürburgring was what a mad scientist might have come up with if he'd put together all the most dangerous elements together in a single, and singular, racetrack. The German circuit meandered for 14.2 miles around the Eifel mountains, which meant it was way too long to be fully staffed by emergency workers. There were more than 170 corners, most of them fast, so there were plenty of opportunities to make a serious mistake. The road was precariously crowned, and it was lined not with guardrails but with gigantic hedges. You never knew when it was going to rain—or what part of the circuit it would rain on, for that matter. "I don't care who you are," Stewart said. "When you're at the 'Ring, the one thing you want to do is get it over. It's that bad. The car leaves the ground—all four wheels—seven times in every lap. I'll not do one more lap in practice there than absolutely necessary. And they all feel that way."[34]

Well, not all of them. Even as the Grand Prix Drivers' Association (GPDA) was agitating to ban racing at Spa and the Nürburgring, plenty of top drivers, including many GPDA members, continued to race there in sports prototypes capable of even higher speeds than F1 cars. The dirty little secret was that, yes, the tracks were irrationally dangerous, but they also tested a racer's mettle in a way that Mickey Mouse circuits couldn't rival. It's no coincidence that Clark was a master of Spa, a track he detested. During Clark's first visit to the circuit, the plucky Brit Archie Scott-Brown was killed in a Lister-Jaguar. Two years later, when

Clark returned in an F1 Lotus, Stirling Moss was critically injured in a practice crash and Chris Bristow and Clark's teammate Alan Stacey died during the race. Despite loathing Spa, Clark won the Belgian Grand Prix four years running, twice in the rain, each time lapping all but one car in the field. Meanwhile, the greatest victory in Stewart's glittering career was at—wait for it—the Nürburgring, where he won the German Grand Prix in 1968 by four minutes despite abysmal conditions in fog and rain. "I never drove in a race like this before and I hope never to again," said Graham Hill, who finished a distant second. "I was really scared at one point."[35]

Then as now, Le Mans was considered one of the crown jewels of racing. Yet in the 1960s and '70s, reviews of the track were mixed, and many Grand Prix drivers chose not to race there. Twenty-four hours is a slog, and it was even more tiring back in the days when there were only two codrivers rather than three or four. The speed differentials between the front-running prototypes and the water beetles competing for the Index of Thermal Efficiency were outrageous. So was the disparity in driving skills between the top pros and the rank amateurs. Then there was the madness of racing on a track where nearly half of the lap was spent wide-open throttle on the 3.7-mile-long Mulsanne Straight, with trees on either side of the road. "You could tell they were safety-conscious because they painted the poplars white about twelve feet up so you could see them at night,"[36] Hobbs said sarcastically. In 1967, during practice, Bruce McLaren whistled through the Mulsanne Kink without lifting in his Ford GT Mark IV, a car capable of 220 mph. "I know why you waited 'til after dark to set that lap record," his codriver, Lloyd Ruby, told McLaren. "You just couldn't stand to look at them trees!"[37]

But the section that really unnerved drivers was Maison Blanche, or White House. Cars would come out of Arnage and accelerate down a long straight, slightly downhill, blasting past tidy gardens where residents watched casually from lawn chairs. Cars would get light as they crested a small bridge, then slalomed through Maison Blanche, with an impenetrable stone wall on one side and a pointless wire fence on the other. "The White House turns were the most dangerous I've ever driven on," Sam Posey said. "It's an ess bend through concrete buildings, and you took it at 150 mph. The first time I went to Le Mans, [John Woolfe] was killed there on the first lap of the race. Welcome to Le Mans."[38]

If there was one single race that summed up the sorry state of motorsports safety in the mid-1960s, it was the French Grand Prix at Rouen-les-Essarts in 1968. Honda had developed an all-new F1 car, the RA302, featuring an unconventional air-cooled V-8 in an unusual magnesium-skinned chassis. Team leader John Surtees had tested the car and felt it wasn't ready for prime time. But the French arm of Honda wanted the car in its home Grand Prix for promotional purposes, and when Surtees refused to drive it, versatile French journeyman Jo Schlesser was hired for the RA302's debut. It wasn't a match made in heaven.

Rouen was a fast and flowing natural road circuit best known for a tricky series of downhill sweepers between the unprotected pits and the Nouveau Monde Hairpin. It was there that Louis Klemantaski had shot his arresting image of Juan Manuel Fangio holding his Maserati 250F in a glorious four-wheel drift during the French Grand Prix in 1957. The track was a throwback to the circuits of the earliest days of motorsports, which is to say that there were virtually no efforts made to protect drivers, crewmen, or spectators. After the Formula 2 race in 1967, Stewart and Clark had presented the organizers with a list of safety recommendations. About half of them were implemented before the French Grand Prix in 1968. One that was ignored was a request to add a barrier outside the second of the downhill sweepers.

Although Schlesser didn't get to test the RA302, he knew his way around Rouen, having finished third there in the F2 race the previous year. He qualified second to last, six seconds off Surtees's time in the RA301—a creditable performance considering his lack of seat time in the Honda, not to mention the car's own shortcomings. Light rain was falling when the race was flagged off. Schlesser, carrying about forty gallons of fuel, proceeded cautiously on the slick track. But on the second lap, he ran wide around the first of the sweepers after the pits. This put him out of position for the right-hander. As he eased the car back across the track, he got into a tank slapper and lost control. He left the road at 70 to 80 mph. Instead of hitting the guardrail that

Clark and Stewart had requested, the Honda rode up a natural earth bank angled at about forty degrees. This launched Schlesser into a cartwheel and a half-gainer toward spectators "protected" by wooden posts and wire fencing.

Even as the car was spinning through the air, fuel was spraying out of the gas tank, and nearly a dozen onlookers were injured, though none seriously. There was a huge *whoosh!*, and the Honda erupted. By the time it landed upside down and slumped back to the edge of the track, it was burning so ferociously that the hay bales caught fire. Corner workers, seemingly stunned, were slow to react, and when the first small fire extinguisher was deployed, the stream was aimed at spectators, not the blazing car, where Schlesser was still inside the cockpit. Eventually, firefighters in asbestos suits arrived and began spraying the car with foam. Before they could extinguish the fire, they ran out of retardant, so they switched to water. This just made the situation worse—much, much worse. To save weight, the RA302 had been skinned in magnesium. The downside of magnesium is that it burns easily and fiercely and hitting it with water causes flames to flare up. As firefighters continued to douse the car, there was a series of white-hot explosions as the inferno intensified. Eventually, chains and grappling hooks were used to pull the car off the track, still inverted, with a motionless and—one could only hope—lifeless Schlesser draped over the cockpit. At this point, the Honda wasn't a race car; it was a furnace.

Meanwhile, fuel had gushed out of the gas tank and streamed halfway across the track, where it ignited. Jo Siffert and Johnny Servoz-Gavin drove through a curtain of fire. With emergency vehicles and workers on the track, the rest of the field slowed down and navigated carefully through the debris. Even so, Hulme, McLaren, Rindt, and Pedro Rodriguez suffered tire damage, and the lens of Surtees's goggles was dislodged. "For the whole race, we could smell burning flesh," said fellow Frenchman Jean-Pierre Beltoise. "Each time we arrived at the bend, it was horrible."[39] At no point was the race stopped, yet the fire burned for fifteen minutes, with flames flickering thirty feet high and filling the air with dense, black smoke. "You see this sort of thing happening on every circuit," BRM team manager Louis Stanley said contemptuously. "The ineptness has to be seen to be believed."[40]

Astonishingly—or maybe not so astonishingly, considering contemporary attitudes—there was no major fallout from the fatal accident. No immediate changes were made in the rules regulating driver gear or circuit safety, and the fire extinguishers required in 1969 did nothing to prevent the death of Piers Courage in a similar fire almost exactly two years after Schlesser was killed. But there was an odd postscript, datelined Santa Ana, California. There, in the All American Racers shop, mechanic/fabricator Terry Malone was working on a second-generation Eagle F1 car. He'd already built a magnesium tub to designer Tony Southgate's specifications. A few days after Schlesser's fatal accident, Malone heard from Gurney. "Dan told me that the mag tub had to disappear," Malone recalled, "and it went up in the loft for fifty years."[41]

HARD HATS

"If you have a $10 head, wear a $10 helmet."

So went Bell's catchy advertising slogan of the 1970s, and truer words have seldom been written. By that metric, early racers had heads worth a couple of bucks, at most—or nothing at all. Although goggles were used almost from the dawn of motorsports, many first-generation drivers went bareheaded. When helmets finally appeared, they were made of linen, canvas, or leather, and they were designed mostly to keep dirt and oil out of the driver's hair rather than to provide protection in a crash.

British physician Eric Gardner is credited with designing the first motorcycle helmet in 1914, and it was required equipment for that year's Isle of Man TT—a perverse irony considering the race's atrocious safety record. In the decades that followed, a pair of posh British hatmakers established the standard for racing helmets. So-called Cromwells, named after Oliver Cromwell, the Lord Protector, were made by Helmets Ltd., which had been established in 1924 to supply sunshading headgear to colonial administrators serving in distant reaches of the empire. In 1926, after dirt track racing was imported from Australia, the company created a line of helmets made of cotton twill coated with shellac specifically for motorsports. Meanwhile, Herbert Johnson of Bond Street in London, which billed itself as "Hatters to the late King George VI," dated back to 1889, when it began fashioning silk-velvet top hats for the British aristocracy. It added cork race helmets to its lineup in the 1930s at the behest of Lt. Col. Goldie Garner, a World War I hero famous for his land-speed-record runs in a series of MG streamliners.

These early British lids were known generically as "pudding basin" or "pudding bowl" helmets because that's what they looked like. Canvas flaps covered the ears, and leather was used to provide interior webbing and a chin strap. A bill was typically attached, and some drivers—most notably 1958 world champion Mike Hawthorn—added a visor. Light and dapper, the Cromwells and Herbert Johnsons were also used as polo helmets, and they were highly prized by road racers hoping to emulate the savoir faire of exemplars like Stirling Moss and Juan Manuel Fangio. They were equally fashionable with circle track racers in the United States despite the fact that they didn't inspire much confidence. "The early helmets were just a little better than the box they came in," said Henry Banks, who won national midget championships before becoming USAC's longtime director of competition.[42] For many years, Phil Hill was a devotee of imported cork helmets even though he knew they couldn't pass what he called the drop test. "You know, you just put the helmet under your armpit and drop it. It breaks," he explained.[43] He was wearing a polo-style helmet in the German Grand Prix in 1958, when fellow factory Ferrari driver Peter Collins died of massive head wounds after his car somersaulted at Pflanzgarten. "Mike Hawthorn brought Peter's [battered] helmet up to the room," Hill recalled. "I don't think I ever used the corker after that."[44]

Helmets were taken more seriously on this side of the Atlantic. World War I fighter ace-to-be Eddie Rickenbacker wore a steel helmet at the Indy 500 in 1916. Although metal headgear didn't catch on, helmets became mandatory at the Indianapolis Motor Speedway in 1935. (The FIA didn't require them until 1952.) But the big breakthrough came in 1947, when a pair of aviation medicine scientists, Charles F. Lombard and Herman P. Roth, patented an energy-absorbent helmet featuring a hard plastic outer shell and a crushable foam interior. This new design was used first by US Air Force test pilots, and it quickly percolated down to highway patrolmen, firefighters, and, yes, race car drivers.

Jo Bonnier, left, and Wolfgang von Trips sport polo-style "pudding bowl" helmets in the Porsche pits at Goodwood in 1959. By this time, most American drivers had gravitated to models that extended below the ears. With their polo shirts, white trousers, suede loafers, and stringback gloves, Bonnier and von Trips exemplified the gentleman drivers of the era. *Revs Institute / George Phillips Photograph Collection*

In 1952, Hal Minyard and Johnny McMurray applied this technology to what they sold as the McHal Helmet. "It took us four months before we came up with a hat that worked," Minyard said. "I wanted to make one just for myself, something that would come down around the side of the head and low across the back of the head. When I wore it for the first time at a midget race at Phoenix, everyone wanted one."[45] McHal-style lids became known as "jet" helmets as opposed to Cromwell/Herbert Johnson polo helmets. McHals remained in vogue in USAC well into the late 1960s even though they didn't meet the stringent standards adopted by the SCCA.

The most successful manufacturer of jet helmets was Bell, owned by Roy Richter. A talented machinist and patternmaker, Richter had been a leading builder of midgets and Big Cars—what are now called sprint cars—before World War II. In 1945, he bought Bell Auto Parts, a Southern California speed shop that catered to the hot rod and racing industries. Richter expanded the inventory to include everything from immensely popular Bell one-piece steering wheels to Cromwell polo hats, and the shop was billed as "Auto Racing's General Store." Helmets were the next frontier. Richter and an employee, Frank Heacox, a motorcyclist who'd flown Navy fighters in the war, spent months studying the helmets on the market. Then they fabricated a laminated shell with several layers of "aircraft quality" fiberglass filled with polyurethane foam.

Thanks to Richter's contacts in the insular racing world and his shop's broad reach beyond it, the Bell 500 was an instant hit when it debuted in 1954. The first customers were motorcyclists. Then Bill Stroppe ordered helmets for the factory Lincoln team he was running in the Carrera Panamericana. (If ever a race cried out for better safety gear, the Mexican Road Race was it.) In 1955, Richter's friend Cal Niday used one in the Indy 500. Although he crashed hard and fractured his skull, he publicly credited the Bell 500 with saving his life. Niday's testimonials turned the newly formed Bell Helmet Company into a major player. But there were storm clouds on the horizon.

The most important event in the history of helmet design unfolded in August 1956 at an insignificant SCCA race on a primitive airport circuit near Arcata, a small seaside town near California's northern border with Oregon. In Sunday's small-bore sports car race, Triumph salesman Pete Snell was dicing with a pair of Porsches. One of them rear-ended his TR3, which clouted a hay bale and flipped several times. Snell's helmet shattered upon contact, and he died of head injuries. The volunteer course physician that weekend happened to be Dr. George Snively, director of the medical department at Sacramento County Hospital. Snively himself club-raced an Austin-Healey, and, as fate would have it, he was looking unofficially into helmet design at the time.

Snell's death prompted the San Francisco Region of the SCCA to commission Snively to conduct the first serious study of helmet technology. His findings were scathing. "Almost none of the people concerned with the use, manufacture or sale of helmets in this country had any worthwhile scientific data concerning a helmet's efficiency," he wrote in an article in *Sports Car Illustrated* that ran under the headline "Skull Busting for Safety."[46] Snively tested helmets from Bell, Cromwell, McHal, Anderson, Gentex, and Toptex, which specialized in the motorcycle police market and was hardly known in the racing world. He rated all but one of them as "inadequate." The winner, surprisingly, was Toptex. Or maybe it shouldn't have been so surprising, since the company was owned by Lombard and Roth, the scientists who'd patented the energy-absorbent helmet ten years earlier. The Toptex secret was a completely nonresilient inner liner called expanded polystyrene, which absorbed rather than transmitted energy. Snively subsequently cofounded the Pete Snell Memorial Fund, which morphed into the Snell Foundation. In 1958, the foundation issued its first standards for helmet safety, and, to this day, a Snell certificate is required to race in most series in North America. (The FIA would also get into the helmet certification game, but not until many, many years had passed.)

Richter was appalled that the Bell 500 had flunked Snively's test. He immediately stopped production and negotiated an exclusive licensing agreement with Toptex to use expanded polystyrene. The new Bell 500-TX helmet was the first to meet Snell requirements. Although the racing space was filled with too many niche firms for any one company to monopolize the market, the 500-TX quickly became the yardstick by which all helmets were measured, both in the United States and overseas. In the British Paddy Hopkirk Motor Accessories catalog, for example, it was referred to simply as the "famous" Bell helmet.

It seems fitting that Bell should introduce the next big breakthrough in motorsports headgear—the full-face helmet. The Bell Star, as it was dubbed, was developed in 1966 and used by bikers in Southern California the next year. The first automotive convert was Dan Gurney, who, not coincidentally, was a SoCal motorcycle devotee. Gurney had started thinking about face protection when he embarked on his road-racing career in the late 1950s. "I was in Frank Arciero's 4.9-liter Ferrari, and I was trying to overtake a car ahead of me which fired a stone from under a rear tire," he recalled. "It went right through the windscreen. It was more akin to a bullet than a pebble. I thought, 'That would've really smarted!'"[47] By the time he moved to Europe to race for Ferrari in 1959, he'd commissioned a leather face mask inspired by the ones used by Top Fuel drag racers. "It made him look like a knight from the Middle Ages," said his wife, Evi Gurney. "But they made so much fun of it that he didn't wear it."[48]

A decade later, while attending a dirt track bike race at Ascot Speedway in Los Angeles, Gurney found the helmet he'd been looking for—a Bell Star, which extended below the chin, thereby protecting the nose, mouth, and cheeks. He wore the full-face helmet while finishing second in the Indy 500 in 1968. Then, two months later, he introduced the Bell Star to Formula 1 at the British Grand Prix. By modern standards, the helmet looked crude and blocky. The eye port was narrow and the shape simplistic, like a fiberglass thimble with a hole in the middle. Also, helmet painters weren't a thing back then, and the Bell Star came in any color as long as it was black. Critics snarkily called it the "spaceman" helmet, and there weren't too many other early adopters besides Gurney and his protégé, Swede Savage.

Still, the benefits of full-face helmets were so obvious that it was just a matter of time before they became standard equipment. As circle track stalwart Tom Bigelow explained, "I went to a full-face helmet as soon as they come out. If I'd had one a couple of years sooner, I'd still have my front teeth."[49] Another oval specialist, Steve Chassey, got the message during a sprint car race in 1969. "Going down to the front stretch, I saw one of the ram horns on Billy Wilkerson's injectors fly up," he recalled. "He ran it over and spit it back, and it hit me in the face and bloodied my nose and bruised me up. So the next week, I went down to Bell Helmets and got an orange full-face helmet."[50]

The last driver to win the Indy 500 while wearing an open-face helmet was Mario Andretti, in 1969, and by 1973 every driver in the race was using a Bell Star. In F1, Jochen Rindt was one of the final holdouts. Actually, he experimented with a full-face helmet but shelved it because he found it too constricting, and he wasn't wearing one when he was killed at Monza in 1970. Brian Redman soldiered on with open-face helmets until demolishing a Porsche 908/3 at the Targa Florio in 1971. "Before the race, engineer Helmut Flegl said to me, 'Brian, if you must have zee accident, do not crash on zee right side'—because that's where the fuel tank was," Redman recalled. "I got about twenty-two miles around the forty-four-mile circuit when the steering broke, and I hit a stone kilometer post right in the fuel tank, and the car exploded. My face and neck were badly burned. If I'd been wearing a full-face helmet, I would have probably gotten away with relatively light burns. So I should have kept up with the latest safety equipment."[51]

Helmets underwent a host of upgrades during the next half-century—lighter and stronger shells, energy-absorbing flame-retardant linings, flip-up visors, and sexier shapes that made them a perfect canvas for wild air-brushed art. Richter missed most of this action; he sold off his helmet business in 1971 and died in 1983. Still, no single figure played a more important role in establishing the architecture that underpins contemporary helmet design. When he died, his memorabilia collection included a photo of Hall of Fame sprint car champ Billy Wilkerson, signed with an inscription: "To the man that has saved more heads than a psychiatrist."[52]

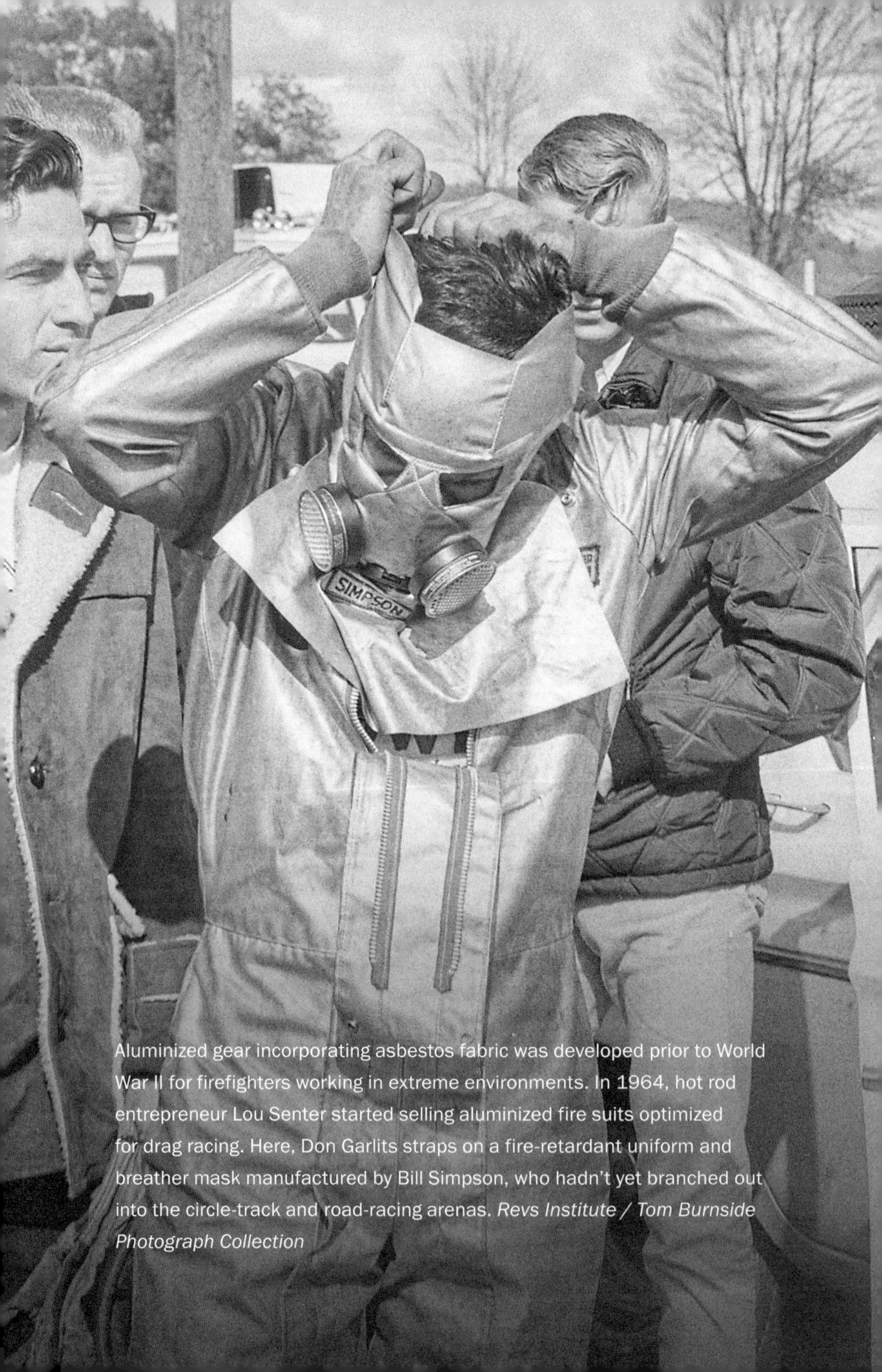

Aluminized gear incorporating asbestos fabric was developed prior to World War II for firefighters working in extreme environments. In 1964, hot rod entrepreneur Lou Senter started selling aluminized fire suits optimized for drag racing. Here, Don Garlits straps on a fire-retardant uniform and breather mask manufactured by Bill Simpson, who hadn't yet branched out into the circle-track and road-racing arenas. *Revs Institute / Tom Burnside Photograph Collection*

CHAPTER FOUR

WHERE THERE'S SMOKE . . .

The start of the Indianapolis 500 is a turbulent, treacherous, heart-in-your-mouth affair. Put thirty-three of the world's most combative drivers and fastest cars on a narrow span of pavement enclosed by concrete barriers, then watch them funnel frantically into Turn One two and three abreast. Can you say, "accident waiting to happen"?

Some drivers take advantage of the chaos to make up a few places. Under normal circumstances, Johnny Rutherford would have been one of them. In the summer of 1964, Lone Star J.R. was a hard-charging badass from Texas clawing his way through the sprint car jungle, and he favored a take-no-prisoners approach from the moment the green flag waved. But this was only his second Indy 500, and his first visit to the Speedway the previous year had ended after forty-three forgettable laps. So as the field bunched up heading into the first turn, he ceded a position to two-time pole sitter Eddie Sachs, a veteran who already had two podium finishes to his credit, then slotted in behind him. *I'll just stick with Eddie*, Rutherford thought. *He usually goes to the front, so I'll see if I can stay with him.*[1]

On the second lap, as he arced down toward the apex of Turn Two behind Sachs, Rutherford saw a red car diving underneath him with two wheels in the grass, and he could hear its V-8 engine shrieking over the insistent thrum of his four-cylinder Offy. The driver, Rutherford knew, was Dave MacDonald, a sports car tyro making his first start at Indy. Rutherford had never raced against him, but he was impressed by his commitment. "He was really standing on it," he recalled, "and I thought, *Boy, this guy's either going to crash or he's going to win this thing*."[2]

Hold that thought.

The three cars formed a tableau of Indy's past, present, and future. Rutherford was in a majestic but ponderous front-engine roadster built by A.J. Watson around a chassis design that dated conceptually back to 1952 and an Offenhauser engine whose earliest iteration had debuted in 1934. Sachs and MacDonald were both running four-cam Ford V-8s that were brand-new for 1964. Although Sachs, like Rutherford, had fought his way up through the midget and sprint car ranks, his mount was a rear-engine Halibrand Shrike inspired by the Formula 1 cars being raced in Europe. MacDonald was in another rear-engine car, this one an oddity created by hot rodder Mickey Thompson, with wide, aerodynamic bodywork. It looked like a pancake on wheels. Railbirds called it "the roller skate." It wasn't a compliment.

The three cars had converged here in the provincial Midwestern town of Speedway, Indiana, for the event justifiably billed as the "Greatest Spectacle in Racing." The Indy 500 was, by far, the best-attended, highest profile, and most lucrative race in the world. It was the brainchild of automotive pioneer Carl Fisher, who'd earned a fortune as the owner of the Prest-O-Lite headlight company. In 1909, he spearheaded a project to build a 2.5-mile rectangular test track on a huge plot of land in the shadow of Indianapolis, which was challenging Detroit for dominance in the nascent automobile industry. Although Fisher envisioned the facility as a proving ground for car manufacturers, it was immediately co-opted for racing. After a few false starts, the crushed-stone-and-tar track was paved with 3.2 million locally sourced bricks, and on Memorial Day in 1911, the resurfaced Indianapolis Motor Speedway, christened "the Brickyard," hosted its first five-hundred-mile race. Ray Harroun won it in his taxicab-yellow Marmon Wasp, and a tradition was born.

Indy epitomized the uniquely American approach to racing. In the rest of the world, races were usually staged on public roads closed for the occasion. Although several significant road races were run in the United States shortly after the turn of the century, this format didn't resonate with American spectators, who lacked the patience to watch cars whiz past once every few minutes—or once, period, in the case of point-to-point races. As fate would have it, the country already had hundreds of racetracks dotting county fairgrounds from coast to coast. True, they'd been built for horse racing, but they worked just as well for horseless carriages. So dirt ovals, ranging from grand mile-long circuits in Milwaukee and Springfield to quarter-mile bullrings in Podunkville, USA, became the backbone of American motorsports.

The Depression gutted the racing world along with the rest of the country; in 1938, while unemployed laborers lined up by the thousands at soup kitchens, the national championship schedule was trimmed to a grand total of two races. But with the return to prosperity after World War II, the sport enjoyed a renaissance. The Championship Trail, as it was known, expanded to about a dozen races a year. Almost all of them were contested on dirt tracks, where robust cars with high centers of gravity were the hot setup. But Indy paid more prize money than the rest of the races put together. And there was no way to put a value on the prestige it carried. "If you never win another dollar in racing the rest of your life, you will still be someone," cigar-chomping 1958 winner Jimmy Bryan said. "You will always be famous. Men will envy you. Women will chase you. Wherever you go, people will look at you and point you out to others. People will buy your name. When you're old and tired and scared and ready to die, you will still be someone who once won the 500."[3]

Even though the cars would race on paved tracks only a couple of times a year, car owners with deep pockets commissioned low-slung pavement machines with the solitary purpose of winning Indy. In 1952, Frank Kurtis, who ran the nation's largest race car factory, established a new template with his Kurtis-Kraft 500A. Offsetting the driveline and canting the engine to the left allowed driver Bill Vukovich to hunker down in the cockpit and reduce the height of the hood, which produced sleeker aerodynamic bodywork. It also lowered the center of gravity, which improved the handling, as did shifting 150 pounds more weight to the left-side tires. The rakish good looks and high beltline of the Kurtis prompted the nickname "roadster." Vuky won Indy in 1953 and 1954, and he should have won in 1952 and 1955. In years to come, builders like A.J. Watson, Quin Epperly, Lujie Lesovsky, and Eddie Kuzma improved incrementally on the 500A. But "incrementally" is the key here. The builders were magnificent fabricators and mechanics rather than academically trained engineers and designers, and while the improvements they introduced every year were ingenious, they weren't game changers. In 1952, the fastest qualifying speed was turned by a supercharged Novi at 139.03 miles per hour. In 1961, Sachs claimed the pole at a speed of 147.481. In a sport as fast-paced as racing, gaining 8 mph over a ten-year stretch didn't seem like much progress.

Reigning Indy 500 champ Rodger Ward saw the future foretold when he raced a Kurtis-Kraft midget (!) in the US Grand Prix at Sebring in 1959, qualifying 43.8 seconds (!!) off the pole. Immediately recognizing the potential of the rear-engine F1 cars, he contacted a British transplant named Dr. Frank Falkner. Trained at Cambridge, Falkner had moved to California to pursue a career as a pediatrician and biology professor at Cal Berkeley, but he remained tight with members of the Formula 1 fraternity. (Years later, he would help his protégé, Danny Sullivan, get an F1 ride with his old mate, Ken Tyrrell.) Falkner was friends with John Cooper, who'd sparked a car-design revolution by putting the horse behind the cart—that is, moving the engine from its traditional position in front of the cockpit to a more advantageous spot behind the driver. Cooper's rear-engine car was lower, lighter, and far more agile than its voluptuous front-engine rivals. Australian Jack Brabham drove a Cooper T51 to the world championship in 1959, and he was cruising to a second title in the upgraded low-line T53 in 1960 when Falkner convinced Cooper to make a pit stop in Indianapolis before continuing on to Riverside for the US Grand Prix. Driving the car in F1 form and giving away more than 100 cubic inches in engine capacity, Brabham flat-footed it around the track while turning a lap at 144.8 mph, which would have put him eighth on the grid in the 500.

Falkner introduced Cooper to Jim Kimberly, the scion of the Kimberly-Clark paper goods fortune. An SCCA stalwart and competent road racer, "Gentleman Jim" paid $20,000—twice what the team would make in an F1 season—to finance construction of a Cooper lightly modified for Indy with a longer frame, an offset suspension, seat belts, a roll bar, and a Coventry-Climax engine punched out to 2.7 liters. (The Offys displaced 4.2 liters.) Racing what looked like a minnow in a school of great white sharks, Brabham qualified thirteenth and finished ninth despite using only 6,000 rpm to save tires. If he'd been able to push the engine to its 6,750 rpm redline, he might have won the race—and, with it, nearly $120,000 in prize money. The upshot was obvious: A rear-engine car designed and built specifically for Indy would instantly render the front-engine roadsters obsolete. But change is hard, even when resistance is futile, so the Speedway cognoscenti turned a blind eye to the writing on the wall. Once again, it remained for another outsider, the protean Mickey Thompson, to take the next step in the Indy makeover.

A prototypical SoCal hot rodder with unlimited ambition and a seemingly infinite inventory of ideas, Thompson was credited with putting the driver behind the rear axle to create the slingshot dragster that would dominate drag racing until the 1970s. In 1960, he'd gone to Bonneville with a streamliner packing four supercharged Pontiacs V-8s, and while he didn't set an official world record because the Challenger 1 broke before he could make the required return run, he still managed a one-way pass at 406.60 mph—the fastest speed ever recorded on land until jet-powered land-speed-record cars took off. In 1962, he embarked on a quest to conquer Indy with a scratch-built rear-engine car designed by John Crosthwaite, a Brit who'd sharpened his skills at Cooper and Lotus. Instead of fitting the engine bay with a standard-issue Offy, Thompson opted for a hopped-up Buick V-8. To drive the car, Thompson again ventured beyond the circle track world and hired a fellow Southern Californian, Dan Gurney, who was establishing his credentials as the fastest American in F1. Gurney qualified eighth with a shot of nitro and was running ninth when the transaxle let go.

Not bad, Gurney thought, for a team with virtually no circuit racing experience. Which got him thinking. What if, he wondered, he were working with guys who were on the leading edge of rear-engine race car design? Gurney cajoled Colin Chapman, the founder and resident genius at Team Lotus, into spending a few days at the Speedway. When he got to Indy, Chapman was appalled by what he saw in the wooden garages of Gasoline Alley. "I thought I'd gone back 15 years," he said. "Having seen these old-fashioned and antiquated cars trundling around, I thought, 'Well, all you've got to do is get an engine with about half the power of these great lumps of junk, build a decent chassis and you've won the race.'"[4]

Then came one of those serendipitous confluences of events that changes everything. Even as visions of sugarplum fairies bearing bushels of prize money were dancing in Chapman's head, the Ford Motor Company was contemplating a return to Indy. In 1935, to publicize his new flathead V-8, Henry Ford had financed a wildly optimistic project promoted by Preston Tucker to commission Harry Miller, the colossus of American racing between the wars, to design and build a fleet of cars to conquer Indy. Ten Miller-Fords were ordered. Six were built. Four qualified. None finished. The calamity permanently soured Henry on racing. It was only after his grandson, Henry II, aka "the Deuce," took the reins of the family business that Ford decided to return to Indy with a new small-block V-8.

Gurney put Ford in touch with Chapman. A structural engineer by training, Chapman had rewritten the rules governing Grand Prix design when he unveiled the Lotus 25 at the start of the 1962 season. Unlike the ladder-frame cars of the prewar era and the tube-frame cars popularized after World War II, the Lotus 25 featured a so-called monocoque structure, with the driver sitting in a central tub and the skin of the body forming the rest of the chassis. A monocoque is both stronger and lighter than the alternatives, which is why it's still used to this day in almost all forms of racing, assuming the rules permit it. Chapman created a made-for-Indy version of the Lotus 25, and he stuck a Ford V-8 behind the driver. In 1963, Gurney and Jim Clark drove a pair of these Lotus-Fords in the 500. Clark finished second, and he would have won if race leader Parnelli Jones had been black-flagged for leaking oil—a controversial no-call that critics called a case of home cooking.

By 1964, you didn't need to be a fortune teller to see what the future held. Twelve of the thirty-three starters were in rear-engine cars, seven of them powered by the stout four-cam version of the Ford V-8. Despite the obvious advantages of the rear-engine entries, diehards derided them as "funny cars" and chose to stick with their front-engine dinosaurs. "These new cars just seem like a bunch of sticks strung together with chicken wire," A.J. Foyt declared.[5] Paradoxically, the seeming fragility of the rear-engine cars meant they often fared better in crashes because the wheels tended to shear off, dissipating energy that would otherwise have been transmitted to the driver. Roadsters, on the other hand, were prone to flipping and gyrating like a crazed gymnast on a tumbling run.

Sachs was one of the few members of the old guard who'd defected to the funny car camp, in his case driving a rear-engine Shrike commissioned by Ted Halibrand of magnesium wheel fame. Chapman was back with Lotus-Fords for Clark and Gurney. Thompson returned as well with his streamlined roller skates. Aerodynamics were a black art in those days, and Thompson hadn't mastered it, which translated into cars that were always threatening to spin in the corners. Making matters worse, USAC, which sanctioned Indy car racing, refused to let him run the smaller-than-usual wheels the cars had been designed to use. Heftier rubber did nothing to improve the handling. But Thompson thought he had an ace in the hole—a driver who, as one rival said, "was the most talented guy in the world for running an oversteering car."[6]

Crew cut and baby-faced, MacDonald looked like an *American Graffiti* character sprung to life. He'd started off drag racing while working as a dealership mechanic in exurban Los Angeles, then graduated to road racing with the SCCA and immediately established himself as the hottest solid-axle Corvette driver on the West Coast. This led to a gig as the top Cobra shoe on the all-conquering Shelby American team and a one-off NASCAR drive that would have earned him a win in the prestigious Riverside race if his transmission hadn't crumbled. Then, driving a rear-engine King Cobra sports racer, he trounced fields including two F1 world champions and two Indy 500 winners to sweep the big-money year-end sports car races at Riverside and Laguna Seca. "He had a tremendous ability to jump in anything and go like hell," said Joe Freitas, a rival Corvette driver. "He could have raced at the beginning of the century, and he could have raced today. I think he would have raced a Sherman tank. Come to think of it, he would have driven a soapbox derby car if it looked like it had some potential."[7]

Rad versus trad. At Indy in 1964, sports car ace Dave MacDonald practices in Mickey Thompson's ultra-wide, rear-engine, full-bodied "roller skate." Behind him is Texas oval-meister Jim McElreath in an old-school Kurtis-Kraft 500K roadster with a Novi crammed into the engine bay. If there was one attribute shared by the two cars, it's that both of them turned out to be technical dead ends. *Revs Institute / Robert Tronolone Photograph Collection*

Thompson hired MacDonald, in part, precisely because he didn't have any experience at Indy, so he wouldn't bring any preconceived notions with him to the Speedway. Most of the veterans who tested the roller skates didn't care for Thompson's heretical creations. Grand Prix veteran Masten Gregory hung one of them on the wall during practice, and several Indy car pros walked away from potential rides after getting spooked by the evil handling characteristics. Although MacDonald sucked it up to put his car in the show in a respectable fourteenth starting spot, he confided to friends and family that the car didn't feel right.

His King Cobra crew chief, Wally Peat, begged him to walk away. "I tried and tried and tried," he said. "But Dave was the type of guy who, when he said something, that was it. He wouldn't quit."[8]

Nor was MacDonald the type of guy who would stroke it just to earn an easy payday. He passed six cars on the first lap and was popping out of line to overtake Walt Hansgen on the second when Hansgen moved left to pass Jim Hurtubise. MacDonald juked farther left to avoid Hansgen. As he did, the rear end broke loose. MacDonald slid broadside through the short chute with the brakes locked up and the steering cranked to full opposite lock. But none of these inputs affected his trajectory. At this point, he wasn't driving a car; he was riding a missile. It exploded into the inside wall. The rubber fuel bladder tore near the filler cap, sloshing gasoline over the hot exhaust pipes and igniting. Blazing like a Viking funeral pyre, MacDonald's car caromed back across the track, trailing a wall of dense black smoke and bright-orange flames in its wake. Two cars whistled past, miraculously unscathed. Right behind them were Sachs, Rutherford, Ronnie Duman, and Bobby Unser, nose to tail, converging with MacDonald's fireball.

"There was probably a three-foot gap between his tailpipes and the outside wall, and I was hard on the brakes right on Eddie's bumper," Rutherford recalled. "At the last instant, Eddie turned to the left just a little bit and hit MacDonald. Both of those cars were full of gasoline, and when he impacted, it felt like somebody had jerked open the door of a blast furnace. It was incredible. Eddie's car reared up at the back, and I went under it, and his right-rear tire put a tire mark on the nose of my Watson."[9] Later, back in Gasoline Alley, Rutherford's crew found a sandy lump with a piece of string looped through it in the engine bay. It turned out to be the lemon that Sachs wore around his neck to suck on during pit stops and caution periods.

Rutherford, Duman, and Unser drove straight through the fire. All three were burned, though not critically. Brabham, who'd qualified farther back, was in the next group of cars to confront the conflagration. "That was about the most terrifying experience I've ever had," he said. "It was an absolute inferno; the flames rose probably 50 feet into the air, and to feel yourself going virtually blindfolded through the middle of that and knowing there is nothing you can do about it is terrible. It was just an unbelievably good sight to come out on the other side and see the track again. I didn't go back for a long time after 1964."[10]

Sachs was killed instantly after T-boning the roller skate. MacDonald, hideously burned, was transported to Methodist Hospital in Indianapolis, but he was pronounced dead nearly three hours after the accident. Meanwhile, the race was red-flagged while impenetrable black smoke billowed angrily into the blue sky, making the Speedway look more like a war zone than a racetrack. Nearly two hours passed while the fire and cleanup crews repaired the damage. Despite the unprecedented delay, there was no talk about canceling the race. Frankly, the notion of pulling the plug to honor the dead never occurred to anybody. In those days, the show went on, no matter what. The races had continued even as the bodies were being collected after the catastrophes at Le Mans in 1955, the Mille Miglia in 1957, and the Italian Grand Prix in 1961. The victors were crowned, and the dead were buried, and then the carnival moved on to its next stop. So at 3:32 p.m., the Indy 500 resumed, and after completing 197 more laps, Foyt took the checkered flag. In Victory Circle, in front of the Borg-Warner Trophy, he glumly brandished a fresh-off-the-press copy of the *Indianapolis Star.* The banner headline on the front page read: FOYT WINNER IN 500. SACHS, MACDONALD DIE.

This was the worst accident in 500 history, which was saying something considering Indy's abominable record. It wasn't so much a matter of how many people had died; it was *how* they'd died—one driver killed by unspeakably violent blunt-force trauma, the other burned almost beyond recognition, all broadcast live on closed-circuit television and captured in grotesque photos that ran in newspapers and magazines from coast to coast. There were plenty of lamentations and recriminations, but nothing really changed. The essential problem was that cars were going faster, which meant that they were releasing more kinetic energy when they hit an immovable object, be it a concrete wall or a telephone pole. So the accident that claimed the lives of Sachs and MacDonald wasn't a one-off. It was a harbinger of things to come.

By longstanding tradition, the Indy car circus moved to the Milwaukee Mile a week after the 500. Hurtubise was running third in a front-engine roadster behind Ward and Foyt. A crowd favorite known as Herk—short for Hercules—for his strength and courage, Hurtubise had achieved cult hero status as he battled with his great friend and rival, Parnelli Jones, in the IMCA sprint car series. At Indy the previous year, he'd qualified second to Jones in the Novi, adored by the fans for the scream of its supercharged engine. When Ward slowed unexpectedly with a seized bearing, Hurtubise ran over Foyt's right-rear tire and flew like a fighter being shot off the deck of an aircraft carrier. "I peeled over like a P-51, grabbed the wheel and crouched down," Hurtubise recalled. "When I hit, my right rear tire came off and smashed me in the chest. It broke three ribs, punctured a lung and knocked me out. That's the last I remember until they were carrying me to the ambulance."[11]

The car erupted into flames when it landed. Since the accident occurred on the front straight, the safety crew was there immediately. Even so, Hurtubise was critically burned over nearly half his body. Practically all the skin on his hands was gone, leaving the tendons and bones exposed. "I told [the doctors] that I was a guy who made a living grabbing hold of something round," Hurtubise said. "I told them to fix my hands so I could do that."[12] Later, he joked to the press, "I told the doctors just to shape them so I could grab a steering wheel and hold a bottle of beer."[13] It took Hurtubise nearly a year to recover, and while he won a handful of races after that—the first, in storybook fashion, at Milwaukee in a USAC stock car show—he was never the same driver after the wreck.

Two months later, the Championship Trail led to the one-mile dirt oval at Springfield. A quarter of the way through the race, a roadster driven by Bill Horstmeyer, a little-known midget driver making his first Champ Car start, brushed the fence in Turn Four. The car flipped, rolled several times, and finally came to rest upside down just short of the pits. As mechanics rushed to the car, it exploded. The fire was so intense that it took several minutes for firefighters to tamp it down enough so that rescuers could reach the cockpit. Horstmeyer died after being pulled out of the smoldering wreckage.

Two months after that, rising star Bobby Marshman was testing tires in an ex–Jim Clark Lotus 29 at Phoenix International Raceway. Although Marshman had gone through the traditional midget and sprint car apprenticeship, he'd adapted quickly to rear-engine funny cars. At Indy earlier in the year, he'd qualified second and effortlessly led for thirty-three laps before breaking while pulling away from Clark and the rest of the field. At Phoenix, he crashed hard after the throttle reportedly stuck at 145 mph. The inferno that resulted after he hit the wall was so fierce that it set the guardrail and grass on fire, and it took firefighters wearing Air Force–issue asbestos suits a minute to yank him from the cockpit. Making matters even worse, hydraulic action had forced fuel out of the center tank and directly onto Marshman, who was burned over 90 percent of his body. After examining him, a doctor said, "There is no skin left that is suitable for grafting."[14] Marshman died six days later at the Brooke Army Burn Center in San Antonio, where Hurtubise was still recovering from his wreck at Milwaukee.

Marshman's death closed the book on one of the most nightmarish years in Indy car history. But the Championship Trail wasn't the only series where fire was wreaking havoc. A week before the accident that claimed the lives of MacDonald and Sachs, NASCAR was at Charlotte Motor Speedway for the World 600. The pole speed was a whopping 8.5 mph faster than the previous year. Early in the race, Ned Jarrett and Junior Johnson were running side by side through Turns One and Two. Johnson inadvertently tapped Jarrett, who spun into the inside wall. "I could see [my car] was on fire in my rear-view mirror," Jarrett recalled. "So my biggest concern in that wreck was, 'Get this thing stopped and get out of here.'"[15]

Fireball Roberts was right behind them. Tall and good-looking, with a memorable nickname derived from his days as a star baseball pitcher, Roberts is often described as the best driver never to win a NASCAR championship. Blinded by tire smoke, he followed Jarrett into the concrete barrier. Roberts's car flipped and landed on its roof, and he was still strapped in the seat when fuel leaking into the cockpit from the punctured gas tank caught fire. Jarrett, who'd extricated himself from his own burning car, heard Roberts yelling at him: "Oh my God, Ned, help me, I'm on fire!"[16] By the time Jarrett was able to pull him to safety, Roberts's uniform was soaked with fuel, and Roberts himself was a human flame. "The next time I came around, I recognized Fireball's car," Richard Petty said. "He was on the ground, and Ned was trying to tear off his burning clothes. The next time around, I couldn't look."[17]

With burns over three-quarters of his body, Roberts lingered for five weeks before dying in the hospital.

Fire might be the most harrowing of man's primal fears. The terror it inspires is especially acute if you're in a confined space—say a race car motoring along at 150 mph or, even worse, a race car that's been so badly balled up in a crash that you can't get out of it. During this era, drivers steadfastly braved a wide variety of potentially deadly safety hazards, from runoff areas dotted with trees and steep gullies to roll bars too low and flimsy to protect them in the case of a rollover. But fire is where they drew the line. "There isn't a driver alive, macho or not, who's not afraid of getting his ass burned up," said Bill Simpson, who built a safety empire based on this insight.[18] Or as early NASCAR champion Tim Flock put it, more colorfully, "There's one thing that all drivers worry about, and that's catching fire. I've seen eight or nine of 'em get it like that—a crack-up, a big blaze, and all you ever see are the hands reaching out the window. You never get over something like that. It's almost put me buggy a couple of times."[19]

Vic Elford, one of racing's greatest all-arounders, was an early adopter of fire-retardant Nomex race wear: fire suit, underwear, gloves, boots, balaclava. Although he was best known for his exploits in sports prototypes and rallying, he also ran a handful of NASCAR races. As he was swaddling himself in Nomex before his first stock car event, the Daytona 500 in 1969, he was confronted by Buddy Baker. A good ol' boy of prodigious proportions, Baker was particularly formidable on the fastest of the superspeedways. "Where's he think he's going?" he facetiously asked the assembled drivers. "To the mooooon?"[20]

Two years later, when Elford returned for another shot at the Daytona 500, he found Baker wearing Nomex everything. Why? The previous year, Baker had been running second in the Alabama 500 at Talladega Superspeedway, the fastest racetrack in the world. A tire shredded at 190 mph and knocked a fitting off the oil cooler. Oil seeped out and ignited. The underside of the car was engulfed in flames that burned through the floorboard. Baker spun the car on the grass apron to get it slowed down and dove out of the passenger side window after suffering second-degree burns to his legs and face. "It was the scariest thing that ever happened to me," he said later. "I don't really mind losing this time. I'm just happy to be alive."[21]

Fire was such an intractable problem largely because the technology to effectively combat it didn't yet exist. But as drivers continued to die and fans were increasingly horrified by the ugly scenes immortalized in newspapers and on television, it became clear that Something Had To Be Done. Contemporary observers may be surprised to learn that most of the credit for upgrading car safety in the 1960s belongs not to the FIA but to USAC. These days, the FIA is the most powerful sanctioning body in the world, and promoting safety is an essential feature of its brand. USAC, meanwhile, has seen its influence decline dramatically. Once the sanctioning body of the Indy 500 and the Championship Trail, it now lords over a much-diminished kingdom of sprint cars, midgets, and Silver Crown cars, which are modern versions of the old dirt Champ Cars raced by Foyt, Jones, and Hurtubise. But in the 1960s and '70s, it was USAC rather than the FIA that led the charge to make racing safer.

While Buddy Baker was running hard near the end of the Alabama 500 at Talladega in 1970, a tire shredded, knocking out an oil fitting of his Dodge Daytona, and the cockpit of his winged warrior was engulfed in flames. After spinning the car in the infield, Baker wriggled out and hopped into a nearby panel truck that drove him to the hospital—with his burned right leg hanging out the window. *Cotton Owens Garage*

The United States Auto Club was formed in 1956. Up until that point the Automobile Association of America had been the main sanctioning body of American motorsports. The AAA began overseeing racing through the newly formed Contest Board in 1902, when automobiles were playthings of wealthy sportsmen. Even as the sport became more mainstream—and, to the chagrin of the ruling class, more blue-collar—the AAA governed as a haughty tyrant, branding unaffiliated tracks as outlaws and blackballing drivers who ignored its edicts. Although he was already a well-known race promoter in Los Angeles, J.C. Agajanian, who would later own two Indy 500 winners, wasn't even allowed into Gasoline Alley during his first visit to the Indianapolis Motor Speedway. In 1947, when Bill France sought AAA sanction for his fledgling stock car series, he was not-so-politely told to get lost. Seven years later, when he snuck into Gasoline Alley with a borrowed credential, he was humiliatingly escorted out by security guards. Afterward, Harry McQuinn, chief steward of the race, declared disdainfully, "We have a long-standing disagreement with NASCAR on what constitutes good racing."[22]

The AAA abandoned motorsports after a shocking two-week stretch during the summer of 1955, when two-time world champion Alberto Ascari crashed fatally during a test session, Vukovich died while leading the Indy 500, and Frenchman Pierre Levegh was killed at Le Mans along with at least eighty spectators. This tragic trifecta prompted the AAA to quit racing and concentrate on road cars. Tony Hulman, the owner of the Indianapolis Motor Speedway, initiated the meeting that established USAC in 1955. Veteran driver Duane Carter was elected director of competition—a sign that the new organization would have a more collegial relationship with racers and promoters than its imperious predecessor. From the start, promoting safety was a primary component of USAC's vision for the sport. One of its first acts was to slow Indy cars down by trimming engine size by fifteen cubic inches for 1957. And it retained the AAA's reputation for enforcing the world's most stringent standards for race car construction.

"Those old guys who ran USAC were always thinking about safety," said former Indy car mechanic Mike Lashmett. "Wonderful men like Art Pillsbury and Frankie DelRoy and Shim Malone had been around since the '20s and '30s, so they'd seen it all. Death wasn't acceptable to them. USAC was very strict as far as the rules were concerned. A car had to be put together properly. You had to have your Magnaflux papers. All the fasteners had to be Grade 8 or better, meaning they were at least aircraft quality. Everything had to be safety-wired. Otherwise, they weren't gonna let you run. Those guys were ardent about safety. I mean, there was no goofing around."[23]

Indy car mechanics were appalled by the shoddy quality of the first rear-engine cars to arrive from England. Mission-critical components were often brazed rather than welded, making them more susceptible to breaking under extreme loads. Instead of using aircraft-quality fasteners, European formula cars were filled with the sort of nuts and bolts found at big-box hardware stores. Military-spec AN (for Army-Navy) fittings, which were commonplace in American race cars, were largely unknown in Europe. Engineer Peter Bryant, who's best known for his Can-Am designs, began his career in Formula 1 before moving to the States to work on Thompson's star-crossed Indy car program. "Compared with the contemporary Indy cars," he said, "the F1 cars were death traps."[24]

The barrage of fire-related deaths and injuries in 1964 prompted USAC officials to take action. First, they banned center-mounted fuel tanks in front of the drivers like the one that burst when Marshman crashed, drenching him in gasoline. Next, fuel tank capacity was limited to seventy-five gallons, and a minimum of two pit stops was mandated for the Indy 500. This eliminated the major advantage of gasoline—better fuel mileage—and had the practical effect of causing all competitors to fill their fuel tanks with alcohol. But this mitigated the problem rather than solving it. Yes, alcohol wasn't as explosive as gasoline, but alcohol fires had killed Horstmeyer and badly burned Hurtubise, Jones, and Jim McElreath during the previous six months. The real issue wasn't the fuel; it was the fuel tank.

USAC increased the required thickness of the steel or aluminum sheets forming the shell of the fuel tank. But the big news was that fuel had to be stored in a rubber bag inside the metal tank, which was now known as a fuel cell, in accordance with contemporary aviation practice. British companies such as FPT (Fireproof Tanks) and Marston Excelsior were already supplying bladders for rear-engine formula cars, but they didn't inspire much confidence. "The original ones were so thin that they leaked before we put them in the car," said Howden Ganley, who worked as a mechanic on McLaren F1 cars before becoming an F1 driver in his own right. "So they were a bit of a disaster."[25]

At the time, Firestone and Goodyear were just beginning their titanic battle for race tire supremacy in the Indy car world as well as F1 and NASCAR. As it happened, both companies had aviation divisions that sold fuel cells for airplanes, based on the self-sealing fuel tanks used in combat aircraft during World War II. Firestone and Goodyear fuel cells modified for racing were available to Indy car teams in 1965, and twenty-two-gallon fuel cells were mandated in NASCAR in 1966. (Prior to that, stock cars used the standard gas tanks found in daily drivers.) In 1968, SCCA required fuel cells for its faster classes. Before long, Goodyear and Firestone were facing competition. Among their first rivals were Donn Allen, an Indy car mechanic who later ran the Shelby American race shop. Then came Aero Tec Labs, which sold its first fuel cell for a Formula Ford in 1970 and still does business as ATL.

In 1970, the FIA required fuel cells in Formula 1. The next year, the rule was extended to Group 5 sports prototypes. For the 1971 season, the FIA also adopted the far more rigorous American standard for fuel-cell performance of four hundred pounds of tensile strength, twenty-five pounds of tear strength, and fifty pounds of puncture strength. (Previously, the FIA had required only ninety pounds of tensile strength, twenty pounds of tear strength, and twenty-five pounds of puncture strength.) Still, fuel cells weren't foolproof, and bladders were known to fail if enough force, or the right kind of force, was applied to them, as Mel Kenyon found out at the freshly paved and reconfigured Langhorne Speedway in 1965.

The new version of Langhorne wasn't quite as murderous as the dirt track iteration had been. The whoop-de-doo section known as Puke Hollow was gone, and the new D-shaped layout meant there was a straightaway to catch your breath. Kenyon was early in a fifty-year-long driving career that would see him crowned as the unofficial King of the Midgets. With his brother, Don, wrenching on his cars, Kenyon had moved up to the Championship Trail. Two weeks earlier, he'd finished third at the Milwaukee Mile. At Langhorne, he qualified near the back in an elderly roadster that had been retrofitted with one of the first of the new generation of fuel cells.

Kenyon normally wore a fireman's suit in his midget. Although it was bulky and didn't breathe well, this wasn't an issue in midget races, which were short and often run at night. But the Champ Car race was a one hundred miler, scheduled to last about an hour, and the weather was sweltering on race day. "I took off the fireman's suit because, in the ninety-five-degree heat, I thought I'd never finish the race," Kenyon said.[26] Instead, he opted for a traditional Hinchman jumpsuit made of "flameproof" cotton, which was supposed to—or, more accurately, was said to—protect drivers from fire for ten seconds.

Twenty-six laps into the race, Kenyon lost his engine. As he slowed with his hand in the air, Hurtubise, who'd recently recovered from the burns he'd suffered the previous year, spun in Kenyon's oil and tagged Ralph Liguori. Ligouri rear-ended Kenyon's car and punctured its fuel cell. The hit also slammed Kenyon's head into the roll bar. He was unconscious while the car was engulfed in flames. A firefighter who tried to pull him out of the cockpit was scorched and later treated for smoke inhalation. By the time Joe Leonard, who'd spun to avoid the accident, and two observers rescued him, Kenyon had suffered burns over 60 percent of his body. "That ten-second suit I had on didn't last long in a five-minute fire," Kenyon said, chuckling grimly.[27]

Although he lost most of the fingers on his left hand, Kenyon recovered after a long stay at the same burn center in San Antonio where Hurtubise and Marshman had been treated. His brother and father designed a glove with a grommet in the palm that hooked to a stud in the steering wheel. With it, Kenyon would win more than one hundred USAC midget features before retiring at age seventy-six. But his experience highlighted two essential points: First, fuel cells weren't infallible. And second, protecting the driver was just as important as protecting the car.

Well into the 1950s, many drivers still raced in T-shirts and polo shirts. Hell, Dick Kraft, creator of the Bug, the world's first purpose-built dragster, went bare-chested (though he wore a makeshift seat belt and

Fire was a constant—and terrifying—threat in the 1960s. Not only were the cars "mobile bombs," in the words of driver-turned-FIA-President Max Mosley, but track workers rarely had the skills or equipment to extinguish fires once they started. Phil Hill escaped unharmed after crashing in the Austrian Grand Prix in 1964, but he could only stand by and watch as his Cooper T66 burned to the ground. *Revs Institute / George Phillips Photograph Collection*

war surplus goggles). By the 1960s, cotton uniforms were de rigueur for professional drivers—typically powder-blue Dunlop suits in Europe and white Hinchmans in the United States. DIYers would dip their suits in a solution of boric acid, a practice that produced more peace of mind than actual protection from fire. Uniforms advertised as "flameproof" were increasingly popular, even required by some sanctioning bodies. They featured cotton that had been treated with a proprietary chemical, the most popular trademarked as Proban. Hype notwithstanding, these suits couldn't stand up to a serious fire. Although Kenyon referred to his uniform as a "ten-second suit," *Car and Driver* reported that, in a

2,500-degree fire, a driver wearing "flameproof" cotton would feel heat in less than a second and start to blister in 2.5 seconds.

Uniforms with a layer of asbestos covered with an aluminized fabric had been developed for firefighters working at airports and in extreme environments. In 1964, Lou Senter of Ansen Automotive, one of the first aftermarket companies catering to the hot rod industry, offered a version with a fireproof hood, air filters, and gloves. He found some takers in the drag racing world, especially the guys driving front-engine rails, who were literally in the line of fire when an engine popped or a blower blew, dousing them with hot oil and combustible nitromethane. But the aluminized suits were too hot and bulky to be worn in any race longer than a quarter mile. Fiberglass was another alternative since it didn't burn, which made it perfect for a flash fire. Unfortunately, it transferred heat through thermal conductance, so if a driver was trapped in a fire for more than a few seconds, he would start getting cooked like a potato baked in foil.

The breakthrough in uniform design was the product of research done by a woman who had no association with or apparent interest in racing. Her name was Alice Stoll, and she was a research physiologist who specialized in aerospace medicine. While working at the Naval Air Development Center in Warminster, Pennsylvania, Stoll patented a device that tested, analyzed, and compared the fire-resisting properties of various materials. Her research showed that treating fabric with fire-retardant chemicals like boric acid or Proban was a losing proposition. The way to go, she found, was to clothe human beings in fabrics that were inherently fire-resistant precisely because they were made with fire-resistant fibers.

Chemists at DuPont took the ball from Stoll and ran with it. Wilfred Sweeny is credited with inventing the product later trademarked as Nomex. In technical terms, it's a synthetic aromatic polyamide polymer. Unless you're a chemist, all you need to know is that it's a man-made material that can withstand temperatures up to 700 degrees Fahrenheit. Unlike cotton, it stops burning when the flame is removed. Unlike nylon, it doesn't melt. Unlike fiberglass, it absorbs heat rather than transmitting it to the skin. As Sweeny's patent filing stated, "In fiber form the polymers of this invention may be used for high temperature heat and electrical insulation, protective clothing and curtains, filtration media, packing and gasketing materials, brake linings and clutch facings."[28]

Another DuPont chemist, Wayne Sorenson, figured out how to transform Nomex into a short-spun yarn similar to cotton. The downside was that the fuzzy texture made uniforms hard to clean. A few years later, DuPont upgraded to a filament yarn with a satiny finish. But it wasn't until the early 1970s that Nomex came in any color other than white or off-white. Other companies developed Nomex alternatives of their own, such as Durette and Kynol, and Mark Donohue hawked gold fire suits made of a flame-retardant material trademarked as Fypro through his Racemark brand. But Nomex became so ubiquitous that it's now used generically to mean any fire-resistant fabric, much as Kleenex is used to refer to facial tissues of all descriptions.

Even before it was available on a retail basis, Nomex was being used by NASA and the US Navy. DuPont quickly realized that automobile racing was a growth opportunity. In 1965, company reps visited the Hinchman factory in Indianapolis. Although Hinchman has since been overshadowed by suppliers such as Simpson, Sparco, and Stand 21, it ruled the American uniform market at the time. J.B. Hinchman had gotten into the business after supplying pristine white coveralls for the Indy 500 in 1925 to Pete DePaolo, who gave the company a burst of free publicity by winning the race. By mid-century, Hinchman was the default choice for Indy car, sprint car, and midget drivers, and the brand was so well-known that its suits were also worn by stars as diverse as Clark, Petty, and the king of cool, Steve McQueen.

In its March 1966 issue, *Car and Driver* ran a long feature story about the new kid on the block. "Nomex. Remember that name," Steve Smith wrote. "If you drive a race car, Nomex could save your life."[29] The article noted that several vendors, including Hinchman, were already selling Nomex uniforms, and it stated flat out that this new material was vastly superior to anything else on the market. But since these were early days, and the technology was still being perfected, drivers were advised to wear not only a Nomex uniform but also Nomex undies. It would be years before improved versions of Nomex, coupled with the development of stronger needles and more capable sewing machines, made double- and triple-layer suits possible.

Bill Simpson got into the act in 1968. A racer himself and a promotional savant, Simpson lit himself and his Nomex suit on fire in Pit Lane at Indy in 1969 to demonstrate how much faith he had in his products—and to shut up Foyt, who'd been giving him grief all month for being a loudmouthed hippie. At the same time, Firestone and Goodyear saw Nomex uniforms as a way to protect their investment in their contracted drivers while advertising the company brand. Starting in the late 1960s, virtually every driver at Indy wore a Nomex suit with either red stripes running from the collar, along the shoulders, and down the sleeves (Firestone) or a pair of vertical red, yellow, and blue stripes emblazoned on the left side of the chest (Goodyear).

The only downside of Nomex was the price: Nomex uniforms cost two to three times as much as "flameproof" cotton, which was about twice as much as untreated cotton. A time-honored racing axiom holds that a lot of guys who would readily spend $10,000 to go one second faster wouldn't invest ten cents on safety. So when the SCCA announced that it was requiring drivers to wear Nomex gear in 1968, the self-styled rugged individualists among its membership suffered a collective meltdown. "Fireproof socks! What next? I thought I came to drive a racing car, not to walk on a bloody bed of coals!"[30] Willie Schuldt ranted in a letter to the editor of *Autoweek*. This prompted a snarky response from Peter A. Lake, who'd been singed in a wreck in his Elva-BMW during an SCCA national at Virginia International Raceway. "At the risk of sounding melodramatic, let me say, Mr. Schuldt, there is nothing quite like the thrill of breathing in flames while pondering your legs enveloped in burning gasoline," he wrote. "Be a good boy, Mr. Schuldt, wear your fireproof socks, and don't make the insurance rates go up any more."[31]

Ultimately, what sold drivers on Nomex was that it worked. They knew better than anybody that crashes were bound to happen, and fuel cells or not, they knew that cars were bound to catch fire. Nomex gave them a fighting chance to survive no matter how wicked the flames. This was demonstrated not just to the drivers but also to tens of thousands of TV viewers during a rare live television broadcast of the 150-mile Champ Car race at Langhorne in 1970. This was to be the last major race at the unloved track where Mel Kenyon had been critically burned in 1965. The next year, USAC drivers would vote to boycott a scheduled

Indy car event, and Langhorne was repurposed as the foundation of a shopping center.

The Langhorne 150 opened with a bang as two tailenders tangled on the first lap. As soon as the track went green again on lap ten, Sammy Sessions, a sprint car stud struggling to establish a toehold in Indy cars, lost the rear end of his year-old Gerhardt-Offy and crunched the wall. The right-side fuel tank exploded into a fireball. The car then ricocheted across the track and wedged underneath the Pit Lane guardrail. "I'm trapped!"[32] Sessions yelled, pointing into the cockpit with smoldering gloves. Intense heat prevented the first wave of would-be rescuers from approaching the cockpit. Even after firefighters sprayed the car with fire-retarding chemicals, it continued to burn furiously for three minutes, and it took another two minutes for more than a dozen men armed with crowbars to free Sessions's foot and drag him out of the red-hot cockpit. As he watched Sessions being transported to the hospital, where he would undergo minor surgery for burns to his hands, a firefighter said, "There goes one of the world's luckiest men. He shouldn't be alive."[33]

Five years earlier, he wouldn't have been.

THE GONZO SAFETY MAVERICK

The 1971 Champ Car season was scheduled to open with what turned out to be a one-time-only race in Argentina. USAC had chartered a plane to fly the teams down to South America. The flight was leaving at 9 a.m., and USAC chief steward Dick King issued a stern warning that anybody who was late would be left behind.

Come nine o'clock, one driver was missing. True to his word, King ordered the plane to take off. As the pilot started taxiing, he spotted a passenger car speeding down the center of the runway. The car screeched to a stop, and out jumped Bill Simpson, late for the plane, but primed for adventure. "That was Bill," his one-time Indy car teammate Tom Bigelow said with a laugh. "He was a wild man. But he was a lot of fun."[34]

Simpson didn't invent safety gear, but he did something more important: He invented the modern safety gear industry. Roy Richter sold helmets. Jim Diest sold harnesses. Lew Hinchman sold fire suits.

Simpson made and sold *everything*. "My vision was to have one place where you could buy all your safety equipment," he explained.[35] Unlike his rivals, he catered to the entire spectrum of racing, from blue-collar dirt tracks to posh road-racing circuits, from drag racing to off-road enduros, from steely-eyed pros to track-day wannabes. More than any other single figure, he made safety part of the ethos of the sport.

"He was the guy who forced us to start thinking about safety," Mario Andretti said. "Until then, it wasn't macho to worry about stuff like that."[36] Rick Mears, who was wearing Simpson's wicked-looking Darth Vader–style helmet when he won Indy in 1979, stated the case even more baldly: "He's probably done more for racing than anybody else in the sport."[37]

Simpson succeeded in part because he was a racer himself, so he understood both what drivers wanted and what they needed—directives that were sometimes at odds. He prospered because he had a knack for promotion, and he was a larger-than-life figure who commanded attention. Friends described him as smart, generous, loyal, hard-working, and honest to a fault. Also exasperating, egocentric, belligerent, hot-tempered, vulgar, and just plain obstinate. As a longtime acquaintance once put it, "For an asshole that big to succeed in business the way he has, he's got to be a genius."[38]

Thanks to his personality and his business practices, Simpson collected enemies the way some people amass 1/43-scale models. He retired in 2010 in the wake of allegations that he'd used counterfeit components and fake certification labels. This came as no surprise to his rivals, who claimed that he unlawfully copied their designs, used inadequate materials in his products, and routinely resorted to harassment and intimidation. "Bill Simpson was not a nice person, as many who worked for him can attest, and built his business by stealing other people's ideas or contracts," said Philippe de Lespinay, the US rep for Stand 21, which has long been on the leading edge of helmet and fire suit design.[39]

Self-interest drove Simpson into the safety business. While drag racing as a teenager, a brake handle snapped off during a pass and he blew through a shut-down zone, ending up with two broken arms and a nasty burn. Diest had already gotten into the parachute business, and war surplus chutes were readily available, but Simpson thought he had a better idea. He studied a parachute rigger's manual, rented a sewing machine, bought a bunch of rip-stop nylon, and made a thirty-foot-diameter crossform chute in his garage.

Simpson jumped into the back seat of his '55 Chevy Nomad station wagon while his best friend, Mike Sorokin, who would later achieve stardom driving the Surfers Top Fuel car, got behind the wheel. On a long downhill stretch on a street in Redondo Beach, with the wagon bouncing along at 100 mph, Simpson tossed his homemade parachute out the back window. It worked so well that it lifted up the rear wheels, and the Chevy crashed into a tree nursery at the bottom of the hill. When a cop asked what happened, Sorokin told him, "You know, I don't think that airplane was high enough when they pushed us out."[40] Not for the last time did one of Simpson's escapades land him in jail.

Simpson bought a few sewing machines, hired a couple of seamstresses, and went into business as Simpson Drag Chutes. Before long, he'd branched out into making aluminized fire suits and leather masks for Top Fuel and Top Gas drivers, who, in the days before full-face helmets, used to get pelted with hot oil, unburned fuel, and, on occasion, broken engine parts. But it was still a low-rent operation. "I went to Simpson's house to buy one of his silver suits," said John Morton, who had a brief fling with drag racing—driving, coincidently, the Surfers Top Fuel digger—before going on to a long and successful career in road racing. "He was sewing his own suits in his house. Right off of his living room was a sewing machine. I also got a hood that made you look like a Ku Klux Klansman."[41]

At that point, Simpson's clientele was strictly drag racers. His horizons widened after a friend convinced him to take a road racing class at the Jim Russell Driving School. As it happened, he got kicked out after his friend flipped a school car. But the experience inspired Simpson to start racing single-seaters with the SCCA. While he was playing around with Formula Continentals, he befriended fellow club racer Pete Conrad. Yeah, Pete Conrad, the astronaut. "He was pretty good but he used to crash a lot," Simpson said. "Anyway, he said NASA had started using this material made by DuPont in the Mercury program to protect the capsule when it reentered the atmosphere."[42]

Conrad arranged a meeting with DuPont executives. Simpson's first big customer was Goodyear, which bought Nomex suits bearing its logo as fast as Simpson could sew them and distributed them free of charge to its contracted drivers. (Firestone drivers used Hinchman wares.) The drivers were a tougher sell because Simpson was a dope-smoking long-hair, whose in-your-face persona didn't sit well with the USAC lifers. In 1969, in the run-up to the 500, Simpson set himself on fire while wearing a borrowed uniform. "The only problem was that they poured

Safety maverick Bill Simpson was one of the loudest and most polarizing figures in the world of racing. But love him or hate him, everybody agreed that he put his money where his big mouth was. During the run-up to the Indy 500 in 1969, he demonstrated the fire-retardant qualities of his Nomex suit for drivers, crewmen, media types, race officials, and one joker roasting a wiener over the methanol flames. *Indianapolis Motor Speedway*

too much gasoline on me, and I was wearing a clear visor, which was a mistake," he recalled. "The fire sunburned my eyes and the radiant heat cooked my eyebrows."[43] Otherwise, he was unhurt. Simpson still had critics after that, but nobody questioned his bona fides.

The demonstration impressed everybody except Simpson himself. "That was kind of a candy-ass light," he said.[44] In later years, he staged ever more spectacular exhibitions. He got so nonchalant about them that, before one stunt, he forgot to remove his heavy gold bracelet. Halfway through the demonstration, he started fanning his arm. When the flames were doused, he yelled, "Goddammit! I burned the fuck out of myself!"[45] He bore a scar on his wrist from the superheated precious metal for the rest of his life.

Simpson moved up to Indy cars in 1968 and ran several seasons on the Championship Trail, netting a handful of top-ten finishes. The Indianapolis 500 was his great white whale. He raced cars at the Speedway for eight consecutive years, making the show only once, finishing thirteenth in 1974. Even if he'd been in first-class equipment, he knew he wouldn't have been a front-runner. "My lifestyle didn't allow me to be a top race driver," he admitted. "Smoking, drinking, fighting, partying, chasing women—I wasn't willing to sacrifice all that."[46]

Nevertheless, his experience on the track informed his approach to safety. A wreck at Trenton inspired him to introduce wider seat belts. Another incident, when he ran up the back of a slower car because he couldn't see the driver's raised hand, prompted him to color his gloves red. After being knocked out in a practice crash at Indy, he started selling his own helmets in 1974. The fact that he strapped himself into the cockpit wearing his own gear cemented his credibility. "I'm a racer," he would say. "I'm here. Where's Mr. Bell?"[47]

Although Simpson's early success was built on Indy car, short track racing, road racing, and drag racing, his company's growth in the 1990s was fueled by the burgeoning popularity of NASCAR. In 2001, thirty-nine of the forty-three starters in the Daytona 500 were wearing Simpson gear. The most prominent was Dale Earnhardt, who died of a basal skull fracture after what appeared to be a humdrum crash on the last lap of the race. Simpson seat belts were blamed for his death, a charge that Simpson challenged by pointing out that NASCAR had never investigated the widespread rumor that Earnhardt never bothered to properly cinch down his harness.

Simpson filed an $8.5 million defamation of character suit against NASCAR, but both sides kissed and made up after the case was settled out of court. The seat belt issue was forgotten, and the HANS device became standard equipment in NASCAR—and just about every other form of racing. Still, the fallout from Earnhardt's death forced Simpson to resign from his own company. In 2002, the instant a noncompete clause expired, he opened Impact Racing, which offered a full line of safety gear and competed head-to-head against the company that still bore his name. He sold Impact in 2010 after claims that the company was selling uncertified products and died in 2024, at age seventy-nine, a member of the last generation of racers who competed when fatal crashes were the rule rather than the exception.

"In the 1950s and '60s, *everything* was dangerous: stock cars, sports cars, open-wheel cars, drag cars. They all killed their share of us," Simpson said. "Everything was substandard. The helmets sucked. The restraints sucked. Fire suits did not exist. There was a rule about wearing belts, but I don't remember anyone ever leaning into the car to check on that. So if you wanted to race you developed a cavalier attitude about life, because that was the only way to deal with it."[48]

Simpson didn't change the racing world by himself. But in his inimitable way, alternately charming and abrasive, he made it a better place. As Parnelli Jones once said, "He doesn't always say it the most polite way, but sometimes you have to be outspoken to get the job done. I don't know where racing would be without him."[49]

Early efforts to cover racing on television were makeshift affairs—clearly illustrated by this photo of a cameraman from KRON-TV, the NBC affiliate in San Francisco, camped out just past the start-finish line at Laguna Seca Raceway during an SCCA regional in 1961. Road racing proved to be a challenge for television to cover, so as ABC beefed up its motorsports portfolio, the network generally focused on oval tracks. *Revs Institute / William Hewitt Photograph Collection*

CHAPTER FIVE

THE UNBLINKING EYE OF TELEVISION

In one of those delicious ironies that make the study of history so entertaining, what we now know as television was invented in 1927 by a young man who'd grown up in a log cabin without electricity. For the next twenty years, radio remained king, and television was merely a curiosity; in 1943, there were only six thousand TV sets in the entire country. But the 1950s turned out to be a golden age of television. The template for the sit-com and late-night television show were created, and programming ranged from highbrow theatrical productions to the silliest game shows imaginable. By the end of the decade, more than 90 percent of American households had at least one television set.

From the beginning, sports were an indispensable part of television programming. Baseball, naturally, was the biggest attraction; at the time, it was still the national pastime, and from a technical standpoint, it was easy to cover. But TV also transformed boxing and professional wrestling into major sports, and according to football lore, the sudden-death overtime game between the Baltimore Colts and New York Giants in 1958 ignited what proved to be an ongoing obsession with the NFL.

With the demise of the Dumont Television Network in 1955, the American broadcast landscape was dominated by three rivals. NBC was the oldest, most powerful, and most profitable network. CBS, though second in line, enjoyed the stature conferred on it by respected newsmen such as Edward R. Murrow and Eric Sevareid. ABC was a dismal third, with the fewest stations, dreariest schedule, and thinnest bankroll. In the sleek offices of 30 Rockefeller Plaza, complacent NBC executives joked that ABC stood for "Almost Broadcasting Network." Ouch!

To raise its game, ABC contracted with a Harvard Phi Beta Kappa, Edgar Scherick, to produce its sports programming. He was shrewd, excitable, and inscrutable; colleagues described him as "a high-strung Mad Hatter."[1] One of his first hires was a dapper, quick-witted, politically adroit young assistant named Roone Arledge, who'd been unhappily working on a puppet show at NBC before moving to ABC. At the time, college football was the only prestige property in the network's sports portfolio. Scherick and Arledge embarked on a two-tiered strategy. First, they planned to add some razzle-dazzle to their staid football coverage. Second, since they didn't have the money or clout to compete with NBC and CBS for top-tier events, they decided to perform an act of business jujitsu, drawing strength from their weaknesses.

Instead of going after the biggies, Arledge and Scherick chased lesser-known sports that Americans knew little about—in some cases, had never even *heard* of. The fees to broadcast them were minimal. Better still, in an era before social media and 24/7 news coverage, viewers wouldn't know ahead of time who'd won and lost. The idea was to cover an event over the weekend, spend the week editing the footage into dramatic, easily digestible segments, and then broadcast them a week later on a new sports omnibus show to be given an attractive time slot on Saturday afternoon. "Sports were life condensed, all its drama, struggle, heartbreak, and triumph embodied in artificial contests," Arledge wrote later about what was, at the time, a novel concept. "Television could capture it all, and in the 1960s, there was a chance to do it creatively. I wanted to make the game more intimate, and a lot more human."[2]

Sounds great—or at least it does now. But when Arledge broached this plan with veteran announcer Curt Gowdy while they were sharing a hotel room—a sign of ABC's financial straits—during a college football game assignment, Gowdy wasn't impressed. "That's the craziest idea I ever heard of," he said, rolling over to go to sleep. "It'll never work."[3]

Wide World of Sports debuted on April 29, 1961, and it aired weekly until 1997. (Gowdy was one of its many celebrated alumni.) During that stretch, broadcaster Jim McKay's timeless voice-over intro—"the thrill of victory and the agony of defeat"—became one of the country's best-known (and most mocked) catchphrases. In later years, *Wide World of Sports* would focus on major league events, but early on, the programming ranged from the sublime to the ridiculous: track and field to barrel jumping, PGA golf to dogsled racing, heavyweight boxing to rattlesnake hunting. Automobile racing fit perfectly into the eclectic mix Arledge and Scherick had in mind.

On May 27, 1961, the fifth installment of *Wide World of Sports* featured the Indianapolis 500—time trials, that is, not the race. Indy had been covered on the radio as early as 1922. In 1949 and 1950, the race was broadcast live on local station WBFM-TV. After that, though, Speedway president (and three-time 500 winner) Wilbur Shaw banned live television coverage because he thought it was eating into ticket sales at the gate. In 1955 and 1956, the NBC *News Caravan* ran tape-delayed highlights a few hours after the race, but the broadcast didn't generate any lasting enthusiasm.

In 1961, ABC broadcast two hours of highlights along with plenty of interviews and a tribute to Tony Bettenhausen, who'd been killed in a wreck during practice earlier in the month. Although it was a tidy package, it lacked the dynamic wheel-to-wheel action that could produce the thrill of victory, much less the agony of defeat. In search of an actual race to broadcast, Arledge flew to Paris to line up coverage of the 24 Hours of Le Mans. "I spoke almost no French, and in fact had almost no money to spend," he wrote. "No matter. I believe I was the first American ever to make a pitch for television rights, and the words 'American Broadcasting Company' in this instance worked wonders."[4]

Road races were already being filmed on the continent and beamed all over Europe. For a piddling $10,000, Arledge secured the rights to broadcast Le Mans, and he hired Stirling Moss as the race analyst. Articulate and unflappable, Moss was being interviewed by Jim McKay almost until the instant he had to run across the track to jump into the Ferrari 250 GT SWB he was codriving with Graham Hill. Although the Ferrari broke in the middle of the night, the broadcast was a hit. Arledge and Scherick were so pleased that they decided to air another race the next month—the Firecracker 250 at Daytona International Speedway. But they ran into a little problem in the form of Bill France, NASCAR's not-so-benevolent dictator.

The previous year, CBS had taken a flyer on covering Speedweek, an array of races culminating in the Daytona 500. The network had dispatched fifty technicians and two of its biggest guns to Florida—news anchorman Walter Cronkite and director of programing Art Peck. Both of them were serious car guys. Peck was a founder of the elite Madison Avenue Sports Car Driving & Chowder Society, which met monthly at Sardi's Restaurant in Midtown Manhattan, and Cronkite had raced a Lancia Appia Zagato in the 12 Hours of Sebring in 1959. Unfortunately, what they knew about stock car racing in general, and NASCAR in particular, could fit inside the tire stem of a Goodyear Blue Streak, and the broadcast bombed.

"The reviews were devastating, just criminally bad," recalled Chris Economaki, the owner and editor-in-chief of *National Speed Sport News*.[5] Two weeks later, NBC added insult to injury by devoting less than five minutes on the *Today Show* to a made-for-TV race at Daytona dubbed the Autolite Challenge. France was incensed by the coverage, which seemed to confirm the unflattering view that NASCAR was a second-rate regional series, and when ABC execs came calling in 1961, he was inclined to blow them off. To placate France, Arledge and Scherick agreed to hire Economaki to provide expert commentary.

Much to everybody's surprise, the shotgun wedding grew into an enduring, and mutually rewarding, love affair. Economaki brought with him a granular understanding of the sport and access to the racing fraternity, and his ebullient personality and willingness to ask pointed questions made him a natural for television. But most important of all, he gave ABC instant credibility among racers. Of course, this cut both ways. Although *National Speed Sport News* billed itself as the racing bible, it was actually a weekly broadsheet on newsprint with modest circulation numbers that served more like an industry newsletter. By giving Economaki a platform in front of millions of television viewers, ABC transformed him into a major player on the racing scene, and he became the face of motorsports for the general public.

Economaki wore many hats, but he was a fan first and foremost. He'd attended his first race when he was nine and immediately decided on a career in motorsports. He started selling the predecessor to *National Speed Sport News* when he was thirteen. The next year, he began writing a weekly column, which he would continue to bang out on a manual Royal typewriter for the next sixty-plus years. He rose to editor in chief in 1950 and soon became the owner as well. The magazine's brief was to cover everything from the big pro races at Indy and Daytona to modifieds and midgets at bullrings nestled deep in flyover country. Economaki presciently put a then-little-known dirt track racer by the name of Anthony Joseph Foyt on the cover in 1956, and he applied his deep knowledge of the sport to helping craft ABC's presence in the racing world.

At the time, motorsports were largely ignored by daily newspapers and general-interest weekly and monthly magazines. Yes, the car magazines enthusiastically covered racing back in those days—far more so than now—but the stories were one, two, sometimes three months old by the time they reached newsstands and mailboxes. Unless you had access to a wire service teletype machine, results were virtually impossible to find until long after the fact. And if you wanted to actually *see* the action, you had to attend the race in person.

Dick Wallen was one of the first filmmakers to figuratively bring the mountain to Muhammad. In 1958, he spent $300 on a 16mm camera that he used to earn fifty dollars by filming the Los Angeles Times Grand Prix at Riverside. By 1961, he'd gone into business (using a more sustainable financial model) shooting, editing, and selling movies about USAC open-wheel races, from sprint cars on the dirt at Du Quoin to roadsters on the bricks at Indianapolis. "In the Sixties," Wallen recalled, "people were starved for any kind of films that showed real racing cars. We used to put on shows in the summer during the racing season. I'd go into a town, make arrangements to rent a hall, do the promotion, sell tickets to one or two thousand people, then split the gate fifty-fifty with the driver who worked the show with me."[6]

In 1964, the Music Corporation of American unveiled closed-circuit television coverage of the Indy 500. The broadcast featured twelve cameras, thirty microphones, and nine announcers led by Charlie Brockman, a mainstay of the Indianapolis Motor Speedway Radio team. Black-and-white footage was beamed to one hundred cities—a total of 161 venues ranging from movie theaters to sports arenas. MCA would continue to broadcast from Indy each year until 1970. Attendance was modest, and, financially, the shows were never much more than break-even propositions. Yes, watching racing in a movie theater was better than not watching it at all. But what people really wanted was the ability to see the action from the comfort of their living room, and this was an itch that could be scratched only by television.

In the three years after it launched, *Wide World of Sports* featured a dozen races: Indy cars, stock cars, and Formula 1. Then, in 1965, ABC

Wide World of Sports debuted on April 29, 1961. The next month, during the fifth installment, racing was featured for the first time in the form of the Indy 500 time trials. By December 1963, the *Wide World of Sports* operation was a well-oiled machine, capable of covering races from Monaco to Daytona to, in this case, the city of Nassau for the Bahamas Speed Weeks. *Revs Institute / Duke O. Manor Photograph Collection*

went all in on motorsports with four NASCAR races, two Grands Prix from Monaco and the Nürburgring, a Champ Car race on the dirt in Sacramento, and, for the first time ever, a national broadcast of the Indy 500. No, it wasn't live, and when the footage was aired a week after the fact, the race was edited down to a forty-five-minute segment that shared the time slot with the World Pocket Billiards Championship. Even so, it was still a big deal. ABC broadcast the race every year thereafter until losing the contract to NBC in 2019.

In 1967, ABC decided to raise the ante yet again by broadcasting a race in glorious color rather than pedestrian black and white. The guinea pig would be the Monaco Grand Prix, the most glamorous race in the world, contested on arcaded streets snaking past the yachts and gilded villas of the French Riviera. Reigning world champion Jack Brabham qualified on the pole in his Repco-Brabham. Next to him, in a scarlet-red Ferrari 312 with a snarling V-12, was Lorenzo Bandini. An affable and easygoing Italian, Bandini had been promoted to team leader the previous year after prickly Englishman John Surtees quit unexpectedly over a political dispute. In France and at Watkins Glen, Bandini had been leading when his car broke. Now, in the second race of the new season, he was under immense pressure from Enzo Ferrari and the rabidly nationalistic Italian press to seal the deal and put Ferrari back in the winner's circle.

During practice, Bandini tagged the wall at Mirabeau and broke a steering arm. Instead of waiting for the wrecker to arrive, he endeared himself to his crew by finding some baling wire and borrowing a pair of pliers from a spectator, then MacGyvering a fix to drive the car back to the pits. During the final practice session, he went fast enough to qualify on the front row. When the green flag fell, Bandini scooted into the lead before skidding on oil on lap two and briefly falling back. But a quarter of the way through the one-hundred-lap race, he was running second to Denny Hulme in the second Brabham.

In the second half of the race, Bandini put his head down and made a run at Hulme. But after reducing the gap to seven seconds, he stopped making progress, and Hulme began pulling away again as Bandini started missing shifts and apexes. Looking back, it seems likely that he'd gotten tired of horsing his heavy Ferrari around the serpentine circuit while chasing the lighter, nimbler Brabham. The race was a lot longer back then, lasting more than two-and-a-half hours; nowadays, it's more like an hour and forty minutes. And as color commentator Phil Hill had told McKay at the start of the ABC broadcast, "One hundred laps around the circuit is really one of the most tiring things you can do."

On lap eighty-two, Bandini roared out of the tunnel in fifth gear—this was the fastest part of the track—and hurtled down toward the harbor. Braking hard, he clipped the curb on the right and ricocheted toward the water. In years past, Alberto Ascari and Paul Hawkins had spun through the "wall" of hay bales erected in front of the railing and into the harbor below, where they were rescued by frogmen stationed in the water. If there had been a guardrail lining this obviously dangerous stretch of track, as there was the next year, Bandini would have glanced off it, at worst damaging his suspension. Instead, he sliced through the hay bales and speared a sturdy iron bollard. The impact was vicious, shearing off two wheels. The Ferrari went up in flames as it turned over, trapping Bandini underneath. "Good lord, look at that," Hill murmured, audibly horrified, as he watched the footage on the screen.[7]

The rescue operations that followed reached a level of ineptitude that verged on criminal negligence. As David Phipps wrote acidly in his year-end review in *Autocourse*, "Lorenzo Bandini was allowed to die at Monaco."[8] (*Road & Track*, in a tone-deaf assessment, described the scene as a "comic opera."[9]) Firefighters didn't reach the scene until a minute after the accident, and when they got there, their civilian gear prevented them from getting close enough to the fire to have any impact on the blaze. It didn't help that the blades of the helicopter hovering overhead, shooting footage for the European TV broadcast, literally fanned the flames. The smoke was so thick that drivers had to tiptoe past the scene of the accident in first gear. "You couldn't see a bloody thing," Hulme said later. "When I went past the first time, I didn't know whether he was in it or not—I wouldn't even look, actually, because I reckoned nothing would put you off more than seeing a bloke burning inside a car, and he was burning for two laps."[10] And yet the race went on.

At first, corner workers thought Bandini had been thrown clear. When they finally realized that he was still in the car, they belatedly used ropes to laboriously right the Ferrari. Thankfully, Bandini had been knocked unconscious. But he lay slumped in the low-sided cockpit, fully exposed, his body horribly burned and covered with fire-retardant spray. Four agonizing minutes passed before the fire was extinguished and he was yanked from the car. Shortly after he was laid on the track like a sack of unwanted potatoes, the fuel tank exploded, and the car—and Bandini—caught fire a second time.

Wide World of Sports caught it all on film. In grisly color.

With a fractured chest and third-degree burns over 70 percent of his body, Bandini died three days later. *New York Times* television critic Jack Gould eviscerated the network for its coverage in a column that ran under the headline, "A.B.C.'s Cameras Insist on Gruesome Detail." As he wrote, "The manner of the reportage, particularly since there was time to do whatever editing might be dictated by the requirements of good taste, left much to be desired. To replay the scene in the stop-action technique common to televised sports was quite unnecessary. And the scenes of Bandini's body being dragged down the street and then being covered by flames for a second time bordered on the macabre, especially in vivid color TV. To any viewer of normal intelligence, the dimension of the disaster was self-evident in the original explosion, and the recourse to more camera work didn't serve any purpose of providing essential information. That Bandini died had been reported days before A.B.C. showed its tape."[11]

Detailed coverage of big wrecks is still a staple of racing broadcasts, and accidents are replayed endlessly in slow motion to analyze exactly what happened. But when it appears that somebody might have been seriously injured, the protocol these days is to cut away from the scene to avoid showing emergency crews dealing with a life-threatening situation. This wasn't how television directors worked in the 1960s and '70s. "The aesthetic was that danger was essential to the sport," said Sam Posey, a fine road racer who became even better known as a TV broadcaster, "and television reflected that belief."[12]

Back then, sensationalism wasn't a bug in the program. It *was* the program. *Wide World of Sports* was in the business of electrifying its audience, whether showcasing a star-spangled motorcyclist soar over a row of parked cars or filming photogenic young divers leap off the cliffs of Acapulco. Lurid spectacle was fundamental to racing's appeal to ABC, and in an age before instant replay, the very real possibility of disaster was a hook that kept viewers pinned to their seats. The forbidding consequences of failure also made racing seem like a more serious endeavor than other *Wide World of Sports* staples like wrist wrestling and log rolling. Long before NBC coined the phrase, racing was "Must See TV" for a certain segment of its audience. Bandini's death was the first automotive fatality to be broadcast on the program, but it wouldn't be the last.

A year later, while covering the Rex Mays 300 at Riverside, ABC demonstrated just how complacently it had ignored Gould's condemnation. During the season-ending Indy car race, Lou Sell, a local dentist who'd just won the SCCA's professional Formula A championship, snap-spun on oil at the end of the long backstraight. In a sickening rerun of Bandini's accident, Sell's Eagle turned over, trapping him underneath while the car caught fire. It took several minutes for the ineffectual safety crew to put out the flames with their puny fire extinguishers. The camera lingered voyeuristically on the scene, then zoomed in for a close-up on the cockpit as the mangled car was righted. "I'm certainly afraid of what we're going to see now," Economaki said in the hushed tone broadcasters reserve for reporting on tragedies.[13] Against all odds, Sell was alive and kicking, and he laboriously levered himself out of the cockpit to reveal a badly charred two-piece uniform. "Well, that's a pleasant surprise, isn't it?" Economaki said. Was it? You could imagine the director gnashing his teeth in the production booth because the shot hadn't been more ghoulish.

Of course, critics like Gould weren't contemptuous only of ABC's coverage of racing. He was also a proud member of that tribe of haters who despised the sport itself. As he wrote, with venom dripping from his typewriter, "The viewer who fails to share the mad frenzy for racing automobiles over such a treacherous course as the Monte Carlo streets might be equally revolted by the apparent mores of the pastime that calls itself a sport."[14]

But even racing's most fervent fans tended to be equally critical of ABC. No automotive journalist ever wielded a more poisonous pen than *Car and Driver* editor Brock Yates. "Thanks, Mr. Arledge," he wrote archly in the wake of Sell's accident, "for another triumph in good taste and our best wishes to you and your crew in your eager search for violence and bloodshed in sport. Perhaps, on some quiet week in the future, you could bring back your wonderous footage of the 1967 Lorenzo Bandini crash at Monaco—sort of a 'Golden Oldie' for all the sickies out there who missed it the first time."[15]

Television's focus on catastrophe fed into the annoying and misguided trope (insert eye roll here) that people watched racing only for the wrecks. Less than three months later, ABC was at it again. In a support race for the Daytona 500, Don MacTavish hit a guardrail, which ripped off the front end of his Mercury Comet. An oncoming car speared the exposed cockpit, killing MacTavish instantly. *Autoweek* called it "one of the most horrifying accidents ever seen in auto racing."[16] Even though the race itself didn't merit inclusion in *Wide World of Sports*, the wreck was teased several times, and a graphic clip was eventually broadcast on the show. "It has become abundantly clear," *Autoweek* declared, "that the sham show on ABC being peddled under the phony mantle of glorifying the world of sports is based primarily on the tawdry sensationalism policy of getting ratings in viewership by any means possible."

While it's easy—and fair—to criticize the network for its morbid coverage, it's worth noting that, at the time, combat footage from the jungles of Vietnam was being transmitted on the nightly news. What rankled racing fans even more than the fixation on death was the perceived ineptitude of the broadcasts, from cameras that always seemed to be in the wrong place to announcers who didn't seem to know what they were talking about. And as if that weren't bad enough, there was also a sense that the broadcasts were dumbed down to appeal to TV viewers who'd turned on the program knowing nothing about the sport.

The announcers for the Super Bowl never bothered to explain what a first down was, nor did the on-air talent covering the World Series waste time unpacking what a relief pitcher did. The presumption was that viewers already knew the rules and many of the nuances of the games. At ABC, the producers behaved as though their audience consisted mostly of aliens from outer space who were seeing racing for the first time and needed instructions about the basics. Every broadcast seemed to feature a breakdown of a pit stop or an explanation—with graphics!—of drafting. The audience was treated like third graders rather than adults.

By the end of the decade, ABC faced competition from small production companies that started putting together racing broadcasts of their own and selling them to independent TV stations around the country. But with fewer resources and less experience, their coverage was even worse than the network's programming. Here's *Car and Driver* again: "Nickel-dime operations being anchored by announcers who are woefully ignorant about either racing or TV production, or both, have resulted in a string of real dozers—shows that rightly end up behind

During the 1960s and '70s, when racing became a staple of television programming, Chris Economaki was the public face of the sport. Besides being a core member of the *Wide World of Sports* broadcast team, Economaki was also the owner and editor-in-chief of *National Speed Sport News*, which was often called "the bible" of American motorsports since it covered everything from the Indy 500 to Saturday night midget shows in Nowheresville, USA. *Indianapolis Motor Speedway*

reruns of *Tarzan and the Enraged Springboks* in audience surveys and could send racing to the same limbo as the Roller Derby unless somebody takes the time to learn what it's all about. The recent job during the Trenton 200 is a case in point. Two hours of spoon players on the *Ted Mack Show* wouldn't have approached it for sheer boring ineptitude."[17]

There was even a fear in some quarters that too much television coverage would homogenize the sport by turning it into a dull, predictable, made-for-the-boob-tube spectacle like bowling and—God forbid!—professional wrestling. Yates constantly railed about the dangers posed by promoters and sanctioning bodies who were, in his opinion, selling their souls to appeal to TV. Better, he argued, for fans to attend races in person than watch meticulously edited clips beamed over the airwaves. "We may be disorganized and confused, and we may lack status with the so-called Sports Establishment," he wrote, "but at least we in motor racing don't have the leeches from television on our backs—and for that we can be abundantly grateful."[18]

Still, the relationship between TV and the racing community fell under the heading of Can't Live With 'Em, Can't Live Without 'Em. After decades of being marginalized as the boorish devotees of a motorized geek show, racing fans couldn't help but feel validated by the attention suddenly being paid to motorsports. And while grousing about television has long been a favorite pastime in the United States, most fans were willing to cut ABC some slack even if its coverage left something—okay, a lot—to be desired. As John Bond, publisher of *Road & Track* and very much the voice of the establishment, wrote about *Wide World of Sports*'s coverage of Le Mans in 1965, "Phil Hill's pertinent comments were great and for once we had a professional commentator, Jim McKay, who knew what he was talking about. They were an excellent choice and everyone we know appreciated the job they did."[19] It was a sign of the times that even Yates, who zealously embraced his role as the anti–John Bond, was eventually seduced by the siren song of network television. After years of relentlessly denouncing ABC in print for a wide variety of sins, he embarked on a second career doing on-air TV commentary as CBS's Chris Economaki doppelgänger.

And why not? During the 1960s and '70s, television broadened the reach of the sport to an extent that would have been unfathomable a generation earlier. This period marked the dawn of an age when television viewers, rather than paying spectators, became the sport's principal audience. TV brought racing to millions of fans who'd never seen it before and weren't likely to travel to the Milwaukee Mile, much less the Terre Haute Action Track. These new eyeballs suddenly made racing more attractive to sponsors large and small. Two of the major advertisers on *Wide World of Sports* were R.J. Reynolds and Brown & Williamson; in years to come, money from these and other tobacco companies would become the lifeblood of the racing industry.

This was progress, wasn't it? More fans meant more advertisers. More advertisers meant more money. More money meant more professionalism and R&D, which translated into more speed, which led to more excitement and competition. But with all these shiny benefits came one sinister consequence: Put all the ingredients together, and you had a recipe for more danger, more accidents, more death and destruction. It was easy to blame television for spotlighting the carnage with such apparent glee. But ABC wasn't the reason that drivers—and track officials and spectators—were being killed. Its coverage was a symptom, not a cause.

The first step in any addiction-recovery program is to admit that you have a problem. Nothing was going to change in racing until the leaders of the motorsports world—sanctioning bodies, promoters, race officials, fans, and even the drivers themselves—admitted that something was wrong. Then, after acknowledging the magnitude of the problem, they would have to look inward and ask some awkward questions about their seemingly endless tolerance for tragedy. Until then, public outrage would continue to grow as the burial plots in the motorsports graveyard continued to multiply.

THE ART OF RACING

Characterizing the zeitgeist of a particular place in time is like trying to catch lightning in a bottle. What may have been the Summer of Love in Haight-Ashbury in 1967 was something altogether different to the thousands of construction workers who were out on strike in Rochester, New York, and the phrase would have sounded like a slap in the face if it had been applied to July in Detroit, where forty-three people died in one of the worst race riots in American history. So it might be presumptuous to suggest that the general public's perception of racing changed during the decade from the mid-1960s to the mid-1970s. But there's no denying the fact there was a cultural shift in the way the sport was depicted. Once dismissed as vulgar sensationalism, racing was for the first time framed as a subject worthy of a more sophisticated audience.

The Cruel Sport, written and photographed by journalist Robert Daley and published in 1963, is often cited as an early example of a book that sought to provide a more nuanced view of motorsports than the pulp fiction and B movies of the era. The knock on it, according to critics, is that Daley perpetuated rather than fact-checked some of the most pervasive myths about racing and why men do it. So it was Tom Wolfe, the man in the white suit, who pushed motorsports onto a more rarified stage with a magazine article regarded as one of the touchstones of New Journalism. In the March 1965 issue of *Esquire*, a bastion of the New York City literati, Wolfe profiled NASCAR's Junior Johnson, the driver credited with inventing drafting. The rambling headline distilled the flavor of the piece: "The Last American Hero Is Junior Johnson. Yes! He is a coon hunter, a rich man, an ex-whiskey runner, a good old boy who hard-charges stock cars at 175 m.p.h. Mother dog! He is the lead-footed chicken farmer from Ronda, the true vision of the New South."[20] As with *The Right Stuff*, Wolfe's history of the Mercury space program, the *Esquire* piece about Johnson couldn't always be trusted on all the details—pesky little facts!—but it nailed most of the big-picture stuff.

The change in racing's status was also reflected in Hollywood. Racing had been depicted in dozens of movies since *The Speed Kings*, a 1913 comedy short featuring real-life racers Barney Oldfield and "Terrible" Teddy Tetzlaff. In the decades that followed, racing films incorporated a lowbrow smorgasbord of thrills, slapstick, romantic entanglements, and crashes galore. A handful of movies, it's true, benefited from big-budget productions with A-list actors such as Clark Gable, Barbara Stanwyck, James Cagney, and Kirk Douglas. But almost without exception, they were melodramas or comedies set in a racing milieu. It wasn't until the 1960s and '70s that motion pictures *about* racing reached American movie theaters. The alpha and omega of this development were *Grand Prix* and *Le Mans. Grand Prix* was a character-driven, plot-heavy blockbuster that trafficked in every motorsports cliché known to man; *Le Mans* was a plotless, seemingly pointless box-office bomb that nevertheless managed to represent the most genuine vision of racing ever put on feature film. Although they could hardly have been more different, both were fruit of the same tree.

In 1965, director John Frankenheimer and actor Steve McQueen hatched a plan to make a movie about Grand Prix racing. After McQueen had a falling out with the producer, he and Frankenheimer went their separate ways and immediately scrambled to line up circuits for shooting on location. McQueen signed up the Nürburgring and Reims for his project, tentatively titled *Day of the Champion*. Frankenheimer got the rest of the racetracks for *Grand Prix*. As it happened, *Day of the Champion* was stillborn, and McQueen made *The Sand Pebbles* instead, leaving Frankenheimer with the field to himself. Members of the Formula 1 circus were ambivalent about his movie. On one hand, they were flattered to be featured in such a big production, though only two drivers, Phil and Graham Hill, got speaking parts. (That's Phil, as Yamura driver Tim Randolph, emoting commendably as he yells to Toshiro Mifune at Brands Hatch, "He's on fire!") But they were annoyed by having to share space and track time with the film crew, and they weren't impressed by Frankenheimer's decision to use dinky Formula 3 cars with fake exhaust as stand-ins for Grand Prix machines. As an exasperated Henry Manney III wrote in his Belgian Grand Prix report in *Road & Track*, "Practice was the usual shambles, complicated by the cinema company people again, who were under everyone's feet staging scenes with ghastly dialogue, worse acting, and laughable situations."[21]

Shot in 70mm Super Panavision and made with a large-for-the-day $9 million budget, *Grand Prix* ran nearly three hours—long enough to require an intermission. It was initially shown in only the biggest movie palaces, which helped it earn $20.8 million in box office receipts, ranking eighth among all films in 1966. Reviewers raved about the racing scenes but slammed the acting and dialogue. As critic Pauline Kael wrote, "The crashes are the best thing in the movie, they're really gorgeous, so we don't mind losing a few of the actors, though the picture could more easily have spared James Garner who seems to be taking the whole thing much too seriously, and Miss [Eva Marie] Saint who is as flat and anxious as a mother in a soap opera."[22] Coincidentally, Kael also panned *The Sand Pebbles* in the same review.

McQueen finally got around to making his racing movie, now titled *Le Mans*, in 1970. Although his initial plan to compete in a Porsche 917 was nixed by his insurance company, McQueen shot a ton of footage during the actual 24 Hours of Le Mans. When the race was over, he rented the track and hired forty-one professional drivers and a fleet of authentic 917s and Ferrari 512s to make the movie. (Racing fans will be relieved to learn that the 917 that appears to be comprehensively wrecked in the movie was actually an old Lola T70 coupe.) The crashes were so realistic that David Piper lost half of one leg, and Derek Bell was burned while making the film. McQueen's obsession caused the movie to go way over the budget, and the experience cost him his marriage and his production company.

Film critics didn't know what to make of *Le Mans*, which, on many levels, hardly seems to be a movie at all. McQueen, the putative star, doesn't speak until thirty-eight minutes into the film, and the entirety of the dialogue can be reproduced on two or three pages. "Dramatically, the picture is a bore," the *New York Times* reviewer wrote dismissively.[23] And that's true. But at a certain level, that misses the point and fails to explain why the movie has become a totem for generations of racing fans. As Aubrey Day explained in *Motor Sport*, "It is more tone poem than movie. A symphony of images that suggest a storyline. It's been described as brilliant, boring, metaphysical. A vanity project. A midlife crisis on film. It may be all of those things."[24] If nothing else, McQueen and *Le Mans* gave us a bumper sticker—and a T-shirt—for the ages: "Racing is life. Anything before or after is just waiting."

Meanwhile, the fine arts community also began to show some interest in racing in the 1970s. Oh, there had always been talented painters who specialized in motorsports, from Walter Gotschke to Michael Turner to Bill Neale. And LeRoy Nieman, the go-to artist of the sporting set, naturally added racing to his oeuvre, depicting Indy and Le Mans in his colorful, wildly expressive paintings. But the sort of artists whose work was represented in museums and top-shelf galleries avoided the subject—until 1975, when BMW commissioned sculptor Alexander Calder, famed for his mobiles, to paint a 3.0-liter CSL Batmobile that was going to be raced at Le Mans. Since then, the company has commissioned nineteen more art cars, starting with artists Frank Stella, Roy Lichtenstein, and Andy Warhol and continuing in more recent years with David Hockney, Jenny Holzer, and Jeff Koons.

Alexander Calder was a celebrated American artist best known for monumental-yet-delicate-looking sculptures he dubbed "mobiles." Hervé Poulain, rear left, was a French auctioneer who wanted to race at Le Mans. In 1975, he persuaded BMW to commission Calder to paint one of its 3.0 CSLs in his signature style—and let Poulain drive it. Although the so-called Batmobile DNFed, the episode inaugurated a BMW art car tradition that continues to this day. *BMW NA*

But the first of the art cars was the result of a harebrained scheme hatched by French amateur racer (and auctioneer) Hervé Poulain.

Poulain figured he could barter a car painted by Calder, who'd already turned a Braniff Boeing 727 into a "flying mobile," for a ride at Le Mans. Surprisingly, BMW's corporate honchos signed off on the concept, and Calder was sent a three-foot-long model to play with. Sam Posey was the obvious choice to partner with Poulain. As a boy, he'd visited Calder's studio in Connecticut, and he was an accomplished painter in his own right. Plus, he had plenty of experience in Batmobiles, and he loved the way this particular one turned out. "It looked fun," he said. "The primary colors just warmed you up."[25]

Posey had been told that the car wasn't going to last for twenty-four hours, so he was determined to put in a flyer during qualifying. He got his chance just before midnight. "As I came out of Tertre Rouge," he recalled, "a prototype just *edged* past me, so I pulled in behind him, took the shift *way* past redline, and drafted him the whole way down the Mulsanne Straight." It was, he said, "the most perfect lap I ever drove."[26] It put him a remarkable tenth on the grid, a hulking production car in a sea of petite prototypes. Calder was at Le Mans, bewildered by the prerace festivities and hopelessly out of place in his L.L. Bean shirt and paint-splattered jeans. He sidled up to Posey. "You look like a nice young man," he said. "What the fuck is going on?"[27]

It wouldn't be the last time the meeting of art and science caused a cloud of confusion.

American Masten Gregory was renowned for his thick glasses, deep voice, fearless driving, and a penchant for jumping out of cars just before they crashed. This captures Gregory's pretzeled Tojeiro-Jaguar after his wreck in the Tourist Trophy at Goodwood in 1959. The unbelted Gregory suffered a broken collarbone after being catapulted fifteen feet in the air and landing on an earthen bank. *Revs Institute / George Phillips Photograph Collection*

CHAPTER SIX

BUCKLING UP

The all-American Scarab Formula 1 team arrived at Monaco in 1960 with a pair of pristine, perfectly proportioned Grand Prix cars built to exacting aerospace standards. Their long hoods shrouded four-cylinder engines with desmodromic valvetrains designed by Leo Goossen, the engineer who'd cut his teeth as a draftsman for prewar giant Harry Miller. The cars had been built at great expense by a team of master craftsmen hired by Lance Reventlow, the only son of the original "poor little rich girl," Woolworth heiress Barbara Hutton. They were painted in a radiant shade of metallic blue created by hot rod customizer Von Dutch, and they looked like sleeker versions of the Maserati 250F. Which was, of course, a huge problem since the Maserati hadn't won a race in three years and every other contemporary F1 car featured chassis with the engine behind the driver, not in front of him. The Scarabs shared a garage with the reigning world championship Cooper team, so even before practice began on Thursday, mechanic/fabricator Phil Remington knew how the movie was going to end. As he recalled, "The workmanship on our cars was really nice—they were beautiful—but when you looked at the general layout of their cars and how simple everything was, you could see that we were out to lunch."[1]

Sure enough, the Scarabs handled poorly, braked badly, and were dead-slow down the straights—a triple threat! Reventlow and Chuck Daigh were more than ten seconds off the pace. But since neither of them had any experience in Formula 1, it wasn't clear how much time was being lost by the drivers as opposed to the cars. To get a more accurate read on the Scarabs' deficiencies, Reventlow asked Stirling Moss to turn a couple of laps in his car. Moss graciously agreed. But as he approached the cockpit, he spotted a weirdly alien sight.

Seat belts.

Like most American race cars of the era, the Scarabs were fitted with lap belts as well as shoulder harnesses. And why not? Seat belts had been around ever since pioneering British aviator George Cayley fitted his gliders with lap restraints during the nineteenth century, and the first patent for a seat belt—granted to New Yorker Edward J. Claghorn, for horse-drawn carriages—was issued in 1885. In 1911, US Army Lieutenant Benjamin Foulois lashed himself to the seat of his Wright Model A Military Flyer in 1911 with a leather cavalry strap. By 1928, seat belts were required in all American airplanes, and four-point lap-and-shoulder harnesses were regulation gear in military aviation during World War II. The automobile industry was slower to see the light. It wasn't until 1948 that Nash became the first manufacturer to offer seat belts in its cars, and the real breakthrough didn't arrive until 1959, when Nils Bohlin, a Swede who'd designed aircraft ejection seats at Saab before becoming chief safety engineer at Volvo, patented the three-point belt that quickly became the industry standard. Starting in 1968, every passenger car sold in the United States had to be equipped with three-point lap-and-shoulder restraints.

Credit for bringing seat belts to racing is usually awarded to the colorful speed demon Barney Oldfield, who fashioned a restraint system out of a parachute harness in 1922. In 1954, the SCCA required seat belts for all race cars, no matter how pedestrian, and by the 1960s, restraints—typically including shoulder belts—were the norm in USAC and NASCAR. To be sure, safety wasn't the only concern. Shoulder harnesses or Sam Browne–style belts fitted diagonally across the chest prevented sprint car and midget drivers from being tossed out of their cockpits while they were bounding over deeply rutted dirt tracks, and

NASCAR drivers needed something to keep them planted in flimsy seats that had been scavenged from VW Beetles and Dodge vans. Still, for whatever reason, it would have been unusual to find a top-level professional driver in the United States racing without seat belts by the middle of the decade.

In Europe, the situation was reversed. Among road racers, conventional wisdom held that, given the opportunity, the most prudent course of action for a driver facing an imminent accident was to jump out of the cockpit, like an aviator bailing out of a stricken airplane. "We all knew the cars would deform in a crash," Richard Attwood explained. "That's why belts weren't really thought of as being a particularly good idea, especially if the car caught fire."[2] The most accomplished practitioner of the skydiving technique was Masten Gregory, "The Kansas City Flash," who famously leapt out of a Lister-Jaguar at Silverstone in 1958 and a Tojeiro-Jag at Goodwood the next year. Crew chief Peter Bryant remembered doing a seat fitting with him before the Tasman Series, the off-season formula car races held in Australia and New Zealand. Gregory suddenly jumped to a standing position and leaped out of the cockpit and onto the floor. Bryant was alarmed, thinking that maybe the car had caught fire. But Gregory calmly stuck a stick of red licorice in his mouth and drawled, in his magnificent basso profundo, "Don't worry. I always check out the escape route when I drive a different car."[3]

These days, the FIA is a champion in the field of safety, and it's fair to say that no sanctioning body has done more to advance the cause over the past three decades. But during the 1960s, it was a follower rather than a leader, and it's equally fair to say that the FIA was a major obstacle on the road leading toward a safer form of racing. "In those days, Formula One was way behind Indy car racing, way behind," said three-time Indy winner Bobby Unser, who drove BRMs at Monza and Mosport in 1968. "Their technologies weren't up with ours. Safety was, I venture to say, 10 years behind in those days. They used to kill drivers like popped popcorn."[4] And that was more or less acceptable because drivers weren't the FIA's principal constituency. On the contrary, the organization represented the power brokers who ran the sport, and it served primarily as a rubber stamp for track owners and race promoters rather than an advocate for the participants. Ultimately, the FIA was a political organization, and everything it did—or didn't do—has to be seen through the prism of politics.

In the years after World War II, a strictly delineated class structure still dominated European society. Attitudes about professionalism in sport were embodied by the veddy, veddy British series of "Gentlemen v Players" cricket matches, which pitted well-heeled amateurs against working-class pros from 1806 until the games were abolished in 1963. Although American society was more egalitarian, sports car racers were thought to be more sophisticated and dignified than the blue-collar denizens of the oval track world. "It was the gentleman's era of sport car racing (except for Southern California, where they instinctively knew better)," Leon Mandel wrote in *Autoweek* about the early years of the SCCA. "Gentlemen tend not only to exclude everyone else from their arcane pastimes, but they tend to run those pastimes badly. There is something very competitive about competition, and into the sport crept a few outrageous types who actually wanted to win. Ken Miles, say, or Walt Hansgen. From there to expense money was a short step, albeit one accompanied by howls of protest from the Gentlemanly Establishment. From expense money came prize money, and from there—flat-out professional racing."[5]

In Europe, aristocrats sat at the top of the motorsports pyramid. These were blue bloods who had been in charge of racing since it first took formal shape, and they made their decisions behind closed doors in private rooms filled with the scent of cigar smoke and inherited privilege. Next came the manufacturers and constructors. Some, like Sir William Lyons of Jaguar and Sir David Brown of Aston Martin, were members of the ruling class, but many more—Enzo Ferrari, Colin Chapman, Jack Brabham, and so on—were self-made men. They were clever and industrious, yes, but unlike the patricians above them, they were concerned with the grubby business of making money, which made them players rather than gentlemen. If constructors were the entrepreneurs of the sport, then the drivers were the tradesmen—racing's equivalent of plumbers and electricians. There were some authentic noblemen among them, from Prince Bira to Wolfgang von Trips, but most of them were mercenaries. They were paid for their expertise, and in the case of luminaries like Moss, Fangio, and Clark, they were paid extremely well. But they were treated like cogs in the machine, and there was no shortage of replacements if one complained or failed altogether. The mechanics were at the bottom of the totem pole. Worked hard and paid poorly, they were expected to doff their caps to their betters. Job security? Workman's compensation? Overtime wages? No. Are you insane? Don't even think about it. As Jim Chapman, who started as a shop mechanic and worked just about everywhere before cofounding Swift Race Cars, put it, "One of the guys at Team Lotus—I'm not going to name names—said Colin [Chapman] looks upon us as turnips. Whenever he needs new turnips, he can just pull them out of the field."[6]

The first automobiles were playthings, and the first races were contested mostly by playboys and resourceful tinkerers fascinated by this new form of technology. Aristocrats quickly formed national racing clubs such as the Royal Automobile Club (RAC) in England and the Automobile Club de France (ACF) to promulgate rules for competition. In 1904, the RAC, the ACF, and four other European clubs met in Homberg, Germany, to organize the Gordon Bennett Cup. Out of that meeting came the formation of the Association Internationale des Automobile Clubs Reconnus (AIACR), or the International Association of Recognized Automobile Clubs, in Paris later that year. In 1922, AIACR established the Commission Sportive Internationale, commonly referred to as the CSI, which was responsible for writing and enforcing the International Sporting Code that governed competition. When racing resumed after World War II, AIACR was renamed the Fédération Internationale de l'Automobile (FIA). The FIA established the World Championship for Drivers in 1950 and the World Championship for Sports Cars and European Rally Championship in 1953. The World Touring Car Championship was inaugurated in 1963.

About sixty countries were affiliated with the FIA. Many of them—countries such as Kuwait, Vietnam, and Senegal—had little or no racing heritage. The CSI had twelve member countries. Five slots were reserved for the "great manufacturing countries," meaning the United States, the United Kingdom, France, Germany, and Italy.[7] The rest were elected annually for one-year terms, usually by politically motivated power blocs. The CSI had no interest in promoting safety. Only rarely were members active racers, so self-preservation wasn't a motivating factor.

They didn't see a moral case for safety. As a practical matter, making racetracks safer by adding guardrails and hiring emergency personnel would cost a small fortune, and racetrack owners and promoters—who were, in many cases, CSI members themselves—weren't keen on spending large sums of money to prevent drivers from getting hurt. Nor, for that matter, were constructors clamoring for safety regulations, which would have cost them time and money while also making cars slower. The only group with a vested interest in safety were the drivers themselves, and short of instigating a mutiny, which wasn't their inclination, they didn't have enough leverage to force the CSI into taking action.

The disparity in power between the CSI and the people it governed rankled the drivers and constructors, especially as the paternalistic conservatism of the 1950s faltered in the face of the vigorous commercialism of the 1960s. The Grand Prix Drivers' Association was formed in 1961 and the far more formidable Formula 1 Constructors Association (F1CA) three years later. But safety wasn't a top priority on either of these groups' agendas, and they weren't really looking for more power. What they wanted most of all was a bigger slice of the financial pie in terms of prize and appearance money paid by the promoters based on the revenue generated from ticket sales. (In those days, there was hardly any television money and precious little sponsorship income.)

The CSI's indifference to safety was reflected in the FIA's International Sporting Code. Prior to the formation of the GPDA, virtually the only safety regulation on the books was a requirement that drivers wear cork helmets—a rule instituted in 1952, nearly two decades after helmets had been required in the Indy 500. After that, the CSI nibbled around the edges with rules demanding catch cans to prevent oil from being dumped on the track and prohibiting bodywork that would impede drivers when they were trying to get out of their cockpits. Roll bars were mandated in 1961, but the regulations didn't specify technical details about dimensions, materials, or installation, so there were several cases of drivers being killed in rollovers when the roll bars bent or collapsed. The FIA required flame-retardant clothing in 1963, which sounds like a major step in the right direction. Unfortunately, until Nomex became widely available toward the end of the decade, there were no garments able to protect drivers from fire for more than a few seconds. That same year, dual-circuit brakes were also mandated. Which was weird. Not because there was anything wrong with a redundant brake system, but because it seemed to be awfully far down the list of action items if making race cars safer was the goal.

Rules for installing seat belts were approved in 1964. This seemed like an especially good idea in light of the results of failing to publish installation regulations for roll bars. But—and here's the crazy part—the FIA didn't *require* seat belts. That is to say, constructors had to follow certain standards if they chose to use seat belts. But the Sporting Code didn't say they had to be installed in the first place. As a result, nobody bothered with seat belts. Looking back, it's hard to see this as anything but lunacy. This approach may—may—have made a certain amount of sense during the prewar era, when drivers sat on top of cars as much as they sat in them. But it continued to be standard operating procedure even after rear-engine cars became the norm. So when Moss tested the Scarab at Monaco, he didn't wear the seat belts that had been installed in the cockpit; he sat on top of them. The Scarab misadventure ended after one disastrous season in 1960. After that, no other F1 constructor incorporated seat belts into their cars.

It's true that drivers sometimes got away with bailing out of their cars immediately before a wreck. Gregory managed it not once, but twice. There are also the breathtaking images of a stunned Hans Herrmann, sprawled on the pavement at Avus, watching his BRM P25 barrel roll without him in it at the Germany Grand Prix in 1959. But what people often forget is that, the day before Herrmann's miraculous escape, Jean Behra was killed when he was flung from his Porsche RSK and into a flagpole at the top of the banking. Three weeks after Moss refused to wear seat belts at Monte Carlo, he broke his nose and both legs when he was thrown out of his Lotus 18 in a high-speed crash at Burnenville during practice for the Belgian German Grand Prix. In 1964, Dutch nobleman Carel Godin de Beaufort died of massive head, chest, and leg injuries when he flew out of his Porsche 718 during practice for the German Grand Prix. The next year, during the Le Mans Test, Lucky Casner, an airline pilot by trade, was killed when his Maserati 151 left the rain-slicked track at nearly 170 mph, and he was hurled from the enclosed cockpit. (Try to imagine how violent *that* impact must've been.) As late as 1968, 1966 Italian Grand Prix winner Ludovico Scarfiotti died when he was ejected from his Porsche 910/68 Spyder during a German hill climb. And countless more-fortunate drivers were seriously injured when they were pitched out of their cockpits. Yet the resistance to seat belts was so powerful and pervasive that when Jackie Stewart started using them in 1967, he was ridiculed as a "safety kook."[8]

The story of how seat belts came to European road racing has rarely been told, and it stars a figure who's been almost completely overlooked—Dr. Michael Henderson. Raised in a medical family, he'd always assumed that he would become a physician. But Henderson had also been born with the racing gene. While he was in medical school, too poor to buy a race car, he attended races as a fan. Through his friendship with Nick Syrett, later secretary of the GPDA, he began announcing races and writing articles for various magazines. He then cajoled Colin Chapman into giving him the components for a Lotus 7 that he club-raced in 1960.

Because he didn't see a future in the National Health Service, Henderson joined the Royal Air Force. While studying aviation medicine, he had an epiphany. "I began to understand that there was a science of vehicle safety out there, that we didn't have to ignore the fact that people are getting injured in [racing] accidents any more than you'd ignore any other kind of malady or illness," he recalled. "The aviation medicine textbook that we were using at that time was about three inches thick. It was a major book! And yet nothing had been done to adapt any of this material—psychological, physiological, impact resistance, anything—to motor racing."[9]

In 1966, Henderson bought a Mallock MK6 Clubman. In years past, he'd retrofitted a touring car he raced at the Nürburgring and his personal Jaguar XK140C with three-point belts, but he realized that this setup wouldn't work in the Mallock because the "lay-down" driving position, similar to the norm in formula cars of the day, would promote "submarining" under the lap belts in the event of a frontal crash. As it happens, Henderson also had trained as a parachutist. It struck him that the crotch restraint in a military parachute could be added to a standard lap-and-shoulder harness to create antisubmarining protection. He then persuaded Britax, a company now better known for its strollers and car seats, to build the harness to his specifications, with straps looped around the tops of the thighs, thereby creating the first six-point belt used in road racing competition.

Angels should have been singing and trumpets blaring. Instead, there was silence. Henderson then wrote several articles extolling the benefits of seat belts, which generated polite enthusiasm but no real action. So Henderson embarked on Plan C. He persuaded various British racing organizations to feed him information about racing accidents during the upcoming season. The idea was to analyze the data for a book he planned to write. Although the book clearly wasn't bestseller material, publisher Patrick Stephens, a great motorsports enthusiast who specialized in racing titles, agreed to publish it for the good of the sport.

Although hardly anybody recognizes his name, Dr. Michael Henderson was one of the most influential figures in the history of motorsports safety. His book, *Motor Racing in Safety,* published in 1968, was the first to analyze the subject in a systematic way. He also put his then-radical theories into practice in 1966, when he fitted his Mallock U2 Clubman with the world's first six-point racing harness. *Michael Henderson*

Written in 1967 and released in 1968, *Motor Racing in Safety* is the foundational text of the motorsports safety movement. Drawing on his study of 221 accidents, Henderson demolished the myth that jumping out of an out-of-control car was a reasonable course of action and made the affirmative case for using seat belts. To add gravitas to his thesis and, hopefully, generate a few sales while he was at it, Henderson asked BRM team chief Louis Stanley to write the book's foreword. Autocratic and polarizing, Stanley epitomized both the virtues and the foibles of the old-boy network. But to his credit, he'd had done more than anybody to promote safety in the F1 community, most notably by almost single-handedly creating the International Grand Prix Medical Service. Stanley invited Henderson to his large house in the postcard-perfect village of Grantchester, southwest of Cambridge. "Okay," Stanley told Henderson, "convince me." Henderson laid out the data he'd collected and made his case. When he finished, Stanley said, "Right. I agree. I'll put belts in Jackie Stewart's car."[10]

By this time, Henderson was dissatisfied with the locking buckles on the six-point harnesses made by Britax. Coincidentally, his work on a program to upgrade the seat belts in the F-4 Phantoms the RAF was buying from McDonnell Douglas had put him in touch with the GQ Parachute Company. Henderson asked officials at GQ if they could produce the six-point harness that would be installed in Stewart's BRM. GQ told Henderson to contact its chief consultant, a remarkably sui generis figure with the memorable name of Terence "Dumbo" Willans.

Orphaned at thirteen and a bronco buster in Australia while he was still in his teens, Willans had volunteered for the British cavalry when World War II began and trained as a paratrooper. Before his first jump, his instructor yelled, "Uncurl your ears, Dumbo, and fly!"[11] Dumbo he would be for the rest of his life. Willans served as a so-called pathfinder during the war, parachuting behind enemy lines in France, Italy, and Greece. In civilian life, he undertook a series of equally risky high-altitude tests and eventually became known as "the father of British sport parachuting."[12] He later performed the first live-fire ejection seat tests of the Folland Gnat jet fighter, wing walked without a parachute at air shows, and worked as a motion picture stuntman. "He was a lovely guy," said John Fenning, who later became his business partner. "It's an old-fashioned word, but he was a gentleman."[13]

Terence Willans, known universally as "Dumbo," was a colossus of military and sport parachuting. Here, he's about to test an ejection seat in a Folland Gnat jet fighter—an enterprise that, as the saying goes, is even more foolhardy than jumping out of a perfectly good airplane. But his greatest accomplishment may have been introducing seat belts to the European racing world after cofounding Willans Harness Manufacturing Ltd. *Willans Family*

GQ harnesses were available to F1 teams for the 1968 season, and thanks in part to Henderson's book, several drivers were what you might call seat-belt curious. But many still had reservations. The most significant holdout was Jim Clark, who resisted all of Henderson's appeals. "Jimmy absolutely refused to wear a belt," Henderson recalled.[14] This was hard to understand, for two reasons. First, Clark had won the Indy 500 in 1965 while wearing a restraint required by USAC. Also, he'd personally witnessed the consequences of *not* wearing seat belts at Monza, during the Italian GP in 1961, when he'd touched wheels with Wolfgang von Trips, who was killed along with fifteen spectators after hurtling out of his cockpit.

Clark opened the 1968 season by scampering away from the field in South Africa to score his twenty-fifth and final Grand Prix win.

In April, he was at Hockenheim in his Formula 2 Lotus 48. The race is often described as a minor event, but, in fact, in those days, most top Grand Prix drivers also competed in F2. Hockenheim was more or less a dumbed-down version of Spa, with ultra-high-speed blasts through a forest dense with towering pine trees. The air was frosty, and the track was damp during practice. Clark, plagued by a misfire, qualified a lowly eighth. Up-and-comer Derek Bell was thrilled to meet him ("my complete nutter hero," Bell recalled[15]) for the first time and chat with him at the hotel bar ("the most incredible moment of my life up until that point," he added). Bell was astonished that he'd outqualified Clark, and he could hardly believe his ears when the Scotsman told him matter-of-factly, "Don't get too close behind me when you come up to lap me because my car is cutting out intermittently."

Clark's mechanic, Dave "Beaky" Sims, had been futilely chasing the misfire all weekend, even driving the car up and down the road outside the hotel the morning before the race. Still, he thought the real issue was the Firestone rain tires, which were outclassed by the Dunlops. Clark was resigned to a dreary outing mired in mid-pack. "Just give me the time and the laps to go," he told Sims before the start. "Don't expect anything, with the tires and the weather."[16]

On lap five, already well behind the leaders, Clark waved Chris Lambert by. (Three weeks later, Lambert would die in the same BT23C he drove to a fourth-place finish at Hockenheim.) Now running a lonely eighth, Clark was approaching a right-hander at nearly top speed when his Lotus snapped into a tank slapper. Clark fought for control but eventually ran out of steering lock. The car slid off the road at about 140 mph and flattened several saplings before slamming broadside into a mature pine tree. The left side of the cockpit bore the brunt of the impact. The engine and gearbox broke off and ended up fifty feet away from the chassis. Clark was ejected, and his head hit the tree trunk eleven or twelve feet up.

Bell believed the misfire was the cause of the accident. Chris Amon, who finished fifth at Hockenheim, theorized that the suspension failed. Chapman, distraught after the death of his motorsports alter ego, commissioned a formal inquiry, which concluded that a tire had deflated. But for members of the racing brotherhood, why the accident occurred was less important than the fact that it had occurred at all. "Jim Clark's death was something like learning that Pope Paul had been busted for smoking pot," Brock Yates wrote in *Car and Driver.* "It was beyond the realm of comprehension—his level of excellence seemed so high, his experience so solid as to preclude any twist of fate, including mechanical failure, from prompting the final accident."[17]

April 7, 1968, was a come-to-Jesus moment for Clark's colleagues. As Amon said, speaking for many of them, "Jimmy's death was the most profound thing that happened to me in my racing career because I felt if it could happen to him, what chance did the rest of us have?"[18] Although seat belts almost certainly wouldn't have saved Clark's life, doing something to enhance safety made a lot more sense than doing nothing. Over the course of the 1968 season, there was a steady drumbeat of teams fitting seat belts to their cars—BRM first, because of Stanley, then Matra, after Stewart defected to the French equipe, then Cooper, then Brabham. By the end of the year, virtually all F1 drivers were using harnesses. "It confirmed my belief that human beings are sentient," Henderson said. "If given the right information, they understand that there are reasonable things to do."[19]

Interest in seat belts naturally filtered down to less exalted forms of racing. John Fenning was an early convert. Although he'd retired from racing after several seasons in Formula 3, he'd decided to return to the sport on a more casual basis, running hill climbs in a Brabham BT21. But to allay his wife's fears, he agreed to take advantage of all of the available safety gear—a Nomex fire suit, an upgraded helmet, and seat belts. The problem was that, in those days, you couldn't just call your local race shop or mail-order parts supplier and buy a set of restraints. In fact, the only driver Fenning knew who used a formula car harness was his one-time F3 foe, Jackie Stewart. "So I called BRM," he said, "and they told me to get in touch with a company called RSC GQ, and when I called RSC GQ, they told me to get in touch with a Major Dumbo Willans."[20]

Fenning met with Willans when Dumbo was in the area performing ejection-seat tests. Fenning bought a four-point harness and installed it over the weekend. When customers visited Fenning's shop, they'd look in the cockpit and say, "What's that?" and he'd tell them, "It's called a seat belt."[21] More by serendipity than design, he started selling competition harnesses to fellow racers. "After about six months, I said to Dumbo, 'Did you ever think of doing this professionally and stop trying to kill yourself jumping out of airplanes?'" he recalled. "I cajoled him into forming a company. He was the brains, and I was the salesman, for lack of a better word."[22]

Willans Harness Manufacturing Ltd. was the first major player in the racing market, and its signature royal-blue belts could be spotted in virtually every F1 car of the era. As it happened, Henderson had gotten out of the harness business just about the time they were becoming normalized. Instead, he moved to Australia and embarked on a new—and fruitful—career in road car safety, eventually serving as director of traffic safety in New South Wales, where he played a leading role in implementing Australia's mandatory seat-belt-use laws in 1972, a world first. But he never lost touch with his old racing pals. So in January 1969, during the Tasman Series, he had a long conversation about seat belts with Jochen Rindt.

An Austrian who'd dominated F2 for several years, Rindt had just been hired by Chapman to replace Clark to lead Team Lotus. Although he was Stewart's chief rival on the track, Rindt was his most vocal ally on the safety front. Like Stewart, he was adamant that major steps had to be taken to make the sport safer. But he broke with Stewart on one major point. As Henderson recalled, "He said, 'I've read your book, and I agree with everything you say, but you will never get me wearing crotch belts.' I tried to explain that the crotch belts bore safely on the pelvic bone, not at all on some of the body's softest parts, but he remained adamant that his 'goolies' would be severely injured on impact."[23]

Fast-forward to September 5, 1970, during practice for the Italian Grand Prix. Rindt held a huge lead in the world championship standings, thanks to four consecutive victories in the trailblazing Lotus 72, which introduced the wedge shape and side radiators to Formula 1. But with his Cosworth V-8 engine, he couldn't match the pace of the twelve-cylinder Ferraris and BRMs on the long straights at Monza. On Friday, to find some extra speed, Chapman had ordered Lotus Number 2 driver John Miles to run his car without front or rear wings. Miles was ashen when he returned to the pits, and he refused to return to the track. "I'm not driving that car," he said. "It's undrivable."[24] But Rindt was convinced that his preternatural car-control skills would allow him to stay between the lines despite the loss of aerodynamic stability. On Saturday, he practiced without any wings on the car. And he managed to keep the car on the track, barely surviving some lurid slides through the Lesmos.

Toward the end of practice, Rindt powered past Denny Hulme at 190 mph. As he started braking for the Parabolica, near the spot where Clark and von Trips had disastrously interlocked wheels nine years earlier, his Lotus 72 suddenly veered to the left, probably the result of a brake shaft failure. The car hit the guardrail at a shallow angle. But the barrier had been bolted together improperly, and it gave way. Instead of deflecting off the Armco, the wedge nose of the Lotus dug in and tore off. With no crotch belts preventing him from submarining in the cockpit, Rindt slid forward inside the cockpit. As he did, the buckle of the seat belt ruptured his liver and severed his jugular. He was dead before medical assistance arrived.

Despite Rindt's death, the FIA didn't take action to require six-point harnesses. In fact, the sporting regulations still didn't require seat belts of *any* sort. You didn't have to be a safety expert to recognize the criminal folly of this dereliction of duty. And it wasn't as if the FIA could have been surprised. A week before Rindt was killed at the Italian Grand Prix, British amateur Chris Summers—who wore street clothes and refused to use a harness—had perished when he was hurled from his Lola T142 in a Formula 5000 race at Snetterton. Almost exactly a year later, Summers's friend and fellow F5000 racer, Peter Hawtin—who also favored street clothes and declined to wear seat belts—died when he was ejected from his obsolete Cooper T90B at Oulton Park.

It wasn't until 1972 that the FIA finally—finally!—mandated six-point harnesses, long after the vast majority of formula cars were already outfitted with them. It was yet another dispiriting case of the FIA leading from behind on safety.

THE ROAD NOT TAKEN

It's comforting to accept the commonly advanced thesis that the major impediment to improving safety in the 1960s was the lack of safety technology. And that's true in certain cases—Nomex, for example, or HANS devices. But even in the 1960s, people understood that surrounding drivers with flimsy gas tanks and racing on roads lined with telephone poles was dangerous. Obvious solutions were ignored because a certain number of deaths and injuries were accepted as the cost of doing business, much as retail chains factor a certain percentage of pilferage into their business models. This indifference was seen most clearly on the Pininfarina stand at the Geneva International Motor Show in 1969. There, draped by five leggy models with bare midriffs and checkered-flag bell-bottoms, was the future of safety in Formula 1, officially known as the Sigma Grand Prix Safety Car.

The previous season had been one of the deadliest in motorsports history. So Robert Braunschweig, editor of the Swiss magazine *Automobil Revue*, came up with the idea of putting together a multidisciplinary team to create a concept for a safer Formula 1 car. The core members were Ferrari chief engineer Mauro Forghieri; coachbuilder Sergio Pininfarina and his general manager, Renzo Carli; engineering professor Ernst Fiala; journalist (and ex-race car driver) Paul Frère; and physician Michael Henderson, who'd developed the first six-point harness for racing. Enzo Ferrari agreed to provide an obsolete 312 F1 car (the winner of the 1966 Italian Grand Prix) as a test mule. The Sigma designation name-checked a safety sedan that Tom Tjaarda had designed for Pininfarina in 1963. The team met daily for about a week at the Ferrari factory in Maranello and often ate lunch with Il Commendatore in a private room in Il Cavallino restaurant across the street. "We defined exactly what could be done to make a Formula One car as safe as possible with the technology available then," Henderson said. "It was a game changer."[25]

Although group members started with low-hanging fruit, the components they chose were upgraded with clever touches. So they implemented a six-point harness, then added retractable belts and a strap connecting the helmet to the rear bulkhead to serve as a primitive head-and-neck restraint. And when they installed a Graviner fire extinguisher, they specced a heat-sensitive unit that would activate automatically in case of a crash. Fuel cells, provided by Pirelli, were filled with foam to prevent gasoline from sloshing and protected by an independent fire-suppression system. The steering wheel telescoped to avoid crushing the driver's chest in a frontal impact. A low rear wing was mounted just behind the cockpit, then beefed up structurally to double as both an aerodynamic aid and a super-effective roll bar. Also, an electronic data acquisition system developed by Fiala was fitted to provide information about the g-forces drivers absorbed when they crashed. But the most important innovation was articulating the concept of a survival cell for the driver. That is to say, the cockpit was supposed to be the safest part of the chassis, engineered to remain intact no matter how badly a crash damaged the rest of the car. The solution was to make sure that the driver's feet were well behind the front axle line and to surround the cockpit with crush zones—metal structures that would compress or deform to absorb energy that otherwise would have been transmitted directly to the driver.

When the working group signed off on the conceptual design, the project was handed to stylist Paolo Martin. Only twenty-five at the time, he'd already worked at Michelotti and Bertone before joining Pininfarina as a man to watch. When he was given the assignment, he knew next to nothing about racing. As he put it, "When I heard about the program, I was a bit perplexed since no one in the office was experienced or competent in the field of F1."[26] He was even more confused after he saw the material from the concept team. When he asked for some direction from management, he was told, "Dear Martin, do what you want."[27]

Martin salvaged all the mechanical bits from the Ferrari, including a 3.0-liter engine with a bag-of-snakes—or maybe that should be a bowl-of-spaghetti—network of exhaust pipes. He set aside the tubular frame of the 312 and fashioned a monocoque chassis out of aluminum alloy. Two long, hefty spars formed the center section, with bulkheads at the front and back of the cockpit. The spars were bent outward at the front to form a structure that resembled a metal lobster claw. At the rear, the engine and gearbox were enclosed in a separate compartment with what served as a metal bumper at the back. The cockpit was protected on either side by outriggers supported by a series of horizontal struts.

Martin opted for a broad chisel-style nose extending beyond the front tires, and the bodywork at the rear included mud flaps. Large sidepods, hearkening back to the Lancia-Ferrari Grand Prix cars of

The Sigma Grand Prix Safety Car, unveiled at the Geneva International Motor Show in 1969, wasn't even a roller, but it illuminated the road to the future. The innovations it embodied included foam-filled fuel cells, a head-and-neck restraint, an electronic data-acquisition system, and a wing that doubled as a super-stout roll bar. Most important of all, it pioneered the concept of using crush zones to create a survival cell for the driver. *Michael Henderson*

1956 and presaging the ground-effects cars to come, were designed to shroud the fuel cells and prevent drivers from interlocking wheels. After extensive tests of scale models in a wind tunnel, Martin styled a car that was low, wide, and flat, like a ciabatta on wheels. (It looked like a cousin of the roller skates raced by Mickey Thompson at Indianapolis in 1963 and 1964.) At the same time, it seemed futuristic enough to have been featured on *Speed Racer*. Notwithstanding all the race-proven Ferrari mechanical components used in its assembly, the car wasn't a runner. It was strictly a proof of concept meant to demonstrate the possibilities for those brave enough to embrace them.

Although the big news at the Geneva show was the debut of the Porsche 917, the Sigma got its share of attention. Jo Bonnier praised it publicly, and Henderson said Jackie Stewart and Jacky Ickx were complimentary, but David Phipps of *Autoweek* reported that it "received a very lukewarm" reception from the majority of Grand Prix regulars at the show.[28] Lamentably, the FIA, which was the target audience, largely ignored the car and the much safer future that it foretold. Yes, fire extinguishers were required in 1969 and fuel cells the year after that, but they were horribly ineffective. Inexplicably, six-point harnesses weren't mandated until 1972. Although crushable structures were required around the fuel tanks in 1973, the survival cell concept wasn't enshrined in the FIA rulebook until 1981. Crash-data recorders didn't arrive until 1997, and head-and-neck restraints didn't become compulsory until 2003, thirteen years after the life-saving HANS device invented by Robert Hubbard and Jim Downing went on sale.

The only element of the Sigma Grand Prix Safety Car that never appeared in F1 was rear bodywork fashioned to prevent wheels from interlocking. Which begs a few puzzling questions: Why didn't the FIA take the project more seriously? What would have happened if the Sigma model had been adopted sooner? And to paraphrase Bob Dylan, how many deaths would it take before sanctioning bodies acknowledged that too many drivers had died?

Fittingly all alone on the track, Jean-Pierre Beltoise slithers past the Casino de Monte-Carlo during a bravura wet-weather drive to victory in a BRM P160 in the Monaco Grand Prix in 1972—the first F1 win for both the driver and a car wearing Marlboro's signature red-and-white chevron. Beltoise would never win another World Championship race, but Marlboro motored on to even greater glory with McLaren and Ferrari. *Pete Lyons*

CHAPTER SEVEN

TOBACCO ROAD

In the mid-1960s, the Tasman Cup operated as Formula 1 Lite—great drivers, less power. During the off-season, to escape the winter gloom in the United Kingdom, Grand Prix aces would take a busman's holiday to compete in a series of races in Australia and New Zealand. The cars were a mix of F1 and F2 machines fitted with engines chosen to meet the 2.5-liter formula, and while the competition was fierce, the weather was hospitable, the starting money generous, and the atmosphere Down Under relaxed and friendly—a welcome respite from pressure-packed Grand Prix weekends.

In 1968, the entry list included stars such as Jim Clark, Graham Hill, and Chris Amon, along with local hero Frank Gardner. Amon won the first two races in his Ferrari. But at the third race, at Lady Wigwam in New Zealand, there was shock and consternation. Not because Clark outran Amon but because his Lotus 49 wasn't painted British racing green. For as long as anybody could remember, European cars had raced in their national colors: green for Great Britain, blue for France, red for Italy, yellow for Belgium, and so on. But special paint had been flown in from England so Clark's Lotus could be done up in an eye-grabbing red-and-gold livery, with a sailor's head logo advertising—advertising!—Gold Leaf cigarettes. Race officials were scandalized, and they briefly banned the car from the track. But Clark was eventually allowed to run, and he went on to lap all but one car in the field while cantering to a historic victory.

The thirteen-hour time difference between New Zealand and the United Kingdom allowed Gold Leaf to place full-page ads commemorating Clark's win in the Sunday afternoon editions of the London newspapers. The purists were predictably aghast. "One U.S.A.C. practice that still sits uneasily on my digestive tract is the practice of naming cars after their sponsors rather than their manufacturers—the Vita Fresh Orange Juice Special, for example, or the Thermo King Air Conditioner Special," tsk-tsked an editorial in *Motor Sport*, the most hidebound of the British racing magazines.[1] But generally speaking, the reaction was more pro than con. The dynamic Gold Leaf livery looked like a smashing product of the Swinging Sixties—Carnaby Street by way of the Mulsanne Straight—and the people who worked in the racing industry were eager to tap into the deep pockets of a new source of desperately needed revenue. "The Lotus looks great in the red, white and gold colours of the Player's Gold Leaf-Team Lotus sponsorship," Bruce McLaren wrote. "This is what Grand Prix racing is going to look like, and I'm all for it."[2]

The floodgates had been opened—unwittingly—by the CSI a few months earlier. Toward the end of 1967, Esso and British Petroleum had stunned the racing world by announcing that they would no longer be sugar daddies for motorsports, providing sponsorship money and free fuel to favored teams. Faced with the closure of this critical financial pipeline, the CSI rescinded its longstanding rule against displaying commercial advertising on race cars. To mitigate the impact of this about-face, advertisements were to be limited to an eleven-by-five-inch rectangle, or fifty-five square inches. It's hard to know exactly what CSI officials expected would happen next—probably the appearance of a handful of small, tasteful decals promoting automotive products such as spark plugs and, perhaps, automotive-adjacent services such as car insurance. Instead, the new rule unleashed a torrent of cigarette advertising that would dramatically reshape racing by injecting millions of dollars into a sport accustomed to subsisting on only tens of thousands. In years to come, NASCAR would become synonymous with Winston; the McLaren F1 team, with Marlboro; and IMSA sports car racing, with Camel. By the early 1970s, nicotine was as essential to racing as leaded gasoline.

The first racer to recognize the possibilities offered by the new regulations was Colin Chapman, the most entrepreneurial of the British race car constructors. Besides being a brilliant race car engineer and designer, he was also a shrewd businessman who built and sold road cars (and later, boats). On Chapman's behalf, Lotus team manager Andrew Ferguson pitched two hundred large British companies in search of a sponsor. They all passed—which says a lot about the lowly status racing enjoyed circa 1967. But then Chapman benefited from a bit of kismet. It turned out that a mechanic at Lotus Components was dating a secretary at the public relations firm that represented the Imperial Tobacco Company. She told him that John Player & Sons, one of Imperial's cigarette brands, was thinking about sponsoring a race team. As Imperial chairman Geoffrey Kent put it later, "It seemed that the only sport in which the British were doing well was motor racing. So we thought, 'Why don't we sponsor motor racing?'"[3] The contract with Lotus entailed a three-year deal worth about $225,000 annually. At the time, Cosworth DFV engines sold for a mere $17,600, and a solid two-car F1 team could do an entire season for $280,000. Under the circumstances, painting Clark's Lotus 49 in the red, white, and gold colors of the Gold Leaf cigarette brand seemed like a small price to pay.

Notwithstanding all the hoopla about Chapman's decision to climb aboard the tobacco train, sponsorship wasn't new to professional racing. For decades, virtually every car in the Indy 500 had carried some sort of commercial backing, though mostly from small companies making modest financial contributions to the team, and it was customary in NASCAR to display the names of car dealers on the fenders of the cars. But in Europe, advertising was considered crass, and the overt commercialism of sponsorship clashed with the fiction that racing was still a sport rather than a business. Much like Olympic athletes trying to preserve their "amateur" status—nudge nudge, wink wink—drivers were paid appearance money under the table, while teams received free merchandise in addition to small stipends from oil conglomerates, tire companies, brake manufacturers, and a handful of other automotive vendors. It wasn't much, but it was enough to pay the bills when teams were small, the cars were simple, and travel was limited.

The first team to bring significant sponsorship to Formula 1 was BRP, for British Racing Partnership, which had been formed in 1958 by Stirling Moss's father, Alfred, and his son's personal manager, Ken Gregory. Yeoman Credit came on board as a sponsor at the nonchampionship Oulton Park Gold Cup race in 1959 and then did the full F1 season in 1960. The next year, Yeoman Credit established its own team. So Gregory scared up a new sponsor in United Dominions Trust, which was a larger rival of Yeoman Credit (which, confusingly, would become Bowamaker in 1962). UDT also owned Laystall Engineering, a crankshaft manufacturer, so the new team was called UDT-Laystall. BRP didn't fare very well on the track—or off it, for that matter, since it was never treated like a full-fledged constructor—and it disappeared in the middle of the 1964 season.

While major teams sat indolently on the sidelines, a couple of privateers got into the sponsorship game. Perennial backmarker Carel Godin de Beaufort painted his old Porsche 718 orange and campaigned it under the Ecurie Pan Am Airlines flag. Far more noteworthy were the exploits of a resourceful young American named Roger Penske. In 1961, chemical giant DuPont gave him enough money to race a Cooper T53 in the US Grand Prix as the Telar Special. The next year, he returned with a Lotus 24 dubbed the Zerex Special in honor of another DuPont product. He also used the Zerex Special name for an ingenious quasi-legal sports car—the first example of Penske's "unfair advantage"—built on the bones of a wrecked F1 car, which he drove to lucrative victories in the big-time pro sports car races at Riverside and Laguna Seca in 1962. Despite winning four consecutive SCCA national championships and being named *Sports Illustrated*'s Driver of the Year, Penske retired from driving when he was just twenty-eight. But lining up sponsors would be one of his specialties when he went into business as a team owner.

Elsewhere on the commercial front, there was a weird incident at the Italian Grand Prix in 1965. In the paddock at Monza, before the first practice session, Chapman was presented with two cases of salami and, presumably, a thick wad of lire. In return, he provided a third Lotus for a wealthy Italian driver who raced as Geki. A similar scene unfolded in the Brabham camp, where local hero Giancarlo Baghetti was entrusted with a fourth entry. Although both cars carried Rondanini Salumi stickers in practice, the decals were removed before the race. Nevertheless, the episode caused plenty of grumbling in the pits. As Denis Jenkinson reported in *Motor Sport*, "As the Lotus mechanics said, they were not allowed to have Esso transfers on their cars, even though it is Esso petrol money that keeps Team Lotus going, so why should they stick salami adverts on the cars when they don't even eat the stuff?"[4]

Tobacco companies promised to be a better fit for racing than purveyors of processed meats. Even before the British Health Ministry banned tobacco advertising on television in 1965, the Carreras Tobacco Company erected a twenty-foot-tall Craven A cigarette pack in the "village" at Le Mans. By 1967, Carreras was sponsoring sports car races in the UK under its Guards brand as well as international Formula 2 and Formula 3 with Craven A. (The company would later expand its portfolio to include Formula 5000.) That same year, the Canadian Grand Prix was sponsored by Player's, which guaranteed $250,000 to cover the organizers' expenses, including prize money, and spent another $250,000 on promotion. Chapman may have been the first constructor to strike it rich with tobacco money, but there was still plenty of treasure to be plundered.

The first car to race in Formula 1 while advertising a tobacco brand was privateer John Love's two-year-old Brabham, which was painted orange with a brown stripe, to promote Gunston Tobacco at the South African Grand Prix over the New Year's Day weekend in 1968. But Love was a Rhodesian who rarely raced in Europe, and Gunston was a strictly South African brand, so the episode largely passed under the radar. And despite the tumult at Lady Wigwam two weeks later, the debut of the Gold Leaf Lotus 49 wasn't treated by the media or anybody else as stop-the-presses material. But then the Tasman Cup moved to Surfers Paradise in Australia, and all hell broke loose. The conservative Confederation of Australian Motor Sport ordered that the paddock gate be shut to prevent Clark and Hill from competing in a preliminary heat race. Cooler heads prevailed, and race officials backed down, clearing the way for Clark and Hill to finish one-two in the final. But another battle was brewing, and Chapman wouldn't win this one so easily.

In March, the Grand Prix season resumed with the non-championship Race of Champions at Brands Hatch, and traditionalists went bonkers when they saw the Gold Leaf Lotus in living color. As journalist Andrew Marriott recalled, "People said, 'It's disgraceful! Where are the national colors? I'm not sure this should be allowed.'"[5] Sure enough, Hill was black-flagged during the first practice session after complaints from ITV, the television network that was broadcasting the race. Chapman was informed that the sailor's head logo had to go; if not, the broadcast would be canceled. Duct tape was hurriedly slapped over the logo and covered with a Union Jack, along with a "Racing for Britain" slogan. This inspired McLaren mechanic Tyler Alexander to cheekily announce that he was going to paint "Racing for Money" on his team's transporter.[6]

The following month, at a contentious meeting in Frankfurt, race organizers, the Formula 1 Constructors' Association and Grand Prix Drivers' Association president Jo Bonnier agreed that cars no longer had to be painted in national colors. This was simply a case of acknowledging reality on the ground. Gold Leaf had already demonstrated that what really mattered wasn't the size or position of an advertisement; it was the shape and colors of the graphics, which transformed F1 cars into rolling billboards advertising their wares at 150 miles per hour. A handful of diehards continued to fight rear-guard actions. A month after the meeting in Frankfurt, Eurovision refused to broadcast the Monaco Grand Prix because it objected to Gold Leaf signage on Hill's Lotus. But only two months after that, ITV reversed its previous policy—and ignored the BBC's objections—and broadcast the British Grand Prix despite advertising on the cars. The dam had broken, and for very pragmatic reasons. As Eric Dymock wrote in *Autosport*, "Motor racing has been a professional sport for a good many years, yet in its major league it has been loath to relinquish the trappings of amateurism, like this quaint idea that it can make its own rules and hang the expense and hang the trade or industry interests. One accepts the need for ugly trackside advertising; one must also accept a rather undignified search for new sources of revenue for racing."[7]

The Lotus/Gold Leaf partnership was hugely successful. And yet, perplexingly, it didn't inspire any immediate imitators. Other tobacco companies weren't yet convinced that motorsports were a venue where they ought to flex their marketing muscles, and the race car companies were, well, race car companies. Among Chapman's major rivals, Enzo Ferrari, Bruce McLaren, and Jack Brabham were racers first and businessmen second, so they lacked the imagination to see the coming sponsorship bonanza. Matra, funded by Elf and the French government, could afford to take the high road and continue to paint their cars Gallic blue. But BRM's Louis Stanley was cut from a different cloth, and he was determined to get a piece of the sponsorship pie.

British Racing Motors had been founded after World War II in a misguided but admirably patriotic attempt to develop a supercharged V-16 engine for Grand Prix racing. In 1952, it was taken over by industrial tycoon Alfred Owen, owner of the Rubery Owen conglomerate of engineering component suppliers. His brother-in-law, Louis Stanley, who ran the team, calculated that the Owens family had spent £12 million of its own money to prop up BRM over the past two decades. (This translated into roughly $33 million.) So in 1971, Stanley rammed a proposal through a split board of directors to accept a sponsorship deal from Yardley, the cosmetics division of British American Tobacco. The program was modest—$120,000 over two years to support a team that entered three, four, and sometimes even five cars in a Grand Prix. Wearing Yardley's gold, black, and tan colors, BRM finished second in the constructor's championship that season. Ronnie Thomson, the president of Philip Morris Europe, sat up and took notice.

A Scotsman who'd been a world-class athlete, Thomson was a dynamic, young executive who brought a fresh attitude to the company. He quickly realized that the cowboy-themed Marlboro Man advertising motif didn't resonate outside the United States, so he began investigating other marketing strategies. As it happened, Philip Morris owned a small French cigarette manufacturer, Fabriques de Tabac Réunies, and FTR had a small personal sponsorship deal with BRM driver Jo Siffert. In October 1971, Siffert died unnecessarily in the nonchampionship year-end Victory Race at Brands Hatch—sponsored, coincidentally, by Rothmans—after the fire extinguishers manned by corner workers malfunctioned. Thomson dispatched Patrick Duffeler, a new hire who would soon become vice director of Philip Morris's motorsports promotions, to attend the funeral in Switzerland. While he was there, Duffeler brokered a meeting between Thomson and Stanley at Lausanne.

Testy negotiations ensued. As Duffeler recalled, "Stanley was bright but pedantic." And that, Duffeler said, wasn't the worst of his sins. "He was incompetent, number one. Arrogant, number two. And he was rude to people in general, unless he was hoping to get something from them."[8] Not that Stanley was concerned about the impression he made. "Speaking my mind has not always made me popular," he said. "But with Marlboro it was quite simple. We came to an agreement on terms. I went over to Geneva, and they tried to alter the contract. So I told them where to put it even though it was painful. I came back, they changed their mind and they came to the Dorchester and signed."[9]

The deal called for Philip Morris to pay BRM $250,000 a year to run at least three and as many as seven drivers for two years. (Five turned out to be the maximum number of entries at any particular race.) In January, Philip Morris sparked a media blitz by flying one hundred journalists to Nice and then bussing them to Circuit Paul Ricard to watch a BRM P160 wearing red-and-white livery blast out of a giant mockup of a pack of Marlboro cigarettes. Four months later, Jean-Pierre Beltoise scored a magnificent win in torrential rain at Monaco to claim Marlboro's first F1 victory. But the rest of the season was dominated by cars sponsored by a rival cigarette brand.

For 1972, Imperial Tobacco wanted to shift its focus from Gold Leaf to a new upmarket cigarette brand, so the wedge-shaped Lotus 72s were renamed John Player Specials and adorned with an arresting black-and-gold paint scheme. When driver Emerson Fittipaldi first saw the new car, he told Chapman, "Well, it just needs four handles to be a coffin!"[10] As it turned out, the JPS livery set an aesthetic standard that few graphics packages have matched in the half-century since. Better still, Fittipaldi was crowned world champion at the end of season.

The old guard was outraged by the commodification of the sport. "One cannot condone the adoption of this Indianapolis-type practice in Formula 1," Mike Kettlewell wrote in *Autocourse*, the annual publication that served as the semi-official English-language record of European motorsports. "One naturally accepts the fact that commercialism is all-important in Formula 1, but it cannot be allowed to get too out of hand. Will drivers change their names next in the style of the pop groups?"[11] Imagine Kettlewell's dismay when the British Grand Prix was officially billed as the John Player Grand Prix in 1972 and, adding insult to injury, was won by Fittipaldi's John Player Special. Indignation notwithstanding, a veritable avalanche of tobacco advertising was about to bury the sponsorship haters.

For 1973, John Player re-upped with Lotus. In addition to sponsoring BRM for a second year, Philip Morris added Frank Williams's

Formula 1 cars are typically identified alphanumerically. But when Colin Chapman, far right, introduced the successor to the Lotus 72 in 1974, he designated it the John Player Special. Drivers Ronnie Peterson, in the cockpit, and Jacky Ickx, soon discovered that the car was a dog. But that didn't placate the purists, especially since the 1974 race at Silverstone was officially called the John Player Grand Prix. *Revs Institute / Eric della Faille Photograph Collection*

cash-strapped two-car Iso-Ford—now Iso-Marlboro—team to the fold and signed a dozen or so drivers and motorcycle riders to personal-services contracts. "We feel we got enormous value from motor racing in 1972," Thomson announced at a huge preseason press conference in Geneva as the company committed to spending $1 million on racing during the coming year.[12] And Marlboro was just one of the brands looking to plant its flag in motorsports. There was so much low-hanging fruit to be plucked from the tobacco companies that Hill, clearly at the end of his career as a frontline driver, was able to land a sweetheart deal from Embassy cigarettes netting him $250,000 per year for three years.

Despite all the sponsorship money, Hill didn't manage a single points-scoring finish in 1973, while BRM and Williams scored only fourteen measly points between them. This clearly wasn't the return on investment that Marlboro had in mind. By this time, Duffeler had befriended Fittipaldi, who was unhappy with the situation at Lotus since the arrival of Ronnie Peterson as a teammate (and rival). Duffeler received corporate approval to structure a "super team" around Fittipaldi for 1974.[13] A deal with Brabham was rejected because Duffeler didn't trust the team's new owner, Bernie Ecclestone. Instead, he signed a contract worth roughly $500,000 with Teddy Mayer at McLaren and dumped BRM.

Stung by this dismissal, Stanley never forgave Marlboro for introducing what he called "cheque book tactics" that were "undermining the sport"—a charge that rang hollow considering that he was the one who'd invited the fox into the henhouse.[14] Marlboro won a world championship with Fittipaldi in a McLaren M23 in 1974. McLarens wearing the iconic red-and-white colors of Marlboro would win eight more championships in the hands of James Hunt, Niki Lauda, Alain Prost, and Ayrton Senna before Philip Morris shifted its allegiance to Ferrari. BRM, on the other hand, limped into oblivion in 1977. Although the last of the BRMs—the overweight, overmatched P207—didn't have a title sponsor, it did have a nickname: Stanley Steamer, the cruel tag bestowed upon it by wags in the paddock.

The road to nicotine addiction followed a different route in the United States. What screenwriters would call the "inciting incident" was a ceremony at the White House in the spring of 1970, when President Richard M. Nixon signed legislation banning cigarette advertising on radio and television by the end of the year. "The advertising of tobacco products on radio and TV this year was worth two hundred thirty million [dollars] to the networks," Chris Economaki wrote in *National Speed Sport News*. "If racing knows how to treat the tobacco companies there's no reason why a goodly portion of this money cannot be bled into our sport."[15] Economaki could have taken that prediction to the bank. Within two years, Marlboro, Winston, Camel, Viceroy, and L&M would all be major presences on road courses and ovals from coast to coast.

The Liggett & Myers Tobacco Company got there first. In 1969, L&M sponsored the final race of the SCCA's pro Formula 5000 series, officially known as the Continental Championship. The next year, the company put up $110,000 in prize money and promotional resources. When the TV ban went into effect the year after that, L&M became the title sponsor of the series. L&M signage was also prominently displayed in Can-Am racing, first on Jackie Stewart's Lola 260 in 1971 and then on the Roger Penske/Mark Donohue/George Follmer turbocharged Porsches in 1972. Meanwhile, IMSA, SCCA's great antagonist in professional road racing, lined up Camel as a title sponsor in 1972. The money involved was negligible—$10,000 toward a points fund, plus $5,000 to the series champ, and $2,500 to the runner-up. But Camel was in it for the long haul, and its support for IMSA stretched into the 1990s.

Marlboro wasn't as steadfast, at least in the United States. Philip Morris tested the waters with Indy cars by signing a two-year deal with USAC. In 1970, the company pledged $50,000 to a year-end championship fund. The next year, the series was retitled the Marlboro Championship Trail, with Philip Morris distributing $300,000 to the points leaders. In 1972, the ante was set to be upped to $500,000. But then Viceroy announced plans to step in as the sponsor of Mario Andretti and Al Unser's cars in the Vel's Parnelli Jones Racing team. This infuriated Marlboro, which snippily decided to take its ball and go home.

The Marlboro/USAC debacle inspired a typically blistering but oddly muddled Brock Yates editorial. "We are talking about nickels and dimes," he wrote in *Car and Driver*. "Marlboro bought practically everything in USAC except their mimeograph machine for about the same price of two 30-second spots on a *Gilligan's Island* rerun and NASCAR sold the farm to Winston for pocket money. And now that racing has so eagerly cuddled into bed with this essentially anti-social enterprise, it has made the sport seem even more suspect."[16] Suspect ethically, perhaps. But Yates's commendable distaste for cigarette advertising blinded him to the vital role that tobacco money would play in funding the growth of motorsports in the 1970s.

Nowhere was the impact greater than in NASCAR—a classic case of the night being darkest before the dawn. In 1970, Ford axed its stock car program and Chrysler cut back its support to a single team. (Chevy had quit a few years earlier.) Doom and gloom were the order of the day. "It was as low a point as you could get in NASCAR," Humpy Wheeler said. "It was just terrible."[17] Junior Johnson, one of the foundational heroes of the sport, threatened to close his race shop. But before taking any drastic action, he made a pilgrimage to the R.J. Reynolds Tobacco Company headquarters in nearby Winston-Salem. There were already strong ties between RJR and stock car racing. Bowman Gray Stadium, billed as the home of longest-running weekly races on the NASCAR schedule, had been named after the father of the company's current CEO. So Johnson found himself pitching a receptive audience. Too receptive, as it turned out. When he asked for $100,000 in sponsorship money, he was told, "Man, we're lookin' to spend millions."[18] To which Johnson replied, "Well, then, I ought to get you together with Bill France at NASCAR. You need to sponsor the whole series."

In December 1970, after months of meetings with France, RJR announced that it would offer a $165,000 purse for the upcoming summer race at Talladega, to be known as the Winston 500. In return for adding $100,000 to the points championship, the series was renamed Winston Grand National. RJR also agreed to spend at least $500,000 on national advertising and promotional campaigns for NASCAR. This went over so well that, in 1972, the points fund was increased to $500,000 and the series was restyled as Winston Cup. "It was a huge help for all of us," said Dave Marcis. "They cleaned up the racetracks. They cleaned up the bathrooms. They painted everything. The purses went up. They gave us a much, much better point fund. It was fantastic."[19]

Winston wasn't merely the title sponsor of NASCAR. It was also a partner whose executives understood that, as NASCAR flourished, so would their brand. During the 1970s, RJR pioneered what's now known as sports marketing activation—the process of engaging customers and increasing brand awareness with activities that go beyond conventional advertising. There were Winston promotions, Winston giveaways, Winston paraphernalia, Winston trophy girls. Camel, which was one of RJR's other premium brands, got the same treatment. "One day, the phone rang, and it's this young man from Camel," recalled longtime West Coast promoter Ken Clapp, who later became a NASCAR executive. "He said, 'Ken, I got money I got to get rid of before the budget closes down. You got anyplace I could spend seventy-five grand?' I said, 'Well, we could build an air-conditioned VIP press facility with restrooms at San Jose.' He said, 'Let's do it, but you've got to get an invoice to me today. I've got to get rid of this money *right now*.'" Clapp chuckled. "There's never been a sponsor in racing like Winston, not even close. I could call them and present an idea, and as long as it was constructive and it made sense and it would sell tobacco, I didn't get nos. I got yeses."[20]

In 1972, Bill France Jr. took over from his father, Big Bill, as NASCAR's supreme leader. Fears that the mild-mannered son wouldn't have the moxie or the backbone to ride herd over the wild stallions of stock car racing were quickly alleviated. "Our drivers' meetings used to be in the Goodyear Building at Daytona," said Donnie Allison, who, with his brother Bobby, was one of the core members of the so-called Alabama Gang. "Big Bill would come in, and Billy Junior would stand over in the corner, leaning against the wall. I never heard him say a word at one of those drivers' meeting—but he took it all in. Big Bill was the boss, and he wanted everybody to know he was the boss, and he didn't mind telling you he was the boss, which is all well and good. Bill Junior was a different horse. Bill France Senior might have started NASCAR, but Bill France Junior *built* NASCAR. The knowledge he got from his dad, and his own practical experience and common sense, got it to where it is."[21]

Despite resistance from members of the old guard, Bill Junior quickly jettisoned dirt tracks from the Winston Cup schedule, leaving "only" thirty-one races, all of them longer than 250 miles. Besides being easier on the teams, the reduced scheduled accentuated the positive. "They wanted to clean up the racing, make it more family-oriented," said longtime NASCAR crewman Kenny Troutt. "Winston spent a *lot* of money, and you could immediately see the effect that had on NASCAR. They took it to the next level. Like at Martinsville, they cleaned up the grandstands, painted the walls, and put flowers all around the deal, made it more attractive."[22]

The decision to sever stock car racing from its hardscrabble dirt track roots helped France promote NASCAR as an upscale brand able to attract a new generation of nonautomotive sponsors. Which it did, as advertisers ranging from Tide to Budweiser flocked to the sport in years to come. But it all began with Winston. As Richard Petty put it later, "RJR came to the races and looked up in the stands and saw their customers. They brought their business partners to the track, and they looked up in the stands and said, 'Those are my customers, too.'"[23]

Racing was a godsend for Big Tobacco. With so many brands of cigarettes on the market and the differences between them relatively small, marketing was the most effective way to stand out from the competition. Motorsports provided a perfect venue for companies that no longer had access to the airwaves. Not only could cigarette makers pay for signage at the tracks and liveries on the cars, but they could also distribute their products to a captive audience that was already inclined to smoke. The calculations were a lot different for the manufacturers of, say, lawnmowers and washing machines. For a lot of nonautomotive sponsors that were thinking of investing in racing, the numbers didn't add up.

In the days before the internet, the standard metric in advertising was CPM, which stands for the cost per thousand ad impressions to reach potential customers. Traditionally, it was based on eyeballs for television broadcasts and readers and/or subscribers for newspapers and magazines. The more people you reach, the lower your CPM. Thanks to television, modern Formula 1 races are seen by about seventy million viewers worldwide while NASCAR races average nearly three million per event. But in the 1960s, TV coverage of motorsports was just getting off the ground, so viewership numbers were negligible. Although enthusiast magazines covered racing, well, enthusiastically, they were niche publications that didn't command the reach that mainstream marketing executives craved. That left the paying customers who actually attended the races, and those numbers varied wildly, depending on the track, the date, and the event. Attendance for the Indy 500 was said to be about 350,000 on race day. Most road-race promoters would have been thrilled to get a tenth as many spectators over the course of an entire race weekend. In 1970, Marlboro sponsored the Lime Rock Trans-Am race. Even though this was at the peak of the series' popularity, tobacco executives left Connecticut with a bad case of buyer's remorse. As Tom Keim, Marlboro's assistant brand manager, explained, "Spending $25,000 to reach 25,000 spectators is costly and difficult to justify."[24]

Sponsorship was an easier sell in the United States than in Europe. Among American racers, advertising wasn't derided as being vulgar or reluctantly accepted as a necessary evil. On the contrary, it was welcomed with a bear hug by every sanctioning body except the hoity-toity SCCA, which was one reason motorsports were far more egalitarian in the States than they were overseas. By the 1920s, several of the cars entered at Indy were funded, at least in part, by aftermarket vendors such as Package Cable (spark plugs), Boyle (valves), and Perfect Circle (piston rings). Fast-forward to the 1960s, and virtually every Indy car—and sprint car and midget—was known by a name rather than an alphanumeric designation. So instead of cars like the Honda RA301 or Matra-Simca MS670B, the open-wheel oval track world featured the Bowes Seal Fast Special, the Fike Plumbing Special, and the Konstant Hot Special. In 1965, Jim Hurtubise even raced a Novi at Indianapolis with sponsorship from Tombstone Life.

The problem was that these sponsors didn't pay much money. Most of them were relatively small companies whose owners were themselves hardcore race fans. They weren't looking to burnish their brand image as much as they wanted to help out friends and get closer to the action. In many cases, such as Al Dean and Dean Van Lines, the "sponsor" was actually the wealthy businessman who owned the team, usually operating at a loss. Cars didn't wear liveries designed to display corporate colors and logos, à la the Gold Leaf Lotuses. Rarely did sponsors get more than their names lettered somewhere on the fuselage. After Parnelli Jones won Indy in 1963, Willard Batteries gave his car owner, J.C. Agajanian, a check for $25,000. Agajanian's son, Cary, recalled, "That was the first time he ever got any money from a sponsor, and he was ecstatic—to think that anybody would pay to put his name on the car!"[25]

The first modern sponsor to make a huge splash at Indy was STP, a mysterious engine additive that was said to enhance performance while curing a host of ills. Precisely because the ingredients of this alleged elixir were secret, STP had plenty of skeptics, so selling it to the general public required a lot of promotion. As it happened, the president of the company was the ideal man for the job. Andy Granatelli was large *in* life and larger *than* life, a born showman and a legitimate racer. Before World War II, Granatelli had promoted successful midget shows at Soldier Field, the capacious stadium where the Chicago Bears played. After the war, he entered a flathead Mercury-powered special that finished twenty-first in the 500, and he later crashed while trying to qualify the car himself.

In 1962, Granatelli bought a trio of Novis, the great coulda, woulda, shoulda fan favorites whose supercharged V-8 emitted a spine-tingling shriek that first thrilled spectators in 1941. The cars raced in 1963 while sporting a couple of STP decals. The next year, Granatelli pulled out all the stops while indulging his P.T. Barnum fantasies. The Novi driven by Bobby Unser was painted STP fire-engine red and festooned with STP stickers. All of the crewmen wore matching uniforms—white with small STP logos that resembled polka dots. Critics sneered that the outfits looked like children's pajamas (which they did). But instead of wilting in the face of public ridicule, Granatelli doubled down by sauntering around Gasoline Alley in a garish XXL business suit featuring the same pattern.

Lamentably, Unser was eliminated in the first-lap crash that claimed the lives of Dave MacDonald and Eddie Sachs. In 1965, the STP Novis finished nineteenth and dead last. The year after that, Granatelli switched his allegiance to a proven winner. Reigning champion Jim Clark's Lotus 38 was duly painted STP red, but he finished second to Graham Hill after a dispute over the lap count. In 1967, Parnelli

Garish sponsorship was nothing new to Indy, but Andy Granatelli raised the bar to levels never before imagined. In 1965, besides painting Jim Hurtubise's Novi Dayglo STP red, he also outfitted his crew in STP outfits that looked more like pajamas than uniforms. Not to be outdone by his underlings, he strolled around the premises in a business suit in the same STP pattern. Alas, the Novi's transmission broke on the first lap. *Indianapolis Motor Speedway*

Jones broke while leading three laps from the checkered flag in his STP-sponsored turbine. The next year, Joe Leonard's all-new STP turbine crapped out nine laps short of winning. It wasn't until 1969 that Granatelli finally hit pay dirt in the STP-sponsored Brawner Hawk driven by Mario Andretti. After the race, while celebrating in Victory Circle, Granatelli planted a sloppy smooch on Andretti's grimy cheek, thereby creating one of the most indelible images in Indy 500 history.

Granatelli's unquenchable thirst for publicity didn't go over well with the old-timers. It didn't help that he'd sued USAC over the rules governing turbines. And railbirds rolled their eyes when he titled his autobiography *They Call Me Mister 500*, even though nobody actually called him "Mister 500" and his cars had finished last more times than they finished first. Still, Granatelli's bombastic personality and promotional acumen propelled his little-known oil-and-gas additive to national prominence. By 1967, the company was recording $43 million in annual sales, and two years later, it went public and was listed on the American Stock Exchange.

In 1970, when Andretti decided to fulfill his dream of racing in Formula 1, STP sponsorship went with him. Not only was Andretti's March 701 painted in STP livery, but so were the team cars of Chris Amon and Jo Siffert. STP remained March's principal sponsor for the next three years. Although hard numbers are difficult to pin down, it appears likely that Granatelli never spent more than about $60,000 a year in F1—a substantial sum of money but far less than Imperial Tobacco was paying Lotus or BRM was getting from Yardley and then Marlboro. Granatelli's critics happily pointed out that his return on investment was pretty paltry, at least if the cost-benefit analysis was based solely on race results. But the progress he made in terms of brand awareness and market penetration was incalculable, and other would-be sponsors started gravitating to the sport.

Anyway, F1 was just a sideshow to Granatelli. Here in the States, he already had most of the country covered with the Indy car circuit. But reaching race fans in the Southeast meant finding a stock car driver to sponsor. After Granatelli surveyed the field, he had his man—Richard Petty, who'd been named NASCAR's Most Popular Driver four times over the past nine years. "Here's the deal," he told Petty. "$250,000 for a sponsorship, and we want to advertise you all over the country."[26] This was at the end of 1971, after the Detroit manufacturers had bailed from NASCAR, and money was scarce. Petty didn't have to be asked twice. The only sticking point was the color of the car. Petty preferred his signature electric blue; Granatelli was adamant about Day-Glo STP red. They compromised on a two-tone livery, red and blue, with prominent STP decals. Oh, and there was one addendum. "It's written into the contract that Andy doesn't kiss *me* after any wins," Petty said.[27]

Racing was a natural fit for STP. But companies with no ostensible interest in motorsports were also starting to see it as effective tool to reach potential customers. S.C. Johnson & Sons was an American conglomerate that worked out of striking corporate headquarters in Wisconsin designed by Frank Lloyd Wright. Although its portfolio was focused on household products such as Pledge and Glade, it also sold an automotive cleaner known as J-Wax or J/Wax. In previous years, the company had sponsored a wide variety of popular radio and televisions shows including *Fibber McGee and Molly* and *The Red Skelton Show*. In 1966, company president Sam Johnson had a brainstorm while meeting with his public relations firm. "Hey," he said, "maybe we ought to be in auto racing."[28]

As fate would have it, the SCCA had recently decided to put together a real-deal, serious-money, no-holds-barred sports car series with six races in North America after the European season was over. For its $25,000 contribution to the year-end prize fund, Johnson became the title sponsor of the Canadian-American Challenge Cup Series Presented by J/Wax. John Surtees earned $78,000 for winning the inaugural championship. Prize money jumped by 40 percent in 1967, and so did the profile of the series. Besides placing ads featuring Can-Am racing, Johnson ran radio promotions and arranged speaking engagements for its suave official spokesman, Stirling Moss. By 1970, the series had become so popular and lucrative that the Bruce and Denny Show—teammates McLaren and fellow Kiwi Denny Hulme—earned more than $300,000 for finishing one-two in the championship standings. The payday was big enough, in fact, to fund the team's entire F1 and Indy car programs.

After the 1971 season ended, Johnson pulled the rug out from under the series when it decided that it had gotten all it wanted out of Can-Am. SCCA began a frantic search for a new title sponsor. Gallo, the winemaker, tentatively raised its hand. "Within two days," *Autoweek* reported, "the company was besieged with 46 proposals; the hat-in-hand applicants ranged from a drag strip in central Pennsylvania to a Super Vee driver in Phoenix. The Gallo reaction: Forget the whole thing."[29] The next suitor was the fragrance company Leeming-Pacquin, which was introducing a new line of male cosmetics called Roman Brio. The rumor mill pegged the sponsorship figures at somewhere between $600,000 and $750,000. In the end, it was zero. Without a title sponsor, Can-Am limped along until being euthanized in the middle of the 1974 season. "The message is simple," Yates wrote in *Car and Driver.* "No racing series should be peddled to sponsors in the first place, because sponsors are by nature capricious allies and should not be counted on for more than temporary support."[30]

Yates, so progressive when it came to the subject of safety in racing, was positively antediluvian when it came to sponsorship. But putting his head in the sand couldn't change the fact that the modern motorsports ecosystem we take for granted today was built on a foundation paid for with millions of dollars provided by sponsors ranging from cigarettes to condoms. By Darwinian evolution, a new subspecies of racing professional came into being: the sponsor finder. There was Mark McCormack, the founder of International Management Group, now known as IMG, whose clients included Rindt, Amon, and Peter Revson; Chuck Barnes, the architect of Sports Headliners, who had Andretti, Jones, Foyt, and the Unser brothers on his roster; Kent Telford, who brought UOP (for Universal Oil Products) to Shadow after starting his search with companies beginning with the letter "A" and working his way through the alphabet; and ex-Firestone PR guy Jim Cook, who was instrumental in getting two competing model car companies—Hot Wheels and Johnny Lightning—to make major financial commitments to racing.

Roger Penske was one of the beneficiaries of the sponsorship boom. "When we formed our race team in 1966 we never viewed it as a profit center," he said. "We raced because we loved the competition and the opportunity to prove ourselves against the very best in the sport. We quickly realized that sponsorship and building relationships with our partners through racing was a winning formula."[31] For most of the team's early years, Penske flew the royal-blue flag of Sun Oil in Can-Am, Trans-Am, and USAC. In 1972, his turbocharged Porsche

917/10s raced in L&M colors. Later, his Indy cars wore the red-and-white livery of Marlboro for nearly two decades.

Sponsorship had an even more transformative impact on Formula 1 and sports car racing in Europe. Prior to 1968, racing was largely an upper-crust sport because the financial barrier to entry was so high. "You see, sponsorship wasn't allowed by the blue blazer, gold button brigade at the RAC," bucks-down racer Guy Edwards wrote. "No sticker much bigger than a string of postage stamps was permitted to sully a racing car, and the only way a driver could really get going was if he had access to private money or hung around the Steering Wheel Club socialising his way into the seat of a car owned by a wealthy entrant. This was all very well up to a point and great if you were part of the 'establishment,' but if you weren't God help you."[32]

Edwards literally wrote the book on motorsports sponsorship. (Yep, it's titled *Sponsorship and the World of Motor Racing*.) Edwards was a racing "nutter," in British argot, who lacked the funds or the contacts to make a career out of motorsports. But when sponsorship was legalized, he realized that, if he could craft a business plan showing a plausible return on investment, he could get other people to foot the bill for his racing program—and that's just what he did. In 1969, he persuaded Tor Line, a Swedish freight shipper, to sponsor his Chevron B8. The next year, Philips, the electronics conglomerate, paid him to campaign an Astra RNR2 Group 6 car. In 1971, he raced at Le Mans with backing from Philips, Camel, and Texaco. Over the next two years, his Lola 290 and 292 were financed by Barclays Bank. By 1974, he'd put together enough sponsorship to broker a deal for a seat in the Embassy Hill Grand Prix team. Edwards was a very talented driver, but without commercial patronage, he probably wouldn't have progressed much beyond club racing.

Sponsorship was equally critical to team owners. In 1968, Frank Williams was eking out a meager living buying and selling race cars and doing the Formula 2 season on the cheap with driver Piers Courage. The next year, Williams lined up funding from a machine tool company called T.W. Ward and moved up to Formula 1. By 1971, Williams had Henri Pescarolo driving a March 711 cosponsored by Ward ($36,000), French brake fluid manufacturer Motul ($91,000), and Italian toymaker Politoys ($24,000). The following year, Politoys funded a bespoke chassis ($96,000) and Motul re-signed to keep Pescarolo in the cockpit ($96,000), while Ward kicked in at least $24,000. The financial arrangements got even more complicated in 1973, when tobacco sponsorship forced Williams to enter his cars as Iso-Marlboros. To keep the team afloat, ten different drivers were employed—or, more often, paid the team—to race the cars. While Williams and other also-rans scrambled to snag sponsorship from companies like an Argentine meat purveyor, an Italian ceramics firm, and a British tea supplier, the top-dog teams put together more profitable deals with top-tier corporations. In 1972, Yardley signed on with McLaren for $240,000 and Martini & Rossi spent $200,000 to help the all-new Techno F1 operation get off the ground. By the time the Grand Prix caravan reached Monte Carlo in 1973, twenty-two of the twenty-five entries brandished some sort of nonautomotive decals.

The erudite, nonconformist British journalist LJK Setright looked upon the scene with the disdain and sorrow of Edmund Burke, patron saint of modern conservatism, casting his bleak gaze upon the excesses of the French Revolution. "It is business now, big booming business, and motor racing will very likely continue to get worse as the business gets better," he wrote. "Everybody in it seems to be taking a cue from the United States, where it has always been like that, where the cars have always looked, sounded, and behaved just like each other, where all that has mattered has been the drivers' names—and those of the sponsors who pay to use their cars as mobile advertisement hoardings, and who in 1972 were threatening to take over the sponsorship and therefore the virtual control of the entire Grand Prix season. America has long been accustomed to this sort of circus act, and it may or may not be fair to see in this vulgar ignorance of the sport's finer points a reflection of the crass commercialism of the American automobile industry."[33]

Setright longed for the days when, as he put it, "grown men in linen helmets sat up in high-sounding high-smelling supercharged cars of architectural grace and animal ferocity, whose bursts of sound jabbed and bounded back from town walls or timbered slopes as they traced the course of real roads at places like Berne, Bari, Albi, Sam Remo, Syracuse or Jersey. They carried no advertising but ran under their national colours; they were more likely to pay entrance fees than to demand starting money."[34] And then came the poisonous coda: "Motor sport is dead."

To be sure, one version was gone, supplanted by a more corporate iteration where the bottom line was a balance sheet. There's no question that some of the romance had been lost in this transition. But in return, motorsports became more accessible to more people. Also, a lot more profitable. It was now possible, if you were a successful enough driver or a savvy enough car owner, to become rich from racing. But most of the money that flowed into the sport didn't end up lining deep pockets. It was funneled back into the teams, to hire more people, to build more cars, to undertake more R&D. As a result, the sport became more professional, and the difference was visible in the most obvious ways.

"When Roger Penske came to Indianapolis, he put floors down and cabinets on the walls in Gasoline Alley," said Carl Hungness, who published the indispensable *Indianapolis 500 Yearbook* for many years. "His crew looked like executives with black slacks and white shirts. He had the first clean garage. Then everybody had clean garages. He had the first enclosed hauler. Then everybody had enclosed haulers."[35] In Europe, a similar role was played by McLaren owner-to-be Ron Dennis, as he shifted from working as a race mechanic to running his own team. "When he started doing Formula 2, the presentation of his cars and his transporter was so different from the regular English teams," said Tim Schenken, one of his first two drivers. "In English teams, if you went into the transporter, you'd be careful not to touch anything so you didn't get grease on your overalls. People nicknamed Ron Dennis Team Clean or, rather cruelly, Team Briefcase."[36] All the same, Dennis's fastidious attention to even the smallest details helped him secure the sponsorship he needed to stay in business.

The heightened regard for professionalism produced not only spiffier-looking teams but also more competitive racing. Consider these qualifying times for the British Grand Prix at Silverstone. In 1953, the gap between first and tenth was 6.0 seconds. Between first and twentieth was 16.0 seconds. Ten years later, the gaps had been cut in half, to 2.4 seconds and 8.2 seconds. In 1973, they were halved again, to 1.2 seconds and 2.8 seconds. It may not be entirely coincidental that this was the year of the infamous race where nine cars were involved in a first-lap melee that left Andrea de Adamich with a broken ankle. With drivers having to come ever closer to the limit, more accidents were inevitable. Car-to-car contact, which had been almost unthinkable just a decade earlier, was now a regular occurrence. And yet safety remained almost an afterthought in the minds of the pooh-bahs in charge of the sport. It was mostly a matter of luck, not skill, that determined whether a driver would walk away from a shunt or whether it would send him to his grave.

TOY STORY

Jim Cook's sport was football. He was a graduate assistant under illustrious Ohio State University football coach Woody Hayes, then worked as an assistant coach while attending law school at the University of Akron. But back then, Akron was known as the Rubber Capital of the World, not the Football Capital of the World. So after graduating, like so many of the locals entering the workforce, Cook ended up getting a job at one of the four major tire companies in town—in his case, Firestone.

Cook worked his way up the corporate ladder until moving to Southern California in 1968 to head the company's West Coast public relations operation. The next year, after going into business for himself, he was hired by Vel's Parnelli Jones Racing (VPJ) to scare up some sponsorship, and he thought the model car market might be a good place to start. As it happens, he wasn't the first guy to come up with this idea.

In 1964, the L.M. Cox Manufacturing Company made a deal with Jim Hall to sell slot car versions of the Chaparral 2A, 2D, and 2E as well as scale models of the 2A and 2C. This was at the beginning of the slot car craze, and Cox promoted the hell out of its products with eye-catching magazine ads. "Exact replica of the 1965 Sebring winner from blueprints checked and approved by Jim Hall," the copy read. "It's all car, all real. So real that when you see it on the track, you listen for the booming roar of the 325 cu. in., 425-hp engine."[37]

Hall received a small royalty for each car sold. Since nearly a million model Chaparrals were sold over the next few years, he earned more than $100,000 from the deal. Cox ended up paying for a substantial portion of the Chaparral budget, which also benefited from engineering support from General Motors, tire-testing money from Firestone, and sponsorship from Shell and Bosch. "Now, I'm not here to say we made money," Hall said, "but we maybe came pretty damn close."[38]

By the time Cook started searching for sponsors, the slot car boom had gone bust, so his first port of call was the Southern California industry giant, Mattel. Although the company's biggest seller was Barbie, it was also making bundles of money with its Hot Wheels model cars, which had debuted in 1968. The next year, Cook pitched Mattel with a proposal for Hot Wheels to sponsor VPJ at Indy. Company founders Ruth and Elliot Handler liked the idea. But they decided to go instead with a mongoose who said he could deliver a snake and give Mattel a drag racing rivalry that would sell Hot Wheels by the millions.

The Snake was Top Fuel superhero Don Prudhomme. Long and lanky, he was lightning quick off the line, hence his nickname. The Mongoose was his longtime adversary, Tom McEwen. Famed engine builder Ed Donovan had suggested the moniker because a mongoose was the only thing faster than a snake. Like the phony feuds cooked up in professional wrestling, the Snake versus Mongoose storyline was match-racing gold. In real life, Prudhomme and McEwen weren't enemies, but they were polar opposites. Prudhomme was terse and calculating, a fierce competitor who hated losing more than he enjoyed winning. McEwen was an outgoing free spirit who had a knack for promotion.

By happy coincidence, McEwen's stepfather was a high-powered attorney who happened to represent Mattel. McEwen wrangled a meeting with Mattel executives. After a second meeting including Prudhomme, Mattel decided to sponsor the duo and create Hot Wheels versions of the cars that would be raced by the Snake and the Mongoose. When McEwen explained that Prudhomme would have to run a Funny Car, Prudhomme almost balked—almost. "By the time I realized the scale of what he had in mind, I would have driven a taxicab to make it happen," Prudhomme said. "It was huge."[39]

At the time, there were only a handful of nonautomotive sponsors in drag racing, and most drag racers lived from hand to mouth. Prize

In 1970, drag racing enjoyed a spike of mainstream popularity thanks to Mattel's manufactured feud between Tom "The Mongoose" McEwen, left, and Don "The Snake" Prudhomme. Neither of their Funny Cars—a Plymouth Duster for McEwen and a Hemi 'Cuda for Prudhomme—was particularly successful in NHRA competition. But the Snake-versus-Mongoose rivalry was match-racing gold, and Hot Wheels models of their race cars sold like hotcakes.
Revs Institute / Pete Biro Photograph Collection

money offered at nationally sanctioned events was barely enough to cover bills, so drivers hoping to earn a living from the sport crisscrossed the country competing in match races at drag strips big and small, on the fringes of big cities and in locations so remote that you needed a compass to find them. Even for big names, $1,000 for a match-racing show would have been considered a stellar payday. By way of contrast, Mattel paid McEwen and Prudhomme $30,000 apiece for the first year of their three-year deal. Knowing that their decals would appear not only on the race cars but also the Hot Wheels models, several associate sponsors also signed up for between $5,000 and $25,000. The Snake and the Mongoose earned $100,000 in 1970, plus match-racing appearance money and royalties for each model sold.

Mattel aggressively marketed the Snake and Mongoose Show with Hot Wheels events in every city where they barnstormed. The immense success of the program brought other sponsors to drag racing, big ones like Coca-Cola and Wonder Bread. In 1975, Winston signed on as the NHRA's title sponsor, and it immediately marked its new territory with its signature colors. "Track operators around the country would call Winston and say, 'Send me four hundred gallons of red and white paint,'" former NHRA competition director Steve Gibbs said. "Next thing you knew, every concession stand, every timing tower, and every guardrail was painted red and white, with Winston signs all over the place."[40]

And what about Jim Cook, the sponsor-finder whose grand plan to get Hot Wheels to sponsor Vel's Parnelli Jones at the Indy 500 had been snaked away by McEwen? He decided to turn lemons into lemonade by pitching Mattel's biggest rival in the model car market. "I met with Henry Orenstein, the president of Topper Toys, which made the Johnny Lightning model cars," Cook said. "I presented him with the names of six drivers to sponsor. He said he liked the idea, but he couldn't sponsor all six. He asked me, 'If your life was on the line, which one would you choose?' I told him, 'Al Unser.'"[41]

Good call. Racing a P.J. Colt entered by VPJ as the Johnny Lightning Special, Unser qualified on the pole in 1970 and led 190 laps en route to the first of his four Indy 500 wins. The contract with Topper Toys was worth about $500,000, with another $271,697 in prize money for winning Indy, plus royalties on model car sales—a stunning windfall by the standards of the era.

"In the past, we would put names on a car for as little as $10,000 or $20,000," Cook said. "Bringing in Johnny Lightning completely changed Indy car racing. It really escalated the costs of racing. They all blamed me for commercializing the sport too much, but it made the racing better."[42]

Although Jackie Stewart flaunted the plumage of the Swinging Sixties—long hair, big sideburns, aviator sunglasses, fisherman's cap—he was equally at home in a yellow *Wide World of Sports* blazer or a subdued Saville Row business suit. Here, at Monaco in 1971, he went flag to flag before changing into formal attire for dinner with Prince Rainier and Princess Grace.
Revs Institute / Eric della Faille Photograph Collection

CHAPTER EIGHT

THE FLYING SCOT VERSUS THE ODD DUCK

If there's one circuit that generates almost universal raves from contemporary drivers, it's Spa-Francorchamps. Makes sense. With dramatic elevation changes, quaint local color, and a series of rewarding high-speed corners, Spa is a throwback to an age when, according to T-shirt wisdom, sex was safe and racing was dangerous. Drivers regarded Spa differently in the more perilous days before the racetrack was defanged by the redesign of 1979. Back then, drivers loved and hated Spa in roughly equal measure. But all of them regarded it warily, like a regal and seemingly docile lion apt to deliver a fatal bite with hardly any warning.

Among natural road courses, only the Nordschleife, with its unparalleled length and succession of blind corners, was more challenging than Spa. But no track was more daunting, by suck-it-up standards. These days, Eau Rouge is considered one of the most intimidating turns in modern motorsports. In 1966, it was overshadowed by not one, not two, but three more formidable corners. Stavelot was a wicked-fast, slightly banked right-hander that American Chuck Daigh once called "the scariest corner in the world."[1] Burnenville was an even faster downhill sweeper with a ditch awaiting anybody unfortunate enough to, in current parlance, exceed track limits. And then there was the Masta Kink, which was taken flat only by the bravest of the brave, holding their breath, with their right foot quivering. How dangerous was Spa? Well, during the Belgian Grand Prix in 1960, two drivers were killed—both at Burnenville—and Stirling Moss was critically injured at the same corner, while a fourth driver's career ended after he was thrown from his car in a practice crash at Stavelot.

Even now, it's hard to process just how deliriously fast Spa was back in the day. In 1973, Jacky Ickx clocked a lap in his Ferrari 312 PB sports prototype at an average speed of 163.674 miles per hour. Again, that's an *average* speed, despite coming to a virtual stop for the hairpin at La Source. Yet aside from the pit complex and grandstands along the front straight, there was almost nothing to suggest that Spa was a racetrack at all. In contrast with modern, purpose-built circuits, it was cobbled together out of two-lane public roads that undulated past hedges, trees, road markers, light fixtures, telephone poles, brick walls, garages, stone farmhouses, and even a bus stop, all built right up to the edge of the pavement. There were no catch fences and hardly any guardrails, just a handful of hay bales scattered here and there in front of immovable objects, and several sections of road were delineated by tall, right-angle curbs that seemed to be designed expressly to send wayward race cars corkscrewing into oblivion.

The Belgian Grand Prix promised to be something special in 1966. For the previous five years, F1 had been governed by a 1.5-liter formula. (The deplorable 1960 Belgian GP was one of the reasons the FIA had mandated smaller engines in 1961.) Chassis technology had entered the modern age during the 1.5-liter era, as monocoques and fully independent suspensions became the norm, but with engines limited to 91.5 puny cubic inches, speeds topped out at a less-than-spine-tingling 165 mph. For 1966, the FIA had doubled engine size to 3.0 liters. The Return to Power, it was called. Ferrari had developed a new V-12 engine, and team leader John Surtees duly put his car on the pole at Spa, shattering the lap record by seven seconds—"a time so startling,"

Henry Manney III reported in *Road & Track*, "that it wasn't even in the program table of speeds."[2]

Had this been 2026, the field would have been flagged off the grid for a parade lap the instant the Rolex clock overhead ticked over to 3 p.m. But in 1966, Grands Prix weren't run with the metronomic precision demanded by the sporting regulations laid out so meticulously by the FIA. Back then, races were organized by the host country's national racing club, each with its own peccadillos. There was no global television audience to worry about, so the start times were based on—well, nobody knew what, exactly, they were based on. And in 1966, there was an additional complication in the form of Hollywood director John Frankenheimer and the crew filming the motion picture *Grand Prix*. Actors and extras were clogging up the pits and paddock, a helicopter was hovering overhead to capture the action, and American world champion Phil Hill was in the cockpit of a McLaren with an oversized Ford engine that had been modified to carry a bulky motion picture camera so Frankenheimer could incorporate some revelatory driver's-eye footage into his movie. As a result of all the prerace chaos, there wasn't time for a parade lap. On the grid, drivers joked darkly that the organizers didn't want them to drive slowly around the circuit because that would give them a chance to recognize just how diabolical the place was.

This wasn't a laughing matter. At Spa, the lack of a reconnoitering lap was an unsettling proposition because the weather in the Ardennes Forest was so capricious. Rain was always a threat this time of year, and because the circuit was so long—8.8 miles—it could be perfectly dry in one section of the track and drenched in another. Conditions were dry and cool on Sunday afternoon. But shortly before the start, rain was reported at Stavelot, prompting a couple of teams to make a last-minute switch to rain tires. Still, it wasn't clear how heavy or pervasive the storm was, so the drivers had no idea what to expect as they swept downhill past the pits and threaded through Eau Rouge.

Surtees was leading when he hit rain at Burnenville. His Ferrari lurched sideways, but he caught it and continued on, and after a quick 360, Jack Brabham chased after him. Jo Bonnier spun into a hay bale. His Cooper skidded to a stop hanging halfway over a ledge, teetering like a seesaw, and he had to inch *very* carefully out of the cockpit and over the rear deck to prevent his car from tipping over and free-falling fifteen feet. Mike Spence went off trying to avoid Bonnier. Jo Siffert braked hard to avoid both Bonnier and Spence and was rear-ended by Denny Hulme. Although none of them was hurt, all four drivers retired. Meanwhile, Bob Bondurant and Graham Hill, who'd also left the track in the melee, pressed on regardless.

As they approached the Masta Kink, the leaders hit what Jackie Stewart later described as "a river of water."[3] Jochen Rindt, running second to Surtees, gyrated wildly—nine times, according to wide-eyed spectators—but miraculously avoided hitting anything. Stewart was next in line. He aquaplaned off the track, flattened a woodcutter's hut, and scythed through a telephone pole before careening over an eight-foot drop and landing on the lower patio of a farmhouse, with the chassis of his BRM pretzeled around him. A fuel line ruptured, turning the cockpit into a bathtub filled with gasoline. Stewart had broken his collarbone and several ribs, but the real problem was that the steering wheel prevented him from escaping. All it would take, he knew, was a single electrical spark or fuel running over the hot exhaust, and he would suffer the same fate as Dick Seaman, the most prominent of the prewar British Grand Prix drivers, who'd died of burns suffered while he was trapped in his Mercedes-Benz after hitting a tree elsewhere on this same circuit in 1939.

As Stewart was glumly considering his prospects, he heard a voice from above. "Jackie? Are you down there? Jackie?"[4]

It was Graham Hill, who'd spun harmlessly after hitting the same stream and stopped to investigate after seeing Stewart's car. He was joined by Bondurant, whose car had flipped and landed upside down, bridging a ravine. (He hopped out of the car after spectators turned it over.) Hill realized that they needed a wrench to remove Stewart's steering wheel. Bondurant ran across the track and borrowed a set of wrenches from spectators who'd parked their cars nearby. After unbolting the steering wheel, Hill and Bondurant levered Stewart out of the cockpit, carried him to a barn next to the farmhouse, and laid him on the back of a hay truck. Another thirty minutes passed before an ambulance arrived. Only then was Stewart transported to what he called the "so-called medical centre at Spa," a filthy facility with cigarette butts littering the floor where he was dumped on a canvas stretcher that could have been a relic from the Battle of the Bulge fought nearby.[5]

Eight cars were eliminated on the first lap. "It was raining so hard that I passed a few cars," Phil Hill said. Having gotten all the necessary film footage, he gratefully wheeled into the pits and announced that he'd witnessed "a massacre."[6] Amazingly, Stewart was the only driver hurt, and not critically. But the experience was a road-to-Damascus moment for the young Scotsman. It crystallized his misgivings about the pathetic medical facilities, lethal racetracks, and flimsy race cars that were commonplace back then, and it convinced him that the sport needed fundamental changes. By the end of the decade, he would emerge not only as a global superstar but also as the very public—and very divisive—face of a controversial safety crusade that transformed race cars, race circuits, and racing itself.

John Young "Jackie" Stewart's path from a small village near Glasgow to three world championships and a knighthood followed all the hallmarks of a hero's journey. As a child, he had to overcome a case of dyslexia so severe that he could hardly read his own name, and he quit school when he was sixteen to apprentice as a mechanic in his father's garage. Later came the disappointment of failing to make the British trap shooting team for the Olympics in 1960. Then there was his family's resistance to him pursuing a career in motorsports because his older brother had retired after a pair of serious racing accidents. As a result, Stewart didn't get a chance to drive an open-wheel single-seater until he was twenty-five. But from the moment he climbed into that Cooper T72, he was on the express train to stardom.

It was March 1964, and a biting wind was blowing across the paddock at Goodwood. Ken Tyrrell, a rugged, no-nonsense timber merchant who ran a Formula Junior team with factory backing, had acquired a T72 with plans to move up to the new Formula 3 series. After seeing Stewart's success in a series of Ecurie Ecosse sports cars, Tyrrell decided to give him a test. Since the car was new, Tyrrell asked Bruce McLaren, who'd already won a couple of F1 races in Grand Prix Coopers, to set a reasonable bogey time. Stewart went out and immediately beat it. McLaren jumped back in the cockpit and, trying harder, lowered the lap time ever further. When Stewart again went faster than McLaren, Tyrrell knew he had a keeper, and he tried to lock him up in a long-term contract.

Tyrrell offered Stewart $28,000 a year in return for 10 percent of all the prize money and bonuses he earned over the next five years. If Stewart wanted to keep prize money and bonuses, Tyrrell said he would pay him only fourteen dollars a year. At the time, Stewart was making sixty-two dollars a week working at the family garage. In later years, to the consternation of the establishment, Stewart would adopt the look of the "mods"—long hair, big sideburns, bell-bottomed pants—but at heart, he always remained a prototypically canny Scot. "I reasoned that if he wanted me to pay him 10 percent of my bonus earnings there must be more money in this business than I was aware of," he said.[7] He opted for the fourteen-dollars-a-year deal and never regretted it.

In Stewart's first F3 race, in blinding rain at Snetterton, he started on the pole and led by forty-eight seconds (!) after three laps, then coasted to the first of seven wins (in eight races) and the championship. The following year, he signed with BRM and beat his much more accomplished teammate, Graham Hill, to take the Italian Grand Prix. He started the 1966 season by winning at Monaco and was leading the Indy 500 when his engine broke less than ten laps from the finish. At that point, he was universally acknowledged as the heir apparent to his countryman, Jim Clark. But then came the wreck at Spa, and Stewart's priorities changed as promoting safety became his lodestar.

Stewart started by looking out for Number One. First, he taped a wrench to his steering wheel to avoid a repeat of the debacle at Spa. The following year, he became the first F1 driver to wear a seat belt. In 1968, after Clark and several other prominent drivers were killed, he hired his own physician to accompany him to races. Then, as president of the Grand Prix Drivers' Association, he began threatening to boycott races if promoters didn't implement safety measures such as guardrails. A joke started making the rounds: How do you find the way to Jackie's Stewart's house? Just follow the Armco. The humor was lost on Stewart's increasingly indignant critics, who berated him as a cowardly agitator who needed to shut up and do his job. "Really we have had enough of this timidity of his," a disgruntled reader wrote to *Motor Sport*. "I suggest that he retire to Switzerland and leave motor racing to the men."[8]

As the Greek tragedians demonstrated two millennia ago, every great protagonist demands an equally formidable antagonist. For Stewart, it was a bespectacled journalist with a long, wispy beard for whom the word "eccentric" might have been coined. Denis Sargent Jenkinson, known by the byline DSJ to readers of *Motor Sport*, was the magazine's longtime European correspondent. From April to September, he would cover races by speeding around the continent on a series of high-performance vehicles ranging from a Norton Manx to an E-type Jaguar. In his private life, Jenks was an odd duck. He lived in a small cottage with a domesticated sparrow, an extraordinary library of automotive books, and a wrecking yard's worth of car and motorcycle parts. He had one dinner plate, one chair, and no running water. Lighting was provided by 6-volt bulbs hooked to a generator powered by a Fiat 500 that was parked outside. He lived for racing and fast motoring. This is a man who once tested a Formula 2 Lotus on public roads on Christmas Day because he figured the police would be less likely to be on the prowl.

There were some obvious differences between Stewart and Jenkinson in terms of style and attitude, but most of them came down to the fact that they were products of different generations, with different mores. Stewart, paradoxically, was the more conservative of the two—a committed capitalist despite the Swinging Sixties plumage, while Jenkinson was, if anything, an anarchist with no interest in business or politics. What's more striking in retrospect is how similar they were in so many ways. Both of them were small in stature yet large in character, willing to take on and maintain unpopular positions no matter how fierce the criticism. Both of them were cosmopolitan characters comfortable in the world beyond the borders of the British Isles. And both of them were repudiations of the stereotypes that their enemies constructed for them.

Detractors called Stewart a pampered baby who lacked the cojones to race on circuits that had been mastered by the titans of an earlier age. Yet it was Stewart who scored a win for the ages at the Nordschleife, finishing *four minutes* ahead of his closest competitor in the German

Grand Prix in 1968, in rain so heavy and fog so thick that BRM team manager Louis Stanley wrote, "Only a miracle prevented several major accidents that could have left a trail of spectator deaths and injuries."[9] Then, in 1973, during practice for the South African Grand Prix, Stewart's foot went to the floor in the brake zone at the end of the long front straight at Kyalami. He spun the car at 180 mph but still went through three layers of catch fencing before his Tyrrell ground to a stop, inches before his helmet would have hit an embankment. "There may be people who feel offended by safety gear, but had not Stewart himself suggested the placement of those wire fences in this location a couple of years earlier . . . well, there wouldn't be a Jackie Stewart to kick around anymore," Pete Lyons reported in *Autoweek*.[10] Not only did Stewart stick around for the race, but he won it going away.

As for Jenkinson, critics dismissed him as an antiquated blowhard as callous and ill-informed as the generals who'd ordered tens of thousands of young men to their pointless deaths during World War I. In fact, Jenkinson had been a conscientious objector during World War II, and he was a genuine and highly respected speed demon. He was the sidecar rider when motorcyclist Eric Oliver won a world championship in 1949. In 1955, he served as Stirling Moss's navigator during their epic victory in the Mille Miglia in a Mercedes-Benz 300 SLR. Before the race, Jenkinson invented the modern version of rally pace notes. Afterward, *Motor Sport* published his long first-person account of the event—an article that's generally acknowledged as one of the most memorable pieces in the history of motorsports journalism.

Jenkinson was the author of *The Racing Driver*, which was the first book to look deeply at the technique and psychology of motorsports. In it, he popularized the concept of "tenths," as in ten-tenths being balls to the wall and, say, five-tenths meaning wanking around like a poseur. He relished nothing more than a driver who could "tiger," a term he used as both a noun and a verb to refer to someone who could grab a car by the scruff of the neck and make it go faster than reason—or, it seemed, the laws of physics—would permit. Moss was his paragon, not only for his unparalleled speed but also for his equanimity while driving flat-out, leaving no margin for error, even when he knew that a mistake could have serious, and perhaps fatal, consequences.

Stewart was elected president of the GPDA in 1968. Previously, the job had been held by Jo Bonnier, an urbane gentleman racer old enough to have raced against Fangio, Moss, and prewar great Louis Chiron. During Bonnier's tenure, the GPDA's chief concern had been negotiating more starting money and prize money for the drivers. When Stewart succeeded him, safety became the union's focus. Speaking with his squeaky Scottish burr, Stewart gave voice to the convictions that most of his fellow drivers shared but were reluctant to say out loud—namely that drastic action had to be taken to make circuits less dangerous. At the end of the 1968 season, he wrote a remarkable essay in *Autocourse* titled "Circuit Safety," which served as the opening salvo in the war between JYS and DSJ.

"I earn my living from being a racing driver," Stewart wrote. "I want to retain my interest in motor racing through being able to continue as a competitive driver for many years to come. This I feel will be more possible if I try to suggest improvements that will allow me to have accidents without serious consequence. I don't pretend to think that I will have no motor racing accidents, but I would like to feel that if and when they do occur I have a reasonable chance of survival. I am not above making mistakes, and it is wrong for anyone to suggest that a Grand Prix driver should always drive within his limits. No human being is without the possibility of making errors, and I don't see why death should be a necessary consequence of human error."[11]

To modern sensibilities, this sounds like a truth as self-evident as all men being created equal. But in Jenkinson's eyes, Stewart's statement of first principles challenged the existential foundation of the sport. "I have seen a matador killed and I have also seen a racing driver killed. To reach the ultimate one must 'Dice with Death' and often Death claims a victim, but when he does so under such circumstances let us not bewail the fact, but rather salute and admire a man who died doing his utmost in his own specialised sphere," Jenkinson wrote. "Man has always strived for the unknown, it is that small factor beyond his knowledge that keeps him going, without it he would deteriorate. Remove the challenge and you remove the reason, whether it be to go faster than anyone else in a straight line, whether it be to accelerate faster than anyone else, or corner faster, or brake later; there has to be a challenge."[12]

In Stewart's article in *Autocourse*, he outlined changes that the drivers wanted at various circuits on the F1 calendar. Most of the track owners agreed to implement at least some of the upgrades. But the GPDA couldn't reach an agreement with the Royal Automobile Club of Belgium regarding Spa-Francorchamps. So in 1969, the drivers boycotted the Belgian Grand Prix, and the F1 round at Spa was canceled. Jenkinson thought the decision was disgraceful. As he wrote, "I have always thought that one of the endearing features of a Grand Prix driver was that he had GUTS and would accept a challenge that normal people like you and I would not be brave enough to face; now I am not so sure."[13]

Even in a British press corps replete with eccentric characters, Denis Jenkinson stood out as one of a kind. Known to readers of *Motor Sport* by the byline "DSJ," Jenks rode shotgun when Stirling Moss drove a Mercedes-Benz 300 SLR to a storied victory in the Mille Miglia in 1955. Although Jenkinson wasn't anti-safety, per se, he insisted that racing without risk wasn't racing at all. *Revs Institute / Max LeGrand Photograph Collection*

Ironically, several of the drivers who boycotted the race competed in the 1000 Kilometers at Spa later that year even though the 5.0-liter sports prototypes were even faster than the 3.0-liter F1 cars. Some of them, most notably Mexican Pedro Rodriguez, were fatalists who considered most safety regulations pointless. Others, like Jacky Ickx, professed to be unfazed by the terrors of Burnenville or Stavelot. And then there were those who were drawn like moths to a flame. "I remember Jackie Stewart hollering at me about defying the Grand Prix Drivers' Association boycott to race at Spa," Howden Ganley recalled. "I said, 'Jackie, but you'd raced there and I never had, so I had to do it.' It turned out that I loved Spa. For me, it was second only to the old Nürburgring."[14]

Although Jenkinson never missed an opportunity to crow about the defectors from the GPDA's party line, the truth of the matter is that most of the drivers privately agreed with Stewart, though, for a variety of reasons—self-interest, self-consciousness, self-preservation—they declined to speak out publicly. As Ganley said, looking back at his own behavior, "Sadly, I was a bit ambivalent, and to my regret I did not support Jackie. I mean, I went along with him. But I was not vociferous about it. I was kind of like, 'Okay, that's great, Jackie. Do what you want to do, and I'll vote for you.' But I wasn't getting up on the pedestal and shouting about it."[15]

Stewart was reviled as the personification of the lily-livered, money-grubbing, self-centered drivers who were supposedly ruining racing. He was name-checked in vitriolic letters to the editor and jeered by members of the old guard. Retired driver Innes Ireland, who'd given Team Lotus its first Grand Prix victory in 1961, would stroll past Stewart on the grid, flapping his arms like a chicken. Back in Ireland's day, remember, drivers didn't even wear what he described as "hysterical" safety belts.[16] "Stewart was the one who started all this crap, going on about his blood-group on his underpants and things," he said. "You think it's a good idea?"[17] Moss was another ex-driver who couldn't understand what all the fuss was about. "They are emasculating our sport with safety demands," he declared. "Over the years, we looked upon road racing as exactly that—road racing. When there was a curb on a turn, we made damn sure we didn't slide into it. Today, drivers insist curbing be removed."[18]

To his credit, although Jenkinson routinely bad-mouthed Stewart as the "beady-eyed little Scot," he never let his contempt for the man corrupt his appreciation for the driver.[19] "I don't think anyone will argue when I say that Stewart is easily the best driver in Formula One racing today," he wrote in his report about the Race of Champions at Brands Hatch in 1971. "To watch his skill and reflexes at work on the wet track was to watch an artist at work and it was a joy to behold."[20] And yet as perceptive as Jenkinson was as a race observer, he was like a horse wearing blinders when it came to the subject of safety. Commenting on a four-week span in the summer of 1970 when Bruce McLaren, Piers Courage, Hans Laine, and Derrick Williams died in four separate road-racing incidents, he wrote, "I am well aware that motor racing, or any other form of racing, is dangerous, bloody dangerous, but that is what makes it exciting for spectators and competitors alike, and I know we have recently had a series of nasty accidents, but, for goodness sake, we must not get hysterical."[21]

But people *did* get hysterical, and Stewart was able to leverage the hysteria to effect major changes. In 1971, the Nordschleife was revamped before being allowed back on the F1 calendar. The Belgian Grand Prix at Spa, which had been reinstated the previous year, was canceled again. Ditto for Mexico, which had been marred the year before by out-of-control spectators sitting on the edge of the racetrack, as if they were attending a rock concert rather than a motor race. In 1972, the Dutch Grand Prix was canceled when the organizers failed to upgrade Zandvoort, and the Belgian Grand Prix was moved to Nivelles.

Like a time traveler transported to an alien future, Jenkinson was bewildered by the transformation Stewart had wrought. Speaking about a chicane that had been added in an effort to save Spa in 1970, he wrote, "Later, when I saw Jackie Stewart, who is the leader of the anti-Spa brigade, I asked him what purpose the GPDA chicane served, apart from adding some braking and gear-changing to the scene, as the cars seemed to be going just as fast down the *Masta* straight. His reply was that the chicane made *Malmedy* corner safer. I was speechless. It was the first time I had heard that *Malmedy* was a dangerous corner. 'Oh, yes,' said the pious little Scot, 'it was very dangerous.' I didn't know whether to laugh or cry, I was so confused. I thought the danger they were

When rain started falling shortly after the Belgian Grand Prix was flagged off in 1966, Spa-Francorchamps was transformed from a racetrack into a minefield. Seven of the fifteen starters crashed on the first lap. Jo Bonnier's Cooper-Maserati ended up teetering on the edge of a parapet. Sweeping past is the Cooper T81 driven by Jochen Rindt, who finished second despite a lurid spin involving nine (!!!) 360s. *Revs Institute / Eric della Faille Photograph Collection*

bleating about was the high speed, and suddenly here I was being told a corner was dangerous. In my humble opinion a corner is as dangerous (or safe) as the driver cares to make it. When race planning with those two Champions, Eric Oliver on sidecars and Stirling Moss on sports cars, if we thought a corner was dangerous we didn't have it altered, we said 'That one is dodgy, we must treat it with respect.' So *Malmedy* corner is dangerous. The leader of the GPDA milk-and-water brigade and his chums have made some remarkable statements in the past, but that is the best yet."[22]

Despite the barbs and widespread disapproval, Stewart refused to be silenced. What was so remarkable—and admirable—about his crusade was that he was essentially a one-man band. Oh, technically, he was speaking on behalf of the GPDA. But for all intents and purposes, he *was* the GPDA, and his influence came not from the backing of the drivers' union he represented but from the strength of his convictions, the power of his personality, and his dogged pursuit of his goals, no matter how unpopular or seemingly unreasonable they might be. His singular impact on the racing world came into sharp focus when he crossed the Atlantic to drive a Lola T260 in the Can-Am series in 1971.

The GPDA had no official jurisdiction over anything but Formula 1. But that didn't stop Stewart from declaring that he would withdraw from the race at Mid-Ohio unless track owner Les Griebling removed the trees planted smack-dab in the middle of the runoff area for the fast left-hander at the end of the front straight. Nobody came out in support of Stewart. "Oh, Jackie," Moss said. "If you're so concerned about the damn tree, just don't hit it."[23] Fellow driver Chuck Parsons added, "If *he* doesn't want to drive [the Lola T260], *I'll* drive it."[24] To Murray Williamson, the SCCA's assistant director of pro racing, the issue was money, not safety. "We know problems exist at many of our tracks," he admitted, "but we can't ask a track owner to make major changes all at once. He would go out of business."[25] As for Griebling, he was overheard muttering darkly, "I ain't cutting down no fucking trees for no sawn-off Scotsman."[26] David Hobbs was nonplussed by the prerace histrionics. "And guess what?" he said. "On Saturday, when we all arrived, the trees were gone."[27]

It had taken a crew working overnight to clear the area, but it was a good thing they did it. On the first lap of the race, Denny Hulme went off and spun right over the spot where the biggest tree had been. "Without that tree being knocked down, we could probably have had another fatality," Stewart said.[28] And just to rub salt in the wounds of his detractors, Stewart won not only the battle but also the race. To Hobbs, Stewart's political clout was even more impressive than his driving. "If I had told them that those trees have to go, they would have said,

'Well, don't come then,'" Hobbs said. "But they weren't about to say that to Jackie Stewart."[29]

Stewart's reputation as the self-appointed safety czar preceded him as the series progressed. At Edmonton, he demanded that some concrete barriers be replaced by catch fencing. They were. Then, at Laguna Seca, he was puzzled by the trees *inside* the guardrail at the fast left-hander at the top of the hill. "The trees were there to protect the barriers from the drivers," he joked.[30] At his request, they were cut down. So were the telephone poles that lined the mile-long backstraight at Riverside Raceway, which was the next stop on the Can-Am calendar. The instant makeovers prompted the *San Francisco Chronicle's* racing columnist Gordon Martin to ask, "Can auto racing afford Jackie Stewart?"[31] The better question: Could it not?

By 1972, Stewart felt confident enough to beard the lion in its den. In an extraordinary letter published in the August issue of *Motor Sport*, he wrote, "What Denis Jenkinson thinks or says concerns me little. To me he is a fence-sitter, doing little or nothing to secure a future for our sport. The readers of *Motor Sport*, however, are much more important. I would like to say to them that whatever criticism I get will make no difference at all to my personal effort to make motor racing, of all classes, safer for as many people as possible within our sport. There is nothing more tragically sad than mourning a man who has died under circumstances which could have been avoided had someone done something beforehand. It therefore always angers me to hear of people who oppose an effort to make our sport safer and therefore reduce the tragic losses that we have all painfully experienced. Such men to me are hypocrites, the only consolation being that in years to come they will probably be looked back on as cranks."[32]

Stewart forecast the future with uncanny accuracy. Jenkinson is often described as the most perceptive and authoritative race reporter in F1 history, and he served as a sort of mentor for a long line of distinguished motorsports journalists. But when it comes to safety, he's now remembered as a crackpot, whereas Stewart is regarded as a hero, and rightfully so. Later on, Bernie Ecclestone, Max Mosley, and Dr. Sid Watkins would pick up the torch. But it was Stewart who lit the fire and almost single-handedly kept it burning through one of the darkest periods of Grand Prix history.

Richard Attwood retired at age thirty-one, only a year after winning Le Mans in a Porsche 917, precisely because he believed that the longer he raced, the more likely it was that his number would come up. "Jackie Stewart was the only person to say anything, and he didn't have any support from any other driver," he said. "We thought that he was being—I don't know, I suppose we thought it was a namby-pamby type of thing. But he was right, and we were wrong. Because, you know, he improved things really, really quickly. He gets a lot of credit for it, but he probably doesn't get *enough* credit for it."[33]

It's said that you should never argue with a man who buys ink by the barrel. But in the war between DSJ and JYS, the beady-eyed little Scot scored an unconditional victory.

SLOW-WALKING AT LE MANS

Every war has its heroes and villains. In the safety battles of the 1960s and '70s, Jacky Ickx played both roles.

The young Ickx was central casting's idea of a Grand Prix driver. Lithe, sophisticated, and Hollywood handsome, he spoke delightfully fractured English with a beguiling French accent. He was marked as a rising star when he qualified third-fastest in the German Grand Prix at the Nürburgring in 1967 despite driving an underpowered Formula 2 car. The next year, after joining Ferrari, he confirmed his status by scoring a magnificent victory in the rain at the French Grand Prix. He would go on to win eight more Grands Prix, six 24 Hours of Le Mans, and the Paris-Dakar Rally in 1983. But with these peaks came some tragic valleys. Although he wasn't to blame, he was involved in no fewer than five fatal accidents during his long career. And he courted controversy early on as the standard-bearer for the faction of conservatives who fought most strenuously against efforts to make racing safer.

Ickx's contrarian views were the product of both nature and nurture. He was the son of prominent Belgian motorsports journalist Jacques Ickx. After a 1958 season that had seen the racing deaths of stars including Peter Collins, Luigi Musso, Stuart Lewis-Evans, Archie Scott-Brown, and Pat O'Connor, Ickx père had been inspired to write a curious essay in *Automobile Year* extolling the virtues of allowing young people to take risks, even if it meant getting killed. As it happened,

Henry Ford II, far right in the foreground, has just dropped the French tricolor to initiate the traditional Le Mans start in 1966. The driver closest to the camera is Dan Gurney, who'd qualified on the pole in his Ford GT Mark II. The run-and-gun approach was abandoned after John Woolfe was killed on the first lap of race in 1969, when he crashed before buckling his seat belt. *Revs Institute / Max LeGrand Photograph Collection*

his son fared best on the riskiest circuits—Le Mans, the Nordschleife, and especially, his home track, Spa-Francorchamps. This put Ickx fils in an awkward position when the GPDA voted to boycott the Belgian Grand Prix in 1969. Because he objected to the timing of the boycott, he resigned from the drivers' union. "I left the GPDA not because of the idea [of promoting safety]," he explained later. "The idea was perfect, and a lot of people have done well for it. And I'm the first to say that in the 1968 Grand Prix in Canada, it was a GPDA safety-fence that saved my life. I disagreed with the politics, that's all."[34]

Ickx's attitude about safety was far more nuanced than a simple yay or nay, but subtlety is one of the first casualties of war. Even as Ickx was pilloried by pro-safety advocates for breaking with the GPDA, he was acclaimed by those who were determined to preserve the traditions of motorsports, no matter how deadly they might be. So imagine the surprise of those implacable diehards when, only a few months later, Ickx smashed one of racing's most beloved customs while striking a hammer blow for safety at Le Circuit de la Sarthe.

The Automobile Club de l'Ouest (ACO) staged the world's first twenty-four-hour endurance race at Le Mans in 1923. At the time, road races generally began with standing starts and oval races with rolling starts. In 1925, the idiosyncratic ACO chose to go its own way. Cars were lined up diagonally on the edge of the road along the Mulsanne Straight while the drivers were positioned on the other side of the track. When the French tricolor dropped, the drivers ran across the pavement, jumped in their cars, and raced off. Voilà! The Le Mans start! In subsequent years, the start was wisely moved to a more accessible position at the start-finish line, in front of the pits and across from the main grandstands. And that's how the race began for the next four and a half decades.

Picture the Le Mans start. Fifty or so drivers crouched nervously in their stations, marked by circles. Already fully amped up, their hearts pounding, they sprinted across the track, leapt into their cockpits, cranked the starters, fed in some throttle—too much, probably—dumped the clutches, and slithered onto the track, fishtailing wildly and grabbing gears as they accelerated onto a narrow stretch of pavement in a smoky, throbbing, multicolored mass. It was spectacular. It was also insane. After all, what did it matter who led the first few seconds of a race that would drone on for twenty-four hours? But sense and sensibility were no match for pride and glory. Stirling Moss, who was invariably the fastest man on the track, practiced his Le Mans start to make sure that he also made the fastest getaway. And it's said that Porsche placed the ignition to the left of the steering wheel—where it's still found today on its street cars—so drivers would have their right hands free for the gear shift lever.

Murphy's Law always played a role at the start. Drivers ran to the wrong car. Or they jumped and missed the right car. Or they jumped into the right car and put their leg through the steering wheel. Or the gear shift lever got caught in their trousers. (We're looking at you, Juan Manuel Fangio!) Or an attack of red mist led to a spin. Fender benders were common in the melee immediately after the flag fell. Sometimes, the flubs had far-reaching effects. When Ken Miles hurriedly slammed the door of his Ford GT Mark II in 1966, it didn't close properly, and the unscheduled pit stop he made to fix it played an indirect role in his controversial second-place finish. Two years later, the improperly latched door of another Ford GT40 blew open at 175 mph while Belgian Willy Mairesse was blasting down the Mulsanne Straight. The car was demolished when it flew into a barrier. Mairesse was in a coma for two weeks and later committed suicide after it became apparent that his injuries would prevent him from racing again.

Ickx missed the race where his countryman was hurt because he was injured himself, recovering from a broken leg suffered during qualifying for the Canadian Grand Prix. When he returned to Le Mans in 1969, he had a new attitude about the race. As he said, "I decided that jumping in a car and running it at more than 200 mph without putting your seat belts on, when they had already been proven to be a huge step ahead in safety, looked to me to be totally crazy. So I decided to do something unexpected."[35] When the flagged dropped on Saturday afternoon, he planned to walk, rather than run, to his car. "I must admit I never talked to anyone about it because they would have considered it to be very bad idea and advised me not to do it," he said. "That's the advantage of being young—you have no fear. I thought it was better to keep it to myself so I wouldn't be disturbed. So it was a total surprise."[36]

Nobody understood what Ickx was doing when they saw him saunter across the track—if they noticed him at all. Most eyes were riveted on the action at the front of the field, and contemporary race reports made only a cursory reference to Ickx's silent protest, if they mentioned it at all. His John Wyer team was obviously caught unawares, judging from the frantic action in his pit while he calmly buckled his harness. Rolf Stommelen, who slid so far sideways at the start that he appeared to be looking out the side window of his Porsche 917, was slicing through Tertre Route by the time Ickx got onto the track. Which was fine with Ickx. "It's much nicer to be a hunter than being chased by someone," he explained. "When you are last, you can do a lot of overtaking, and the race is very attractive."[37]

Ickx's leisurely stroll probably would have been dismissed as a stunt if it hadn't been followed by another unscripted incident, this one with much more tragic consequences. Privateer John Woolfe was a gentleman driver who'd raced at Le Mans for the first time the previous year in a Chevron B12 fitted with an old Repco F1 engine that made a bit more than 300 horsepower. For this year's race, he'd bought one of Porsche's brand-new, largely unsorted 917s. Besides packing a flat-12 rated at 520 horsepower, the aerodynamically unstable 917 was so twitchy that most of the factory drivers tried to weasel out of racing it. After the Le Mans start, Woolfe managed to get ahead of Chris Amon's Ferrari 312 P and stay there during the 3.7-mile-long blast down the Mulsanne Straight. (No chicanes in those days.) Amon was much quicker going through the corners at Indianapolis and Arnage, but the 917 was sliding so alarmingly that he decided to hang back. After hitting the bump at Maison Blanche—universally regarded as the most dangerous section of the track—Woolfe dropped a wheel on the grass. The Porsche swerved into a guardrail and disintegrated, and the unbelted Woolfe died after being thrown from the cockpit. Amon was lucky to escape with minor burns when he ran over the Porsche's fuel tank, which exploded when the Ferrari speared it. The race was won, after a thrilling finish, by none other than Ickx. "We started last, and we finished first," he said. "And because I won, I suppose I was forgiven."[38]

It's hard to imagine that either Woolfe's unfortunate death or Ickx's unexpected stroll, taken alone, would have had a serious impact on the race. But taken together, they told a cautionary tale, and it didn't take long for the ACO to tease out the moral of the story. In 1970, the cars were lined up diagonally in front of the pits, but with the drivers safely belted into their seats. The next year, the ACO junked tradition altogether and went with the Indianapolis-style rolling start that's used to this day.

Although Ickx usually gets credit for ending the Le Mans start, he believes the honor belongs to Woolfe. "I was only the inspiration," he said. "John paid with his life."[39]

After the startling success of the McLaren M16s the previous year, everybody showed up with wings at Indy in 1972. Vel's Parnelli Jones Racing tried to leapfrog the competition by hiring Maurice Phillippe, who'd helped design the groundbreaking Lotus 72 F1 car. Phillippe thought dihedral airfoils would produce extra downforce in high-speed corners. They didn't, and by the time Joe Leonard started the race, the wicked-looking fuselage-mounted wings had been clipped. *Indianapolis Motor Speedway*

CHAPTER NINE

FEAR OF FLYING

History is full of inflection points when the course of human events could have shifted in a radically different direction. What if Gavrilo Princip's Browning semi-automatic pistol had jammed when he fired it at Archduke Franz Ferdinand? What if the US Supreme Court had allowed a recount to proceed in Florida in the 2000 presidential election? What if, as was once asked of a panel on *Saturday Night Live*, Napoleon had commanded a B-52 at Waterloo?

Okay, it's pretty clear how *Le Grand Armée* would have fared with a jet-powered bomber providing air support against Wellington's infantry. But what if race officials at the Nürburgring had been more open-minded and discerning when Michael May showed up at the 1000 Kilometers in 1956 with a Porsche 550 Spyder sporting what appeared to be a section of an airplane wing mounted directly above the cockpit?

Unfortunately, the wing had two strikes against it from the start. First, to contemporary eyes, the appendage looked bizarre. Second, May was a precocious Swiss engineer with a gloriously contrarian bent, which is to say an unknown quantity and quite possibly dangerous. He reasoned that if an airfoil shaped to serve as the wing of an airplane produced lift, then turning it over would generate antilift, or what we now call downforce. *Motor Sport*'s racing scribe Denis Jenkinson immediately understood how it was supposed to work. "An experiment that could have a future is this upside-down mounted aerofoil controlled by the driver of the Porsche Spyder to apply increased loading on the tyres when cornering," he wrote.[1]

The car was fast in practice—too fast. Porsche's domineering team manager, Huschke von Hanstein, wasn't happy to see an unheralded privateer outrunning his factory cars. He browbeat the organizers into outlawing the wing because it supposedly posed a threat to spectators and other drivers, and the car was permitted to race only after the device was removed. The next month, May took his winged 550 to Monza for the Supercortemaggiore, but officials there wouldn't even allow it on the track. So the dawn of racing's aero revolution would be delayed by nearly a decade by skeptics too unimaginative to gaze into the future.

Now, it should be noted that wings weren't entirely new to racing. A pair of airfoils had appeared on Fritz von Opel's rocket-powered Rak 2 as early as 1928, and wings were attached to a Mercedes-Benz land-speed-record car in 1938. In the United States, Jim Cushman raced a supermodified—think sprint car with a roll cage—with a wing designed by George and Floyd Miller mounted over the cockpit at Columbus Motor Speedway in 1958. (The car was known, fittingly, as the Aero Dynamic Special.) But it wasn't until the early 1970s, after roll cages were required, that wings became a regular addition to sprint cars.

In 1961, car builder Bob Osiecki decided to make a run at the $10,000 prize Bill France was offering for the first car to exceed 180 miles per hour at Daytona International Speedway. He acquired an ex–Pat O'Connor Indy 500 roadster and retrofitted it with a big-block Chrysler bored out to 450 cubic inches. Upgraded with a supercharger, the bulky V-8 made 800 horsepower, so oomph wasn't an issue. But Osiecki knew that two Indy cars had already crashed fatally on the high banks. In a quest to improve high-speed stability, he enlisted the aid of Georgia Tech University, where students built a mock-up with stubby airfoils on either side of the car, like wings on the fuselage of an airplane, and tested it in a wind tunnel. Despite this scientific approach, the roadster—Mad Dog IV—was a handful, and at least a half-dozen drivers got some seat time before they decided that running the car flat-out on the banking would have a deleterious effect on their life expectancy. Osiecki finally hired Art Malone, a braver-than-Dick-Tracy drag racer with no Indy car experience. After four laps, the tires were virtually shredded—but not before Malone earned his pay (and then some) by turning a lap at 181.561 mph, 26 mph faster than the pole speed in that year's Daytona 500.

Around this time, wings gravitated to the drag racing arena on Jack Chrisman's Howard Cams Special, a Top Gas rail also known as Twin Bears because it had a pair of blown, poked-and-stroked small-block Chevys mounted side by side in front of the driver. No wind tunnel testing for this baby, just a sheet of plywood mounted at a roughly forty-five-degree angle between the front axle and the engine to prevent wheelies. The next year, small wings started sprouting over the front axles of Top Fuel slingshots. Then, in 1963, Don "Big Daddy" Garlits showed up at Pomona with a big wing mounted on slender struts over the blower of Swamp Rat V. After sweet-talking officials into allowing him to run the car, he won the Winternationals, beating none other than Art Malone in the final, while laying down an 8.26-second run and flashing through the lights at 186 mph.

Road racers came late to the wings-and-things party. One of the first figures to systematically investigate a new approach was Carlo Chiti, who'd earned a degree in aeronautical engineering before running the technical department at Ferrari. In 1961, he created the company's first rear-engine race car, the sleek 246 SP sports racer. During early testing at Modena, factory driver Richie Ginther noticed that the high windscreen required by Le Mans regulations created a low-pressure zone that caused exhaust fumes to be sucked back into the cockpit. Drawing on the aerodynamic expertise he'd developed during stints at Douglas Aircraft and as a helicopter mechanic in Korea, Ginther suggested that the team fabricate a four-inch-tall strip of aluminum and mount it across the rear deck. Ginther's so-called fence not only kept exhaust fumes out of the cockpit; it also helped plant the rear end of the car and cured the 246 SP's early instability problems. What was soon dubbed a "spoiler" debuted on the Ferrari at Sebring in March. The following month, the extra downforce generated by this aerodynamic aid helped the car score its maiden victory in the Targa Florio.

It didn't take long for other racers to start riveting spoilers to their cars as a quick fix to eliminate rear-end lift. But nobody understood the full ramifications of this breakthrough. Almost since the invention of the automobile, designers had been obsessed by the efficiency of streamlined bodywork. Physics tells us that drag is proportional to the square of speed, while power is proportional to the *cube* of speed. Therefore, it's exponentially easier to go faster by reducing drag than it is by increasing horsepower. So when they could, designers fashioned smooth bodies in teardrop shapes with the smallest frontal area possible. That's why, by the 1960s, most Formula 1 cars looked like cigars suspended on exposed wheels, with drivers in semi-reclining positions to minimize wind resistance.

The drag-is-evil philosophy persisted for several more years. Even as late as 1968, when Porsche started developing the 917 sports prototype, the design team did all it could to reduce drag. This turned out to be a be-careful-what-you-wish-for proposition. With a 4.5-liter flat-12 engine producing 520 horsepower and bodywork generating virtually no downforce, the car was terrifying at high speeds. "Bloody hell, it was absolutely horrendous," said Richard Attwood, who raced a long-tail 917 at Le Mans in 1969. "I've never had such a bad time in a car for so long. It lifted everywhere. If it had rained, either I would have come in and said, 'I can't drive this car anymore,' or I would have died."[2] In the race, British privateer John Woolfe *was* killed after crashing fatally at Maison Blanche before completing his first lap. Only then did Porsche begin seriously addressing the car's handling flaws. The next year, Attwood won Le Mans in a much-more-tractable short-tail 917K with codriver Hans Herrmann.

The first sign that a new aerodynamic age was dawning appeared in the fall of 1966. The Canadian-American Challenge Series had been inaugurated the previous week at St. Jovite. Now, the circus had moved to the sand dunes of Bridgehampton. The night before practice was scheduled to begin, John Morton was in a diner near the track. In years to come, Morton would become far more successful as a driver. But at the time, he was working as a crew chief for actor Dan Blocker's tiny operation. As he and another crew chief were eating dinner, they saw the Chaparral team roll in. Sitting on top of the open trailer was a white car with a gigantic black appendage rising three feet above the rear deck. "What the hell is that?" Morton asked. After batting the question around for a while, he concluded, "It looks like a car with a tire rack on top of it."[3]

What it was, in fact, was a new chapter in automobile racing.

The car was Jim Hall's Chaparral 2E, and what Morton had taken for a tire rack was actually a giant airfoil. Designed to generate hundreds of pounds of downforce at speed, it also generated tons of curiosity at rest. "A shock wave went through the paddock when they pulled up with that double-axle trailer, everything white and that car sitting there with an enormous wing on it," recalled Sam Posey, who was racing a conventional McLaren-Elva Mark II. "It was awesome. I mean it completely changed the game. The Chaparral not only looked incredible, it also looked beautiful. It was everything a race car could be or should be. It took an incredible leap forward. Now, they had their troubles, but what the hell. They stopped everybody in their tracks."[4] Or as Hall remembered, "The pictures that you see are really funny. Dan [Gurney] and all of the good drivers were laying underneath it and looking all around."[5]

Hall was the ringmaster of the comedy unfolding at Bridgehampton as well as the chief architect of the coming aero revolution. Tall and lanky, often photographed wearing a cowboy hat, Hall looked like the prototypical Texas rancher. Shortly before he turned eighteen, he inherited an oil fortune when his parents died in a plane crash. He soon started road racing in an ever-more-exotic series of Ferraris and Maseratis, many of them procured from longtime friend and fellow Texan Carroll Shelby. After a few years, he realized that he was never going to beat the factories by buying customer cars. No, dominating the competition—and that was his goal—meant he needed a unique alternative. So in 1961, he bought an all-new, tube-frame, small-block-Chevy-powered sports car created by famed builders Dick Troutman and Tom Barnes. At Hall's suggestion, it was dubbed the Chaparral, a small bird better known as the roadrunner.

At first glance, Hall seemed to be following the trajectory of another rich kid, Lance Reventlow, who'd funded the development of the Scarabs. And as it happened, Troutman and Barnes had been two of the principal builders of Reventlow's cars. But there was one huge difference between Hall and Reventlow—between Hall and anybody else in the motorsports world. He'd earned a degree in mechanical engineering from the prestigious California Institute of Technology, aka Caltech. Also, he was a pilot whose logbook included plenty of time in high-performance airplanes, including the P-51 Mustang, and his experience with the aerodynamics of flight would come in handy when he turned his attention to designing race cars.

The original Chaparral was essentially a new-and-improved version of the Scarab. The problem was that the Scarab had been designed in 1957. By the time Hall began racing the so-called Chaparral 1, its front-engine design had been rendered obsolete by lighter, nimbler mid-engine cars from Cooper and Lotus. Hall didn't want to buy somebody else's car, nor did he want to copy somebody else's design. Which meant . . . and then the light bulb went on. "Up until then," he said, "I took things as they were and just manipulated the controls. I really hadn't applied any of my mechanical engineering background before. I just assumed that Colin Chapman and Enzo Ferrari knew how to build race cars and I didn't, and that was that."[6]

By this time, Hall had partnered up with another Texas wildcatter-cum-racer, Hap Sharp. They'd set up an operation in the small West Texas city of Midland, in the heart of the highest-producing oil field in the country. Along with various buildings and a race shop, the property encompassed a featureless 1.8-mile test track appropriately dubbed Rattlesnake Raceway. All they needed was a car. Thinking *way* outside the box, they contacted structural engineer Andy Green, who was working on the B-58 Hustler, a Mach 2 bomber being built by Convair in Fort Worth. Green was eager to save enough money to start a side hustle fashioning sailboats out of fiberglass. Sharp told him that he and Hall might have a job for him. Intrigued but mystified, Green flew with Sharp to Midland, where Hall explained that they wanted him to design the chassis for a new race car. A chassis? Green was mortified. He'd been operating under the assumption that they wanted some ideas about using composites to erect portable buildings to provide shade in the oil patch. "I don't know anything about cars," he blurted.[7]

"That's just what we want," Hall assured him. "We don't want anybody with any preconceived ideas."

Drawing upon his ideas for boats, Green came up with a design based on "torque boxes"—structures that are triangulated to resist twisting force, or torque, when a car accelerates, brakes, or turns. Green envisioned a chassis assembled from eleven torque boxes arranged around a central tub housing the cockpit. Typically, torque boxes are constructed out of sheet metal. But since his expertise was in composites, Green designed the entire chassis out of fiberglass-reinforced plastic. Colin Chapman gets credit for creating the first modern monocoque race car—the Lotus 25, which debuted in 1962. A year later, knowing nothing about Chapman's work in England, Green conceptualized the first fiberglass monocoque.

Before crafting the body, Hall wanted data from a wind tunnel. Then as now, access to wind tunnels was extremely limited, especially if you were a novice race car builder based in a city whose greatest claim to fame was having the tallest building (twenty-two stories) between Fort Worth and Phoenix. But through racing, Hall had met Frank Winchell, the brilliant engineer who ramrodded Chevrolet's high-powered Research and Development Department. Hall invited Winchell to visit his operation down in Midland, and then Hall got a tour of Chevy R&D. They quickly realized that each had something to offer the other. The General Motors Technical Center outside Detroit was full of esoteric test equipment and a bevy of crack engineers such as Jim Musser, Jim Kinsler, and Jerry Mrlik. Chaparral had a test track and two superb test drivers, and the fact that it was so far removed from the center of the automobile industry meant that experimental projects could be tested there with no fear of outsiders getting a peek at what was going on.

The exact parameters of the deal between GM and Chaparral Cars were never publicly divulged, and that's the way both parties preferred it. Like any successful poker player, Hall held his cards close to his vest. As for Chevrolet, the company wasn't "officially" involved in racing at the time, which is why *Chevrolet = Racing*, the excellent book written about this period by former Chevy R&D engineer Paul van Valkenburgh, was subtitled *Fourteen Years of Raucous Silence.* Although there's no question that Chaparral benefited from a lot of Chevy development and support, Hall was adamant that the majority of the most important breakthroughs were made in Midland. As he put it, "My experience as a pilot helped me because I had an understanding of the forces on the airplane. When I started analyzing the aerodynamics of race cars myself, I think I ended up knowing about as much about it as anybody."[8]

Hall incorporated the wind tunnel data he got from Chevy into the design of fiberglass bodywork for the all-new Chaparral 2. (Despite the nomenclature, he considered this the first "real" Chaparral.) For the next two years, the car dominated the US Road Racing Series, which was a dress rehearsal for Can-Am, even as the team incorporated a host of upgrades including a front splitter, a rear spoiler, and ducts to channel air over the body. "By the end of '64, we had cars that were balanced from 40 miles an hour to 140 miles an hour, and they were the fastest racing cars in the world," Hall said. "We decided to build a lighter car for the 1965 season. We put a big flap on the back of it, but it made so much drag that, even though we were lapping faster than the other cars, guys could pass us on the straightaway. So we could go fast on the straightaway again, we put a little movable flap on the back of it, and we kept making that flap bigger and bigger and bigger. And we finally got to the point that we were pushing down so hard on the car that it bottomed it out. So I said, 'You know what? If we put the force into the rear wheel hub, we won't have that problem anymore.' And that's what we did."[9]

The result was the high wing that debuted on the Chaparral 2E at Bridgehampton in 1966. The concept was so radical and the prospects so dramatic that a patent for an "aerodynamic spoiler for automotive vehicles" was issued to Hall, Musser, Winchell, and Mrlik.[10] "What really impressed me about the high-wing Can-Am car, the 2E, was that they put the downforce directly on the wheel, through the suspension, rather than on the body," reported Phil Hill, who'd been hired to drive one of the two Chaparrals. "I had been at Ferrari, and they had been putting downforce on the body with an air dam on the rear deck. With that rear wing, the Chaparral felt like it was really planted. The 2E was very easy to drive, left foot on the brake and right foot on the go pedal. There was no clutch, just a two-speed fluid torque converter. When you weren't braking, you kept your left foot on the fail-safe pedal. This kept the wing flat. When you took your foot off the pedal, the wing automatically flipped to the high-downforce position. You could feel the difference immediately. It lowered the top speed by at least 25 mph."[11]

Hall was fastest in qualifying at Bridgehampton, but he gave his car to Hill—and vacated the pole—after the wing mount on his teammate's car broke in practice. Hill was running second in the race when the wing got stuck in the high-downforce position, and the loss of top-end speed relegated him to a fourth-place finish. This proved to be a harbinger of things to come. The 2Es were quick but fickle, and Hill netted the team's

Phil Hill sits patiently in the cockpit while mechanics Randy Gilbert, left, and Karl Schmid do some last-minute wrenching on the Chaparral 2E. The Can-Am race at Bridgehampton in 1966 marked the debut of the car—and its outrageous wing—as well as the dawn of a new era when aerodynamics would be the principal driver of car design and cornering speeds would climb at an unprecedented rate. *International Motor Racing Research Center – Photographic Collections*

only win, at Laguna Seca. The next year, Hall upgraded the 2E into an extraordinarily advanced endurance-racing Chaparral dubbed the 2F. The car was faster than its more successful rivals, the Ford GT Mark IV and Ferrari 330 P4, but transaxle woes translated into repeated DNFs. Only in the last race of the season, the BOAC 500 at Brands Hatch, did it hold together, allowing Hill to win the final race of his career.

The weirdest thing about the high-wing Chaparrals isn't that they didn't win more races despite being a technological leap ahead of the competition. It's that more people didn't copy them. You would have thought that the deacons of the Formula 1 design brotherhood would have immediately jumped on the bandwagon. But no wings sprouted in Europe in 1966 or 1967. Even teams that had been outrun by the Chaparrals in Can-Am and the Championship of Makes ignored the implications of Hall's discovery. In fact, Mauro Forghieri of Ferrari, who was responsible for introducing wings to F1, expressly denied that he was inspired by the Chaparrals.

Wings belatedly found their way to the Grand Prix world by a circuitous route that ran through Rolla Vollstedt's shop in Portland. Best known for giving Janet Guthrie her first ride at the Speedway in 1976, Vollstedt was a longtime Indy car entrant who designed and built his own cars on a tight budget and ran them for several years with progressive upgrades that kept them marginally competitive. In 1967, he fabricated a pair of handsome monocoques drawing on elements of contemporary Lotus and Brabham practice. Although the cars looked good, they suffered through a disastrous season. But at the last race of the year, the Rex Mays 300 at Riverside, Vollstedt had a trick up his sleeve. Two of them, actually.

The first was a road-course ringer behind the wheel. When his plan to hire Mark Donohue fell through, the colorful Vollstedt persuaded execs at Firestone and Riverside to kick in enough money to entice Jim Clark to Southern California for the race. The second was some intriguing aero upgrades—mustache spoilers on the nose and a wing at the back. Well, not a high wing like the one on the Chaparral. Vollstedt's airfoil was a simple piece of sheet metal that was roughly two feet square, sharply upturned at the rear end and mounted on top of the bundle-of-snakes exhaust of the four-cam Indy Ford engine. Dan Gurney was the acknowledged master of Riverside; for years, he'd dominated races there in Indy cars, stock cars, and sports cars. As expected, he put his Eagle on the pole and led from the start. But much to everybody's amazement, Clark, who'd qualified second-quick, hung right with him in Vollstedt's heretofore uncompetitive nag. And then, even more shockingly, Clark passed Gurney just before missing a shift and overrevving the engine, which dropped a valve.

No doubt, Clark's estimable driving skills were a major reason he'd been able to keep up with Gurney. But the wing almost certainly helped. (George Follmer finished sixth in the other winged Vollstedt entry.) Clark took this knowledge with him when he traveled to New Zealand for the Tasman Series. At Teretonga Park, at Clark's suggestion, mechanics fashioned a wing out of the remnant of a helicopter rotor and mounted it to the gearbox of the Lotus 49 with two heim joints. Colin Chapman didn't appreciate this unauthorized design change, and he ordered the wing removed before Clark could test it on the track—but not before a young Ferrari engineer snapped a few photos.

While Chapman didn't like mechanics treading on his turf, he wasn't going to let his ego get in the way winning races. At the Spanish Grand Prix, the first continental race of the F1 season, Lotus brought adjustable front wings but didn't use them. Two weeks later, at Monaco, the front wings were used. Also, the bodywork of the Lotus 49 had been extended past the engine, rising up at the tail to form a wedge resembling a more elegant variation of—wait for it—the wing on the Vollstedt-Ford that Clark had raced at Riverside. Graham Hill qualified on the pole and won the race. Merely a coincidence? Forghieri obviously didn't think so.

The next race was at Spa. There, Chris Amon's Ferrari 312 was fitted with a true airfoil mounted over the V-12 engine. Forghieri insisted that the impetus came not from the Chaparral or the spy photo shot by the Ferrari engineer in New Zealand but from none other than Michael May, the Swiss aerodynamics pioneer who'd given up on wings after his experiences with his Porsche 550 back in 1956 and who was now working informally as a fuel-injection consultant at Ferrari. Like they say, what goes around comes around. The effect of the wing was startling. During practice, Amon closed on Brian Redman's Cooper T86B as they approached Stavelot. "I can remember going by him into the corner, with my foot buried right in it, as he was braking and changing down," Amon said. "The thing felt tremendous."[12] He was fastest by *3.7 seconds*—an eternity in F1—during Friday practice. Jack Brabham got the memo and hastily attached airfoil-type wings behind the engines of his and Jochen Rindt's cars. It rained on Saturday, which rendered the lap times irrelevant. In the race, Amon's Ferrari and both Brabhams broke, and Bruce McLaren gave his eponymous team its first Grand Prix victory in an M7A with a spoiler riveted to a structure behind the engine.

Thus commenced the Battle for Aero Supremacy. Not another race passed where a new wrinkle wasn't introduced. It wasn't immediately clear whether this was a testament to the technical ingenuity of Formula 1 or to one-upmanship run amok. Wings moved farther forward and farther back. They grew wider and taller, then wider and taller still. They were attached to the bodywork. They were attached to the hubs. They were fixed. They were adjustable. The system operated by compressed air. Or by electrohydraulics. Or via cable or bungee cord. The drivers moved the wings as they saw fit, or the wings moved automatically, depending on whether the brakes were applied, or fifth gear was selected, or the moon was in the seventh house of the seventh sun and Jupiter was aligned with Mars. By the fall of 1968, every car sported wings varied enough to confound an ornithologist.

Some outsiders wondered if it was all just a game of monkey see, monkey do, and skeptics suggested that the major benefit of wings was that they made the drivers feel more confident. The teams knew better. At Monza, a wingless BRM emerged from Curva Grande—the intimidating sweeper at the end of the pit straight—at 156 mph. With a wing, the exit speed was 168 mph. Tire temperature, meanwhile, climbed from 130 degrees to 160 degrees, which demonstrated how much more grip was being developed. Lap times were an even better barometer. McLaren reported early in the wing-development game that aero aids were worth one to one-and-a-half seconds a lap. By the final race of the season in Mexico City, the fastest lap, recorded by Jo Siffert in a high-wing Lotus 49, was nearly four seconds faster than Clark had gone in an aerodynamically clean version of the same car the previous year.

Wings were great, everybody agreed. Exactly why, nobody knew for sure. "We didn't have any wind tunnels," said Herbie Blash, a longtime FIA official who was then a mechanic at Lotus. "It was just, 'Stick this on' and 'Stick that on.' Colin was flying his own plane, so he obviously understood aerodynamics to a certain degree. But we had no real technical knowledge about what would work and what wouldn't work."[13] And what empirical data existed was derived almost entirely from what happened when new untested parts were deployed on race weekends.

Fast-and-dirty prototype development has a lot going for it, but it also means taking the bad with the good. In the case of wings, failure *was* an option, and it occurred early and often. By the time the teams reached Rouen for the French Grand Prix, Chapman had soured on the small, vestigial wing that debuted at Monaco. Now, in typical Chapman fashion, he'd fitted his Lotus 49Bs with the biggest, tallest, most outrageous wings in Formula 1. In the garage, young Jackie Oliver, who'd been hurriedly drafted into the team after Clark's death, pushed on the airfoil, which made a disquieting *boinggg!* sound as it visibly vibrated on the slender mounting struts. "Is that all right?" he asked.[14] To which Chapman scornfully replied, "Lad, when you sit on an airplane and you look out the window when it takes off, the wing is flexing because that's what keeps it from breaking."

Oliver shelved his doubts, and when he headed out for practice, he was pleased to experience "fantastic" levels of grip—briefly.[15] On his third flying lap, streaking past the grandstands at 190 mph, he closed on Attwood's BRM, which was just coming out of the pits. As Attwood moved over to allow Oliver to pass, the turbulent air behind him tilted back the wing of the Lotus so that it was generating lift instead of downforce. Uh-oh. The rear wheels levitated off the ground, and the car walloped a low wall so hard that the gearbox, transaxle, and rear wheels broke off as a single assembly, leaving Oliver dazed and confused in what was pretty much the only part of the chassis that hadn't been destroyed.

Chapman, who had a fractious relationship with most of his drivers unless they were named Clark or Andretti, blamed Oliver for losing control. Despite the accident, and even though several observers told

Chapman that they'd seen the Lotus's wings flexing conspicuously at speed, he opted for even higher airfoils at the next race, Brands Hatch. The wings survived the British Grand Prix; in fact, Oliver would have won if his transmission hadn't disintegrated while he was leading. This time, John Surtees was the one with wing woes. After the freshly mounted airfoil on his Honda RA301 snapped off, he finished the race with the naked struts blowing in the wind and a set of bald rear tires, thanks to the sudden lack of grip. At the US Grand Prix, the rear wing of Rindt's Brabham BT26 collapsed at both ends so that it looked like a tepee built with an erector set. At the next race, in Mexico, a strut on local hero Moisés Solana's Lotus 49B broke, forcing him to pit to have the wing ripped off and trashed.

By the time the 1969 season began in South Africa, F1 was deep in the throes of wing mania. Lotus, Brabham, and Matra all showed

Shortly after wings arrived in Formula 1 in 1968, so did wing failures. During practice before the US Grand Prix, driver Jochen Rindt, in helmet, and car designer Ron Tauranac, to his immediate right, study the broken airfoil on their Brabham BT26. The following season, Rindt would break his nose and suffer a concussion after the high, hub-mounted wing of his Lotus 49B collapsed during the Spanish Grand Prix. *Revs Institute / Karl Ludvigsen Photograph Collection*

up with biplane arrangements—two sets of high wings, front and rear. During practice, Kyalami looked more like an airport than a racetrack. The wings of two of the Lotuses and both the Brabhams failed during practice or the race. Still, Jackie Stewart won in a biplane-equipped Matra MS10, outrunning Hill in his twin-wing Lotus. At Montjuïc Park, the twisty street circuit in Barcelona hosting the Spanish Grand Prix, Chapman reasoned that he needed even bigger wings. After practice on Friday, Lotus mechanics worked into the night fabricating six-inch-wide extensions with fiberglass and foam to either side of the rear wing. "No testing, no scrutineering," said mechanic Beaky Sims. "It shows what you could do back then."

Despite the lack of testing, the Lotuses qualified one-three in the hands of Rindt and Hill. Rindt led from the flag and walked away from the field. As he started his ninth lap, Hill's wing collapsed after he crested the bump on the front straight at 160 mph, and his car was demolished when it rammed into the guardrail on the left and ricocheted into the Armco on the right. Hill was unhurt. But as Sims ran out from the pits, Hill saw the wing sagging on Rindt's car. "His wing is going! His wing is going!" he yelled. "Beaky, get back to the pits and tell Chapman to bring him in."[16] Too late. When Sims was halfway there, he heard a huge crash as Rindt's wing failed. Rindt cannoned into Hill's wrecked Lotus and then vaulted onto the guardrail. If the launch angle had been slightly higher, he would have landed in the crowd. As it was, Sims said, "The nose of the car was bent up like a banana. We couldn't get [Rindt] out, and we could hear the battery shorting, and we could smell fuel. Finally, Graham got astride the car and just *yanked* him out."[17]

Most race reports noted that Rindt wasn't seriously hurt, which was true, but that minimized the brutality of the crash. Rindt's helmet and the roll bar had been ground down while he was sliding along upside down, and he was trapped in the cockpit for forty seconds while fuel was leaking. When he was pulled out of the cockpit, he was covered with blood from a broken nose—this was before full-race helmets had been widely adopted—and he'd suffered a concussion severe enough to require hospitalization. Also, one firefighter broke his leg, and a second broke his arm. The accident inspired Rindt to write an open letter from his hospital bed arguing that wings ought to be banned.

"Basically I have two reasons why I am against them," he wrote. "1. Wings have nothing to do with a motor car. They are completely out of place and will never be used on a road-going production car. Please note, I mean wings and not spoilers, which are incorporated into the bodywork. You can say that they bring colour to racing, and I cannot argue against that; but after all F1 racing is meant to be a serious business and not a hot rod show. 2. Wings are dangerous, first to the driver, secondly to the spectators."[18] As an aside, he also foreshadowed the eternal gripe about wings—that turbulent air from the leading car impedes the car running in its wake, making it harder to pass and generally stinking up the show.

Rindt had plenty of company in the anti-wing camp. Two weeks before the debacle at Monjuïc Park, while attending a Formula 2 race at Pau, CSI president Maurice Baumgartner had seen a wing fall off Jean-Pierre Beltoise's Matra as it passed the pits. The next month, at the Monaco Grand Prix, Baumgartner convened all the entrants after the first practice session and announced that he'd reluctantly decided to ban rear airfoils, effective immediately, limiting front wings to canards on the nose. Ken Tyrrell was irate because, he said, the Matra had been designed with wings in mind, so running them without airfoils would be dangerous. Brabham, meanwhile, was irritated because the decision caught the teams by surprise. But this wasn't a hill the constructors were willing to die on. And, frankly, most people agreed privately that the wing thing had gotten out of hand. So there were no complaints when, a week later, the CSI made the ban official. As its communiqué stated, "This danger is as serious for the spectators as for the pilots."[19]

By midseason, rear wings had returned to F1, but they were smaller and lower, similar in concept, if not execution, to what we have today. Pundits confidently predicted that the perennial search for grip would force designers to shift their attention to four-wheel drive, and some of them did. But four-wheel drive turned out to be a cul de sac. Instead, constructors looked for ways to make smaller wings more effective, mostly by routing the air properly over the bodywork—one of the keys to the Lotus 72's long run as a championship contender. But as the Lotus 78 and Lotus 79 would show at the end of the decade, the best way to generate downforce was to control the way air flowed *under* the car. With the development of "ground effects," virtually no form of motorsports would ever be the same.

By this time, high wings were about to find a new home in a less chichi neighborhood, NASCAR's relatively low-tech Grand National series. From its earliest days, stock car racing had been largely a short track phenomenon, with dirt being the preferred surface. By 1967, dirt was on its way out, but Richard Petty still was able to cruise to the championship in his Plymouth Belvedere—while winning twenty-seven races—by cleaning up on bullrings like Occoneechee Speedway and Middle Georgia Raceway. The problem, from the perspective of Chrysler marketing mavens, was that Petty was outclassed on the superspeedways that generated the biggest buzz. So for 1968, the Mopar brass decided to develop a car to kick Ford's butt at Daytona, Charlotte, Atlanta, and Darlington.

Although the sleek Dodge Charger looked like a winner, it was saddled with one speed-killing flaw—flying buttresses that produced tons of drag. The aerodynamicists in Chrysler's Special Vehicles Group persuaded the production-car designers to install a flush-mounted backlight and grill to dramatically improve air flow over the bodywork of a homologation special dubbed the Charger 500. What they didn't realize was that their counterparts at Ford had embarked on an even more radical makeover of its own midsized fastbacks. To begin with, Ford fabricators rolled the rocker panels, which allowed the race cars to sit lower to the ground, and fashioned sleeker front bumpers. Then they extended and drooped the noses to reduce drag while creating downforce. The Ford Torino Talladega and the wilder Mercury Spoiler II ruled Grand National during the 1968 season. The situation got so ugly that Petty announced that he was abandoning Chrysler and defecting to its crosstown rival—a betrayal as unthinkable as Abraham Lincoln joining the Confederacy.

Led by Larry Rathgeb, the Chrysler Special Vehicles Group pursued a nuclear option. The goal was to increase superspeedway lap speed by 5 mph. The two possibilities were finding 85 more horsepower or generating 15 percent less drag. The team chose Door Number Two. Extending the nose by eighteen inches and shaping it into a pointy beak solved the drag issue, while an aggressive lip spoiler produced two hundred pounds of downforce. But this created a new problem: A conventional rear spoiler wouldn't make enough downforce to balance the car. Instead, the aero wizards suggested installing an airfoil with streamlined vertical supports. After testing, they settled on a humongous rear wing fifty-eight inches across and 7.5 inches wide mounted 23.5 inches above the rear end. It could be adjusted from plus-two degrees to minus-ten degrees, at which point it generated more than six hundred pounds of downforce.

No stylists were involved in the design of what was to be christened the Dodge Charger Daytona. That threatened to kill the project because homologating the car would mean selling it in Dodge showrooms, and it looked like . . . well, let's just say nobody was going to mistake it for one of the Chrysler 300 "letter series" beauties. Fearing the worst, Rathgeb showed sketches to Dodge vice president and general manager Bob McCurry, who had to sign off on the project. "God, it looks awful," McCurry said. "Will it win races?" When Rathgeb said it would, McCurry told him, "Well, damn it—go ahead and build it!"[20]

The Daytona didn't race until September 1969, which coincided with the opening of Alabama International Motor Speedway. Bill France had built the high-bank oval in Talladega with the express purpose of being the fastest racetrack in the world. Mission accomplished. Driving a high-wing Daytona, Charlie Glotzbach qualified on the pole with a lap at 199.466 mph. The speed was not only mind-bending but also tire-shredding, so much so that all but one of the top drivers boycotted the race. Last-minute replacement Richard Brickhouse gave a Daytona a win in its maiden outing. The car was so successful that the Plymouth Road Runner got a similar but somewhat more artful makeover the next year, and the upgraded SuperBird was the winningest speedway car of the 1970 Grand National season.

In his first race in the car, never having even tested it before, Pete Hamilton won the Daytona 500 in an electric-blue SuperBird owned by Petty Enterprises. (King Richard had returned to the Mopar fold to take advantage of the new Plymouth.) Bobby Isaac won the championship in a Daytona prepared by irascible crew chief Harry Hyde, who was the inspiration for the Robert Duvall character in *Days of Thunder*. "My goodness," Hyde said of the Daytona, "it had good downforce, and then you had the big ol' piece coming down the side there that would hold the side forces in. You could hang that car out constantly two, two-and-a-half feet and just keep riding, and it would stay right there. It was a perfectly balanced car."[21] As for the SuperBird, according to Petty, "It was all but impossible to spin one of them out at speed."[22]

Still, speed was an issue. The combination of maximal horsepower and minimal drag had caused speeds at Daytona to climb about 20 mph over the previous five years. In early 1970, only eighteen laps into his first Grand National race, Talmadge Prince was killed at Daytona in a year-old Dodge Daytona—the first death in NASCAR on a banked oval since 1965. Although the 200 mph barrier was never officially breached, NASCAR officials got spooked by the thought of a car hurtling into the crowd. In the middle of the 1970 season, they mandated the use of a restrictor plate between the carburetor and the intake manifold to rein in engine power. At the end of the year, the winged warriors were effectively outlawed by a new rule requiring them to be fitted with small-block motors while nonwing cars could run big blocks. "You know, NASCAR was right in parking that car," Hyde said later. "At the time I thought it was a cruel act, but we didn't know how to be careful. We would have had them going so fast that it wouldn't even have been safe to sit in the grandstand."[23]

But before it was consigned to history's dustbin, the Dodge Daytona scored a public relations coup for the ages. "I got a call from Frank Wylie at Dodge PR," Rathgeb recalled. "He wanted to know if we could go 200 miles per hour at Talladega, and I said, 'Of course, we can.'"[24] On March 24, 1970, Rathgeb entrusted a specially prepared Daytona to Buddy Baker, a gregarious giant who excelled on superspeedways. His early laps weren't encouraging. "Buddy didn't think we could break 200," Rathgeb said. "To keep him occupied, we gave him a roll of tape, and he taped up every opening on that car."[25]

On his thirtieth lap, running wide open, Baker clocked a lap at 200.091mph. When he pitted, the crew stripped off the tape he'd applied. Four laps later, Baker went quicker still—a lap of 47.773 seconds, or 200.447 mph. "The car was so good I was flat-out around the track," said Baker, who would go on to win four 500-milers at Talladega, as well as the 1980 Daytona 500. "I could have gone a lot faster than 200. I said, 'Let's go to it and really set 'em a record.' They said, 'Well, the next barrier is 300 miles per hour; do you want to break that one?' And I told them, 'Nooo! Scratch my name off that trophy.'"[26] Thanks to restrictor plates, no stock car would exceed 200 mph during a race weekend for another twelve years.

But even as wings were being clipped in NASCAR, they were spreading in Indy cars. The timeline dated back to 1962, when Smokey Yunick brought a roadster to the Indianapolis Motor Speedway with a giant airfoil mounted in front of the cockpit. The drag slowed the car on the straights enough to cancel out the extra speed driver Jim Rathmann could carry through the corners, so it was shelved before the 500. In 1966, several Champ Car races featured a rear-engine Jerry Eisert car with a rear wing, but neither Al Unser nor Ronnie Duman achieved much success with it. After the tumult of the early 1960s, occasioned by the arrival of rear-engine cars from Europe, Indy car design had stagnated. There were some intriguing developments on the powerplant front, namely the introduction of turbines and turbocharging, but most of the cars followed the same F1-esque cigar-shaped mold. After the FIA banned movable aerodynamic devices in 1969, USAC followed suit. It also added regulations meant to discourage the development of stand-alone rear wings and prevent the aero revolution from spreading to Indy. But you know what they say about the best-laid plans, right?

If nothing else, their name suggested that the Eagles built at All American Racers ought to have wings. In 1971, Dan Gurney fitted his latest creation with an airfoil mounted directly behind Bobby Unser's helmet so that it could masquerade as an engine cover. AAR went to Phoenix International Raceway, a fast and vicious one-mile oval, for a preseason test. Out of the box, the car was a pig, and three days of testing in scorching desert heat didn't improve its manners. "Boss, you're supposed to be able to come up with something," Unser complained to Gurney. "Can't you come up with anything, for crying out loud?"[27]

Grasping at straws. Gurney remembered how his former teammate Richie Ginther had once solved the handling woes of a Ferrari 246 SP by slapping a crude spoiler on the rear deck. Gurney ordered his crew to cut a strip of aluminum and fold it lengthwise to form a ninety-degree angle. Then, they pop-riveted the L-shaped tab to the trailing edge of the wing to deflect air coming off the airfoil. Unser thought the exercise was a waste of time—until he got back into the cockpit. "I took that son of a bitch out and made less than one lap," he said, "and I had just discovered the biggest thing ever in race car handling."[28] The miracle fix was dubbed a "Gurney flap" in the Big Eagle's honor. (Widely used in aviation, this aerodynamic aid is known generically as a wickerbill.) Unser qualified on the pole at Phoenix and six of the eleven other races on the schedule. But not at Indy. Because when he got to the Speedway, he ran into an even more creative interpretation of the rules.

Like every other F1 designer, Gordon Coppuck had been wowed by the Lotus 72 that Rindt drove to a posthumous world championship in 1970. During the off-season, he used its basic architecture—chisel nose, wedge profile, and side-mounted radiators—as the template for the all-new McLaren M16 Indy car. But to get around the ban on stand-alone wings, he extended a strip of bodywork over the turbocharged Offy and used it as the mount for an integrated airfoil that extended beyond the gearbox and rear tires. Because the wing was much farther back than the one on the Eagle and because Coppuck had optimized the airflow both over and under it, the McLaren was much more efficient than the Eagle, despite the Gurney flap. At Indy, the airfoil doubled rear downforce and caused cornering speeds to jump by 4 mph. Mark Donohue practiced at 180 mph-plus in a Roger Penske–owned M16, and Peter Revson qualified on the pole in a Team McLaren car at 178.696 mph. Unser was third-fastest, but he wasn't in the same zip code.

After Indy, the American version of wing mania took off, as crew chiefs scrambled to add airfoils to their cars. "There used to be—and still is—a pretty thick book of NASA wing sections, and we all used to thumb through it," said Mike Devin, who was Johnny Rutherford's crew chief at the time. "The wing section that I chose was off an airplane they call a Beaver, which they fly in Alaska for short takeoffs and landings. So it was a pretty aggressive wing. I just scaled it down. For the front wing, I made something that looked good. It was pretty flat on top and had a small belly on the bottom, but we weren't looking for a lot from the front in those days. And if it didn't work it, we would put a little wickerbill on it, and that would bring it to life. So it was all just trial and error."[29]

Still, Donohue dominated the next two superspeedway races at Pocono and Michigan. By the time the Championship Trail reached Ontario, which was a slightly faster version of Indianapolis, he'd raised the bar to 185 mph and change—7.5 mph faster than the previous year. The big speed numbers generated a lot of publicity, which everybody agreed was a good thing. So at the end of the season, USAC decided to go with the flow and allow free-standing wings as long as they didn't move and weren't attached to the suspension.

The new rules forced everybody to overhaul their cars yet again. In 1972, the hot setup was to mount the rear wing as far back as possible to increase the efficiency of the airfoil. The Vel's Parnelli Jones Racing team tried to steal a march on the competition by hiring Maurice Phillippe, who'd worked with Chapman on the Lotus 72. Phillippe sketched out an inventive design incorporating a pair of very, very cool-looking dihedral wings attached diagonally to the fuselage on either side of the driver. The idea was to increase downforce in the turns. Unfortunately, they didn't work worth a damn, and they were hacked off like dead tree branches in an attempt to find some more speed at Indy. While the VPJ Parnellis struggled, the Eagles were soaring.

The all-new Eagle was principally the work of Roman Slobodynskyj, a freethinker who'd been plucked from Southern California's vibrant aerospace industry. Building upon the success of the M16 would have been a safe and sensible approach. But Slobodynskyj attacked the problem from a different direction. "I starting thinking backward," he said. "Way back then, the cars carried seventy-five gallons of fuel. That's a pretty large volume, so that dictated a lot of the design. As the fuel burns off, it changes the handling. So my idea was to concentrate as much of the fuel as possible around the CG [center of gravity] so the change would not be as dramatic as the fuel was used. That also led me to put the radiators close to the CG to get the weight distribution close to 40:60, which we were aiming for. We also thought about polar moments, so we tried to keep the mass of the components as closely wrapped up as possible."[30]

Although both cars featured a chisel nose, the Eagle was wider and less angular than the McLaren. The radiators were tucked into sidepods, which were flat instead of wedge-shaped to encourage better airflow back to the coffee table-sized rear wing. At 200 mph, the car generated about 1,500 pounds of downforce—twice as much as the 1971-spec M16. There wasn't anything unique about the suspension, but the geometry worked perfectly. So did the rest of the Eagle, which turned out to be one of those golden race cars that hit every sweet spot—downforce versus drag, aero grip versus mechanical grip, speed versus drivability.

At the first test, at Ontario, the car was bog slow on the straights. During lunch, Gurney glumly asked Slobodynskyj, "Hey, Roman, how long would it take you to redesign the car?"[31] After some poking around, the crew realized that the engine was sour. When the team returned with a good motor, Unser immediately started turning shockingly fast laps, eventually topping out north of 196 mph. During the test session, a phone rang at the VPJ shop in Indianapolis. Crew chief George Bignotti answered it, then didn't say much other than an occasional "Uh-huh" before hanging up. "I don't know who the hell that was," he announced, "but he must've been playing a prank. He said Bobby Unser just went 197 miles an hour at Ontario."[32]

It was inconceivable. But it was true. In 1972, Unser claimed the pole at Indy at 195.940 mph—17 mph faster than the previous year, 26 mph faster than two years earlier. By comparison, during the fifteen-year stretch between 1956 and 1970, the pole speed increased only 24.6 mph. Unser set track records in six consecutive races, and his AAR teammate, Jerry Grant, broke the 200 mph barrier at Ontario. Contrary to conventional wisdom, the newfound speed came not on the straights but in the corners. In fact, straight-line speeds dropped even as lap speeds increased. Consider these Indy numbers from the past decade:

CHASSIS	LAP SPEED	CORNER SPEED	STRAIGHT SPEED
1963 Watson	149 mph	140 mph	160 mph
1968 Eagle	169 mph	156 mph	200 mph
1970 P.J. Colt	170 mph	158 mph	200 mph
1971 McLaren	179 mph	163 mph	217 mph
1972 Eagle	196 mph	183 mph	206 mph

Although Donohue won the Indy 500 in a Penske M16 over Grant's Eagle, McLaren clearly had some catching up to do. During the off-season, the team overhauled the rear end of the car. "The car felt so good, and it was so well balanced," said Rutherford, who was now leading the team, "that it's the first time I'd ever been able to go around the speedway with my foot flat on the floor."[33] After clocking laps at 200 mph during practice, J.R. qualified at "only" 198.413 mph. Of course, that doesn't seem quite as impressive when you realize that Bobby Unser had taken the pole at the high-bank Texas World Speedway at 212.766 mph. And there seemed to be no limit in sight.

But with great speed comes great consequences, especially since the extra pace was found in the corners, where it was more likely that drivers would lose control. In 1972, during practice at Indy, Jim Malloy's Eagle slammed head-on into the wall in Turn Three, and he died four days later without regaining consciousness. Two months later, Merle Bettenhausen's right arm was ripped off when his M16 knock-off scraped the wall at Michigan International Speedway. The next season was even worse. Little-known Bob Criss, taking his first-ever laps in a Champ car, died during a preseason test session at Phoenix. Then, before qualifying at Indy, veteran (and grandfather) Art Pollard was killed after wrecking his Eagle in Turn One. The Speedway was the site of more tragedy later in the month, when Gurney's one-time protégé, Swede Savage, wrecked his Eagle in Turn Four shortly after losing the lead of the 500. He was only twenty-six when he died in the hospital five weeks later.

You didn't need a degree in differential calculus to see where the trend line was heading. USAC immediately trimmed the width of rear wings from sixty-four inches to fifty-five inches, then cut another eleven inches in 1974. Also, pop-off valves were introduced to restrict the power of the turbocharged Fords and Offenhausers. Thanks to these constraints, an official lap at 200 mph wouldn't be recorded at Indy until 1978. On the other hand, no other drivers would die in an Indy car until Gordon Smiley was killed at Indianapolis in 1982. This eight-year stretch without any fatalities was the longest in Champ Car's history up until that point.

THE CHARGE OF THE TURBO BRIGADE

They called him "Herbie Horsepower" because his name was Herb Porter, and he worshipped at the altar of forced induction. For nearly two decades, he was a prophet wandering in the wilderness, preaching a gospel that the racing world ignored. Then, in 1968, he built the turbo Offy that propelled Bobby Unser to victory in the Indianapolis 500, silencing his critics, converting the skeptics, and ushering in a new approach to engine design. He continued to work on race motors until he died in 1997, at eighty-three, universally regarded as a high priest of turbocharging but too crusty, cranky, and just plain ornery to be beloved. "I don't know what would happen if Porter were still around because he wouldn't shut up about anything," said longtime mechanic and racing executive Roger Bailey, who credits Porter with teaching him how to build Offys. "Today, most people don't believe there's a bear, let alone that it shits in the woods. Porter would have told them right off the bat where the bear came from, what it was doing, and who's picking up the poop. There were no ifs, ands, or buts with him. It was, 'This is how it's going to be.'"[34]

During World War II, Porter served as a staff sergeant overhauling P-40 and P-51 fighters, and he developed a deep appreciation for the superchargers on their screaming Rolls-Royce Merlin V-12s. After the war, he went to work as an engine builder and crew chief. He fitted a sprint car with a Roots-style supercharger in 1949 and, later, a centrifugal blower. Encouraged by the speed of these cars, he built a blown Offy that Andy Linden used to qualify on the front row at Indy in 1952. (The car was aptly named the Miracle Power Special.) But the engine puked after twenty laps, and Linden was classified thirty-third and last. Like the heroes of Greek myth, Porter's supercharged cars tended to be spectacular but short-lived. The only car faster than Porter's in qualifying was the turbocharged Cummins Diesel. The diesel broke early, too, but the turbo attached to it would have a lasting impact on Porter's career.

A supercharger creates horsepower by forcing more air into the cylinders. It's typically driven by a belt, gear, or chain run off the engine. This drive mechanism exacts a penalty by sapping a certain amount of power. A turbocharger, by way of contrast, is driven by exhaust gases that would otherwise flow out the tail pipe, so the extra power it

Forced-induction guru Herb Porter, second from left, brought modern turbocharging to Indianapolis in 1966 with an elderly Watson roadster retrofitted with a Rube Goldberg–like tangle of tubing that didn't fit under the hood. Blasting down the straights at 200 mph but plagued by turbo lag in the corners, Bobby Grim became the second-to-last driver to put a front-engine car into the show—barely—but he was eliminated in the big first-lap crash. *Indianapolis Motor Speedway*

produces is more or less free. The downside, at least early on, was that it took some time for the turbo to spool up, so there was a lag between depressing the throttle and actually accelerating. It was also difficult to tune the turbo to work well across a broad range of engine speeds.

Nevertheless, turbos started to appear on trucks and tractors in the 1950s, and in 1962, General Motors felt emboldened to apply the technology to the Oldsmobile Jetfire. Engineer Bob DeBisschop was hired by Garrett AiResearch to make it work. It didn't, or at least not well enough to succeed in the consumer market. Throttle lag was a drag, and the turbo didn't do much at low speed. On the other hand, it worked *really* well at high speed, which suggested that it might have a future on big ovals where engines worked in a relatively narrow rev band. But this remained the stuff of idle bench-racing sessions until the arrival of a brand-new V-8 from Ford in 1963 threatened the longtime dominion of the Offy.

Although the Offy had scored its first win at the Speedway in 1935, its underlying architecture went back a lot further than that—to 1912, when a double-overhead-cam, four-valves-per-cylinder Peugeot won the French Grand Prix. In 1919, Ballot used a similar setup in its straight-8 Indy racer. The next year, Harry A. Miller designed his own twin-cam straight-8. With an integrated block and head and a one-piece barrel-type crankcase, this engine proved to be among the most successful—and aesthetically satisfying—artifacts in motorsports history. Engineer Leo Goossen was responsible for the drafting, and shop foreman Fred Offenhauser oversaw the engine build. What a triumvirate! It should come as no surprise that Millers dominated the sport for years to come.

Boat racing was big in the Roaring Twenties, so Miller fashioned at 310-cubic-inch version of his straight-8 for hydroplanes in 1925. The next year, he cut it in half to create the 151-cubic-inch four-cylinder Miller Marine engine. Over the years, this would be enlarged for automotive use to various sizes ranging from 200 to 270 cubic inches. After Miller went bust during the Depression, Offenhauser opened his own shop, filling it with equipment from his old boss. A 260, now known as an Offy, won Indy in 1935. After World War II, 220 Offys ruled sprint car racing until the small-block Chevy arrived in the early 1960s. Meanwhile, 255 and 270 Offys won every Champ Car race except Pikes Peak from October 1946 to August 1963. And from 1953 to 1960, every car that qualified at Indy was either an Offy or a Novi, which had been designed by Goossen and built initially at Offenhauser's shop.

But no empire lasts forever. The barbarians started pounding on the gates in 1961, when Jack Brabham showed up with a lightly modified Coventry-Climax Grand Prix engine. The next year, Mickey Thompson brought a stock-block Buick. But 1963 was the year that the Offy dynasty seemed poised for a fall, due to the arrival of a much better fortified tribe of marauders from Dearborn. The first Ford V-8 was a race version of its Fairlane powerplant, and Jim Clark drove it to a second-place finish. The next year, Ford returned with a four-cam iteration that was the culmination of a $10 million development program. It had 75 horsepower and 2,000 rpm on the Offy, and that was running on straight methanol, without any "pop," or nitromethane. All the front-runners broke, and A.J. Foyt and his Offy picked up the pieces at Indy. But by 1965, he and all the other fast guys would be racing four-cam Indy Fords.

The Offy empire struck back on two fronts—supercharging and turbocharging. Dick Jones, who ran the Champion Spark Plugs competition program, hated the Ford engine because it used Autolite spark plugs. So he borrowed a 220 Offy sprint car motor, sleeved it down to 171 cubic inches, and rigged up a GMC 4-71 Roots-type blower driven by a toothed Gilmer belt. With help from Goossen and Dale Drake, he got it up to 545 horsepower. Parnelli Jones broke the lap record at Phoenix in a private test in 1966 and qualified fourth at Indy. But neither he nor the other three drivers with supercharged Offys did much in the race. Development pretty much ceased after that because it soon became clear that the turbo had more upside potential.

Over at AiResearch, DeBisschop had realized that the street-car world wasn't ready for turbocharging (or vice versa), but he reasoned that it was a natural for the racing environment. He got in touch with Porter, who was now a respected crew chief running conventional Offys. Herbie Horsepower was game to experiment. Working out of Porter's shop, he, DeBisschop, and Stu Hilborn (of fuel-injection fame) fitted an off-the-shelf TE06 turbo designed for an Allis-Chalmers diesel tractor to a spare Offy. Before long, they were making 600 horsepower on the Champion dyno. Yowza! Porter crammed the engine in an old Watson roadster with the turbo and a Rube Goldberg–like network of large pipes and tubes hung out the side of the cockpit. With Bobby Grim behind the wheel, the car thundered down the front straight at Indianapolis at 200 mph and belched flames on overrun in the corners. Grim described it as "an absolute plumber's nightmare of two sets of injector nozzles, one adjusted for unblown, the other for when the blower kicked in. Which meant that at low speeds, the roadster was a slobbering idiot—pop, spit, slobber, it barely ran at all. Then all of a sudden, *BLAM!* The turbo kicked in, and it was hold-onto-your-ass."[35] Grim was the only roadster driver to qualify. In the race, he got boxed in by the huge start-line crash. "I couldn't have gotten out of there with a helicopter," he said.

It didn't matter. A stand had been made, and a counterattack commenced. Brute force was never an issue, but the addition of a wastegate and other detail upgrades improved drivability. In the opening race of the 1967 season, Lloyd Ruby scored the turbo Offy's first USAC win, going flag to flag at Phoenix. The next year, Porter worked with DeBisschop and Jud Philips on Bobby Unser's turbocharged Eagle. Unser won Indy, and Offys powered nine of the first eleven finishers. By 1969, Ford was turbocharging its formerly unbeatable four-cam motor. But in a strange twist of fate, the old-school, heavy-duty design of the Offy—especially the robust bottom end—allowed it to absorb stratospheric levels of boost better than the Ford, which was hobbled by its improperly sized intake ports. As longtime Indy car mechanic John Anderson explained, "The Fords couldn't breathe as well as an Offy. I mean, they weren't bad, but, you know, an Offy had only four big slugs and four valves per cylinder, so it could ingest much more air than a four-cam Ford and then burn it. That's why they were just so successful."[36]

In 1973, Bailey built the turbo Offy powering Johnny Rutherford and his Team McLaren M16C. "In those days, there was no limit on the manifold pressure," Bailey said. "We had a 120-inch manifold pressure gauge, and we bent the needle. Our Heenan & Froude 490 dyno pegged out at 1350 horsepower, and that engine on the dyno went *way* past that. We'll never know the true horsepower. But Rutherford always said that he could spin the wheels on the short chute at the Speedway."[37] J.R. qualified on the pole at a record 198.413 mph, with one lap at a tick over 199 mph. "It was shortly after that that USAC came out with the pop-off valves," Bailey said. "They said the speeds were getting out of control, and they wanted to keep them down to sensible levels."[38] The turbo Offy maintained its crown until a turbocharged version of the Cosworth F1 engine, dubbed the DFX, arrived in the late 1970s.

Road courses were a tougher nut to crack since the mix of low-speed and high-speed sections required so much more flexibility from an engine. Credit for the first successful application belongs to BMW, which won the European Touring Car Championship in 1969 with a 2002 accessorized with a KKK turbo, after which forced induction was promptly banned. But it was Porsche that put the technology on the international map with the 917/10 Can-Am car. The turbo conversion wasn't undertaken in the adventuresome spirit of exploring new technological territory; it was simply to guarantee a reasonable financial return on investment after new rules prevented the normally aspirated 917 from competing at Le Mans and the rest of the Championship of Makes series. "Porsche was a very small company in those days, and we had spent a lot of money on the 917," program manager Helmut Flegl said. "So the question was, 'What could we do with the car?' And the Can-Am had a very short rulebook."[39]

Can-Am was the last of the anything-goes race series. Virtually since it had been inaugurated, Can-Am was dominated by McLarens packing American pushrod V-8s hogged out to 7.0 and 8.0 liters. Although the 5.0-liter flat-12 in the 917 had been the most potent engine in European road racing, it was a knife in the gunfights being fought in Can-Am, as Porsche discovered in 1969 with a spyder version of the Le Mans racer. The 917 PA, as it was dubbed, was significantly lighter than the coupe, but it still didn't have enough horsepower to run with the big dogs. Two years later, Porsche designed a more compact variation specifically for Can-Am. The second verse was the same as the first. The solution was more power—a *lot* more power.

Tests with an experimental flat-16 engine convinced Porsche that it made more sense to turbocharge the existing motor. But R&D chief Ferdinand Piëch wanted a partner with some experience with the technology. Roger Penske was a perfect fit. In 1971, he and his driver/chief engineer/team manager Mark Donohue had raced a turbo Offy at Indy, and their privately run Ferrari 512 M had been faster than the 917s (and the factory Ferraris) at Daytona and Sebring. As a bonus, the young Penske had come to prominence driving Porsche 550s and 718s in SCCA competition. "After Le Mans," Penske recalled, "I got a call from Piëch's wife, who said, 'My husband would like to meet you regarding an opportunity with Porsche.'"[40]

Early tests were discouraging. "The first turbo engine we got over here, it wouldn't idle, it would slobber all over the place, fart, foul the spark plugs," said Woody Woodard, the chief mechanic on Penske's

Can-Am Porsches. "You'd put your foot on the gas, and you'd have to wait five minutes for the turbo to spool up. It was literally undrivable."[41] But after a lot of development and the installation of a recalibrated Bosch fuel-injection unit known internally as "the happy pump," the 917/10 was effectively unbeatable. Although Donohue was injured in a preseason crash, his replacement, George Follmer, schooled the McLarens to win the championship in 1972. For the next year, Porsche developed the follow-on 917/30. In addition to an improved long-wheelbase chassis and more efficient bodywork, the new car featured an even bigger, more powerful turbocharged engine. In race form, the 5.0-liter motor

Blitzkrieg! Mark Donohue put his Porsche 917/30 on the pole by nearly two seconds for the Can-Am race at Road Atlanta in 1973. His only real competition were Porsche's lesser turbopanzers—the 917/10s driven by George Follmer (No. 16), Jody Scheckter (No. 0), and Hurley Haywood (No. 59). The first normally aspirated car was Jackie Oliver's UOP-sponsored Shadow DN2. The Porsches were so dominant that they effectively killed the Can-Am series. *Corporate Archives Porsche AG*

was rated at 1,000 horsepower, whereas the new 5.4 made 1,130 horses without straining. On the Porsche dyno at Weissach, with the boost cranked, figures of 1,400—and, reportedly, 1,500—horsepower were seen. During testing at Paul Ricard, the 917/30 was clocked at 242 mph. Donohue demolished the competition so thoroughly in 1973 that the Can-Am series folded the next year. Donohue telexed Flegl, "p.s., these cars are so good its beyond belief u should pat yourself on the back but ur arms arent long enough."[42] Or as he later confided to a friend, "If I drove this thing as hard as I could for the whole race, I'd end up five laps ahead of everyone."[43]

The Porsche 917/30 came scarily close to fulfilling Donohue's motorsports fantasy of a car powerful enough to spin the tires from the exit of each corner until the entry of the next one. Herbie Horsepower would have been pleased.

David Pearson checks out the elbow-high side-impact bars that car builder Cotton Owens, left, added to the standard NASCAR roll cage in his 1963 Dodge. The only other visible piece of safety equipment is the padded steering wheel. Until Banjo Matthews revolutionized stock car design by fabricating custom chassis in the early 1970s, Grand National race cars were built on the stock frame rails found on street cars. *Cotton Owens Garage*

CHAPTER TEN

SOMETHING WICKED THIS WAY COMES

Clint Brawner was a magnificent machinist and an endlessly resourceful mechanic whose motto was "Man made it; man can fix it."[1] When rival crew chiefs of the roadster era ran into something they couldn't repair, they would drop the broken part in front of Brawner's garage with the expectation that he could work his magic on it. Brawner's other superpower was his ability to identify unsung drivers whom he could groom for stardom. Jimmy Bryan had won only one Indy car race before Brawner hired him to drive for Dean Van Lines in 1954. Working with Brawner, Bryan won three national championships in four years. After Bryan semiretired, Brawner replaced him with a winless Texan by the name of A.J. Foyt. Two years later, when Foyt moved on, Brawner tapped Eddie Sachs. Previously better known as a clown than a racer, Sachs put the Dean Van Lines Special on the pole at Indy for two consecutive years and came within three laps of winning the 500 in 1961.

The relationship between Sachs and Brawner cooled after the Indy that got away, and they split in 1962. To fill the empty seat, Brawner began looking for a driver who was young, ballsy, and malleable. All the top Indy car guys were already spoken for. So Brawner figured his best bet was to find an up-and-comer who was tearing it up in the sprint car ranks, where the cars were nasty, the tracks tricky, and the competition savage.

His first choice was Stan Bowman, who'd just scored his maiden win at the national level. Brawner caught up with him at the USAC sprint car show at the Terre Haute Action Track in June 1962. In a heat race, Bowman's front axle snapped. The car flipped four times, soared over the wall, and landed fifty feet from the track. Bowman died five days later of head injuries. The next month, Brawner made a pilgrimage to Langhorne to scout Hugh Randall. After failing to qualify in a Kurtis old enough to be eligible for vintage racing, Randall hung around, hoping to snag a ride as a relief driver. When not one but two drivers bailed out of another ancient Kurtis that wasn't handling, Randall told the owner, "I'll drive 'er!"[2] On his second lap, he hooked a rut in Puke Hollow and was killed when the car rolled. The month after that, Brawner attended the USAC sprint car race at New Bremen to take a closer look at Donnie Davis, who'd finished a surprising fourth at Indy earlier in the year. After taking the checkered flag, Davis's right-side tires rubbed up against the wall. His car flipped, and though it landed on its wheels, Davis died of a basal skull fracture.

Eventually, Brawner decided that it would be safer to go with a veteran, so he signed Chuck Hulse, a known quantity with a ton of experience. In May 1964, shortly before heading to Indy to drive the Dean Van Lines Special, Hulse entered the USAC sprint car show at the New Bremen track where Davis had been killed. In the feature, Hulse rode over a wheel of a car that had spun in front of him and flipped seventeen times. Although no bones were broken, the violence of the gyrations caused double vision that kept him out of racing for two years. To replace Hulse, Brawner hired the kid who finished fourth at New Bremen, a cocky runt who was barely tall enough to peer over the oversized steering wheel of his sprint car. Good call, as it turned out. Five years later, after winning a pair of national championships, Mario Andretti would give Brawner his only Indy 500 victory as a crew chief. (Creepy footnote: Andretti ran his first USAC sprint car race in a car that he'd seen Bobby Marvin burn to death in a few months earlier. "I could still smell the flesh," he remembered grimly. "It's macabre, but it's true."[3])

Sprint cars were the motorsport jungle's version of the black mamba—powerful, primeval, fast-moving creatures packing a lethal bite. With a power-to-weight ratio better than an Indy car but built on a shorter wheelbase, sprint cars were twitchy, ornery, and murderous when provoked. "In fact, sprint car racing is probably the most dangerous pastime since Irish football," a British transplant wrote, tongue in cheek, in *Car and Driver.*[4] But it was no joke to the men in the cockpit, straddling the transmission tunnel and hanging on for dear life. One of the first things Parnelli Jones did after winning Indy in 1963 was start weaning himself off sprint cars before quitting cold turkey the following year while continuing to race Indy cars, midgets, stock cars, Can-Am prototypes, Trans-Am Mustangs, and off-road vehicles. Mind you, this was one of the gutsiest men ever to don a Hinchman uniform, not to mention the winner of three consecutive sprint car championships. And yet, he once confided, "If there was one part of my career I could have cut out, it would have been running those high banks in a sprint car."[5]

Like many other types of race cars, sprint cars were invented to fill a niche. During the 1920s, with the economy booming, American motorsports were dominated by the elegant creations of Harry Miller. The impossibly slender, jewel-like Millers were impeccably engineered and immaculately built, and they set speed marks on high-bank board tracks that are hard to believe even today, a century later. But when the Roaring Twenties devolved into the Great Depression, nobody could afford machines as sophisticated as the Millers. By 1938, the national championship sanctioned by the AAA consisted of a grand total of two races—the Indy 500 and a one hundred miler on dirt at Syracuse.

Indy was the big enchilada, a single race that paid more money—and conferred more fame and glory—than all the other ones put together, so the guys who competed there kept pavement cars, often refurbished Millers, in their stables. But since most of the tracks around the country were dirt ovals ranging from a quarter mile to a full mile, the laws of natural selection suggested that new species would evolve to race on them. Sure enough, the smaller tracks became the preferred habitat of dramatically downsized cars called midgets. For half-mile and longer tracks, what we now know as sprint cars were developed. Confusingly, they were known as Big Cars to distinguish them from midgets, but they were smaller than the cars that raced at Indy. All three breeds shared the same basic chassis, engine, and body designs, much like clothing sold in small, medium, and large sizes. The exact rules differed by sanctioning body, but for big-picture purposes, Indy cars had wheelbases around one hundred inches; sprint cars, eighty inches; and midgets, seventy inches, with engines sized proportionately.

Sprint cars took off after World War II, but for a variety of reasons, no single sanctioning body secured control of the racing. By the mid-1960s, there were four competing organizations. The United States Automobile Club (USAC) was the most prominent since it was the only one with a national presence. Plus, it had the fearsome high banks at Salem, Winchester, and Dayton known collectively as "the hills." The International Motor Contest Association (IMCA), formed in 1914, focused on the Midwestern country fair circuit. The West Coast was the province of the California Racing Association (CRA) while the United Racing Club (URC) was strictly East Coast.

The sprint cars of the 1960s weren't much different from the ones of the 1950s—or the 1940s, for that matter. The biggest change was that the Offy was being supplanted by the cheaper and higher-revving/more powerful small-block Chevy V-8. No matter which powerplant was fitted, sprint cars remained hellishly dangerous. No fewer than five sprint car drivers were killed in a five-week stretch during the summer of 1966—two in a single wreck at Reading, two more on consecutive days at Calistoga, and a fifth after tangling with two other cars at Tulsa. As the death count rose inexorably, Brock Yates wrote in *Car and Driver*, "Though USAC has made valiant efforts toward safety, sprint car racing remains statistically the most hazardous brand of the sport in the world."[6]

Lap belts were required by most sanctioning bodies, and drivers generally augmented them with either a shoulder harness or a strap across the chest. But this was less about protecting a driver in a crash than keeping him from popping out of the cockpit like the cork from a champagne bottle when the car bounced over ruts and potholes. "You

Past, present, and future. Race winner Gary Bettenhausen has his right-rear tire smoking as he powers underneath Bruce Walkup in a pair of uncaged sprint cars during the USAC show at Winchester Speedway in 1969. Rollie Beale, in a then-rare sprinter sporting a roll cage, chased Bettenhausen home to finish second. With its high banks, high speeds, and rickety wood guardrails, Winchester wasn't a track for the faint of heart. *John Mahoney*

got the hell beat out of you on them old dirt tracks that IMCA had in the Midwest," Jones recalled. "We were running every day and every night, and my whole body was black and blue because there were rocks everywhere and the right front tire would pull up dirt all the time. I used to put cardboard inside my uniform to protect myself."[7]

Drivers were routinely pelted with rocks, stones, and clods of hard-packed dirt that felt like boulders. This was before the full-face helmet had been pioneered by Bell. Drivers wore aviation-style goggles and bandanas or leather shields hooked to their helmet, but the protection they provided was marginal at best. Cosmetic damage wasn't the only concern. It wasn't unheard of for drivers to be stunned after being hit by unidentified flying objects. At Eldora, reigning USAC sprint car champion Johnny Rutherford got nailed by a projectile spit out by Andretti's rear tire. It split his goggles and knocked him out. His car catapulted over the guardrail while his arms were outstretched and raised upright like a referee signaling a made field goal. The car flew another sixty feet before crashing nose first into a gully. Rutherford's arms were badly broken when they slammed against the top of the windshield. "When I was in the hospital, my wife brought me the newspaper," he recalled. "There was a big picture of me, and the caption said, 'Rutherford waves to the crowd as he leaves the racetrack.'"[8]

Although Rutherford chuckled when he told the story, he didn't think it was funny at the time. He didn't race again for more than a year, and the incident set his career back so far that it was seven years before he won another major race. But J.R. was lucky compared with dirt master Don Branson, one of the luminaries of the roadster era. On the eve of his retirement near the end of the 1966 season, "Pappy" passed out after taking a rock to the head during a sprint car show at Ascot Park. His car shot into the fence, caromed back onto the racing line, and was speared by Dick Ascot, a star-in-the-making who'd won his first Champ Car race only two weeks earlier. Both men died in the crash. It was USAC's second sprint car double fatality in five months.

Getting clipped by rocks and clods of dirt was an occupational hazard, but it rarely had such tragic consequences. When things went catastrophically wrong with sprint cars, it was usually a matter of rolling and/or flipping. The fast way around a dirt track involves what's known as backing a car into the corner. The driver pitches the car into the turn so that the back end of the car starts rotating around. He then catches the slide by applying opposite lock and adjusts his line by modulating the throttle. Old-school sprint cars were saddled with unsupple suspensions and high centers of gravity. When they were all crossed up, drifting sideways at an angle often exceeding sixty degrees, they were susceptible to being pitched out of control by factors such as deep ruts, large potholes, or a nudge from a rival. And when a car let go, the willowy frame and solid axles meant that the results were often sickeningly spectacular—end-over-end somersaults that would impress an Olympic gymnast and barrel rolls that would turn a fighter pilot green with envy.

The violence of these wrecks often caused basal skull fractures, a mortal injury that wouldn't be addressed until the HANS device was invented decades later. But roll bars mounted behind the open cockpit made a lot of sense. They started appearing in the 1950s, and USAC mandated them by the end of the decade. Still, this was an imperfect solution even when the roll bar was properly built and installed, which wasn't always the case, whether because of incompetence, stinginess, or the temptation to sacrifice safety to save weight. Eventually, safety-conscious builders started surrounding cockpits with a lattice of steel tubes to protect drivers when they got upside down.

The roll cage wasn't a new concept. NASCAR featured stock ladder-frame chassis until the unibody Ford Fairlane debuted in 1967. (Custom frames didn't become standard stock car equipment until Banjo Matthews began supplying them in the early 1970s.) Because the chassis were so flexible, steel tubing was welded strategically around the cockpit to provide both structural rigidity and crash protection. By 1965, after a grim twelve-month stretch during which four drivers died in stock cars, the elbow-high door bars pioneered by builder Cotton Owens were widely adopted. When stock car leviathan Holman & Moody began working on the Ford GT program in 1966, it installed NASCAR-style chromoly cages in the Mark II Le Mans prototypes. In January 1967, during a preseason test at Daytona, Peter Revson's car scraped the wall and blew a tire. The car took off like an airplane and demolished a light pole twenty-five feet in the air before crashing and crumpling into a jagged metallic ball on the front straight. Astonishingly, Revson was unhurt. "I remember getting out of that thing, opening the door and pulling myself up out of the car, and I've never seen so many shocked people in my life," Revson said later.[9]

In the open-wheel world, primitive roll cages appeared first on so-called supermodifieds, which were a rabid cross between modified stock cars and sprint cars. The first caged sprint car to attract national attention was the Vince Conze–owned sprinter that Jimmy Davies raced at Ascot and Pikes Peak in the early 1960s. The most strident proselytizer for roll cages was the prolific SoCal car builder Don Edmunds, a one-time Indy 500 Rookie of the Year who quit driving after seeing so many of his friends die on the track. By the mid-1960s, he was using a winning slogan to sell cars with bolt-in cages: "The sprint car is a mean, vicious animal," he said. "Tame the animal with a roll cage."[10]

In 1966, longtime CRA president Walt James cited rising insurance costs as the justification for requiring roll cages, but he was nearly burned at the stake for heresy at an emergency meeting, and the regulation was eighty-sixed before it ever took effect. Old-timers and self-professed purists detested roll cages as abominations. "I hate the things," said four-time IMCA sprint car champ Bobby Grim. "I've raced for twenty years without one, I sure don't need a cage now."[11] Andretti was another critic. "They looked like shit," he said, and he worried that the added protection would make drivers more willing to take risks—a concern shared by Jones.[12] "We killed a lot of drivers before we had roll cages on dirt cars," Jones said. "But we had more respect for each other on the track back then. I've always contended that Pikes Peak is the most dangerous racecourse I've ever driven. Well, they've never had a driver fatality there. What happens is, when you start at the bottom, you tell yourself, 'I'm going to make sure I get to the top. If I win, great.'"[13]

Joe Scalzo, the most vivid chronicler of this era, articulated the philosophical resistance to safety advances that seem, in retrospect, to have been no-brainers. "Nobody wanted to pasteurize the racing and make it too safe," he wrote. "Sprint car drivers are hard men, much harder than even the average fan realizes. And what they seem to love best about sprint car racing is its toughness, its way of separating the men from the boys, of being so raw and wild that only relatively few drivers are daring enough to do it. Adding roll cages seemed a way of making the racing so safe that anyone could attempt it."[14]

In 1969, the URC made roll cages optional. James took another stab at mandating them for the CRA, but his proposal was rejected by a vote of 40–25. Around the same time, proposals to require cages were floated month after month at USAC board meetings, but there wasn't quite enough support to implement a new rule. Meanwhile, though, drivers were metaphorically voting with their feet. Mel Kenyon, better known for his wondrous midget exploits, was an early adopter. "I've been bit, and I don't care to get bit again," he said. "I know how it feels. Race drivers are a bunch of professional fools, and I'm one of them. But I do what I can to help myself because the only other person that's looking out for you is the good Lord himself."[15]

Greg Weld, the 1967 USAC sprint car champion, credited a roll cage with saving his life after a fiery wreck on the Salem high banks in 1969. Tom Bigelow was another reluctant convert. "When roll cages first come out, I thought they were for sissies," he said. "Then I flipped a [noncaged] sprint car at Terre Haute in 1969. My head hit the ground several times, and my brain started hemorrhaging. That night, I had another race at New Bremen. I got a bottle of aspirin on the way over there, and I kept gobbling them up to kill the pain. After the race, on the way home, I thought I'd take a couple more but I realized I'd already finished the whole bottle of one hundred. Monday morning, I collapsed, and I was unconscious for two days. Let me tell you: After you take a tumble with the roll cage and you crawl out not being hurt, you think, 'Oh, boy. There's no chance I'm ever going to get in another sprint car without a roll cage.'"[16]

Roll cages were a tougher sell to fans. Everybody agreed that the inelegant metal trellises destroyed the classic good looks of a sprint car. And since spectators weren't the ones with their lives on the line, it was easy for them to scoff at the risks. The general consensus seemed to be that sprint cars were *supposed* to be dangerous. "If you are going to the grocery in haste, you can get hurt or killed," a reader wrote to *National Speed Sport News*. "Granted that getting killed on a shopping trip is inglorious. What better way is there for a racer to die than in a good sprinter with 500 horses under his foot? Who wants all that tubing cluttering up a good hairy racer? Pretty soon these nuts will be asking for rules demanding roll cages on the caskets."[17]

The turning point in the battle over roll cages came on September 1, 1969, a day that will live in racing infamy. Two weeks earlier, newcomer Kenny Gritz had shocked the sprint car world by outrunning Jan Opperman—the King of the Outlaws—to win the prestigious Knoxville Nationals. With this feather in his cap, he showed up at the Nebraska State Fairgrounds in Lincoln with a caged Don Edmunds car. IMCA

Mel Kenyon was an early adopter of roll cages on his midgets and sprint cars. In 1974, he brought a caged Eagle to Indy, shown here in the pits, but the tubing disrupted the flow of air to the rear wing, and the car was dead slow. Therefore, the only driver ever to race at the Speedway with a roll cage was Bruce Walkup, who qualified a creditable fourteenth in 1970 and finished twenty-ninth. *Revs Institute / Bruce R. Craig Photograph Collection*

officials demanded that the cage be removed even though Gritz argued that the bolt-in unit didn't give him a competitive advantage. No dice. Gritz grudgingly unbolted the steel tubing. Thirteen laps into the thirty-lap feature, he slammed into a giant pothole. His car flipped over the retaining wall and landed cockpit first on a concrete abutment. He died instantly, and so did most of the remaining resistance to roll cages.

The sheer perversity of Gritz's death—and the lawsuit that followed—finally made the old guard see reason. IMCA, CRA, and URC all required roll cages on sprint cars starting in 1970. USAC dragged its feet for another year but finally followed suit in 1971. By

1972, the cageless sprint car was extinct. Roll cages were also required on dirt Champ cars (now known as Silver Crown cars) and midgets of every known variety. Not a single driver was killed in a CRA race for two years running—an anomaly so statistically improbable, in light of the CRA's previous track record, that it almost qualified as a miracle.

There was, briefly, a movement to bring the technology to Indy cars. In 1970, Bruce Walkup raced in the 500 in an awkward-looking Mongoose-Offy with rear-view mirrors attached to a roll cage. (A caged Wolverine chassis designed by Edmunds failed to qualify that year, making Walkup the only driver ever to race at Indy with a roll cage.) Four years later, Kenyon and his brother, Don, fashioned a cage for their Eagle. Unfortunately, the tubular structure destroyed the airflow to the rear wing. After calculating that the roll cage was costing them 8 mph, the Kenyons removed it. But the concept never went away completely. In 2018, concerns about cockpit safety in Formula 1 and other open-cockpit cars prompted the FIA to mandate the halo, a three-pronged titanium structure surrounding the driver's head. And starting in 2020, IndyCar required that cockpits be fitted with an aeroscreen, which is a laminated polycarbonate windscreen mounted on a titanium frame. Neither the halo nor the aeroscreen is a roll cage, per se, but all three components share the same philosophical DNA.

The shift to roll cages back in the 1970s caused a lot of angst, and some of it lingers to this day. Not because anybody wanted to see drivers get hurt but because it changed the mindset of the competitors. "It made people a lot braver than they used to be," Steve Chassey said. "Look at the kids driving these things today. They flip them all the time, and they don't get hurt because of the cage. If the cages weren't there, they wouldn't be driving as aggressively as they do now. We had a lot more respect for the other guys. You didn't run into them, and you didn't run over them. You might pinch them here and there, but you wouldn't make contact."[18]

The other major reason roll cages ran into so much pushback is that the sprint car community is as conservative as an Amish settlement. Long after rear-engine chassis revolutionized Indy car racing, sprinters soldiered on as smaller versions of the classic front-engine roadsters—and still do. In 1970, a bespectacled schoolteacher achieved local fame in the Northwest by winning the Canadian American Modified Racing

Association (CAMRA) championship in a car featuring both a rear-mounted engine and four-wheel drive. Nobody paid much attention because CAMRA was a small regional sanctioning body. But in 1973, the unheralded Tom Sneva came east and began waxing USAC fields with a rear-engine sprinter cobbled together out of an antique Huffaker Indy car. Adding insult to injury, Jerry Hansen, a twenty-seven-time SCCA national champion and a major star in the sporty car firmament, won a trio of USAC and IMCA sprint car races in a Lola T192 Formula 5000 car retrofitted with a roll cage. USAC's response? If we can't beat 'em, ban 'em. Outlawing rear-engine chassis preserved the status quo, which saved owners a ton of money in the short term, but at what long-term cost? "If they had allowed rear-engine sprint cars, there would have been more of them," Chassey said. "And then there would have been a lot more of an opportunity for drivers to get into an Indy car because of their experience in a rear-engine car. It was just crazy that they wouldn't allow them."[19]

When it came to wings, on the other hand, resistance was gradually worn down. Aerodynamic appendages first appeared on supermodifieds back in 1958, and by the 1960s, winged super-sprint cars were becoming popular. In 1971, the URC made wings mandatory, and the World of Outlaws series gave winged sprinters a national audience after launching in 1978. Thanks to gigantic wings—and even bigger sideboards—winged sprint cars can carve through the corners much more effectively than nonwing cars. Is faster better? Well, both approaches have their devotees. But there's no question that the winged cars are safer because the massive structure erected over the cockpit serves as a crumple zone when they get upside down, which still happens a lot.

Why were wings embraced while rear-engine chassis were rejected? Probably because wings don't change the fundamental character of the cars. More so than just about any other form of racing, sprint cars remain throwbacks whose primitive nature makes them an appealing alternative to the digital-forward, technology-driven forms of racing that now dominate the sport. For precisely that reason, drivers continue to get hurt and killed in them, just not nearly as often as they did before roll cages were required. To this day, they're still mean, vicious animals. But they've been tamed, in more ways than one.

(ALMOST) ANYTHING GOES

On the surface, Can-Am was road racing's version of sprint cars—big, brawny, in-your-face ground pounders with more grunt than grip. But on a deeper level, they're what Formula 1 claimed to be but actually wasn't, which is to say the ultimate in what-if race car design.

"I thought the Can-Am was a terrific series because there was so much innovation," said Dan Gurney, who scored the last two wins of his career in Can-Am cars in 1970. "It was the other end of the spectrum from a spec series: You never knew when something mysterious was going to come along and render everything obsolete. These days, the cars are designed by the rules as much as the engineers, and that stinks to high heaven. It was a lot more fun when you could strut your creativity. And it was very exciting to know that, if you were smart enough, you could change the balance of power."[20]

The Can-Am series was conceptualized over a bottle of scotch in the home of Bill Fleming, an SCCA lifer who'd run an MG TC in the second race ever staged at Watkins Glen, way back in 1949. The heavy lifting was done by SCCA executive director John Bishop, the prophet who'd led the organization into the land of professional racing. What Bishop envisioned was a series limited only by the human imagination. "All the rules fit on one legal-size piece of paper," said his son, Mitch Bishop. "My dad was in favor of drawing a box and saying, 'Okay, everything inside the box is free. Do whatever you want.'"[21]

Although the rules package was new, the series wasn't without precedent. In 1958, the Los Angeles Times Grand Prix at Riverside had inaugurated a tradition of West Coast tracks hosting sports car races with purses hefty enough to attract European road-racing stars to compete against their American counterparts after the Grand Prix season was over. The races were generally sanctioned by USAC because SCCA was strictly—and strenuously—amateur in those days. In 1963, Bishop and competition director Jim Kaser convinced the SCCA board of directors that they needed to create a professional series of their own. The result was the US Road Racing Championship. The USRRC was successful by the SCCA standards. But since it was held in the middle of the racing season, it didn't attract any international stars. Or much international attention. Or much attention, period. As two-time series champion Mark Donohue put it, "The USRRC was fine, but it was like playing tennis with your wife."[22]

Enter the Canadian-American Challenge Cup for two-seat "unrestricted" sports cars, effectively defined as "anything goes." Jointly sanctioned by the SCCA and the Canadian Automobile Sport Clubs, the series was to feature six races in the United States and Canada

This photo doesn't compute at first glance, and it looks even weirder the longer you study it. That's Shadow owner Don Nichols towering over his AVS Mk I Can-Am car in 1970, with designer/evil genius Trevor Harris nearly supine in the cockpit. Harris minimized frontal area to maximize top speed. The bespoke Firestones were nearly as wide as they were tall, but as the uneven tread wear suggests, the tires didn't work very well. *Trevor Harris*

during an eight-week stretch in the fall of 1966. To tempt Europeans, the organizers amassed a purse, including contingency money, totaling $358,570—the biggest payday, by several orders of magnitude, ever offered for a road-racing series. Johnson Wax provided credibility and promotional muscle when it came on board as the title sponsor, and anointing Stirling Moss as the Challenge Cup commissioner (whatever that meant) lent the proceedings a touch of class.

The first race was at St. Jovite, and the turnout was promising—John Surtees, Bruce McLaren, and Chris Amon (who finished one-two-three) coming from afar and Donohue, Gurney, and Parnelli Jones representing the home team. During practice, Paul Hawkins's Lola T70 did a high-speed back flip after hitting a bump on the backstraight. "You shouldn't try to fly if you don't have a fucking pilot's license," joked his friend, Hugh Dibley, who was himself an airline pilot.[23] The next day, proving that turnabout was fair play, Dibley flipped his own T70. He and Hawkins were charter members of the Can-Am Flying Club.

The pair of blowovers in the first-ever Can-Am race didn't auger well for the future, especially since the cars in the series were the hairiest road racers ever built. In later years, big-block motors would be reamed out to eight liters, and speeds in excess of 200 mph were achieved even on North American tracks, where the straightaways were shorter than the ones in Europe. Yes, there were a number of hellacious wrecks, none more spectacular than the cartwheel that nearly killed Jim Hall at Las Vegas in 1968. But the only driver to die in the Can-Am series was privateer Dick Brown, who crashed during practice for the race at Mosport in 1970. Then again, that's not the whole story. Two weeks before Brown's death, McLaren was killed while testing the new M8D at Goodwood, a circuit that had already been deemed too dangerous for wheel-to-wheel racing. And the following year, Stan Burnett died while testing his homebuilt car at Seattle International Raceway. Still, Can-Am racers benefited from safety regulations that were much stiffer than the ones governing road racing in Europe.

The second race of the series, at Bridgehampton, was enshrined in motorsports history as the event where Hall introduced the modern wing and forever changed the trajectory of the sport. The Chaparral 2E was merely the first of several wild-hair designs to take advantage of the

Can-Am's no-rules-are-good-rules mindset. They weren't all successful; even the revolutionary 2E won only a single race. But each of them deserves a moment in the spotlight. So how about a round of applause for these worthies:

- Trevor Harris's tiny-tired AVS Mk I Shadow, which stood only knee high
- Peter Bryant's Ti22, which was built almost entirely of titanium
- Jack Hoare's Mac's-It Special, which had two-stroke Rotax motors driving each of the four wheels
- Hall's Chaparral 2J "sucker car," which used a two-stroke engine to pioneer the implementation of ground effects
- Porsche's 917/10, which proved that turbocharging could work for road racing

Innovation is all well and good, and sometimes it's great. But tried-and-true designs are the ones that win most of the races. The early years of the Can-Am series were dominated by the clever-but-conventional cars coming out of the McLaren shop in Colnbrook, England. Hall described the M6A, which won the championship in 1967, as "a common car, done uncommonly well," and the same description could be applied to various iterations of the M8 and the M20 to come.[24] Although the McLarens didn't break any new ground, Bruce McLaren and his teammate, Denny Hulme, cleaned up on the racetrack.

In 1970, Hall came up with a concept that would, in theory, crush the McLarens—and every other car on the planet. As he recalled, "I got a fan-mail letter from a young man who had drawn a beanie with four wheels and a propeller on top, and he wrote, 'How about this for downforce?' And I thought to myself, 'Wow, that kid's got something interesting.'"[25] Working with the engineers at Chevrolet R&D, Hall rigged up a two-stroke engine to run a fan that literally sucked the car to the ground. "I tested it at Rattlesnake Raceway, and it was fantastic," he said. "It had so much download that you could actually hang it on the ceiling. You'd get to a corner where you'd been braking at the 3 marker. Hell, you'd go right through the 2 marker, and when you couldn't make yourself drive it any deeper, you'd put your foot on the brake, and you'd

The Chaparral 2J carves through the Esses at Road Atlanta during the Can-Am race in 1970. Vic Elford effortlessly stuck Jim Hall's innovative sucker car on the pole despite stopping to repair an oil leak with an hour to go in qualifying. Although the 2J never won a race, it was so quick, and it obviously had so much potential, that the SCCA banned it at the end of the season. *Bill Warner*

be slowed down to 60 miles an hour before you got to the corner. It was unbelievable!"[26]

Driven by Jackie Stewart and then Vic Elford, the Chaparral 2J showed astonishing pace before being hamstrung by niggling mechanical problems. During qualifying at Riverside for the last race of the season, Elford was a monumental 2.2 seconds faster than Hulme, who'd long since clinched the championship. The sucker car broke yet again in the race, and it never got a chance to redeem itself. Fearful that ground-effects technology would render everything else obsolete, the SCCA banned the 2J, to the eternal frustration of Hall and his team. "The original concept of the Can-Am series was to provide one race series with an absolute minimum of rules to promote engineering innovations," Chaparral engineer Don Gates complained. "Jim Hall's Chaparral Cars is the only entrant that has attempted to fulfill this concept to any degree. Our detractors say that we are not within the spirit of the rule; we contend that they are not within the spirit of the Can-Am series."[27]

Hall split after that. Johnson Wax followed a few years later, and prize money plummeted. But the death knell for the series came, ironically, from another form of technology that rendered the competition obsolete—the turbocharger attached to the flat-12 in the Porsche 917/10. Developed in concert with Mark Donohue and campaigned by Roger Penske, the turbopanzer won the 1972 championship in the hands of George Follmer. The next year, Donohue and Penske returned with the new-and-improved 917/30 and waltzed to another title. By this time, Team McLaren had left the building, and the SCCA turned the lights off on the series in the middle of the 1974 season.

Like the American Civil War, the clash between Goodyear and Firestone pitted brother against brother. Al Unser was a soldier in Firestone's army while Bobby fought for Goodyear. Determined to remain neutral, their father, "Pop" Unser, wore a bespoke "Goodstone" jacket at Indy in 1969. To even the scales, "Mom" Unser dressed up in a "Fireyear" jacket of her own. *Revs Institute / Robert Tronolone Photograph Collection*

CHAPTER ELEVEN

THE TIRE WARS

When you're as rich as J. Frank Harrison Jr., you don't have to flaunt your wealth. Maybe that's why the Firestone guys at Indy didn't know who he was and why they were ready to shine him on when he approached them with a tantalizing business proposition.

It was May 1966. Harrison had entered the Indianapolis 500 with a brand-new car designed and built by crew chief Jerry Eisert. Although he was new to Indy, Harrison had been around racing for a long time, mostly with sports cars—big Maseratis and little Lotuses that cleaned up in SCCA and USAC road races with guys like Lloyd Ruby and Jim Hall behind the wheel. And while he did some racing himself, Harrison was usually content to be the Briggs Cunningham–style patron of the operation, a role he was uniquely qualified to perform.

Harrison's father had been a cousin and business associate of one of the creators of the Coca-Cola empire. Harrison himself was the president of Chattanooga Glass. Remember those green six-and-a-half-ounce bottles Coke used to come in? Chattanooga Glass was the principal supplier for the East Coast. Harrison also owned Dorsey Trailers, which was one of the biggest companies of its kind in the Midwest.

A sharp guy, obviously, and ahead of his time on the car front. In 1963, a month before Colin Chapman changed the course of Indy history at the Speedway, Harrison showed up at Trenton with a rear-engine Lotus 18 Formula 1 chassis cradling a Coventry-Climax engine punched out to 2.7 liters. Although the car was criminally underpowered, Ruby started from the pole and outran a field composed entirely of Offy-powered roadsters until the Colotti gearbox broke after thirty laps in the lead.

Harrison made his debut as an entrant at Indy in 1965 with a space-frame car designed and built by Eisert, but it failed to qualify. The next year, although Eisert upgraded to a monocoque chassis, the Traco-built small-block Chevy didn't have enough juice to get the car up to speed. The four-cam Indy Ford ruled the roost in those days, and all the fast guys had one, but Louis Meyer, who handled Ford's race-engine business, didn't have any motors for sale. On the other hand, Firestone, which was desperate to prevent Goodyear from breaking its decades-long Indy 500 winning streak, had stockpiled several engines just in case any of their contracted teams needed them. So Harrison ambled over to the local Firestone office.

"I understand that you guys have got your arms around a couple of Ford engines," he said.[1]

The Firestone rep was noncommittal. "Yeah."

"Well, how would it be if I could get one of them, and I won't put anything but Firestone tires on my trucks and trailers?"

"Well, how many tires do you buy a year?"

"About two thousand."

That got the rep's attention. "You know what?" he said. "Why don't you get your guys and get your pickup truck and go up to Louis Meyer Incorporated and pick up that Ford engine you just got?"

The lessons to be learned? First, money talks in racing. Always has, always will. Second, the business-to-business strategy was being practiced long before "B2B" deals became a thing in the twenty-first century. Third, and by far the most important, the tire companies exerted an almost immeasurably powerful influence on racing in the 1960s and into the '70s.

History tells us that nothing supercharges the pace of technological development faster than a war, whether between nations or businesses or competing ideologies. In the annals of motorsports, no battles were ever bloodier—metaphorically, for the most part—or more expensive than the ones fought between Firestone, Goodyear, Dunlop, and M&H in USAC, F1, NASCAR, and drag racing. Tires tripled in size, while tire compounds got stickier and treads disappeared. Cornering speeds surged, and accidents followed. But even as the tire manufacturers were spending small fortunes in-house to improve their products, they were spending large fortunes sponsoring drivers and, in some cases, funding entire teams. They trumpeted their successes in "win" ads in magazines and commercials on TV. Even so, the general public never fully appreciated the breadth and depth of the role played by the tire companies. More than any other players in the racing game, tire makers fueled the tremendous commercial growth of the sport in the late 1960s, and their power didn't wane until other big-time sponsors began arriving in appreciable numbers in the early 1970s.

"In 1973, I was with Lloyd Ruby," Mike Devin said. "We had a sponsor in Commander Motorhomes out of Southern California. They picked up the majority of the day-to-day expenses and gave us a truck and a trailer, and we got to keep our prize money to run the team. But Firestone bought me like three Eagles and five engines over a couple of years and gave us a stipend of about $100,000, which was a lot of money in those days. So we were basically a Firestone team."[2] The model worked differently in F1, but the result was pretty much the same. As Jack Brabham recalled, referring to the lean years in Grand Prix racing, "The main thing that saved the sport some years ago was the arrival of the American tyre companies, Firestone and Goodyear. Without the competition between the tyre companies some teams would not have been able to carry on."[3] Case in point: Brabham's $240,000 budget for a two-car team in 1971 was covered almost completely by Goodyear.

Behold the race tire. To those outside the insular racing world, it's a nondescript black rubber doughnut, one indistinguishable from another except for the dimensions and the lettering on the sidewall. To anyone other than a chemical engineer, its properties are mysterious, and its design seems to owe more to alchemy than science. Yet there are few things in life that drivers prize more highly than brand-new tires, with the golden laps that they provide. And for a team manager, constantly sweating over budget numbers that never quite pencil out, there are few deals better than an all-expenses-paid contract with a tire manufacturer.

A clever debater could make a case for the proposition that tires are the single most important component in racing. They're the principal variable where the rubber hits the road, which is to say that the physics of motorsports can be reduced to understanding the behavior of the contact patch—those four roughly rectangular spots where the tires converge with the racing surface, be it asphalt, concrete, dirt, gravel, or water. A computer analysis of F1 results that made the rounds in 1973 suggested that a driver and chassis could affect a ninety-second lap by 0.5 seconds each and an engine by 0.7 seconds while tires supposedly were worth as much as 2.0 seconds. It's not clear how this study was conducted, and the results seem awfully arbitrary. Then again, during the 1980s, teams would gain at least a second by bolting on super-sticky one-lap tires for qualifying, and that time came down almost entirely to the rubber compound.

Precisely because there's so much potential speed in tires, tire development can be a bottomless pit, and when two tire manufacturers decide to square off in a particular arena, the costs tend to be astronomical. That's the major reason most pro series have gone to a spec tire, allowing the tire manufacturers to rule as uncontested monarchs of their private kingdoms—Pirelli in F1, Firestone in IndyCar, Goodyear in NASCAR, and Michelin in IMSA. Typically, tire companies pay sanctioning bodies a fee to secure the right to be the sole supplier of the series, which seems kind of crazy. Then again, the cost of a brokered peace is a hell of a lot cheaper than the price of an all-out war, as the battles fought over Indianapolis would demonstrate.

When Ray Harroun won the first Indy 500 in 1911, his Marmon Wasp was riding on tires that had been manufactured about three hundred miles away in Akron, Ohio, by the Firestone Tire & Rubber Company. Firestones were on the winning car again in 1920 and every year thereafter for the next four and a half decades. The competition melted away over the years until Firestone was left with a monopoly, and progress proceeded at a sluggish pace. Balloon-style tires debuted in 1925, and the status quo persisted for the next quarter-century other than modifying rubber compounds to survive on the abrasive asphalt that replaced the bricks of the Speedway in the late 1930s. In the 1950s, to accommodate the new Indy roadsters, Firestone widened the treads by 50 percent and introduced nylon cords that had been developed during World War II. Still, to modern eyes, the tires look comically tall and narrow, riding on sixteen-inch-diameter wheels at the front and eighteens at the rear. (To reduce wear, the mighty Novi ran *twenty*-inch wheels.) The tires stood about thirty inches high, but the tread width, roughly the size of the actual contact patch, was about five inches, or narrower than a CD case. Since Firestone was the only game in town, there was no reason to invest in upgrades that would dramatically increase cornering speeds, and durability was prized over grip. Eventually, in fact, Firestone would build tires capable of lasting five hundred miles. The tradeoff was that they were as hard as rocks. Drivers called them "flintstones" and joked that if the car started sliding, the tires would throw sparks. Nobody liked them, but everybody used them, so what was the point in complaining?

Everything changed in 1963. The skirmishing began in Southern California, with a shot fired by Mickey Thompson. A human whirlwind wearing a white T-shirt and a buzz cut, Thompson was often described as a hot rodder, which was true as far as it went but about as accurate as calling Bruce Springsteen a guitarist. His modus operandi was to zig when others zagged. In 1963, he showed up at Indy with weirdly streamlined rear-engine cars riding on the tiniest wheels ever seen at the Speedway—twelve inches instead of the normal sixteens and eighteens. Mounted on them were ultrawide tires with a tread width of seven inches at the front and nine at the rear. "Because they are small and I still want good tread life, I just widen the tread," he explained. "I lose some savings on the frontal area, but I gain traction."[4] Thompson had proven this concept at Bonneville with experimental Goodyear tires designed by tire engineer Gene McMannis. He subsequently hired McMannis, who designed a new tire for Thompson's so-called roller skates. Goodyear didn't have an Indy car program—yet—so Thompson agreed to pay some of the development costs if Firestone would manufacture a run of bespoke low-profile tires with a wide tread and soft rubber. Done.

As it happened, Firestone was already committed to building special fifteen-inch tires for the Lotus 29s that Colin Chapman had brought for Dan Gurney and Jim Clark. To be honest, there was no secret technology embedded in these tires; they were smaller than the roadster tires simply because the Lotuses themselves were so much lighter than the hulking front-engine Watson, Kuzma, and Epperly chassis. And like Thompson, the Firestone engineers had widened the footprint to compensate for the loss of height. But when Gurney nearly broke the track record shortly after the track opened, conspiracy theories abounded, and a delegation of angry roadster owners, drivers, and mechanics signed a petition demanding that Firestone withdraw the fifteens or make them available to everybody. Firestone reluctantly agreed to supply the smaller tires, and Parnelli Jones was using four of them on his trusty roadster, Ol' Calhoun, when he took the pole and won the race.

Meanwhile, Firestone was also getting grief from A.J. Foyt. The company had given Smokey Yunick a special tire for his super-lightweight roadster. When Foyt's request for a set of his own was refused, he placed a call to Goodyear's competition manager, Tony Webner. Although Goodyear wasn't playing in the Indy sandbox at the moment, it had the tire to beat in NASCAR. "Listen, we've been runnin' on these skinny cast-iron tires for so long, and puttin' up with no bite on the track, so why don't you all come on down and have a try at it?" Foyt told Webner. "I'll run your tires. And, by the way, bring some of those wide stock car tires with you."[5] Goodyear rented the track for a few weeks after Indy 1963. "Their first batch of tires wasn't much better than the stock car tires they had brought down before the race," Foyt said, "but we had to start somewhere."[6]

The tire wars were about to erupt.

The Goodyear Tire & Rubber Company had been founded in Akron—the Rubber Capital of the World—in 1898, three years before its crosstown rival. Named after Charles Goodyear, the inventor of vulcanized rubber, it was a publicly traded company. This gave it access to greater resources than Firestone, which was still a family-owned concern. Although Goodyear tires had been on the car that won Indy in 1919, the company concentrated on street (and aviation) tires during the next few decades. In 1955, the Carl Kiekhaefer Chrysler 300s ran on Goodyear Police Special tires while spanking the competition in NASCAR. This inspired Goodyear to hire Lee Petty, Richard's father, to conduct tests in 1957 that led to the introduction of the first Stock

Car Special tires. Before long, Goodyear Blue Streaks were dominating stock car racing, scoring a virtual clean sweep of Grand National races in 1962.

But NASCAR was the bush leagues back then, and modified street tires were good enough for the "taxicabs" raced on the Southern circuit. Goodyear's success in the small pond of sports car racing also didn't earn the company much respect from the heavyweights in USAC. Competing for wins at Indy would require a major step up in class. Firestone had more heritage, more institutional knowledge, and more technical expertise. But Goodyear had more money, and corporate executives put it to use by paying Foyt $100,000 to run their tires in 1964. Foyt was the Man in those days, the cockiest, winningest, gnarliest Texan the racing world had ever seen. Jones may have been a tick faster and Jim Hurtubise might have been a touch braver. But nobody could match Foyt's sum of all parts. It didn't matter if it was Indy cars or stock cars, dirt or pavement, sprint races or enduros, Anthony Joseph was the man to beat every time he suited up. Sure enough, he started his annual trek on the Championship Trail by giving Goodyear its first Indy car win by leading all one hundred laps at Phoenix. Then he went flag to flag again at Trenton. But Indy was the big kahuna, and that's where Goodyear's dream season went south.

The 1964 edition of the Indy 500 would prove to be the last stand for the roadsters, and both Foyt and Jones chose to stick with their dinosaurs after testing rear-engine "funny cars." Neither one of them was fast enough to hang with the Lotuses of Clark and Bobby Marshman. But Jones was significantly quicker than Foyt, and tires seemed to be why. Firestone had ramped up its competition department to meet the threat from Goodyear and gone all-in on the lower-profile design that Thompson had used the previous year. While searching through Firestone's R&D archives, tire engineer Bob Martin, who would later run the F1 program, found the design of a tire mold for a corn-planting machine, circa 1934. To clear the furrows in the field, the tires were built so that the center section, holding the tread, drooped instead of forming a conventional crown so that it looked concave when viewed head-on. Under load on the racetrack, the tires flattened out, increasing the contact patch. This type of depressed-crown construction proved to be well suited to the lower-profile tires that were being developed. The only way Goodyear could keep up with Firestone was by using a softer compound that compromised durability. In the middle of the month, a frustrated Foyt switched back to Firestone tires (though he retained his ties to Goodyear). So did the other thirteen drivers who'd been practicing on Goodyears.

Instead of jumping on the Firestone Wide Oval bandwagon, Chapman insisted on running his Lotuses on beefed-up versions of the Dunlop tires he used in F1. Bad call. Although Clark qualified on the pole, the Dunlops couldn't handle the sustained high speeds around the Speedway, and Clark's suspension broke when a tire chunked while he was leading. Gurney's Dunlop-shod sister car was withdrawn just to be safe. Marshman broke. Jones was engulfed in a pit fire. With all the other fast guys gone, Foyt took the lead on lap fifty-four and never relinquished it. (He never changed tires either.) In Victory Circle, still wearing a Goodyear uniform, he graciously thanked Raymond Firestone for his contributions to the sport, but he refused to cash the $15,000 check Firestone wrote to the winner.

Goodyear left the race with egg on its face—and a vow never to be humiliated like that again. Both Goodyear and Firestone established outposts in England to squabble with Dunlop for supremacy in Formula 1, but it was in the United States that the battles were fought with that special ferocity unique to civil wars. In 1965, seventeen of the starters in the 500 were contracted with Firestone, the remaining sixteen with Goodyear. Ditto for 1966. The next year, brothers Bobby and Al Unser found themselves in opposite camps, so their father wore a jacket advertising "Goodstone" while their mother's jacket promoted "Fireyear."

It was a zero-sum game, and the tire companies enlisted as many teams and drivers as they could. Foyt was the deadliest arrow in Goodyear's quiver. The next big addition was Gurney, who'd just formed All American Racers with Carroll Shelby. "He had all the stock," Gurney joked, "and I had all the work."[7] But it was Goodyear that paid most of the freight. Gordon Johncock was another important hire. "I used to do a lot of testing for Goodyear," he said. "They wanted me to have a team, so

When the tire war erupted at Indy in 1964, drivers had to choose sides. Parnelli Jones, left, stuck with Firestone, and the company rewarded him with a chain of tire stores that made him a wealthy man. His great rival, A.J. Foyt, defected to Goodyear—sort of. He switched to the faster Firestones for the race, which he went on to win. But he still wore his Goodyear fire suit in Victory Lane. *Indianapolis Motor Speedway*

I set it up, and they funded it."[8] Since it had been around longer, Firestone had already locked up a lot of the more established studs like Jones, Ruby, and Rodger Ward. But Ward was ready to retire, Jones was getting ready to quit racing open-wheel cars, and Ruby was pushing forty. Firestone needed some new blood. Firestone rep Jim Cook was at Daytona while Ford was testing the Ford GT Mk II Le Mans racer before the start of the 1966 season. When he heard a rumor that Goodyear was making an offer to Mario Andretti, Cook frantically called his bosses in Akron and told them to come up with something better. Andretti was quickly signed to a four-year Firestone deal reportedly worth $250,000 annually. Not that Cook and Firestone always got their man. As he recalled, "We made a deal with Roger Penske, and the son of a gun went across town and made a better deal with Goodyear."[9]

Several other drivers had similar contracts at a time when salaries for the biggest superstars in stick-and-ball sports topped out at around $100,000. The tire company money was on top of the typical arrangement most drivers had with their owners—40 percent of the prize money, 50 percent for a win. Dave Lockton, who worked as a sports agent representing many of these drivers before becoming the founder of Ontario Motor Speedway, said that in 1967 ten of the thirteen best-paid athletes in the world were race car drivers, thanks primarily to tire contracts. "Vel Miletich and Parnelli Jones, A.J. Foyt and Mario Andretti made even more from their other tire deals," Lockton said. "Firestone or Goodyear provided extremely lucrative arrangements enabling them to build chains of Firestone and Goodyear tire stores, where the real estate alone would become worth tens of millions of dollars, and that dwarfed what they were directly pulling down as athletes."[10]

Both Goodyear and Firestone admitted to investing something like $10 million a year on racing in the 1960s. "We could have built a new, fully modern tire plant for what we were spending on racing," Firestone tire engineer Greg Foust said.[11] Money was no object, and winning was everything. At Indy in 1966, Goodyear program manager Leo Mehl was bombarded with calls from the top brass in Akron. "Management kept asking us, 'What's the problem? Do you need more people? Do you need more money? More equipment? What is it?'"[12] The easiest approach, though not necessarily the best, was to sign up as many drivers as possible. "It was the battle for the drivers that screwed it all up," said Humpy Wheeler, who was working for Firestone at this time. "Most of the drivers were honest. But there were no written contracts. You just handed them a check and hoped they honored their commitments. But some of them took money from both companies."[13]

Switching from one manufacturer to the other was common in NASCAR, where the tire deals were much smaller. Firestone had a points fund for its drivers, and both companies offered free tires to favored teams. But the ties that bound a team to a manufacturer weren't very tight. Not only did teams change tires from race to race, but some of them swapped brands *during* races. Still, Le Mans was the site of the most galling tire-company defection. Fees paid by Firestone to test tires kept Bruce McLaren's fledgling team afloat in 1964 and 1965. So when he went to Le Mans in 1966 to drive a Ford GT Mark II for Shelby American, he insisted on using Firestones even though team principal Carroll Shelby was one of Goodyear's biggest competition-tire dealers. Early in the race, the Firestone intermediate tires were junk on the wet-dry track. After falling behind by two laps, McLaren decided to bolt on a set of Goodyears, his Firestone deal be damned. McLaren ending up winning the race—on Goodyears. On the victory rostrum, he quaffed champagne while wearing a sheepish smile and a driver's suit with a prominent Firestone patch.

It was a strange kind of war. Most of the combatants were engineers and chemists, many with advanced degrees, who'd been assigned to the competition department precisely because they were so bright and conscientious. They lived in the same neighborhoods in Akron, and they frequented the same hotels and restaurants on the road. So it wasn't like they were shivving each other in back alleys or hiring hit men to take out the competition. "I knew a lot of the Goodyear guys," Foust said. "We'd go to seven o'clock Mass together, and then we'd see each other at the track. And we respected each other. But Goodyear and Firestone were dire enemies, so there wasn't a whole lotta love between us."[14]

The competition departments expanded, but not as dramatically as the budget numbers would suggest. For better or worse, there was only so much that could be done in the lab. Tire molds took a long time to develop, so they couldn't be modified from race to race, which meant that dimensions such as tread width and aspect ratio remained constant for months at a time. Rubber compounds, on the other hand, could be modified more quickly as company chemists whipped up mysterious concoctions full of hardeners, softeners, oils, waxes, accelerators, stabilizers, and just about every other ingredient short of eye of newt and toe of frog. Even as practice was progressing at Indy in 1965, the Firestone factory continued to churn out new tires. "I kept having to run out to the airport with a station wagon to pick up the sets that had been produced in Akron," Firestone tire engineer Hal Horton recalled. "One time, as I was picking up four tires, the airport guy says to me, 'Boy, it's really something. Goodyear is sending more Firestone tires back to Akron than you're picking up.'"[15]

Both companies foiled future attempts at industrial espionage by creating elaborate systems to track the whereabouts of every tire they produced, and then they doubled down on development. In 1973, Firestone factories spit out ninety-two thousand race tires. Goodyear, meanwhile, produced about three hundred compounds, though only thirty were actually tested on the track. In those predigital days, computer simulations weren't sophisticated enough to accurately predict performance, and only so much could be learned from the in-house test rigs. So both companies embarked on punishing racetrack test programs that kept their people on the road for as much as 250 days a year. "Nobody was harder on tires than Gordie Johncock," said one of Johncock's longtime mechanics, John Anderson. "We seemed to be testing all the time, day and night."[16]

Although some drivers considered tire testing a chore, others, like Andretti, relished the opportunity to get extra seat time and unlock the secrets of tire performance. For mechanics, testing was a win-win. During the offseason, it got them out of the snowy Midwest to sunny racetracks in Arizona and California, and they were paid a daily fee and a per diem. "It wasn't a lot, but it was extra money in our pocket," Mike Lashmett said. "When I was working at Patrick Racing, we'd take one car in a Kaufman trailer and everything we needed to run it, and Gordie would fly in later. It would be me, him, George [Bignotti], George Jr., two or three Goodyear, guys and *lots* of tires. And it just went on all day long."[17]

Relentless development in the laboratory and testing on the racetrack, coupled with the fierce competition between Goodyear and Firestone, led to astonishing technological advances. This was seen most visibly in the radical changes in the size and shape of tires. In 1963, the typical tread width was five inches, and tires were mounted on sixteen-inch wheels at the front and eighteen inchers at the rear. By 1969, fifteen-inch-diameter wheels were pretty much standard, and USAC capped tread width at ten inches in front and fourteen inches in the rear, partly at the request of the tire manufacturers. As Mehl said at the time, "The tires would have been so good that they would have stifled competition, and we didn't want that."[18] Meanwhile, as tire width nearly doubled, the aspect ratio, which describes the relationship between the height of the sidewall and the width of the tire, was cut in half, from 0.70 in 1963 to 0.35 in 1969. A low-profile tire—that is, one with a shorter sidewall coupled with a wider tire—increases the contact patch while raising cornering capability. (As a bonus, it can be mounted on a wheel that leaves room for larger brakes.) In 1963, the fast cars were going through Turn One at Indy at 142 miles per hour. By 1969, they were doing 158 mph. Corner speeds rose even more dramatically in the 1970s, but with the addition of wings, it's hard to isolate how much of the improvement was due to downforce rather than mechanical grip.

Progress comes with a price, and the price isn't always calculated in dollars and cents. "When you get competition, people push the envelope, right?" said John Watson, who went on to win five Formula 1 races after nearly being killed when a tire deflated in a flat-out right-hander during Formula 2 practice at Rouen in 1970.[19] His Brabham BT30 clipped a barrier, and he broke an arm and a leg and fractured an ankle. (Coincidentally, two French Formula 3 drivers were killed and a third critically injured at the track that same weekend.) "There was no conscious decision by any tire company to make an unsafe product," Watson said. "But in the process of trying to get ahead of your competitor, decisions were made, and sometimes, sadly, they were the wrong decisions."[20]

The tragic consequences of unfettered competition were felt first in NASCAR. After seeing Goodyear bring its stock car expertise to Indy, Firestone decided that turnabout was fair play. In 1964, Firestone paid Petty Enterprises $50,000 to run its tires, and several other drivers came on board. At the same time, Chrysler had introduced its thunderous

Hemi. Supporting a two-ton stock car going 170 mph was a tough task, and the tires weren't always up to it. In the Atlanta 500, tires blew almost as fast as they could be mounted. Paul Goldsmith hit the wall after losing a tire while leading. Drivers started calling their tires maypops because that's what they were fixing to do. "I'm afraid that someone may die before any safety measures are taken," Richard Petty declared.[21]

Fireball Roberts was killed at Charlotte six weeks later, and Fred Lorenzen nearly bled to death after crashing at Daytona five weeks after that. "The cars are going too fast for the tracks," Junior Johnson said. "We haven't learned enough to keep the cars handling safely at the speeds we can now travel. And the tire companies are having trouble developing compounds that will give adequate tire wear."[22] For the record, tires had nothing to do with either wreck, but that didn't stop drivers from worrying. As Wheeler recalled, "They couldn't understand why all this stuff was happening, and they were spooked by the whole thing."[23]

Even though the Grand National schedule featured sixty-two races (!) in 1964, the tire companies still found time for testing. In September, during a Goodyear tire test at Charlotte, Jimmy Pardue broke the lap record. On the next lap, a tire exploded. He shot through a wooden guardrail, sailed over a seventy-five-foot embankment, and burrowed, head on, into a chain-link fence 150 yards away before flipping over and landing in a dry creek bed. He died during surgery two hours later. In January 1965, Goodyear orchestrated another big tire test at Daytona. One of the principal players was Billy Wade, who'd landed a sweet ride with Bud Moore's top-flight operation after Joe Weatherly was killed at Riverside in early 1964. Wade enjoyed a solid season highlighted by a miraculous never-to-be-repeated swing through New York and New Jersey where he won four consecutive Grand National races in ten days. At Daytona, a front tire let go, and he was killed when he hit the wall. Ironically, the test had been scheduled to evaluate Goodyear's new inner liner, which was a tube with its own dedicated air supply mounted inside a larger tire. The idea was that, even if the tire blew, the inner liner would produce enough structural rigidity to prevent an accident.

Tire testing in Indy cars proved to be equally dangerous. In October 1964, Jim McElreath was badly burned when he crashed in an Offy-powered Brabham BT12 during a test at Indy, but he recovered quickly enough that he missed only one race. Then, after the season ended at Phoenix International, Marshman hung around to test for Ford, with the Firestone guys helping out. He crashed and burned when the throttle reportedly stuck while he was going 145 mph. "I accompanied him to the hospital," Foust said. "Some people go to the races to see wrecks. Well, those wrecks scared the crap out of us. We knew that our best friends were putting their lives at risk, and we lost a few of them along the way. It was a very traumatic period."[24] Marshman died six days after the accident.

War is a contagion that spreads until one side declares victory or the other loses the will to fight any longer. The tire war had commenced at Indy, then jumped to NASCAR, sports cars, and drag racing. Eventually, it crossed the Atlantic Ocean and established a new beachhead in Europe. In 1964, the Goodyear International Racing Division opened in Wolverhampton, near Birmingham. The next year, Firestone created a competition department of its own in West London. The battles that resulted would be more complicated than the ones being fought in the States because they involved not just two but three combatants—Firestone and Goodyear, naturally, but also Dunlop, the English company that had reigned supreme until the colonial interlopers arrived.

Unlike Indy cars, Formula 1 had long enjoyed competition between tire manufacturers. At various times during the 1950s, Grand Prix cars raced on tires produced by Englebert, Pirelli, Avon, Dunlop, and Continental. By 1959, Dunlop was the only company left standing. Established in 1889, Dunlop Rubber was older than both Firestone and Goodyear. It had helped pioneer the concept of the multinational corporation, and at one point, Fort Dunlop—its corporate complex in Birmingham—was the largest factory in the world.

During the years when Dunlop had a monopoly in F1, development slowed to the point that drivers were able to use the same set of tires for multiple Grands Prix. But with Goodyear setting up shop only a few miles away from Fort Dunlop, the R&D department got busy. In 1964, Dunlop increased the tread width of front tires from four inches to six inches and the rears from five inches to seven inches. The company also began offering thirteen-inch tires along with traditional fifteen inchers. The aspect ratio came down to 0.58, which wasn't quite low-profile—0.50 is the usual line of demarcation—but was getting close. By the end of the season, the state-of-the-art R6 model was probably worth about a second over a ninety-second lap.

During the month between the Italian and US Grands Prix, Goodyear paid BRM twenty-five dollars per mile, plus expenses, to test its new tires at Riverside. Goodyear also made the team an attractive offer to supply tires in 1965. Graham Hill briefly tested the new Goodyears on his spare BRM at Kyalami during the first race of the year but decided to stick with the Dunlop R6. The calculations were different for Dan Gurney, who was driving for Jack Brabham. Goodyear had been instrumental in getting All American Racers off the ground, and Gurney had scored a class win at Le Mans in a Goodyear-shod Cobra Daytona Coupe the previous year. He realized that the Dunlops were faster, but as he explained, "I knew Goodyear was not quite ready for top-line F1 competition, but I also realized that they intended to have a real go. So I decided to take the plunge and pull Jack in as well."[25] Goodyear sweetened the deal by paying Brabham $28,000, which was $28,000 more than he—or any other team—was getting from Dunlop, whose sponsorship was limited to free tires. Goodyear also signed up the struggling Honda team, which was coming off a miserable year in 1964, its inaugural season in F1. This turned out to be a smart move. Although Gurney podiumed in the last five races of the year, it was Richie Ginther who gave Goodyear its first F1 win, aboard the Honda RA272, in the rarified altitude of Mexico City in the final race of the 1.5-liter formula.

Firestone's F1 tires debuted in 1966. Chapman, who'd enjoyed a successful—and profitable—relationship with Firestone at Indy, was the only major team to tie the knot with the newcomer. Not that it really mattered. This was the free love era of F1 tire selection, and monogamy was out of style. Even though Ferrari was contracted with Dunlop, it tested Goodyears and Firestones at Zandvoort, and when Ludovico Scarfiotti won the Italian Grand Prix in his twelve-cylinder Ferrari 312, producing almost hallucinatory levels of joy among the *tifosi*, he gave Firestone its maiden victory in F1. That said, the three tire companies were well matched, with Goodyear winning four races, Dunlop three, and Firestone two. But there were disquieting signs that Dunlop was in danger of being priced out of the game.

In 1967, the Americans were fully up to speed—and speedier than the Brits. While Goodyear and Firestone could crank out new tread patterns and compounds in a few days, Dunlop needed a couple of weeks. At the start of the season, BRM was the only major team aligned with Dunlop. But as the season progressed and the tire performance

Even as Rick Ramsey scored one of the last big wins for the soon-to-be-obsolete front-engine Top Fuel slingshots in the NHRA Supernationals at Ontario Motor Speedway in 1970, his wrinkle-wall Goodyears embodied the future of tire technology. Coupled with the development of more forgiving slipper clutches, the extra traction produced by tires designed to deform—and increase the contact patch—at launch caused elapsed times to plummet. *Revs Institute / Pete Biro Photograph Collection*

gap grew, even BRM jumped ship and signed with Goodyear. Peak humiliation arrived at the British Grand Prix at Silverstone, the central hub of British racing. Gazing down at the grid from the Dunlop Tower, company executives saw only one car on their tires—a sad, outdated Cooper driven by Swiss privateer Silvio Moser, who was making his F1 debut after qualifying next to last, 7.6 seconds off the pole. Dunlop general manager L.J. W. Bailey, who'd been an artillery officer at Dunkirk, ordered the development team into his office and gave them a curt directive: Beat the Americans. It was too late to do anything in 1967, when Firestone (six wins) and Goodyear (five wins) split the spoils. But Bailey's command ensured that 1968 would turn out to be the most competitive season, tire-wise, in F1 history.

After the debacle the previous year, Dunlop was able to sign only one team in 1968, and it was French rather than British. Matra was making its F1 debut. Normally, you wouldn't expect much from a newcomer. But Matra held a trump card in the form of Jackie Stewart, who'd established himself as the best driver on the Grand Prix circuit after Clark died at Hockenheim. To increase its chances of success, Dunlop brought fifty tires per car to the races and put extra effort into developing wet-weather rubber. It hit the jackpot when Stewart won the Dutch Grand Prix in heavy rain and prevailed again in even more abysmal conditions at the Nürburgring. (Curiously, the wet French Grand Prix went to Jacky Ickx in a Firestone-shod Ferrari.) Another Stewart master class at Watkins Glen gave Dunlop three wins for the year against Firestone's six and Goodyear's three. The next year, Dunlop came out on top with six wins.

At this point, it was clear that any tire manufacturer that stood still would be left behind. As journalist José Rosinski wrote, "Racing-tire technology had reached such a level of sophistication that the classical distinctions between rain, damp and dry qualities were no longer sufficiently precise. It had become necessary to add to the equation the notion of matching the tire to the circuit, each circuit naturally presenting a special case for the manufacturer to deal with. Taken to extremes, this meant that they would have to produce a different tire for each circuit, designed to suit not only the atmospheric conditions but also the surface and layout of the track."[26]

In 1970, Dunlop managed only two victories, again, both thanks to Stewart. By this point, the company was negotiating what turned out to be a disastrous merger with Pirelli, and it clearly didn't have the technical or financial means to match Goodyear tire for tire. Dunlop quit racing at the end of the season, with twenty different F1 tire models, eighty-three Grand Prix wins, and eight world championships to its credit. Corporate execs claimed that abandoning the F1 arena would save the company $600,000 a year, which, if accurate, highlights how badly Dunlop was being outspent by its American rivals. In *Motor Sport*, William Boddy put a curmudgeonly spin on Dunlop's decision: "It could well be that Dunlop realise that the supply of tyres for present-day GP projectiles has become a bit of a farce, unacceptable to the public at large, and that this, coupled with the fact that once upon a time drivers used to come to the Fort, helmets in hand as it were, pleading for tyres that would stand up to the tasks they had in mind, whereas, in the seventies, it is the managers, the Mr. 10%s, who arrive with contracts in their fists, asking how much lolly Dunlop will pay to sign up their drivers, which prompted this most unhappy ending of Dunlop's long association with top motor racing."[27]

Dunlop wasn't the only company that saw the writing on the wall. Firestone had been threatening to bail for years. It sometimes seemed as if the main reason it stuck around wasn't because racing made business sense but because the Firestone family couldn't stomach the idea of surrendering to Goodyear. Whatever the reason, Firestone's fortunes in F1 climaxed in 1970, when it won ten races and Goodyear managed only one. *Take that, you bastards!* And Firestone had one more bullet in the chamber for 1971, what one journalist breathlessly described as "the miracle device that, almost secretly used by [Lotus driver Emerson] Fittipaldi at Kyalami's second day of practice, had enabled him, to his amazement, to make a full two seconds improvement on his Thursday times."[28] The slick tire had come to road racing.

The treadless tire seemed to be such a logical end point in the eternal quest for a larger and more effective contact patch that it raised an even more obvious question: Why wasn't it invented sooner? Actually, "invented" is the wrong word since slicks had been standard equipment in drag racing for more than a decade. And to be honest, there was so little tread on the tires by 1971 that going to a full slick didn't send drivers into hyperspace. Grip increased dramatically not simply because the surface was flat, but also because the flat surface was stretched over such a wide area, creating an enormous contact patch.

Tires are a major source of drag in open-wheel cars, and larger tires mean more drag. (As a side note, this is why Firestone produced a one-off tire for the ten-inch wheels that designer/mad scientist Trevor Harris specced for his low-low-*low*-line Shadow Can-Am car in 1970.) To minimize drag, thirteen-inch wheels replaced fifteen inchers as the norm. As the wheels got smaller, the tires got wider. By 1973, tires were roughly nine inches wide at the front and fourteen inches at the rear. With ultralow-profile aspect ratios as low as 0.30, this translated into gargantuan tires measuring twenty inches in diameter at the front and twenty-six inches at the rear.

Much like test pilots exploring new flight regimes, drivers equipped with these huge, super-grippy tires were exposed to behavior they'd never experienced before. "I don't think they understood the technology too well," Howden Ganley said. "In Formula 5000, I encountered this strange vibration running through the car. I complained to the Goodyear engineer, and he said, 'Yeah, we didn't know what causes it, but it's happening in Formula 1, too.' Shortly afterward, I was driving for BRM on Firestones, and I felt this weird vibration. It was so bad that it would flutter your eyeballs, and you'd go blind for a while. Anyway, I went to Silverstone so they could film the tires in slow motion. When I said I'd like to see the film, the engineer told me, 'You do *not* want to see that film. It will really put you off.' So I never did see it. But apparently it was terribly scary stuff."[29]

A deflating tire probably caused the accident that killed Clark in 1968. In 1969, tire failures were blamed for crashes that shattered Brabham's ankle during a test at Silverstone and broke both of Graham Hill's legs at Watkins Glen during the US Grand Prix. The next year, another blown tire left Brabham upside down in the catch fencing at Zandvoort. The typical failure mode worked like this: Tire deflates and spins off the rim at high speed. "Oh, shit!" moment ensues. Retaining screws, sometimes called safety pegs, were drilled into the wheels to secure the tires. But by 1971, tires were being worked so hard that they still came off the wheels on four occasions—at Zandvoort, Andretti and Clay Regazzoni, both in Ferrari 312Bs; at Monza, Rolf Stommelen in a Surtees TS9 (at 180 mph); and at Watkins Glen, Mike Hailwood in another TS9. Although some of the resulting crashes were heavy, none of the drivers were hurt.

In 1972, Firestone beat Goodyear 7–5, thanks to wins by Lotus, Ferrari, and BRM. But Fittipaldi's world-championship-clinching victory in the Italian Grand Prix was the last time Firestone would see a checkered flag in Formula 1, though the company skulked around the Grand Prix circuit for a few more years, supplying back-marker teams and no-hope privateers. In 1975, every car on the grid raced on Goodyears—even the Parnelli VPJ4 driven by Firestone's biggest star (Andretti) and owned by one of its biggest dealers (Jones). The tire wars didn't end with an unconditional surrender. Like old soldiers, they just faded away.

But nature abhors a vacuum, so Goodyear didn't have the field to itself for long. Michelin crashed the F1 party in 1977, and Pirelli showed up fashionably late in 1981. Goodyear was finally driven out of F1 in 1998 by Bridgestone, the Japanese conglomerate whose subsidiaries included—in a crowning irony—Firestone. Then Bridgestone and Michelin duked it out for a couple of years before realizing that there are no winners in a tire war. In 2011, Pirelli became the sole supplier for Formula 1, just as Firestone/Bridgestone is the only player in IndyCar, as is Goodyear in NASCAR and Michelin in IMSA.

And so the swords were beaten into plowshares, and the people were happy. Most of them, anyway. But there are those who pine for the days when the tire companies funded entire race teams and stickier tires materialized magically each race weekend. When it was possible to play one manufacturer against the other and persuade engineers to develop a tire optimized for your particular needs. Alas, it's hard to imagine that history will repeat itself on the tire front. Such is life. And you know what they say: Peace is hell.

AN ENGINE FOR EVERYMAN

The Cosworth DFV doesn't belong on the list of most innovative race engines of all time. It didn't pioneer any revolutionary architecture, didn't feature any groundbreaking metallurgy, didn't change the direction of engine design. It was brilliantly executed, no doubt, and worthy of study and emulation, but relatively conventional, and there's nothing wrong with that. Still, if you put together a list of the most *important* race engines of all time, the Cossie is a consensus first-round pick. Not only because it won 155 of 262 races in an eighteen-year stretch. But because it also was an essential ingredient in fueling the tremendous expansion of Formula 1 in the late 1960s and through the '70s by enabling a host of newcomers to flourish.

"The Cosworth was a modern V-8 engine that was compact, lightweight, gave good horsepower, was fundamentally reliable, and relatively cheap," said John Watson, who scored all five of his Formula 1 wins in DFV-powered cars. "It was in the right place at the right time. It enabled Formula 1 to move on from what had previously been a slightly elitist sport, and it opened up the door to small entrepreneurial motor-racing team owners. Many of the teams that ended up in Formula 1 never would have made it had it not been for Cosworth and, in fairness, Mike Hewland, who made the gearboxes. Formula 1 would never be the business, industry, sport, profession that it is today if it weren't for the Cosworth."[30]

Cosworth is a portmanteau for Mike Costin and Keith Duckworth. Costin was the practical engineer, Duckworth the design genius—and, yes, that's the correct term. They formed Cosworth Engineering in 1958 while they were both working for Colin Chapman. In fact, Costin stayed on at Lotus for several years while Duckworth ran the business. Working in converted stables with no toilet, Duckworth began modifying pushrod Ford Anglia engines for Formula Junior racing. Later, he developed the twin-cam head used successfully on Lotus Cortinas. This led to the SCA, for Single Camshaft Series A, which won Formula 2 championships in 1964 and 1965.

By this time, Coventry Climax, the longtime engine supplier for British Formula 1 teams, had announced that it didn't plan to develop a powerplant for the new 3.0-liter formula scheduled to begin in 1966. Duckworth was already working on an all-new FVA four-valve F2 engine. Chapman, one of racing's greatest idea men, wondered what it would take to put two of them together on a common crankshaft to create a world-beating F1 engine. "Well," Duckworth said, "let's suppose we have to make five engines, do the design, and a bit of development. On the back-of-an-envelope basis, about £100,000 will be needed to do the job properly."[31] Converted to Yankee Benjamins, that was $280,000. Or translated into a universal form of currency, peanuts.

Peanuts, yes, but peanuts that neither of them had. After striking out elsewhere, they approached Walter Hayes. An urbane and charming pipe smoker who'd worked as a powerful Fleet Street editor, he now ran Ford of Great Britain's public relations operation and was so highly regarded within the company that he had a direct line to CEO Henry

Mike Costin, left, and Keith Duckworth, center, were the cofounders of Cosworth. Duckworth was the principal designer of the Cosworth DFV, the robust, compact, and cost-effective 3.0-liter V-8 that won 155 of 262 Formula 1 races between 1967 and 1985 and helped launch more than a dozen F1 teams. Walter Hayes, right, was the dapper Ford executive who persuaded Henry Ford II to fund the development program. *Ford Motor Company*

Ford II. Hayes agreed to pay Duckworth $280,000, but he demanded an F2 engine as well as an F1 motor. "I wanted to see the little one built first, because, frankly, I thought that if the little one worked, then the big one was sure to work," he explained.[32] To get the project approved, he pitched the Deuce directly. "It will be the best £100,000 you ever invested," Hayes told his boss.[33] Bull's-eye.

The Cosworth Double Four Valve was a twin-cam engine with one spark plug per cylinder, cup-type cam followers, dry sump lubrication, and spur gears driving just about everything. The compact dimensions and structural rigidity of the motor were necessary because Chapman planned to use it as a stressed member of his new Lotus 49. Although the free-breathing head design demanded an orthodox pent-roof combustion chamber and flat-top pistons, Duckworth departed from—and rewrote—conventional wisdom by speccing a remarkably narrow (by the standards of the day) included valve angle of thirty-two degrees. Careful attention to porting and crankcase windage paid huge dividends and pointed the way forward. As Duckworth would say later, "In terms of air flow, and flow management, today's F1 engine uses exactly the same principles that I established 25 years earlier."[34]

When it appeared in 1967, the DFV made 405 horsepower at 9,000 rpm. In its debut in the Dutch Grand Prix, Graham Hill was the fastest qualifier in his Lotus 49, while his teammate, Jim Clark, won the race—an exceedingly rare first-time-out win for both car and engine. Clark won three more Grands Prix that season. The DFV was so good, in fact, that Hayes was afraid it might destroy F1. So despite Chapman's objections, he insisted that the engine be offered for sale. Cosworth put it on the market in 1968 at a very friendly price of $17,600. (Depending on the precise spec, a turbo Offy was going for about $22,500 at the time, a four-cam Indy Ford for roughly $27,000, and a turbocharged version for more like $35,000.) DFVs were found in McLarens, Matras, and Lotuses in 1968. Brabham and Williams followed suit in 1969, then March, Tyrrell, Surtees, and de Tomaso the year after that. Before too long, the question was: Which teams *weren't* running Cosworths? Answer: only Ferrari, BRM, and Matra.

Performance upgrades arrived every season: 430 horsepower at 9,500 rpm in 1969, 450 horsepower at 10,000 rpm in 1971, and 460 horsepower at 10,250 rpm in 1973. And yet the price tag remained stable for several years before dropping—yes, dropping—to $15,300 in 1971. It went back up to $16,800 in 1973, but this was still lower than the original cost. Between 1968 and 1973, more than one hundred engines were built. And not once during this stretch did anything other than DFV-powered cars win the constructors' championship.

The availability and relative affordability of the Cosworth was a critical element in the creation of nearly two dozen teams that made it to Formula 1. Granted, some of them barely lasted a blink of the eye. Does Martini ring a bell? Didn't think so. How about Maki and Token? Then again, consider all the teams that won their first F1 races with DFVs providing the power—McLaren, Tyrrell, Matra, March, Shadow, Hesketh, Penske, Williams, Wolf. And there were a bunch of Cosworth teams like Arrows, Surtees, Copersucar, and Ensign that never made it to the top step of the podium but came close on a couple of occasions.

The DFV scored its last win in 1983, with Michele Alboreto driving a Tyrrell to victory in the Detroit Grand Prix. By the time production ceased in 1985, about 380 engines had been built. What ultimately killed the Cosworth wasn't old age; it was turbocharging. But what one hand giveth, the other taketh away. After seeing how the DFV performed in the VPJ4 driven by Mario Andretti, car owner Parnelli Jones thought it might have a future in Indy car racing. He and the Vel's Parnelli Jones Racing team destroked an F1 engine to 2.65 liters and added a turbocharger. Al Unser scored the mongrel motor's first victory in the Pocono 500 in 1976. Duckworth happened to be attending the race as a guest. He was so impressed that, to Jones's eternal indignation, he decided to build Indy car engines in-house.

The Cosworth DFX, as it was designated, instantly rendered the turbo Offy obsolete and won every Indy 500 from 1978 to 1987. It continued to monopolize Indy car racing until the Chevy-badged Ilmor engine debuted in 1986. By the time it was mothballed, DFXs had won 153 Indy car races to go along with the DFV's 155 F1 wins. Somewhere, Walter Hayes was puffing on his pipe and saying, "I told you so."

Richard Petty informs the press that members of the Professional Drivers Association—every top NASCAR driver other than Bobby Issac—were boycotting the inaugural race at the new superspeedway that Bill France had built at Talladega in 1969 because the tires weren't up to the speeds. Petty and the PDA won the battle, but France won the war, and efforts to unionize NASCAR soon fizzled. *Bryant McMurray, courtesy of J. Murrey Atkins Library, UNC Charlotte*

CHAPTER TWELVE

THE STATE OF THE UNIONS

Curtis Turner was as slick a piece of work ever to emerge from the Blue Ridge Mountains. The son of a moonshiner in Floyd County, North Carolina, Turner was trippin' whiskey by the time he was sixteen, earning fifty dollars a keg while snapping bootlegger's turns on Thunder Road to steer clear of the revenuers. "Pops" was tall and solidly built, like a college quarterback after a few years of seasoning, with a granite jaw, twinkling eyes, and a shock of brown hair that broke like a wave on his forehead. Unimpeachable sources claim that he once showed up late for a race at Columbia Speedway, a rough-around-the-edges dirt track in South Carolina, in a brown pinstriped suit, cordovan wing-tipped oxfords, brown silk socks held up by garters, a button-down white shirt, and a banker's tie. After shedding his jacket, he led the first 134 laps before finishing second. Affable and accommodating, with an endless supply of easygoing charm, Turner was the life of extravagant parties that lasted until the police arrived to shut them down or the Canadian Club and Coke ran out. A showman par excellence and an aviator of incomparable ability (if questionable judgment), he once landed his twin-engine Aero Commander on the main street of Easley, South

Carolina, to pick up a bottle of whiskey from a friend, then nearly clipped a police cruiser on his low-level flight out of town. Couple his beyond-the-racetrack exploits with car control skills that amazed even his fellow drivers, and it's not hard to understand why he became stock car racing's first legitimate superstar.

But Turner was more than a good ol' boy partial to Stetsons and aviator sunglasses. He was also an astute businessman with a nose for sweetheart deals and the ability to negotiate a hard bargain. At various points, he ran sawmills, bought and sold timber, dealt in real estate, dabbled in the jukebox business, and owned a small bank. He was shrewd enough to know that there was no money in owning his own race cars, which is why, for most of his career, he collected a paycheck from Ford Motor Company as a factory driver in addition to earning a cut of the prize money he won. But after Bill France built Daytona International Speedway, NASCAR seemed to be on the brink of a period of unprecedented prosperity, and Turner thought it might be a propitious time to get into the racetrack-owning business. Employing financial gymnastics that would have befuddled a Harvard Business School professor, Turner cobbled together a $2.3 million deal and partnered with race promoter (and Bill France antagonist-to-be) Bruton Smith to build a state-of-the-art banked oval on property he owned near Charlotte.

Charlotte Motor Speedway was built in less than a year, with the last of the paving completed a couple of days before the first World 600 was staged in 1960. Thanks to the rough, pockmarked surface and the unusual length of the race, the event was a train wreck. Forty-three of the sixty starters broke, and Joe Lee Johnson won by four laps. (Turner led for twenty-one laps.) Construction cost overruns and a revenue shortfall left Turner drowning in debt. After exhausting more conventional options, he negotiated an $800,000 loan from an unorthodox source—the International Brotherhood of Teamsters. In return, Turner was supposed to form and populate a race car drivers' union.

Organized labor was desperate to find a foothold in the South. A union drive called Operation Dixie had been mounted after World War II, but it failed dismally. Since then, most states south of the Mason-Dixon Line had passed right-to-work laws that blunted the appeal of unions. Now, the Teamsters were gambling that a figure as well-known, respected, and charismatic as Turner could at least organize his fellow drivers, and from this tiny acorn, they hoped, a mighty oak tree might grow. By this time, the track's financial woes had enabled Turner's rivals to elbow him out of the Charlotte management group, and he was eager to play ball with the Teamsters because he figured he could use the union money to buy back control of the speedway.

In the summer of 1961, Turner flew to Chicago to lead the first meeting of the new union. The stated goals were bigger purses, better racetrack facilities, adequate insurance, viable pension plans, and

If Curtis Turner hadn't existed in real life, an enterprising screenwriter would have invented him. Dressed with his customary panache in a plaid jacket and two-tone oxfords, he lounges alongside the step-down Hudson Hornet he drove to victory in the Strictly Stock race at Langhorne Speedway in 1949, outrunning two other early NASCAR heroes, Bob Flock and pole-sitter Red Byron. *Revs Institute / Bruce R. Craig Photograph Collection*

scholarships for the children of drivers killed on the job, as it were. Although drivers from both NASCAR and USAC were said to have joined, the only ones identified by name were Turner and three other early heroes of stock car racing—Tim Flock, Fireball Roberts, and Buck Baker. The next day, Turner issued a statement: "A majority of the drivers on the Grand National Circuit have signed applications and paid initiation dues of $10 for membership in the Federation of Professional Athletes."[1] To which France replied, "No known Teamster member can compete in a NASCAR race. And I'll use a pistol to enforce it."[2]

Just in case he hadn't made himself clear, France convened a meeting with drivers in a vacant building near Bowman Gray Stadium in Winston-Salem. "Gentlemen, before I have this union stuffed down my throat, I will plow up my two-and-a-half-mile track in Daytona Beach and plant corn in the infield," he declared.[3] Speaking hypothetically, he added, "Joe Blow, what are you going to do when Driver X pulls up to you in the second turn of a race, points a pistol at you and asks, 'Have you paid your union dues?'"[4] Then he suspended Turner, Flock, and Roberts for life for "conduct detrimental to auto racing."[5]

After gauging which way the wind was blowing, Roberts quickly resigned from the union and was benevolently reinstated by France. Baker was also permitted to resume racing, though his glory days were behind him. But even as France played the strongman, he wanted to make peace with the rank and file. Before the week was over, he'd created the Grand National Advisory Board with two drivers (Ned Jarrett and Rex White, who also resigned from the union), two NASCAR execs (Ed Otto and Pat Purcell), two car owners (Rex Lovette and Lee Petty), and two track owners/promoters (Clay Earles and Enoch Staley). Flock and Turner refused to crawl back into the fold, and they remained personae non gratae. It wasn't until 1965, after Turner paid a $30,000 fine and ate enough crow to choke an elephant, that France welcomed him back to NASCAR. But by that time, the dream of unionizing drivers was a dim memory.

In retrospect, the Teamsters push had come too soon. Yes, professional baseball, football, and basketball all had unions dating back to the 1950s, but they were relatively toothless until the mid- to late 1960s, when the players started rebelling against the owners and the first strikes were called. The situation was different in NASCAR. The drivers were independent contractors rather than team players, and most of them didn't have contracts to tide them over when they hit hard times. But they didn't like the looks of the landscape as they approached the end of the decade.

Safety was one issue. Drivers weren't thrilled about speeds that were inching upward to 200 miles per hour, especially with a new high-bank oval at Talladega already under construction. "There were a lot of scared race drivers back in those days," Humpy Wheeler recalled.[6] Or as Cale Yarborough said after qualifying on the pole at Daytona in 1968 at 189.222 mph, "You don't drive a car here anymore; you aim it. I used to think Daytona was an easy track, but at 190 mph, it's more dangerous than Indy."[7] Before the 500, another driver confided, "Somebody's going to get it out there today. I only hope it isn't one of my friends."[8] As it happened, nobody was hurt, but half the field crashed or broke.

Money was another concern. Manufacturer support was drying up, and the tire companies were cutting back their sponsorship programs. The Grand National Advisory Board had turned out to be little more than window dressing, so teams and drivers scuffled from race to race, and in 1968, there were a *ton* of races on the Grand National schedule—forty-nine, to be exact. Thirty-seven of them were on short tracks where the amenities were primitive and the pay was paltry. The total purse for the one hundred miler on the dirt at Greenville-Pickens Speedway was $4,940, split between twenty-three entrants. Ten guys went home with one hundred dollars apiece in their pockets—and cars that needed fixing. Granted, some promoters paid "deal money" under the table, but it usually went to the bigger-name drivers. There was grumbling that NASCAR wasn't looking out for the racers, especially the hand-to-mouth independents who survived on prize money. Adding insult to injury, the bathroom facilities at most tracks consisted of metal troughs for the drivers to pee in and portable toilets for their wives and children. "We felt like we deserved a little bit better than that," Donnie Allison said.[9]

A strange confluence of events led to the next step on the rambling road to unionization. After retiring from racing, two-time Grand National champion Ned Jarrett had formed a management and promotion company with local businessman Ramon Pike. Their firm was subsequently bought by Restaurant Associates, a food service titan that operated Mamma Leone's in New York City and helped popularize the concept of theme restaurants. The executive vice president of Restaurant Associates was Larry Fleisher, a high-powered attorney who just happened to be general counsel for the National Basketball Players Association. Fleisher thought NASCAR might be ripe for unionization. Jarrett, so well-liked that he was known as "Gentleman Ned," would have been the perfect emissary. But back in 1961, Jarrett had joined Turner before changing his mind and cutting ties with the union, and he didn't want to butt heads with France again. So Pike was charged with finding a driver willing to spearhead the effort. Richard Petty, come on down!

Petty was at the top of his game behind the wheel, and he'd recently won NASCAR's Most Popular Driver award. He led a five-man delegation to meet Fleisher in New York City. "We told him that we wanted better restrooms and a place for our families and some other things to help out the drivers," Allison recalled. "He said, 'That's very commendable. But the main issue is going to be the money.' Well, we had a pretty good disagreement over that. At that time, we were not interested in getting the purses raised, and that's the gospel truth. Anyway, we ended the conversation with him saying, 'When y'all figure out what you want to do, call me and let me know.' And that was the end of it."[10]

With King Richard serving as president, the Professional Drivers Association (PDA) was formed at an unpublicized meeting in Ann Arbor in the summer of 1969 before the Yankee 600 at Michigan International Speedway. Other members of the executive committee were Yarborough, Allison and his brother Bobby, Elmo Langley, David Pearson, LeeRoy Yarbrough, Charlie Glotzbach, James Hylton, and Pete Hamilton, and just about every prominent driver other than Bobby Isaac joined the union. Fleisher was hired as general counsel. "We are not making any harsh demands," Petty told the press. "We simply feel we should be able to make suggestions and recommendations that will help our situation as well as that of others involved in the sport. We are not seeking a war with NASCAR or with track promoters."[11]

This was a fight France didn't need. He was already bickering with Ford and Chrysler over technical regulations, and promoters, especially at the small tracks, were moaning about rising costs and flat ticket sales. Now, to his immense annoyance, the drivers were giving him a hard time. You could almost hear the exasperation in his voice when he lobbed a volley back at Petty et al.: "NASCAR has been pretty great to this bunch of people. Some of these fellows have gotten to be big heroes, and they have apparently forgotten how they got there," he groused. "We're not planning to change NASCAR. We'll post our prize money, and they're welcome to run if they want to. If not, that's their business."[12]

But even as he traded barbs with the drivers, France had bigger fish to fry. Three years earlier, when NASCAR had been humming along at a healthier clip, he'd negotiated a deal to build a new racetrack in a small town in Alabama felicitously sited near a proposed extension of Interstate Highway 20. Not a short track. Not an intermediate speedway. Not even a superspeedway, or at least not just any superspeedway. No, Talladega International was designed to be the fastest racetrack in the world, with turns banked at a thirty-three-degree angle to allow stock cars to achieve speeds of 200 mph. The track was finished about a month before the first race was scheduled. Coincidentally, this was also around the time that the PDA was being formed. Soon, the track and the union would collide, with incendiary results.

Cars had no problem getting up to speed when the factory teams were invited to conduct prerace tests at Talladega. But at 190 mph, the drivers were getting beaten up by the rough track, suffering nausea, chest pains, and even temporary loss of vision. There were dark rumors that something called the "pogo effect" was to blame—wild, uncontrollable oscillations that sometimes resulted when NASA lit the fuse of its liquid-oxygen-powered rockets. This turned out to be a red herring. That still left France facing another potential showstopper: The tires provided by Firestone and Goodyear were getting chewed up when they ran faster than 180 mph, so drivers couldn't keep the hammer down for more than five or six laps before the rubber started disintegrating.

Meanwhile, the Grand National season kept on keeping on. Despite rumors about a driver boycott at Darlington, the Southern 500 went off without a hitch. By this time, the PDA had more than forty members. Although Petty insisted at a well-attended press conference that no "drastic measures"[13] were planned, he said the union was lobbying for retirement pensions, better insurance, metal guardrails instead of antiquated wood fences, and "comfort facilities,"[14] better known as restrooms, for the drivers and their families at the tracks lacking modern amenities. Purses, intriguingly, weren't mentioned. The following week, at Talladega, relations between France and the drivers would reach a new low.

During practice, driving a high-wing Dodge Daytona, Glotzbach turned a stunning lap at 199.987 mph on his third flyer. The problem is that he damn near destroyed his tires doing it. "They were going too fast. And it was new asphalt, which is always a tough one, so they couldn't keep from blistering tires," recalled Humpy Wheeler, who was repping Firestone. "We did everything we could, even shipped in harder tires from Akron, but they still blistered. Nothing that we tried to do worked, and that's when we decided to pull out. It would have been a bloodbath if we'd stayed in it."[15] France was gutted when he was told that Firestone was withdrawing its tires. He twisted the arms of Goodyear officials to persuade them to stay, and they did—grudgingly. But it was clear that France couldn't stage a genuine race, with drivers running flat out rather than cruising around at a sharply reduced pace to keep the tires from blowing out.

Petty had informed France a week before the race that he didn't think the track was safe. On Friday night, after Glotzbach qualified on the pole at 199.466 mph, the PDA executive committee met and voted to boycott the race. As Petty told reporters, "When you are having tire problems and the track is so rough you can't sit in your car, and you know something is going to break, it's time to do some thinking—especially when you are approaching 200 mph."[16] France pulled out all the stops to persuade the drivers to stay. He even took a USAC-spec stock car onto the track and turned a lap at 159 mph, which impressed exactly nobody. Then he suggested that the drivers voluntarily keep their speeds down to 175 mph to give the fans a show. Ultimately, he lost the support of not only the drivers but also the car owners. "This is a matter of life and death. There's no way I'd put my driver on this race track," said Banjo Matthews, who was a top car builder as well as the owner of Donnie Allison's Ford. "I think, simply, that Bill France made a mistake. We knew a long time ago this track wasn't ready for a race. Wednesday, I recommended that we go home. We built cars to go as fast as they can, to beat the other guy. And when we can't run them like that, it's time to leave."[17]

PDA members convened in the open-air garage on Saturday morning. Wearing sunglasses and serious sideburns, Petty looked imperturbable as he presided over the meeting with arms crossed against his chest. When France tried to force his way in, Yarborough blocked him. Big Bill was an impressive physical specimen, and nobody doubted his courage. But Yarborough was a former Golden Gloves boxer who would famously fight Donnie *and* Bobby Allison simultaneously after wrecking at the end of the Daytona 500 in 1979. France wasn't able to crash the meeting, and the PDA reaffirmed its decision to boycott the race. At 7 p.m., France's voice boomed over the public-address system: "Let the garage area be cleared. Cars that will not run in tomorrow's race must be taken from their stalls immediately and removed from the raceway."[18] As dusk fell, Petty's truck engine sparked to life, and he towed his Torino Talladega back to his shop in Randleman, North Carolina. Other than Isaac, who'd never joined the PDA, virtually all of the Grand National regulars followed Petty's lead.

To fill the field, France brought in the racing version of strike-busting scabs—drivers who'd competed in Saturday's Grand American race for lighter and slower pony cars. "When they boycotted the race, Bill France Senior got us all together and said, 'Look, I'll pay you X amount of dollars if you race tomorrow.' Shoot, any extra money was big money back then. We done it without a thought," said Richard Childress, who would graduate from racing as a scrappy independent in Grand American and Grand National to winning six Winston Cup championships as a team owner with Dale Earnhardt. "Richard Petty came over to talk to us about joining [the PDA] and not racing the next day. But they didn't want us to join before, so we wasn't going to join now."[19] The race went off as scheduled on Sunday with a ragtag collection of entries. Caution flags were thrown every twenty-five laps to prevent tires from blistering. Chrysler offered little-known Richard Brickhouse a ride in the Daytona that Glotzbach had put on the pole. "Brickhouse came to us [PDA members] and said this was his opportunity to drive a good car, and he had to run," Allison recalled. "I told him, 'Richard, you do what you want to do. But no one will ever know you done it.'"[20] Brickhouse won the race—and effectively sabotaged his career in NASCAR.

Afterward, France tried to spin the Talladega 500 as a victory—his victory, that is—against a cabal of spoiled, gutless, money-grubbing drivers. But despite his proven public relations acumen, there was no getting around the fact that the race had been a fiasco. To placate the fans, France offered them a rain check to attend the next Daytona 500, and a lot of them did, which cut deeply into his profits at the biggest moneymaker in his portfolio. But that was a problem for another day. His immediate objective was to shore up support, so he and other NASCAR officials began meeting with constituents—track owners, tire companies, carmakers, even some struggling independent drivers who might, in theory, be willing to abandon the union. He also courted public opinion by trotting out lump-sum prize money figures that made it seem as if the drivers were living in high cotton. In fact, according to the PDA, only thirty to thirty-five of the 150 drivers in NASCAR earned more than $5,000 a year. Disability insurance payouts were forty dollars a week, starting two weeks after an injury was incurred. There were no retirement benefits whatsoever. "A guy devotes his life to racing, and he gets only $7,500 if he gets an arm torn off," Bobby Allison said. "If he gets killed, his wife gets $15,000."[21]

Toward the end of the year, France announced that he'd commissioned a feasibility study to consider a retirement pension program for drivers and agreed to throw extra cash into the year-end prize fund in 1970. To peel low-bucks drivers away from the PDA, he floated a proposal to pay independents for showing up at premier events—deal money by another name. After dangling these carrots, he pulled out his big stick. To prevent another Talladega-style boycott, NASCAR issued a new entry form that required teams to race their cars once they showed up for an event, even if that meant using a substitute driver. "I'm sorry if anybody finds this new rule objectionable," France said, positioning himself as an honest and perfectly reasonable broker, "but if they do, then we don't want them in the event."[22] The rule itself was something of a nothingburger, but the subtext was clear: Get on the bus or get run over.

Winston started pouring money into NASCAR in 1971, and the series was rebranded as the Winston Cup the year after that. France unveiled a shorter schedule structured around better-paying races, and dirt tracks were axed altogether. This was good news for the bigger-name drivers who weren't eager to pound around short ovals for chicken feed. Then, in 1972, NASCAR further sweetened the pot by creating an appearance money program for the top teams—$2,000 for the longer races, $1,000 for the shorter ones. (France shrewdly made race promoters responsible for coming up with the money.) Although there was still plenty of lingering resentment about France's high-handed control of the sport, the ascension of his son Bill Junior to the throne soothed some feathers. While his father tended to be a my-way-or-the-highway leader, Billy was more collegial and congenial, though the results tended to be the same. "If you had a discussion with Bill Junior about something you didn't like," Childress said, "by the time you got finished, you felt he was right after all. He had that way of getting to you."[23] With the younger France running the show, the stock car labor movement ran out of gas. "I have severed all ties with the PDA," Petty announced in 1973. "I feel there is no need for an organization of this type since Bill France Junior has taken over as President of NASCAR."[24]

Safety continued to be a source of anxiety. In 1971, the aero cars that had dominated the previous two seasons were effectively outlawed, and big-block engines were choked down with restrictor plates. This reduced speeds by about 10 mph, but the cars were still spooky fast, especially when they were hurtling around the high banks in the big, tight packs that were the unavoidable product of "plate" racing. Veteran independent Friday Hassler was killed when his Chevrolet Chevelle was mangled in a nasty wreck involving twelve cars during the first of the Twin 125 qualifying races at Daytona in 1972. The next year, Talladega was the site of an even more heart-stopping accident. To goose attendance, the field for the spring race had been increased from fifty to sixty cars, safety be damned. (When the track opened, the limit had been forty cars.) On the ninth lap, twenty-one cars were caught up in a crash that's considered to be the first of the "Big Ones" that are still a regular feature of modern restrictor-plate races. Amazingly, the only driver to be seriously injured was Black pioneer Wendell Scott, who spent a month in the hospital and soon retired from racing.

Unhurt in the crash was reigning Rookie of the Year Larry Smith. Although he wasn't a front-runner, Smith had managed to line up financial backing from Carling Black Label beer—one of the rare non-automotive companies involved in stock car racing—and his car was painted stylishly in his sponsor's black-and-gold colors. Three months later, he was back in Alabama for the Talladega 500. Thirteen laps in, he spun into a concrete retaining wall, probably because of a cut-down tire, and died of what appeared to be a basal skull fracture. About two hours later, in one of the most bizarre incidents in NASCAR history, Isaac—the 1970 Grand National champion and a neighbor of Smith's—heard a voice that told him to get out of the car. He radioed car owner Bud Moore: "Get a relief driver. I quit."[25] He pitted immediately and never raced a Grand National car again.

When it came to trends involving safety, sponsorship, and technology, stock car racing and Indy car racing often marched in lockstep. But not when it came to unions. During this era, Indy car drivers were much better compensated than their counterparts down South. And unlike NASCAR, USAC wasn't an autocracy. It was the United States Automobile *Club*, after all, and while drivers didn't run the show by any stretch of the imagination, they were represented on the board of directors and were able to influence the direction that the organization took.

The only period when USAC drivers appeared to be poised to organize was the summer of 1971. About thirty of them met with PDA officials on several occasions to discuss the benefits of joining the union. Ultimately, this proved to be a dead end. But another subject kept coming up in discussions—the scheduled race at Langhorne. For much of its storied history as the fastest one-mile dirt track in the country, Langhorne had been respected by all and feared by many. In 1965, it was paved and reconfigured from a perfect circle to a D-shaped oval. The makeover was almost universally panned. "Langhorne is definitely the most dangerous course in our schedule, and everybody knows it," Wally Dallenbach declared. "We keep going faster every year. The track is so rough and there are so many blind spots at the speeds we're going, we just don't feel it's safe to run."[26] Although USAC approved the track after a safety inspection, the drivers unanimously voted to boycott the race in 1971. The property was sold and turned into a shopping center shortly afterward.

Drag racing went in a different direction from Indy cars. Like NASCAR, the National Hot Rod Association (NHRA) was run as a fiefdom by its founder, Wally Parks. But the courtly, affable Parks was more of a consensus-builder than Big Bill France, and he preferred to rule with a velvet glove rather than an iron fist. While NASCAR existed for the principal purpose of generating profits for its shareholders—who, by 1971, consisted entirely of the France family—the NHRA had been formed in 1951 as a nonprofit organization to serve the burgeoning ecosystem of hot rodding. Parks wasn't driven primarily by a thirst for revenue, and his allegiance wasn't simply to race promoters and drag strip owners; it was to the higher calling of getting drag racing off the street and repositioning it in the mainstream of American sports. He was equally concerned with automakers, aftermarket suppliers, parts vendors, fans, and, of course, racers. By 1964, the NHRA had fifty-seven thousand members. The vast majority of them were hobbyists who didn't make a living from the sport. Naturally, these amateurs had a different agenda from the relatively small cadre of drag racing professionals. The tension between them was the source of the growing pains the NHRA experienced in the 1960s. As Joe Scalzo wrote in *Motor Trend*, "The NHRA apparently still hasn't made up its mind whether it wants drag racing to be a sport for the racers or one for the cash customers, a dilemma haunting them now for almost a decade."[27]

Drag racing was the youngest of the major forms of motorsports. Not coincidentally, it was also the least profitable. Parks didn't consider this a major problem. He wasn't a hypocrite in the fashion of Avery Brundage, who headed the International Olympic Committee during this era and insisted on a sham form of amateurism even though it was common knowledge that many athletes were being paid illicitly. But Parks saw no reason to cater to professionals when most of his members were drag racing largely for fun, and the entry fees they paid were a solid source of revenue. Even in the big-dog Top Fuel class at the NHRA "majors," the prize money barely qualified as petty cash. To earn a living, drivers would tow from coast to coast to compete in match races where the fees were guaranteed, win, lose, or draw. But as a practical matter, they had to continue to race in the NHRA majors because that's where they established their credibility and earned bragging rights by beating the best of the best.

The long-simmering feud between Parks and Don "Big Daddy" Garlits, the best known and most successful drag racer on the planet, finally boiled over at the US Nationals at Indianapolis Raceway Park in 1971. The Nats were the premier event on the NHRA schedule, and everybody who was anybody was there. Garlits qualified fastest in his Swamp Rat 14, the rail that had revolutionized Top Fuel by putting the engine behind the driver, and he blitzed his competition in each of his first four rounds to make it to the finals. There, he faced off against Steve Carbone, who'd qualified second in his conventional, but now obsolete, slingshot. Carbone knew he couldn't outrun Garlits, so he devised a plan to outwit him.

A drag race can't begin until both drivers have "staged." This involves inching their cars forward close enough to the starting line so that their front wheels break a beam aimed horizontally across the track. Only after both cars have broken this beam, or staged, will the starting lights—aka the Christmas tree—do their thing. Amber bulbs then light up in descending order until the green-for-go bulb pops on. If a car leaves the starting line before the green light flashes, the red light comes on, which means an instant "L" no matter how slowly the other car went. Garlits, being Garlits, liked to stage last as a demonstration of psychological domination. At Indy, to get inside Garlits's head, Carbone let it be known that he wasn't going to stage first, "even if I run out of fuel or the headers melt off the engine."[28]

Top Fuel cars don't like to idle for extended periods because the engines heat up and develop more power—too much power. Also, the clutches get hot, which makes them bite harder and more likely to spin the tires instead of hooking up. Obviously, Carbone faced the same issues Garlits did. But at least he could see the Hemi trembling in front of him and tell how hot it was getting. With the engine behind him, Garlits couldn't. Also, since Carbone figured Garlits would delay staging as long as he could, he had "loosened up" his clutch so that it wouldn't engage as quickly as normal and compensate for the extra

Don "Big Daddy" Garlits is probably the best-known figure in drag racing history, and this photo of him at Lions Drag Strip in 1970 might be the most famous image of his career. It captures the fraught moment when the overstressed two-speed transmission of Swamp Rat 13 exploded, cutting off half his foot. While recuperating, Garlits conceptualized the radical rear-engine Top Fueler that would quickly consign traditional slingshots to history's dustbin. *Tony Thacker Collection*

horsepower being made by his engine. Just as he'd promised, after completing his burnout, Carbone refused to stage. Garlits, driven by ego rather than common sense, followed suit. In one of the most surreal and memorable episodes in Top Fuel history, a roughly three minute standoff ensued in front of the Christmas tree while their high-strung Hemis idled unhappily. Garlits didn't give in until smoke and steam started billowing from his engine. When the lights went green, he impotently spun his tires, and Carbone won after what's now known simply as "The Great Burndown." His payday? A measly $6,100, including contingency money, or less than the cost of an engine rebuild.

At the year-end banquet, Garlits collared Parks in a hallway and told him, "Steve Carbone should have walked out of there with $30,000, not $3,000 [in prize money]."[29] When an agitated Parks argued that paydays that size were years away, Garlits said, "I'm going to have a race of my own next Labor Day weekend, and I'll pay each of the professional classes $25,000 each to win, plus contingency." Parks cackled in his face, but Garlits got the last laugh. The next year, he formed the Professional Racers Association (PRA), with him as president and none other than Carbone as treasurer. Garlits brokered a deal with the American Hot Rod Association, the NHRA's for-profit rival, to put up $200,000 for a race in Tulsa over the Labor Day weekend, heads-up against the Nats. Then he wrote an open letter in *Drag News* inviting unhappy racers to join the rebellion.

The PRA quickly signed up nearly fifty drivers. When *Autoweek* asked Parks why he couldn't match the PRA pay scale, he said, "The concept is not feasible for economic reasons. I can understand the drivers' motivation, but the tracks simply can't afford such big purses."[30] But even as he was making this claim, Parks realized that he'd been outflanked by Garlits, and he needed to come up with some money—real money—to prevent widespread defections to the PRA show in Tulsa. To his credit, that's just what he did. When Gary Beck won Top Fuel at the Nats in 1972, he earned three times as much as Carbone had received the previous year. After that, there was no going back to the old payouts. "Parks never forgave me," Garlits said.[31] The feeling was mutual.

Garlits and the PRA ran their own Labor Day races in 1972. About half of drag racing's headliners entered the event. Some of them even managed to race in both Tulsa and Indy, shuttling from one to the other between runs. But only 37,522 tickets were sold, which was far less than anticipated, and not enough to make the show a financial success. There were diminishing returns the next year, and the year after that the turnout was so feeble that Garlits quit in the middle of the event. He would later form another organization called the Professional Racers Organization, but this, too, failed to challenge the hegemony of the NHRA. By this time, major-league sponsorship was arriving, and in 1975, Winston became the title sponsor of the series. A rising tide raises all boats, and as waves of prosperity swept over drag racing, the drivers decided that they were content to let somebody else take the helm.

The only form of motorsports where a drivers' union had a crucial impact was Formula 1, and even in this case the effectiveness of the organization had less to do with the strength of the institution than the persuasiveness—and pig-headed persistence—of its most prominent member.

The Grand Prix Drivers' Association (GPDA) was formed in Monte Carlo in 1961. It was the successor to the short-lived Union des Pilotes Professionnels Internationaux, which had been created to represent drivers in all forms of racing. It quickly became clear that the drivers at the top of the mountain had different interests from those toiling in the backwaters of motorsports. When the larger union was reconstituted as a more elite association, Stirling Moss was elected president. Dashing and energetic, Moss was the obvious choice. The other heroes of the postwar era—the Fangios, the Ascaris, the Hawthorns, the Taruffis—were all retired or dead. Besides being the most prodigiously talented road racer of his generation, Moss was also the prototype for the modern professional driver. He was a media-friendly personality with a business manager who coordinated his busy schedule and negotiated his many endorsements. Because he was so good in so many types of cars and so well-known to so many different audiences, he commanded lavish appearance fees from race promoters and was compensated generously by car owners. As such, he was a figure worthy of emulation. But because he was such a singular character, following his example was easier said than done. No other drivers were as fast or famous as Moss. Their presence at a race wouldn't draw appreciable numbers of extra fans, so they didn't have the leverage to demand higher appearance fees. Race promoters offered them a certain amount of starting money, and they either accepted it, or they didn't. The GPDA was created to correct this one-sided system by enabling the drivers to negotiate as a monolithic block.

In 1962, a vicious crash at Goodwood ended Moss's career and effectively closed the book on the postwar era of road racing. The meticulously bearded Joakim Bonnier succeeded Moss as GPDA president. The son of a university professor and heir to a Swedish publishing fortune, Bonnier was a tall, elegant, cosmopolitan figure who spoke six languages fluently and was the very personification of the gentleman driver. Today, the term "gentleman driver" refers to a wealthy amateur who's bought a ride that he couldn't have earned on merit alone. But in the 1950s, other than a handful of overt mercenaries like Moss and Fangio, most drivers were gentlemen—not gentlemen of leisure, exactly, but men with enough money to indulge what was, even then, an expensive avocation. Bonnier wasn't championship material, but he was quick enough to have given BRM its first F1 victory, winning the Dutch Grand Prix in 1959.

By the 1960s, most of the gentlemen drivers had been supplanted by pros and shunted to privateer operations near the back of the grid. In 1964, Cooper, Lotus, Brabham, and BRM, which employed most of the top drivers in Grand Prix racing, banded together to form the Formula 1 Constructors' Association (F1CA). F1CA and the GPDA often worked as a tag team to negotiate the amount of starting money to be paid and the number of entry slots to be guaranteed. The deals hammered out with race organizers were named after the cities where they were finalized—the Paris Agreement, the Belgrave Agreement, and so on. Representing the financial interests of drivers was the principal raison d'être of the GPDA well into the 1960s. Advocating for safety? Only half-heartedly. In 1967, in the wake of the ghastly wreck that killed Lorenzo Bandini at Monaco, *Autoweek* editor in chief Leon Mandel asked Denny Hulme what the GPDA could do to address obvious circuit defects and inept emergency crews. The short answer? Not a damn thing. "We're just too small to have any effect," Hulme admitted.[32] Bonnier acknowledged his own impotence when he wrote to the FIA, "The first concern of the GPDA is safety for everybody involved in motor sport, and I am afraid I cannot say that our interests in this respect have always been looked at in the best possible way by the responsible authorities."[33]

At the end of 1967, the GPDA was granted a spot on a subcommittee created by the CSI to promote safety. The new body's role was strictly advisory, and cynics dismissed it as nothing more than an empty promise. And it probably would have been one of those ineffectual groups that issues reports ignored by everybody if the GPDA itself hadn't been overhauled. In 1968, with Bonnier in the twilight of his career as a driver, Jackie Stewart was elected president of the GPDA. Stewart was the contemporary version of Stirling Moss—fast on the track and savvy and eloquent off it, which made him an ideal spokesman for the union. Guaranteeing grid positions remained a thorny issue, especially as the availability of the Cosworth DFV engine allowed a host of new constructors to break into F1 and clog up the paddock. But thanks to Stewart's personal passion—some called it an obsession—for safety, the GPDA shifted its priority to a more existential issue. "Through 1968 and into 1969, we resembled dogs with a bone," he said. "In every interview, at every opportunity, we raised the issue of safety, alternating dire warnings with new demands."[34]

The GPDA began with personal safety, demanding that the CSI require genuinely flame-retardant clothing and six-point harnesses. (It didn't.) Next, the GPDA moved its campaign to more controversial territory—circuit safety. The opening volley was fired at Jarama during the Spanish Grand Prix. After the previous year's race, the GPDA had identified various problems with the circuit, from guardrails that cars could slide under to corners marked with movable cones instead of permanent curbs. As Stewart recalled, "I was personally involved in an accident where my car left the road at a very low speed and it went underneath one of these Armco barriers—in fact it got to the point where the barrier came right up to my crash helmet and knocked the peak off. My head was wedged so tightly between the Armco barrier and the roll over bar that I couldn't even turn it; another six inches forward and that would have been the end of me."[35]

As late as a week before the race was scheduled in 1968, no changes had been made. Stewart later insisted that the GPDA never threatened a formal boycott. Still, the drivers' well-publicized unhappiness, backed up by demands from the CSI, compelled the organizers to make the necessary upgrades, and the race went off on schedule. A month later, at the Belgian Grand Prix, the GPDA circulated a petition asking that the start be delayed in case of heavy rain. Spa, remember, was where Stewart had nearly been killed two years earlier when a downpour drenched the circuit, so this request cut close to the bone. The organizer agreed to honor the unanimous petition. As it happened, the race was dry. But a precedent had been set.

Still, these were mere skirmishes. It wasn't until 1969 that the battle over circuit safety began in earnest. The first target was Spa, which was universally regarded as the riskiest circuit in F1. After Stewart inspected the track, the GPDA demanded additional and improved guardrails. The Royal Automobile Club of Belgium rejected this expensive-to-fulfill request, and the drivers—to everybody's shock—voted to boycott the race. The fallout was brutal, with most magazines and fans slamming the drivers for their feeble "milk-and-water" approach to racing.[36] Belgian prodigy Jacky Ickx, who would later set the all-time lap record at Spa, resigned from the GPDA to protest the boycott. In *The Times*, arguably Great Britian's most influential mainstream daily newspaper, motoring correspondent Geoffrey Charles wrote, "However well intentioned the advocates of greater safety may be, they are slowly eroding one of the basic elements and attractions of the sport for both drivers and spectators—namely the built-in danger. Give the misguided safety fanatics any more freedom . . . and every circuit will become just a harmless watered down nursery track on which only completely protected drivers will dare to race."[37]

Critics like Charles were clearly on the wrong side of history, as the events of the cataclysmic 1970 season would show. In June, after Bruce McLaren was killed in a testing accident at Goodwood and Piers Courage died in particularly monstrous crash at Zandvoort, the GPDA met in Louis Stanley's suite at the Dorchester Hotel in London. "Gentlemen, we have reached a crucial moment," Stewart declared. "Bruce and Piers are dead, and I think it is fair to say both might well have survived if the governing bodies and circuit owners had listened to what we have been saying for the past three years. People say they agree, but nothing gets done. When Piers's car burst into flame, there was not even enough of the appropriate fire-fighting equipment to extinguish the car. This is ridiculous. How long are we going to let the organisers be so careless and disrespectful with our lives? We must do more."[38]

The Nordschleife was next on the GPDA's hit list. The drivers were able to force the German Grand Prix to move to Hockenheim in 1970, which prompted widespread improvements of the Nürburgring. But despite lingering issues with track safety, F1 returned to the Nordschleife the next year and continued to use the circuit until Niki Lauda was nearly killed there in 1976. The GPDA had better luck defanging Spa-Francorchamps. After the Belgian Grand Prix in 1970, F1 abandoned Spa, and it wouldn't come back until 1983, on what was effectively a new racetrack. The third circuit targeted by the GPDA was Autodromo Nazionale di Monza. The drivers demanded major changes after Peter Gethin won the Italian Grand Prix in 1971 at a record average speed of 150.754 mph. The next year, Monza incorporated a pair of inelegant chicanes, and while they were widely reviled, they cut speeds by nearly 20 mph.

In many respects, 1972 was the high-water mark for the GPDA. Like Napoleon's army, marching triumphantly to Moscow before withering away during the long and devastating retreat back to France, the GPDA was losing cohesion and hemorrhaging support. On June 11, 1972, Bonnier was killed in the 24 Hours of Le Mans, which he considered to be the "most dangerous" track in racing.[39] (Since it wasn't on the Grand Prix schedule, the GPDA had no authority over the Circuit de la Sarthe.) By the time he died, Bonnier was no longer racing in Formula 1, so he'd ceased to play a prominent role in the GPDA. Yet his death was a potent symbol of how much still remained to be done.

A more vexing issue was internal dissension. While the GPDA tried to present a united front, critics like Denis Jenkinson loved to give the naysayers a forum. Not that any drivers were antisafety, per se, but there were disputes over tactics and philosophy. Ickx resigned from the organization on several occasions because he objected to the boycotts. John Surtees, still lionized by the *tifosi* as "Il Grande John" for his exploits on MV Agusta Grand Prix motorcycles, criticized the guardrails-everywhere approach, favoring catch fences or runoff areas. The phlegmatic Mexican Pedro Rodriguez, whose younger brother,

Ricardo, had been killed in the Mexican Grand Prix when he was only twenty, was largely unperturbed by safety defects. So was his great rival in Porsche 917s, Jo Siffert. And many drivers were ambivalent about a core tenet of the safety project. On one hand, they didn't want to die simply because they made a mistake or a critical component broke. But on the other hand, they knew that the most dangerous tracks were also ones that tended to be the most rewarding to drive on. As Chris Amon put it after the GPDA boycott of 1971, "It's a pity we're not going to Spa. It's a dicey circuit at the best of times, but immensely satisfying to do a fast lap, which is really what Grand Prix racing is all about."[40]

The fractious internal politics and dwindling influence of the GPDA were showcased during the shambolic prerace activities before the Belgian Grand Prix in 1973. After Spa was banished from the list of approved F1 tracks, the Belgian Grand Prix was staged at Nivelles in 1972. The reviews of this dull circuit had been so meh that the FIA decided to shift the race to Zolder in 1973. Unfortunately, by the time the decision was made, it was too late for the freshly poured pavement to cure. At the Friday morning practice session, the surface was so soft that walking on it left visible footprints, and when the 500-horsepower F1 cars ventured onto the track, their huge rear tires ripped up giant gobs of asphalt and flung them into the air. Two cars crashed, and several others spun. Confronted by angry drivers and car owners, the organizers agreed to cancel the afternoon session so new pavement could be laid.

While steamrollers huffed and puffed, GPDA members bitched and moaned. After the sun had gone down, new GPDA president Denny Hulme emerged from the closed-door meeting and issued a statement calling for the track management to agree *in writing* to postpone or cancel the race if the surface wasn't raceable by 11 a.m. Saturday, or ninety minutes before the next practice session. The deadline passed without any action. GPDA members huddled privately while CSI officials sat on their hands. Some of the drivers had reservations about the proposed boycott. "Let's get on with the event; it's the same for all of us," said fearless Surtees driver Mike "The Bike" Hailwood, winner of twelve Isle of Man TT races before switching his attention from two wheels to four.[41] At 1:35 p.m., Ickx, who wasn't a GPDA member at the moment, wheeled his Ferrari onto the track. Next out was Iso-Marlboro driver Nanni Galli, who justified his decision to defy the GPDA by claiming that he'd arrived too late to attend its meeting. While the two cars circulated around the track, team owners threatened to withhold starting money or even to fire drivers if they didn't climb into their cockpits. To a man, they refused. One of them ostentatiously packed his bags as if to leave. Shortly before 2 p.m., a CSI official miraculously produced a document signed by the organizers agreeing to pay 3.5 million Belgian francs if the track surface proved to be unsatisfactory.

In retrospect, this seemed to be a fig leaf that allowed the GPDA to save face. With all the cars ready to go and two of them already on the track, it would have been almost impossible to sustain a boycott. Practice resumed on Saturday afternoon, and on Sunday, the race was flagged off on schedule. After a scratchy start, the track surface broke up as predicted; it looked, Hulme reported later, "like the dying minutes of a demolition derby."[42] Six cars crashed and only three finished on the lead lap, with Stewart heading a Tyrrell one-two over understudy François Cevert. "The absurdity of the whole situation is that we were bulldozed into racing at Zolder—a track that even club racers had refused to drive on a few weeks earlier!—when the brand-new Nivelles track where we had raced last year was sitting idle only a few miles away," Hulme wrote in *Autosport*. "I came away from Zolder feeling that the drivers had really pushed for a Belgian Grand Prix if it was at all possible, but we wanted to race on a race track that came close to Grand Prix standards rather than a patched goat track."[43]

But the most damaging blow to the GPDA was Stewart's surprise retirement at the pinnacle of his career, announced shortly after Cevert was killed at Watkins Glen at the end of the 1973 season. By that point, although Hulme was officially running the show, Stewart remained the power behind the throne. He was the insurgent who'd launched the safety revolution, and he'd been at the front of the ramparts ever since. Besides being a three-time world champion, he was a commercial powerhouse and a public relations machine, which gave him a bully pulpit that he occupied with great glee. Yes, he'd gotten some help from elder statesmen like Graham Hill, Jack Brabham, and Dan Gurney, but the GPDA operated less like the US Senate than Smokey Robinson and the Miracles, with most of the other drivers content to remain in the background while Stewart occupied center stage, absorbing the brickbats lobbed by his critics.

And there were plenty of critics, starting with circuit owners and race promoters who were apprehensive about the exorbitant costs of upgrading their racetracks. The GPDA didn't help its cause when it proposed banning writers and photographers from the pits, alienating the very people it needed to make its case to the public. As it was, the more traditional journalists resisted any efforts to redefine racing as a thoroughly modern sport rather than a twentieth-century take on medieval jousting. Typifying older members of the press corps was Henry Manney III, *Road & Track*'s longtime F1 correspondent, who contemptuously dismissed the GPDA as a "lofty and self-righteous . . . organization that prates so much about safety."[44]

Through it all, Stewart abided. In public, at least, he never responded to his critics with the ad hominen attacks they were happy to hurl at him. He consistently took the high road, reiterating over and over that all he wanted was what was best for everyone. Looking back from our perspective in 2026, it's easy to say that racing would have put its own house in order eventually, Stewart or no Stewart. And that's true. But it wouldn't have happened as soon or as dramatically. As historian Doug Nye said, "Jackie broke new ground by coming out and saying publicly what he damn well thought instead of going through channels, through the old boy network of behind-the-scenes negotiation, a little bit of French corruption, a little bit of Italian money changing hands. You know, all of that stuff that could have taken years."[45]

After Stewart retired, the GPDA's influence waned. It reached a low point in 1975 at the Spanish Grand Prix, which was run on the Montjuïc Park street circuit where Jochen Rindt and Graham Hill had crashed heavily after suffering wing failures in 1969. On the Thursday before the race, while jogging around the track, Emerson Fittipaldi was horrified to discover that many of the hastily erected guardrails were either entirely unbolted or simply wire-tied to posts. At an emergency meeting of the GPDA, drivers voted to strike until the guardrails were secured properly. Only two drivers defied the boycott and ventured out for practice on Friday; one of them, predictably, was longtime GPDA dissident Jacky Ickx. Thanks to the solidarity of the rest of the drivers, the first practice session on Saturday was canceled while track workers, F1 mechanics, and even Ken Tyrrell prowled around the circuit, hand-tightening bolts with wrenches. To a disgusted Denis Jenkinson, the work stoppage was yet another example of the lunatics running the asylum. "The whole affair had become so sick it was no longer funny and was yet another blow by the Trade Unions and the rising-up of the workers, as Karl Marx warned us would happen," he wrote.[46]

Fed up with the intransigence of the GPDA, the organizers threatened to impound the cars and withhold all payments unless the teams participated in the third and final practice session late Saturday afternoon. Forced to choose between money and safety, the constructors voted with their checkbooks and ordered their drivers to stop screwing around. Despite Fittipaldi's objections, the GPDA meekly capitulated. Fittipaldi, the reigning world champion, registered his displeasure by turning a couple of laps at a snail's pace. Then, instead of racing on Sunday, he flew home to Geneva. "When I landed, there was a TV [crew] waiting," he said. "I thought they wanted to interview me because I'd left the track. But they said, 'Emerson, do you know what happened? It was a tragedy.'"

While leading a chaotic race, the rear wing support of Rolf Stommelen's Hill GH1 failed at about 150 mph. His car cartwheeled over a guardrail and into the crowd. Four people were killed and nearly a dozen seriously injured, Stommelen among then. The race was red-flagged, and Fittipaldi's teammate at McLaren, Jochen Mass, was declared the winner. Yet it was Fittipaldi who came off as a hero for refusing to race, and his example made the GPDA look small and spineless by comparison. Never again would the union play a pivotal role in F1 politics, and it was little more than a rubber stamp by the time it was formally disbanded in 1982.

Like the PDA in NASCAR and the PRA in drag racing, the GPDA fought the law, and the law won. Still, by fighting the good fight, the unions raised public consciousness and forced sanctioning bodies to confront the issues of safety and driver compensation. Ultimately, were they winners or losers? A little bit of both.

TUGGING ON SUPERMAN'S CAPE

NASCAR was born in 1947 in an Art Deco landmark in Daytona Beach during a meeting attended by the biggest movers and shakers in stock car racing. The largely forgotten efforts to create an anti-NASCAR unfolded in a pool hall that doubled as a bar—or maybe it was the other way around—in Darlington, South Carolina, in the fall of 1973. Grimy drivers at the bottom of the Winston Cup food chain had gathered to grab a few cold beers after the Southern 500 and grouse about the lousy financial hand they'd been dealt by Bill France Jr. "I said what we ought to do is go get our cars and go up the road and rent ourselves a track and run the same day as the [next] Southern 500," said Raymond Williams, who was the loudest and most rebellious of the disgruntled drivers. "In my mind, it was going to be a union-type deal. We were stretched for money."[47]

Every form of racing has its haves and have-nots, but in no series was the gulf between them as wide as it was in NASCAR. For many years, Cup fields were filled out by so-called start-and-park entries. These were cars that had no chance of a strong finish. So instead of putting wear and tear on them, much less running the risk of a crash, their drivers would "retire" after a few laps and collect the prize money for "finishing" forty-second or forty-third or whatever. This was a viable business strategy in the 2000s, when last place paid more than $50,000. But it wasn't a money-making proposition in 1973, when even at a premier event at Darlington, more than half of the field earned less than $2,000, and a couple of guys took home less than $1,000.

Although the automakers in Detroit were no longer pumping millions of dollars down a pipeline to NASCAR country, there was still a nucleus of big names like Richard Petty, Cale Yarborough, and the Allisons who drove for established teams owned by Junior Johnson, Bud Moore, and the Wood Brothers. But the garages were occupied mostly by also-rans known generically as independents, which usually meant they were not only the drivers but also the owners, chief mechanics, tow-rig operators, and bottle washers. Like the start-and-parkers to come, they rarely ran flat out, preferring instead to aim for a finish. During the 1960s and into the '70s, this approach made sense from a business standpoint. In those days, it wasn't unusual for half the cars to break, so simply making it to the checkered flag guaranteed a decent payday. This was especially true when there were forty, fifty, sixty races on the Grand National schedule, most of them on dusty dirt tracks that didn't offer enough money or prestige to attract the David Pearsons and Buddy Bakers of the world. In 1971, James Hylton and Cecil Gordon, two of the top independents, nearly beat Petty to the Grand National title even though neither of them won a single race.

In 1972, NASCAR moved the goalposts by reducing the Winston Cup schedule from forty-nine races to thirty-two. Dirt tracks were abandoned, and with them, it seemed, the independents. Most of these minnows had enthusiastically joined the Professional Drivers Association back in 1969, but the union had turned out to be a paper tiger. Williams, a free spirit who'd dubbed himself "Captain America" and painted his red, white, and blue car accordingly, stepped into the breach. With the help of fellow independent Bill Dennis, he rented Trico Speedway, a bare-bones three-eighths-mile bullring in Rougemont, North Carolina, and set November 25, 1973, as the race date. He then arranged for insurance, tires, race fuel, even publicity. "I worked my butt off preparing for that race," he told journalist Jonathan Ingram. "I worked day and night for weeks. My phone bill was horrendous."[48]

According to the race poster Williams put together, the Independent 250 would be showcasing "NASCAR'S FINEST," but it most definitely wouldn't be carrying NASCAR's imprimatur.[49] Although France did nothing to hinder the race, he kept tabs on the preparations from his lair in Daytona Beach. Williams and his confederates did their best not to poke the bear. "This isn't a protest race against NASCAR," Williams insisted in a newspaper interview despite all evidence to the contrary. "What we're trying to prove is that too much of the prize money is in the first few positions. We'd like to see it spread out more."[50]

The rules for the race were minimal—any late-model stock car, any type of engine, any size imaginable. The nineteen entries included all the top independents, from Hylton and Gordon to Elmo Langley and Richard Childress. The pole was claimed by the iconoclastic Dave Marcis, a hard charger from Wisconsin who'd never subscribed to the run-easy-for-a-finish philosophy (and who would go on to win five Cup races during a career that stretched from 1968 to 2002). But the competition promised to be fierce. "I feel like I'm committed to run flat out, and I believe everybody else feels the same way," veteran Jabe Thomas said. "And if that's the case, it will be the first time in years we've done that."[51]

Among the drivers, prerace enthusiasm was sky-high. Unfortunately, the Independent 250 turned out to be less *Days of Thunder* than *Talladega Nights*. Not that it was a joke, but nothing went according to the script. Although Williams had hoped to sell six thousand tickets, threatening weather, a subpar location, the gas crisis, and an inherent lack of star

As late as 1969, most Grand National races were still run on scruffy short tracks like this one at Asheville-Weaverville Speedway. Bobby Isaac won the Western North Carolina 500 by four laps in his winged Dodge Daytona. Independent owner/driver J.D. McDuffie earned $490 for turning 407 laps around the half-mile oval—and went home with a bum transmission in his two-year-old Buick. *Bryant McMurray, courtesy of J. Murrey Atkins Library, UNC Charlotte*

power limited attendance to two thousand. The racing was good, with Gordon taking the win after Marcis made a late pit stop amid confused scoring. "If truth be known, I actually won the race," Marcis insisted. "But Cecil's brother was working for me, so how would it have looked if I challenged the result?"[52] Gordon earned a mere $500 for what turned out to be his first and last "Grand National" victory. "The money doesn't concern me. I won a race today," he said. "We done it, and there ain't been a better race all year."[53]

But racing exists on two different planes—on track and off. And off the track, Williams took a financial beating from which he never recovered. "When I had the first Grand National race," he said, "I had a truck, a trailer, two cars and no engines. A year later, I didn't have no trailer, no truck, no car, no tools, no nothing. I was history. I was historied in 24 weeks."[54] Williams ran only two more Grand National races, winning a grand total of $1,790, before calling it a career. He later likened the experience to fighting a losing battle with City Hall. But the more precise metaphor was tugging on Superman's cape. France hardly felt it, and when he shrugged, Williams went flying into oblivion.

By 1976, the remaining independents were so unhappy that they started noodling over a wildcat strike. After talking things over with Hylton, France put together a program titled "Plan C," which guaranteed the top twenty nonwinning drivers up to $15,000 a year in appearance money. At the time, the big names were getting more like $100,000. So the rich got richer and, as the ancient Greek political philosopher Thucydides once put it, "the weak suffer what they must."

TV Tommy Ivo whets the crowd's appetite in the tire-roasting Top Fueler that broke the 7.0-second barrier in 1962. The digger was known as The Barnstormer, an especially apt name because Ivo spent less time competing in NHRA elimination events than he did crisscrossing the country in a series of dragsters he called "the baddest bears in the woods" as a headliner in match races against local heroes or other traveling pros. *Tony Thacker Collection*

CHAPTER THIRTEEN

A QUARTER MILE TO GLORY

Yellow River Drag Strip was an outlaw track. Not an outlaw in the sense that it was illegal or a lone pariah that operated beyond the norms of polite society. On the contrary. Yellow River was one of a legion of scruffy drag strips that dotted backwaters all over the country, from the overgrown pastures of the rural South to the featureless sprawl of the exurban West. "A lot of them were back in the woods, and you needed a map just to find them," said Don Prudhomme, who visited just about all of them during his long career.[1] What made these tracks outlaws was the fact that they weren't sanctioned by the National Hot Rod Association (NHRA) or the American Hot Rod Association (AHRA). Instead of big-time events featuring full fields of national stars, they catered mostly to local run-what-you-brung competition—a motley mixture of fair-weather drag racers in street-legal cars and semi-pro ringers with more moxie than money.

For outlaw tracks, the money shows were "booked in" slates of match races hyped through newspaper ads, flyers, and radio spots exhorting listeners to "BEEE THERRRRRE!!!" NHRA and AHRA races featured a series of elimination rounds until the two last remaining cars faced off in the final. A typical match race, on the other hand, involved two headliners who were usually paid a flat fee to race heads-up in a best two-out-of-three format. On special occasions, to boost attendance, promoters would put together a "Chicago-style" show with four racers competing on a round-robin basis. And that's exactly what drew five thousand fans to Yellow River Drag Strip in Covington, Georgia, on Sunday, March 2, 1969.

The attraction was a quartet of Funny Cars featuring blown, big-block, nitro-gulping engines in tube-frame chassis covered by fiberglass, flip-top bodies that resembled muscle cars of the era. Good ones blasted through the quarter mile in eight seconds while going out the back door at more than 180 miles per hour. They weren't quite as fast as Top Fuel slingshots, but they were more squirrelly going down the track—and more popular with the fans. This made them naturals for the match-race circuit, where spectators were eager to root for their Mopar, Ford, and GM faves.

The three out-of-town invitees at Yellow River were Arnie Beswick in the Tameless Tiger Pontiac GTO, Malcolm Durham in the Strip Blazer Corvair, and Frank Ogelsby in a Cougar owned by "Dyno Don" Nicholson, who'd recently switched to Pro Stock after deciding that Funny Cars were too hairy for his taste. The local stud was Georgian Huston Platt, who campaigned his Camaro as the Dixie Twister. The chassis came from the Logghe Stamping Company, a top Funny Car builder of the day. Although Chrysler Hemis were the engines of choice in this period, Platt's mill was a Chevy V-8 bored and stroked to 498 cubic inches and topped by a GMC 6-71 supercharger.

The drag strip consisted of a narrow, two-lane furrow of asphalt cut through a woody Georgia hollow that now houses a mobile home tract about thirty-five miles east of Atlanta. Although there were chain-link fences and guardrails near the start line, nothing separated the spectators from the rest of the track other than shallow dirt berms. The shut down area was particularly iffy, with a curve right in the middle. The conditions weren't ideal, to put it mildly, but they also weren't especially dubious by the standards of the day, which were, admittedly, not very high. As Platt said later, "There wasn't a track in 10 states that was qualified to run those cars back then."[2]

By midafternoon, the crowd was liquored up and rowdy. Several PA announcements requesting that spectators move away from the track were ignored. At 2:20 p.m., Platt staged in the right lane for his run against Ogelsby. In front of him, the drag strip was flanked by two unbroken lines of people stretching to the finish lights. Platt launched cleanly. But about one thousand feet into the run, he heard a loud bang. He immediately popped his parachute. Although there is a brief clip of amateur video of the wreck, it's too blurry to show exactly what happened. According to drag racing lore, a foolhardy fan moved toward the track to grab a beer can and was swallowed up by the billowing chute. For whatever reason, the Dixie Twister angled to the right and arced over the dirt berm like a crowd-surfing rock star and thudded into a tightly packed mass of humanity. Contemporary reports say the car was going 150 mph when it hit.

In and of itself, the crash wasn't serious. If there had been a decent barrier in place, Platt would have walked away unscathed—which, in fact, he did. But because there was no spectator protection, the results were cataclysmic. Eleven spectators died at the scene, and a twelfth died later in the hospital. The youngest was three years old; the oldest, sixty-five. The rest were in their teens and twenties. More than forty people were injured.

This was the worst tragedy in the history of American motorsports.

Yet behind this simple, declarative sentence is a long, complicated story. Although there was plenty of regional coverage of the accident, the Yellow River catastrophe wasn't a big story in the rest of the country. Today, amazingly, it's almost completely forgotten. Even drag racers who were active at the time have only a hazy recollection that something really ugly occurred on a really sketchy drag strip somewhere far, far away. This is a comment less on the fallibility of memory than the barbaric safety record of drag racing in the 1960s. Sure, twelve dead and forty-plus injured in a single incident are appalling numbers. But this was an era when the drivers of Top Fuel rails and Funny Cars were killed as regularly as Social Security checks were cut. To understand why carnage was so commonplace requires looking back at the roots of the sport.

Racing is encoded into the DNA of Homo sapiens. Running fast was a primary technique for escaping from predators in the African savannah, and, as the old joke goes, I don't have to outrun the bear. I just have to outrun you. So foot races from, say, this tree to that pond were almost certainly one of the first forms of competitive entertainment known to man. But this format didn't translate well to automobiles. Early cars were large, heavy, and underpowered. Transmissions were crude, and tire grip was virtually nonexistent. Acceleration from a standing start was glacial, which made the first generation of cars look unimpressive compared with their equine counterparts.

From the beginning, the standard metric wasn't 0 to 60; it was top speed. The first motorsports celebrity was Belgian Camille Jenatzy, christened "the Red Devil" for breaking the 100-kilometer-an-hour barrier. Even as road circuits and ovals were becoming the dominant rivers of motorsports, land-speed-record racing developed into a small but well-traveled tributary. In the years between the two world wars, aristocratic Englishmen such as Henry Segrave, Malcolm Campbell, George Eyston, and John Cobb emerged as heroes as they pushed their leviathans past 200 mph, 250 mph, 300 mph, and 350 mph.

Land-speed racing followed a different trajectory here in the United States. During the Great Depression, instead of fabricating custom bodies around gigantic airplane engines, an eclectic collection of young, resourceful, self-taught mechanics began stripping down dirt-cheap Model A and Model T Fords and massaging their pedestrian flathead engines with a potent amalgamation of DIY modifications—trick carburetors, custom intake manifolds, magic camshafts, straight pipes. To see how fast their fenderless roadsters would run, these proto-hot rodders ventured north from Los Angeles into the Mojave Desert. There, the Southern California Timing Association (SCTA) and other SoCal car clubs staged speed meets on the dry lake beds of Rosamond, Harper, and best-loved of all, Muroc.

During World War II, Muroc served as a US Army Air Corps training base. After the war, it became the home of America's experimental aircraft program. Lauded as the repository of the Right Stuff, Muroc was the base that launched the Bell X-1 rocket plane, which broke the sound barrier, and the North American X-15, which pierced the edge of space. Because of all the aviation activity, automobile racing at Muroc was banned. Land-speed meets continued to be staged on the dry lake at El Mirage. But in 1949, the SCTA moved its big summer meet to the salt flats at Bonneville, and the heyday of the dry lakes was over.

This wasn't the only change percolating in the late 1940s. When World War II ended, servicemen returned to Southern California with cash in their pockets, first-rate fabrication and mechanic-ing skills in their toolboxes, and an enduring thirst for adventure in their souls. Also, thanks to the staggering growth of the aviation industry during the war years, the region was flush with machine shops and foundries that offered easy access to cutting-edge equipment and materials. The result was the birth of a subculture that was named "hot rodding," and a vast aftermarket speed-parts industry grew up to support it. For a core group of hot rodders, land-speed racing remained the sine qua non of the sport, and they made annual pilgrimages to the holy land at Bonneville. But Utah was a long way from Los Angeles, especially in the days before the interstate highway system was built. Accommodations were spartan, and since the salt flats were so vast, the action didn't lend itself to spectator viewing.

Predictably, other forms of grassroots racing sprang up closer to home. Various formats were used in various locations. But the format that seemed the most natural was racing from a standing start—the automotive version of cavemen running from this tree to that pond. What's generally considered to be the first modern drag race was staged on Sunday, April 10, 1949, on a service road of the Santa Barbara Municipal Airport, between two veterans of the dry lakes scene. The favorite was Tom Cobbs, heir to a tobacco fortune, who'd shortened a '34 Ford frame, clothed it with channeled '29 Ford Model A roadster bodywork, and added a '29 DeSoto grille as an aesthetic flourish. Under the hood was a 239-cubic-inch Mercury flathead topped by a then-rare, fearsome 3-71 Jimmy blower cannibalized from a GMC bus. Facing off against him was Fran Hernandez, shop manager for Vic Edelbrock, who was one of the leading lights of the thriving go-fast parts business sector. The fenders of his Deuce coupe had been unbolted, and the Merc V-8 had been bored and stroked to 296 cubic inches. What nobody realized was that Edelbrock had started experimenting with nitromethane, the miracle potion that still powers Top Fuel dragsters and Funny Cars. When the flag fell, Cobbs smoked his tires, and Hernandez pulled out a gap that couldn't be closed. He had his car on the trailer before anybody could investigate any further.

Even though the Hernandez–Cobbs grudge match has been immortalized as "the day drag racing began," the sport officially dates from the following year.[3] In 1950, the owners of Santa Ana Municipal Airport, a sleepy airfield about an hour south of LA, agreed to allow cars to race on Sundays on an unused airstrip in return for 10 percent of the gate receipts. The deal had been put together by a triumvirate led by C.J. Hart, better known as "Pappy," a former moonshiner turned used-car dealer. On June 19, about five hundred spectators paid fifty cents per ticket to watch the cars in action, which included Hart's wife, Peggy, in their Model T roadster. "I didn't invent drag racing," Hart insisted later. "Heck, that sort of thing's been going on ever since there was cars."[4] True. But it was the Santa Ana Drags that gave this casual pastime a formal structure.

After some trial and error, the conventions that defined drag racing for decades to come were established—two cars pairing up side by side, then blasting off together toward a finish line a quarter mile, or 1,320 feet, straight down the track. With the creation of this formula, the sport grew at a phenomenal pace. Drag strips popped up like invasive weeds throughout the state, mostly in small towns loitering on the edges of more populated areas—Salinas, Tustin, Lodi, Bakersfield, Newhall, Tracy, Inyokern, the list goes on and on. But these were threadbare operations where the competition was variable and the amenities virtually nonexistent. A substantial segment of the hot rod world preferred to run their cars on Van Nuys Boulevard or the concrete bed of the Los Angeles River, competing for cash, pink slips, or pride. Street racing didn't go over well with either the police or the public, prompting self-righteous and quasi-hysterical demands to crack down on this brand of juvenile delinquency.

Enter Wally Parks. As a prewar lakes racer, he'd been one of the founders of the SCTA, and he ramrodded the effort to bring land-speed racing to Bonneville. Along the way, he befriended a visionary by the name of Robert "Pete" Petersen, who recognized the business opportunities offered by hot rodding. When Petersen launched *Hot Rod* in 1948, he installed Parks as the editor in chief, and the magazine instantly became required reading for the hot rod set. Worried that street racers were giving hot rodding a bad name, Parks wanted to limit competition to established drag strips. The problem was that there was no governing body, so each track owner promulgated his own set of rules, and confusion reigned.

In March 1951, Parks cofounded the National Hot Rod Association to "create order out of chaos."[5] As the longtime NHRA president, he was the drag racing analog of Bill France—an undisputed leader who legitimized a branch of motorsports by bringing it under a single all-powerful umbrella. This wasn't the only similarity between the two men. Like Big Bill, Parks was a tall (six feet, four inches), personable character who cut a dignified figure. Like France, Parks had a very specific vision of the nature and future of his organization, and he clashed with those who wanted to nudge it in a different direction. And like France, he had his detractors, though none who challenged his character. "He always tried to take the high road to make the sport safer, to make it better," said Steve Gibbs, who was an NHRA executive for nearly fifty years. "He wasn't in it for the money. He made good money, a good living. But he could have made a whole lot more if that's all he wanted to do."[6] Like NASCAR, NHRA faced several rivals over the years. But when the dust settled, NASCAR and NHRA were the only ones left standing in their respective domains.

The first drag racing cars were street rods and lakes racers. But the smart guys immediately realized that getting to the 1,320-foot mark first meant that acceleration was more important than sustained top speed. This placed a premium on the power-to-weight ratio. Aerodynamics? Not so much. The first purpose-built dragster was a bodyless T roadster packing a flathead Ford. By the mid-1950s, speed king Mickey Thompson had popularized the slingshot, so-called because the driver sat at the tail end of a ladder-style frame, behind the rear wheels, like a rock in a slingshot.

Eventually, cars were classed according to bodies, chassis, engines, and fuel. (In drag racing parlance, "fuel" classes are limited to cars running anything *but* gasoline, hence the sarcastic quote often attributed to Don

Garlits: "Alcohol is for drinking, gas is for cleaning parts, and nitro is for racing."[7]) Because Parks envisioned NHRA as an organization for enthusiasts rather than professionals, there was a place for everything, from relatively stock production cars to scratch-built slingshots, aka rails or diggers. Speed determined the pecking order. At the top of the hill were slingshots powered by supercharged engines drinking from a gas tank spiked with nitromethane. Known as Top Fuel cars, or generically as "fuelers," these spindly dragsters packed so much "pop" that they usually spun their tires from the start to the finish of a run. Classified as AA/FD, they were the poster child for the competitiveness, technological innovation, and unrivaled spectacle of drag racing.

With this spectacle came spectacular crashes. The NHRA's founding slogan was "Dedicated to Safety," and in 1954, the club secured insurance through Aetna.[8] That summer, the first of three NHRA Safety Safaris began visiting racetracks across the country. The name notwithstanding, the Safety Safaris weren't primarily about, you know, safety. They were to show racetrack owners best practices for running a race event—how to weigh and number the cars, how to stage and time them, how to collect engine oil, how to site the bathrooms. The idea, again, was to create order out of chaos.

Promoting safety was a tougher challenge. Many of the fastest cars were homebuilt contraptions of widely varying quality, and the technology—some of it brilliant, some of it wacky—changed by the week. In 1957, to put a lid on top speed, NHRA banned nitromethane. This had the unintended consequence of raising the profile of the upstart American Hot Rod Association (AHRA), which doubled down on Top Fuel racing. Meanwhile, Lions Drag Strip, the most prominent track in the country, continued to cater to fuel classes. And the most prestigious event of the year, the Smokers Meet at Famoso Raceway, was dominated by fuelers.

Aside from the nitro ban, safety standards were minimal. When Dick Kraft built drag racing's first rail, dubbed "the Bug," he clocked speeds better than 110 mph at the Santa Ana Drags in 1950 while going bare chested—or, when it was really sweltering, stripping down to a bathing suit. By the late 1950s, when fuelers were posting elapsed times in the eight-second range and top speeds faster than 180 mph, the standard "uniform" was a T-shirt and blue jeans. That's what Garlits was wearing when his digger exploded during a match race in 1959 in Chester, South Carolina. "I would have been killed in that fire had my wife not given me a black leather jacket to wear at that event," he recalled. "That was the first time I wore a jacket, and it saved my life. And I had aviation goggles, and that saved my eyes."[9] But he wasn't wearing gloves, and his hands were so badly charred that they looked like incinerated chicken wings. "My God!"[10] the emergency room physician said when Garlits was rolled in. "There's nothing we can do for this man!" Fortunately, he *didn't* do anything, meaning he didn't amputate Garlits's hands, which had been the doctor's initial intention. Instead, Garlits kept his hands submerged in a saline solution for six weeks to guard against infection before resuming a career that would earn him the sobriquet "Big Daddy" and make him the most enduring icon in drag racing history.

Dick Kraft realized that weight, not drag, was the major enemy in drag racing. So he took a 1927 Model T Ford that had been used for pesticide-spraying duty and stripped it down to the frame rails. No body, no front brakes, and, on occasion, no shirt. Mods included a flathead Ford V-8 and a seat fashioned out of two pieces of wood. In 1950, he ran the quarter mile at 113.92 mph. *Tony Thacker Collection*

The first major safety advancement unique to drag racing was the parachute. There's no universal agreement about who introduced it or exactly when it debuted; the sport was so new, and the coverage was so spotty, that a lot of first-time-ever stories carry the whiff of mythology. The most commonly accepted origin story contends that SoCal racer Abe Carson sought help from Irving Air Chute, which had supplied parachutes to the US military and forty-five other nations during World War II. The company wasn't interested, but it allowed one of its employees, Jim Deist, to take the job on a moonlighting basis.

A former lakes racer himself, Deist started experimenting with an army-surplus parachute on a paved but not-yet-opened section of an interstate highway near his home in Burbank. The parachute was so effective that, when it was deployed, it yanked the rear bumper off his Ford station wagon. Next, Bob Muravez, a local racer who drove a series of twin-engine diggers known as Freight Trains while using the *nom de course* Floyd Lippencott Jr., tested a modified version at the San Fernando Drag Strip. "At that time, I was running about 150 [mph] consistently," Muravez said. "There was no lever for the chute. The D ring was taped to my shoulder harness, and I pulled it when I went through the lights. *Pow!* When I got back to the pits, Jim said, 'What do you think?' I pulled off my leather jacket, and I had bruises from the straps. My goggles had two little dots on them. I told him, 'Jim, I think those are my eyeballs.'"[11]

Another SoCal hot rodder, Bill Simpson, developed a smaller, gentler ribbon-style, cruciform parachute designed especially for drag racing. By the end of the decade, he and Deist had become the principal suppliers of safety gear in the drag racing and land-speed-record spaces, starting with parachutes, then branching out into seat belts, fire-retardant suits and gloves, hardware, and, in Simpson's case, helmets. Besides being bitter rivals, they were yin and yang personified. "Jim Diest was easygoing, laid-back, kind of a jolly, old grandfather," said Carl Olson, a Top Fuel driver who later became a highly respected safety maven. "Bill Simpson was a raving maniac."[12] Nevertheless, they both prospered because there were plenty of customers to go around. As Simpson recalled, "The cars were evolving so fast that there was always something new that could get you hurt. Parts broke, tires blew, wheels came apart, frames collapsed. For a while we had problems with clutches blowing up so violently that they'd cut a car right in half. And sometime they'd cut off a guy's feet, too."[13]

The elevated risks didn't translate into bigger paydays. Besides being the newest form of motorsports, drag racing was also the least lucrative. It had developed as a grassroots sport, and there were those who believed it should remain a largely amateur hobby or, at best, a break-even proposition. "Wally always said, 'When we start paying [prize] money, the sport will be ruined,'" Garlits said.[14] In those days, it cost from $6,000 to $8,000 to build and campaign a Top Fuel car. Yet in 1964, when Garlits won Top Fuel at the Nationals, which was the biggest race on the NHRA calendar, his take was $500 in cash, plus a 1965 Mustang, a 195-piece Craftsman tool set, a set of Firestone tires, and a bunch of other merchandise. And this was a stupendous jackpot, by contemporary yardsticks. At local shows, the usual prize for winning Top Fuel was $500—not in cash, mind you, but in a savings bond that was worth only $375 if you redeemed it right away.

Genius, right? Drag racing trailblazer Lou Baney had come up with the bond idea while running the drag strip in Saugus and competing with Hart's track in Santa Ana. "C.J. had started giving trophies away, so we decided to give out a $25 war bond (which only cost us $18.75) for Top Eliminator, and at a really big meet we'd give out a $100 bond," Baney said. "Well, wouldn't you know it, we'd offer the $100 bond or $75 cash, and the drag racers back then were just like racers today, because they always took the cash. I don't think we ever actually gave away a war bond at one of our races."[15]

That was Baney speaking as a promoter in the early 1950s. By the mid-1960s, when he was a big-time car owner, he was singing a different tune. "I feel that anyone who races a fueler, if they were to put as much time, effort and diligence into a job as they put into their car, would end up with 50 times as much money as they end up with from racing," he said.[16] Case in point: While the baby-faced Don Prudhomme was accumulating an unbelievable 200–9 win-loss record (or maybe it was 236–7, record keeping being an imperfect science in those days) in the legendary Greer-Black-Prudhomme fueler, he continued to work his day job as a car painter. "The money I won driving the Greer car, that was just fun money," Prudhomme said. "The first time I started to make pretty good money was when I went match racing. There was one year we run about seventy events, up and down the road. [Tommy] Ivo would do like one hundred of them."[17]

"TV Tommy" was the first superstar of drag racing, but he didn't achieve celebrity status by winning NHRA nationals or the big Smokers Meet. No doubt, it helped that Ivo was a well-known child actor who continued to make movies and appear regularly on television into his twenties. Also, he was a natural showman, not to mention a fearless racer who set a bunch of records in a series of cars that he referred to collectively as "the baddest bears in the woods."[18] In 1960, he was featured on magazine covers in a twin-engine slingshot, the idea being that two gas motors were better than one nitro mill. While he was on summer hiatus from the TV show *Margie*, he got a call from a promoter back east. "Listen," the promoter said, "if you want to come back here and run your car on our tracks, we'll give you a race every weekend—ten weekends in a row for $500 a race."[19] Ivo promptly signed on the dotted line.

Ivo did his own wrenching, but he couldn't go it alone. To join him on the road, he hired a teenage car painter who lived nearby—a fresh-faced kid named Don Prudhomme. Neither one of them looked old enough to shave. Using Ivo's Cadillac coupe to tow the dragster on a single-axle open trailer, they hit fifteen tracks around the country. At a lot of them, the fans were so jazzed to see a twin-engine car—packing a parachute, no less!—that Ivo made exhibition passes with nobody in the other lane. Two years later, he hit the road again for an extended tour with a new fueler. "They'd pay me $1,000 and the local guy $500, but it was a foregone conclusion who was going to win," he said. "So I told them, 'Why don't you spend an extra $500 to get Garlits instead of a local guy, and then you'll make $5,000.' And they did. And I raced that darned guy about fifty times a year."[20]

Ivo only occasionally bothered to compete in NHRA events, which paid next to nothing. Instead, he put together a little black book of promoters and track owners, and these contacts kept him busy year-round while fattening his wallet. Before long, match racing was such a big thing that there were a handful of agents who lined up shows at tracks big and small all across the country. These shows were a godsend for touring pros, but the money also came in handy for local hot shoes recruited to run against the booked-in gunslingers.

By 1964, there were no more than three hundred Top Fuel cars around the country, most built to similar specs since the vast majority of weirdo "innovations" had been track-tested and rejected. The typical chassis was a long, narrow, ladder-style frame about eighteen inches wide at the cockpit, sometimes sheathed in bodywork, sometimes left bare. At the front were laced moped wheels; at the rear, tall narrow slicks. The driver hung out the ass end of the car in an open capsule surrounded by a roll bar with a central down-tube. In front of him, obscuring his vision, was a 392-cubic-inch cast-iron Chrysler Hemi, topped with a 6-71 GMC blower and blowing flames out of so-called zoomies—J-shaped exhaust headers that routed tire smoke away from the driver and produced downforce to help keep the chassis planted. Good fuelers weighed about 1,500 pounds and made roughly 1,200 horsepower, which translated into seven seconds and 190 mph. Visibility sucked, and the handling wasn't much better. There was none of this modern change-rods-pistons-bearings-and-rings action after every pass. Tires might last a dozen runs. Engines ran until they broke.

By 1964, drag racing was on the verge of a quantum leap. Before the season began, Parks reluctantly rescinded his ban on nitromethane. As a practical matter, AHRA and numerous unaffiliated tracks had been running fuel races already. But the NHRA decision opened the floodgates. The Smokers Meet drew more than one hundred fuelers competing for thirty-two slots in the field, with Connie Kalitta outrunning Garlits in the final. Kalitta's win was the first victory for Goodyear's brand-new drag slick, and it marked the start of a protracted, expensive tire war that caused speeds to soar. During the summer, the 200 mph barrier was finally breached. (Garlits was officially credited with setting the record, but as with many drag racing firsts, this claim is widely disputed.) By the end of the year, 200 mph was old news. The next year, no fewer than fifty-three fuelers competed in Thompson's Gathering of Monsters at Fontana Drag City, which was open only to cars that had already collected 200 mph time slips.

As speeds jumped, so did fatalities. In February 1964, John Wenderski was killed in a freak accident when a gust of wind blew his car off the pavement, flipping into a rocky field. Over the next seven months, five more Top Fuel drivers were killed, along with a passerby who was struck by a rail that had gone out of control. And 1965 was even worse, with nine fatal wrecks. Parachutes failed to deploy. Engines blew. Axles broke. Wheels flew off. To a certain extent, these were foreseeable failures. It didn't help that drivers themselves were so nonchalant when it came to safety. "For most guys, it was a distant second to performance," said Leroy "Doc" Hales, who paid his way through medical school by driving a Funny Car. "Some people even bitched about it. *Oh, God, I gotta have this now? It's gonna cost me a bunch of money.*"[21]

While car safety was marginal, the tracks themselves were death traps. "Fremont had light poles, with nothing protecting you from them," Olson remembered. "Half Moon Bay had a drainage ditch at the end of a very short emergency runoff area, and if you didn't get the car stopped before the end of the track, you'd nosedive into this ditch and hit a dirt bank. That's what killed Denny Milani, who'd driven my car before I bought it. Salinas had a line of fifty-five-gallon drums filled with sand protecting what was designated as the pit area from the racetrack on the left side, and on the right side was barbed wire fence all the way down the track and cattle on the other side. It had a forty-five-degree, right-hand turn with the dip in the middle, a couple hundred feet down the shut-off area. And then where the taxiway intersected with the runway was another line of sand-filled fifty-five-gallon drums. That was one of the most dangerous tracks I ever ran on. But it was all we had. And so we turned a blind eye to how dangerous it was."[22]

As the 426 Hemi, nicknamed "the elephant motor," and the Ford Cammer, named for its overhead-camshaft valvetrain, came online, engines made *way* more power than the tires could handle. In the days before treated drag strip surfaces and super-sticky rubber, it wasn't uncommon for fuelers to smoke the tires for an entire run. The weak link was the clutch. Early on, drag racers went to dual-disc units to handle the torque produced by the engine. Conventional wisdom held that the best clutch was the one that hooked up first, since this would get power to the ground fastest. So most guys used a grippy friction material patented as VelveTouch on their clutch discs. But as engines started developing more torque—a lot more torque—something had to give. Ergo, when the clutch locked up, the tires would spin. Some drivers were more adept than others at slipping the clutch off the line and modulating the throttle during a pass to prevent the tires from breaking traction. But this wasn't easy, and it was hard to pull off run after run.

Enter the slipper clutch. As the names implied, it allowed the clutch to slip a predetermined amount, which prevented the tires from spinning. Instead of smoking the tires all the way down the track, traction was maximized, and speeds increased dramatically. As with so much drag racing history, the invention of the slipper clutch is a murky subject, though it's often attributed to Roland Leong. A native of Hawaii, Leong's first—and last—run in a fueler ended in a harmless crash at Lions. After that, as an owner/mechanic, he campaigned a long series of successful rails and Funny Cars as "The Hawaiian." In 1965, he teamed up with Prudhomme and renowned engine builder Keith Black to win the two most prestigious races on the NHRA calendar—the Winternationals at Pomona and the Nationals at Indianapolis Raceway Park.

The next year, as the story goes, while rebuilding a conventional clutch, Leong inadvertently installed one of the plates backward. This prevented the disc from mating securely with the flywheel. When Mike Snively, who'd replaced Prudhomme, launched the car with the new slipper clutch, he made a surprisingly quick, smokeless run down the track. Armed with this secret weapon, The Hawaiian scored back-to-back wins in the Winternationals and the Nats in 1966. Before long, other racers began reducing spring pressure on the pressure plate to allow clutches to slip. Then, Bruce Crower and Carl Schiefer started selling clutches designed to slip a predetermined amount without any driver input. These slipper clutches revolutionized the sport—for better or worse—by taking a lot of the finesse out of how cars were launched off the line.

Like any mechanical component, clutches will break if they're overstressed. Since the bellhousing that held them was nestled between the feet of the drivers, builders realized early on that it would be a good idea to encase the clutch in a protective metal cocoon called a clutch can. This was fine for conventional clutches, but with the advent of the slipper clutch and the tremendous buildup of heat inside the bellhousing, a hydroformed-aluminum clutch can, or even one made of welded steel, was no longer adequate. As Black said, "The thing had become so dangerous that you might as well [have handed] the driver a hand grenade with the pin pulled."[23]

The grenade exploded at the end of 1967 while Mike Sorokin, onetime boon companion of Bill Simpson and a past Hawaiian shoe, was running a fueler at Orange County International Raceway. The clutch exploded, and the flywheel severed the car in two pieces. The cockpit tumbled down the track like a wobbly basketball with Sorokin strapped half in and half out of the cockpit. It was one of the most gruesome accidents in drag racing history, and it prompted the NHRA to issue an order to "make all clutches safe, or go back to smoking the tires."[24]

Independently, the Speed Equipment Manufacturers Association (SEMA), which had been formed a decade earlier by aftermarket parts vendors such as Edelbrock and Diest, created a technical committee to vet the parts being used by drag racers. "It was ultimately determined that the first and most important element of controlling the problem was to develop some minimum standards for the products themselves because there was a lot of junk out there," said Olson, who was the drag racing representative on the committee.[25] The first set of criteria governed clutches and flywheels. Clutch containment devices, that is, clutch cans, were next on the list. Still, the SEMA regulations weren't infallible. In 1969, John "the Zookeeper" Mulligan died after his clutch exploded at the Nationals and his fueler was engulfed in a terrible ball of fire, and the next year, at the same track, Jim Nicoll was miraculously unharmed when a runaway flywheel carved his Top Fuel car in half during a *Wide World of Sports* broadcast. (After winning the race, convinced that Nicoll had been killed, a distraught Prudhomme said morosely on camera, "I think I'm quitting."[26]) But the problem was largely solved by the 1970s.

Transmissions, though, were another story. In the late 1950s, everybody started using direct drive. By 1969, when Hemis were making 3,000 horsepower, Garlits theorized that a two-speed transmission might be the way to go. It turned out that a SoCal fueler named Leonard Abbott had built an experimental unit based on '49 Ford overdrive gears, and he was happy to give it to Garlits. "I ran it for three months before anybody realized I had a two-speed," Garlits recalled. "I told everybody the second gear was a reverser that never worked. But then Snake and Roland Leong caught on during a tire test at Indianapolis. Leonard sent the first production two-speed to Prudhomme, which really pissed me off, so that's when I decided to develop my own two-speed with Quarter Master Industries."[27]

Garlits based his transmission on a more modern and seemingly robust Chrysler TorqueFlite. What he didn't realize was that it contained a small sprag that wasn't strong enough to withstand the power of a nitro engine. At Lions in March 1970, when he matted the throttle of Swamp Rat 13, the sprag flipped backward and allowed the transmission drum to spin at three times engine speed. "Well, it couldn't do that," Garlits said. "At about 20,000 rpm, the drum split in two and cut the car in two and cut half my foot off."[28] Start line photos of Garlits and the cockpit kicked up in the air at a seventy-five-degree angle to the chassis are among the most arresting images in drag racing history.

While he spent six weeks recuperating in the hospital, Garlits came up with an idea that would render every Top Fuel car in existence obsolete. Back in Florida, he, Connie Swingle, and Tommy Lemons built a rail with the engine, clutch, and transmission—which is to say, all the stuff that was prone to blowing up real good—*behind* the driver. Rear-engine cars had been tried before without much success because they were so darty going down the track. And, as it happened, Garlits spun his experimental creation over and over during three months of largely fruitless testing. It wasn't until the steering ratio was slowed down that the handling woes were cured. During his first run with the modified steering, Garlits glimpsed a future that was far safer—and faster—than the immediate past. As a bonus, his face wasn't being splattered with hot oil, fuel, and water, and he had a panoramic view of the track in front of him. Garlits and Swamp Rat 14 opened the 1971 season with a pair of runner-up finishes, then won the Winternationals and the March Meet. By 1973, front-engine slingshots were as antiquated as flathead Fords.

But even as Top Fuel cars were becoming safer than ever, a new, more popular—and somewhat controversial—class was generating fresh concerns about safety, or the lack thereof. The genesis of what would eventually be dubbed Funny Cars is, like so many drag racing tales, convoluted and contestable. In some respects, you could almost say that the class created itself. Muscle cars were taking off in the 1960s, so it was only natural that drag racing versions would be developed. A lot of the action in those days came in match races and exhibitions rather than formally sanctioned NHRA and AHRA competition. Instead of obeying the letter of the law, enterprising racers started flouting the rules to win cash money rather than competing for trophies and negligible payouts. Although these mods rendered the cars ineligible for any existing classes, they were a big hit with fans. In 1964, NHRA bowed to the inevitable and created the Factory Experimental class, or F/X. "The name gives clear indication of how the game here is played," ran an editorial in *National Dragster*, NHRA's official magazine. "It's expensive, true, far more than racing in the other stock classes, and is precisely why NHRA set it apart from competition by the individual."[29]

The Ford Thunderbolt was what the NHRA had in mind. Ford built one hundred of these race-spec Fairlanes retrofitted with big-block high-rise 427s, which gave grassroots competitors access to a reasonably affordable, professionally built race car. But Dodge quickly raised the ante with a trio of Chargers packing supercharged 480-cubic-inch Max Wedge engines that marauded across the country with official Mopar backing. This inspired Californian Jack Chrisman to stuff a blown Ford 427 in a Mercury Comet and feed it with nitromethane. He also moved the engine back two feet to improve weight distribution. Chrisman's seminal creation smoked the tires halfway down the track when it debuted at the NHRA Nationals in 1964.

This got Chrysler's attention. At the AHRA Winternationals in 1965, there were seven Dodges and Plymouths powered by blown, nitro-fueled versions of the 426 Hemi. To improve the handling, the front wheels had been moved forward ten inches and the rears fifteen inches. According to drag racing folklore, again unconfirmed, an AHRA announcer said the odd proportions looked "funny." Later that year, Ford unveiled a quartet of Comets with blown Cammers. But unlike the production-based Thunderbolts from only one year earlier, these new cars featured tube-frame chassis, altered wheelbases, and one-piece fiberglass bodies that flipped up as a unit. Dubbed "flip-tops," or "floppers," or just plain "flops," cars built to this template were soon classified as Funny Cars.

Fans couldn't get enough of them. Unlike the rails, gassers, and fuel altereds that had long been treated like drag racing royalty, Funny Cars looked like the models sold in new-car showrooms. Plus, they were spectacular going down the track, breaking the 200 mph barrier in 1969, and they made the same noises as the big-deal Top Fuelers. In 1967, Irwindale ran a Funny Car–only show—a sign of the times. In 1970, when the NHRA rejiggered its race format, Funny Car was enshrined as one of the four pro classes at national events. By this time, it had surpassed Top Fuel not only in terms of popularity but also

Funny Cars are essentially shortened Top Fuelers with fiberglass bodywork hinged at the rear, hence the nicknames "flip-top," "flopper," or just plain "flop." Unlike modern versions, Funny Cars still resembled street cars in 1971. This is the Plymouth Barracuda that Don Prudhomme raced as the Snake II. Assembled on a "Lil'" John Buttera chassis and powered by a Keith Black Hemi, it topped out at 226 mph. *Revs Institute / Pete Biro Photograph Collection*

commercial opportunities. Funny Car events were paying more than $1,000 in contingency while Top Fuel was getting only $150.

Generally speaking, old-timers didn't like them. There was no getting around the fact that Funny Cars looked freakish. They were volatile when they left the line. The enclosed cockpit meant that engine fires were likely to be DEFCON 1 events. Still, Top Fuel diehards like Carl Olson could see where the sport was going. So he bought a Hemi-powered Funny Car, climbed into the cockpit, had the body lowered, and the engine started. "I was looking right at the back of the fuel injector," he recalled. "I couldn't see the front wheels. The TorqueFlite transmission was leaking turkey blood. I let it run for two minutes. When I got out, I put an ad in *Drag News*. That was the entire Funny Car phase of my drag racing career."[30]

Funny Cars were hard to handle and dangerous when provoked. Ford stalwart Les Ritchey was killed in 1966 when a rear axle sheared off during a match race, and Doug Cook of Stone, Woods & Cook fame was critically injured when his car flipped the next year. The no-holds-barred aspect of early Funny Cars was highlighted in 1968 when two drivers died in oddball vehicles, one with an E-type Jaguar body and the other resembling a Cadillac Eldorado. Fire was a constant hazard. Ford factory ace Gas Ronda, who'd been Ritchey's partner, was badly burned in 1970 when his engine let go and transmission fluid burned through the firewall. (It took him nearly a year to recover.) Shortly thereafter, NHRA required that all Funny Cars carry at least five pounds of Freon, and some of the most prominent drivers, such as Tom McEwen, fitted their cars with fully plumbed Halon fire-suppression systems.

Money—real money in the form of corporate dollars—started flowing into the sport at the dawn of the 1970s. The popularity of Funny Cars helped. Coca-Cola sponsored the Funny Car Cavalcade of Stars, which trouped across the country like a rock band on a national tour. To sell Hot Wheels models, Mattel promoted the Snake versus Mongoose match-race series between McEwen and Prudhomme, and Revell was about to enter the fray. Other nonautomotive sponsors included Der Wienerschnitzel, A&W Root Beer, Smirnoff, and even Wonder Bread. First-class tracks with amenities far nicer than the usual bleacher seating and hot dog stands opened in Dallas, Gainesville, and Ontario, California, prompting the NHRA to expand its national schedule from four races to seven and then eight races.

More money meant more competition. But the battles weren't always fought on the drag strip. Like the NHRA, the AHRA had been formed in the 1950s as a nonprofit organization for grassroots racers. But by 1962, it had been commandeered by Jim Tice and reconstituted as a for-profit entity. Big Jim was a bulky, blustery former B-24 pilot who'd gotten his start leading a Studebaker car club called the Slobs. His stated goal was to make money, and promotion was his game. "Jim Tice was the Barnum & Bailey of drag racing," Garlits said. "His main concern was putting what he called 'butts on boards,' meaning people sitting in the stands. Safety wasn't a big issue because he figured the guys who race were professionals who knew how to make their cars as safe as they wanted to. Nobody put a pistol to their heads to get them into their cars. And so if they built a dangerous car, that was their problem."[31]

In 1970, Tice fired a shot across the bow of Wally Parks by creating the Grand American Series of Professional Drag Racing. He cherry-picked an elite group of fuelers who agreed to appear at ten events. In return, they automatically qualified, so they were guaranteed a decent payday no matter how poorly they ran, in addition to competing for a $20,000 championship fund. "AHRA, the sanctioning body that's in the racing BUSINESS, puts up the high dollar 10 times a year in its Grand American series, and the sport's biggest names always seem to come loaded for action," Tice crowed.[32] Meanwhile, Tice got crossways with Larry Carrier, the owner of the über-successful Bristol Dragstrip. Carrier angrily resigned from his position as an AHRA vice president and formed the International Hot Rod Association (IHRA). The IHRA followed most of the practices pioneered by the AHRA. If you were one of the chosen few, the living was easy—prime parking spaces, seeded qualifying, friendly tech inspectors, and so on. Tice and Carrier had such similar business models, in fact, that the former filed a lawsuit against the latter.

The NHRA, meanwhile, stayed steadfastly in its own lane. Its brand was based on providing a level playing field to all comers, no matter how well connected. It also ratcheted up its efforts to raise safety standards, especially for Funny Cars. "Those Funny Cars were dangerous as hell," Prudhomme said. "They'd catch on fire and burn the shit out of you. A lot of guys got burned back in those days."[33] The five-gallon Freon rule did nothing to prevent an epidemic of frightening Funny Car fires in 1972 and into 1973. That April, the NHRA announced a new rule, effective immediately, mandating twenty pounds of Freon or Halon divided into at least two bottles so the fire-extinguishing agent could be shot into both the cockpit and the engine compartment.

But fire continued to be a problem for several more years. Herm Petersen was horrendously burned when the rear axle of his Top Fueler snapped at Orange County International Raceway, and he went topsy-turvy. He survived only because he held his breath for fifty-five seconds while he was being rescued. Even so, he spent three-and-a-half months in a hospital burn unit and underwent countless reconstructive surgeries. Orange County was also the site of another devastating Top Fuel wreck when Kenny Logan lost both legs and a hand after he submarined partly under a guardrail—an accident that hastened the shift to concrete barriers. Another guardrail claimed the life of Pete Robinson during the Winternationals in 1971. A one-time engineering student, "Sneaky Pete" was one of Top Fuel's most inventive innovators, a builder so weight-conscious that he would, as the saying goes, drill a hole in a hole. At Pomona, he'd mounted an experimental skirt under the frame to produce an early form of ground effects. During his final run, his rail veered uncontrollably to the right and disintegrated after hammering the guardrail.

Gibbs, who'd joined the NHRA executive team by this time, realized that safety had to be addressed more proactively, so he oversaw the creation of the TRW Safety Caravan. Despite its impressive name, the unit was so rudimentary that it had no traveling equipment. "Back then, there were only about four races in a season, and we'd ship the timing equipment in a big blue box from place to place," Gibbs recalled. "But when we got to Indianapolis or wherever, we'd have to rent or buy fire extinguishers and trucks to use as emergency vehicles. The tracks might have had some of their own equipment, but we had zero traveling equipment and used volunteer help. Then a company called Weber Clutches provided us with a Jaws of Life, and we reinstituted the Safety Safari primarily because we now had this safety tool that needed to go around the country. And since we were going to do that anyway, we bought a trailer and truck and put in good extinguishers, and we started going around the country with some really first-class safety equipment."[34]

The Safari also got some top-shelf medical expertise in the form of Doc Hales, whose specialty was emergency room medicine. A former Funny Car driver who hung up his Nomex gloves after badly burning his fingers in a wicked drag strip fire—without causing lasting damage, fortunately—Hales attended national events on a volunteer basis, manning emergency vehicles as well as providing medical attention. Fires still occurred, but they were no longer a scourge. "People get burned when they're in a fire for a prolonged period of time," he explained. "We could get to a Funny Car fire within twenty or thirty seconds, at most, from the time it started, and we would have it out in ten or twenty seconds."[35] Thanks in part to the work of the Safety Safari, Robinson would be the last driver to be killed during a NHRA national event until Blaine Johnson died in a Top Fuel car at Indy in 1996.

In December 1972, the last rites were said over Lion's Drag Strip, the iconic SoCal track founded by Mickey Thompson and long managed by C.J. Hart. In many respects, its closing marked the end of an era. Until 1973, each of the NHRA's national races was run on a stand-alone basis. But in 1974, a year-end points championship was established. This theoretically made it possible for teams to earn a living doing the entire series instead of towing race cars all over the country in search of match races. Winston became the title sponsor the next year, and more sponsors, spreading around more money, soon followed.

Was this the future Wally Parks envisioned when he founded the NHRA in 1951? Impossible to say. Ultimately, parents can't control how their children turn out. One way or another, drag racing had come of age.

SLICK OPERATOR

So many of the early icons of drag racing had cool nicknames—from Cha Cha to Grumpy, Jungle Jim to Dandy Dick, The Ace, The Loner, The Greek, The Flyin' Hawaiian—that you have to wonder how a soft-spoken, big-hearted New Englander with the mild-mannered name of Marvin Rifchin earned a spot in the pantheon of hot rod heroes.

"He had a little company in Watertown, Massachusetts, called M&H, and he designed all of his own tires," Top Fuel champion Carl Olson explained. "He had been building oval track tires, but he saw drag racing as an emerging market. Up until then, drag racers had been using recaps that would delaminate and were marginal at best. So he thought, 'I'll design a slick tire for drag racing and see how it works.' Well, it revolutionized drag racing."[36]

In 1958, Rifchin persuaded Don Garlits—Big Daddy himself!—to use a set of new M&H Racemaster slicks on one of his first Swamp Rats. This was before Garlits had solidified his national reputation by smoking the SoCal hotshots, and he was open to suggestions. "He said that I needed a tire that's not recapped," Garlits said. "They were narrow, about six and a half inches wide, but he said that wouldn't matter. I didn't know that much about tires back then and listened to what he had to say."[37]

Garlits won Top Eliminator in a race in South Carolina. He then used M&H slicks to become the first drag racer through the 170 mph, 180 mph, and 200 mph barriers. Rifchin started running full-page ads in *Hot Rod* offering a money-back guarantee. "Maximum Bite," the copy read. "And we've got the records to prove it."[38]

Rifchin didn't invent slick tires. Nobody knows who did. Treadless tires were used on midgets as early as the 1930s. But they weren't purpose-built slicks. They were used tires that had been recapped—a process that involves removing the old tread and replacing it with new rubber. But instead of swapping in new treads for the old ones, the center section was left flat and untreaded. Eureka! The slick tire was born.

Rifchin and his father, Harry, formed the M&H (for Marvin and Harry) Tire Company after World War II. The core business was tire sales and recapping. But Rifchin wanted to ride the postwar wave of short track racing. At the time, midget and stock car racers used untreaded versions of passenger car recaps. Rifchin figured he could do better than that. He developed a more aggressive rubber compound optimized for racing, and he got his regular rubber supplier, Denman Rubber Manufacturing Company of Warren, Ohio, to produce it. He used this racier compound to recap tires, and he then marketed these stickier recaps to the racing community. The tires went over so well that Rifchin was ready to take the next step.

Recap slicks, he knew, were a kludge. A more elegant—and lighter and stronger—solution would be to design a slick from scratch. So Rifchin persuaded Denman to take an existing passenger car mold, ream out the tread, and fill it in with Rifchin's super-duper racing compound. This would then be used to make a prototype. Bingo! By 1957, the M&H slick was so successful with short track racers that Rifchin began searching for new markets.

Drag racing seemed to be virgin territory. The first tires designed specifically for quarter-mile action were the "asphalt slicks" introduced in 1953 by Alex Xydias, proprietor of the famed SoCal Speed Shop.[39] But these weren't really slicks; they were recaps with seven inches of tread that purportedly produced "four times the traction of a regular tire."[40] Several other vendors improved on the SoCal formula and became go-to guys in the drag racing world—Bill Krech of Inglewood Tire Company, Bruce Alexander of Bruce's, Ron Hurst Racing Tires, Bill Moxley, and Bill Casler, to name a few. But all of them were selling recaps masquerading as slicks, while M&H was offering the real deal.

Rifchin ran his first tests in November 1957. The tire performed so well that he tooled up three sizes of drag slicks and went into production in June 1958. The advantages of his tire were unmistakable and inarguable. Whereas a recap incorporated twenty-six pounds of rubber, the M&H Racemaster used only fifteen pounds. Also, Rifchin was able to build the tire mold so the tread was slightly concave at rest, which allowed it to expand into a perfectly flat surface at speed to maximize traction. The only downside was that his slicks cost more than the recaps. And, of course, Rifchin was a newcomer with no drag racing reputation. Getting Garlits on board was a major coup. And when Garlits started cleaning up in 1959, M&H was suddenly on the national map.

For the next few years, M&H had the drag racing market cornered. By the early 1960s, the company offered seven tires for everything from Top Fuel slingshots to hobby racer sportsman cars. "Leo Mehl [who ran Goodyear's racing program] once told me that a drag tire was the toughest tire to build," said Don Prudhomme, who rose to prominence running M&Hs. "They want to tear themselves apart. It's scary how they look at the other end of the track. To develop a tire to hold together

Marvin Rifchin, right, put the M&H Tire Company on the national map in 1958 by introducing the first scratch-built (as opposed to recapped) slicks designed for drag racing. Rifchin's Racemaster tires dominated the sport until Goodyear arrived in the mid-1960s. Rifchin chats with team owner Raymond Leong, who campaigned a long series of race-winning Top Fuelers and Funny Cars as "The Hawaiian." *Revs Institute / Karl Ludvigsen Photograph Collection*

under those circumstances—well, some companies don't want to do it. And some companies *can't* do it."[41]

Goodyear had the know-how, the money, and the will to tackle drag racing. So in 1963, even as it was gearing up to beat Firestone at Indy, the company decided to leverage some of its NASCAR expertise to challenge M&H. Over the Christmas break, Connie "the Bounty Hunter" Kalitta tested the new Blue Streak Dragging Special. A few weeks later, he used the Goodyears to shut down Garlits at the Smokers Meet in at Bakersfield. The battle had been joined.

It was easy to tell the tires apart. The sidewalls on the M&H models featured a series of parallel grooves just beneath the tread. Now known as "pie crusts," these trusses were originally needed to support the tread on recapped tires. Goodyear's secret weapon was smooth sidewalls designed to flex visibly, or "wrinkle," when a car was launched. "The rigid tires were almost like truck tires. They would spin and grab and spin and grab and spin and grab and do a smoky burnout almost all the way down the strip," said Goodyear's current general manager of global racing, Stu Grant, who learned his craft as a compounder working in drag racing. "The launch with a low-psi wrinkle-wall tire was so much stronger because you had a bigger contact patch and your coefficient of friction between the rubber patch and the surface was so much greater."[42] A back-to-back test of the M&H slicks and new wrinkle-wall Blue Streaks conducted by Dick Landy in 1965 in a precursor to the Funny Car showed that Goodyear had a clear-cut edge.

M&H fought back with wrinkle walls of its own. Before long, both companies developed stickier compounds and wider treads so that racers no longer spun the tires for an entire pass. It's hard to separate how much credit goes to tires as opposed to clutches and engines, but elapsed times tumbled over the next few years, from the mid-seven seconds in 1964 to the mid-six seconds in 1968. The pace of development shocked even the racers. "The tire thing, in one sense, has gotten so ridiculous that, if I called up today and got new tires, by the end of the weekend, they would probably be obsolete," Garlits said at the time. "I've had tires come here to Tampa on the airplane, and the same day, they would call and tell me not to run them."[43]

Drivers signed contracts and broke them as the tire companies leapfrogged one another. Firestone dipped its toes in the Top Fuel pond before deciding that the water was too deep. (It would return later with the Drag 500, which was popular in the doorslammer classes.) And that, ultimately, was what sank M&H. As Steve Gibbs put it, "M&H dominated for the longest time—until Goodyear got into drag racing. Then, all of a sudden, people were getting free tires or maybe a little bit of money. That period didn't last too long. But Goodyear had more money than Marvin, and that put him behind the eight ball."[44]

Although M&H's fortunes rose and fell over the next few decades, Rifchin himself remained an ever-present—and widely admired—presence on the drag racing scene. "He was a great guy, a real gentleman," even Goodyear's Grant said.[45] An enthusiast who was willing to get his hands dirty, Rifchin was a friend to all and so fair-minded that he sometimes advised his own customers to use his rivals' tires when he knew his M&Hs couldn't get the job done. But he never stopped trying to build a better product. "As time went on, Goodyear won out," Prudhomme said, "but it was a hell of a fight."[46]

Clad in his signature blazer, BRM team principal Louis Stanley discusses strategy with team manager Tim Parnell. Although Stanley fancied himself the Enzo Ferrari of British racing, his critics thought Colonel Blimp was a more fitting analog. Whatever his flaws, Stanley played a seminal role in bringing both sponsorship and upgraded safety standards to Formula 1. *Revs Institute / Karl Ludvigsen Photograph Collection*

CHAPTER FOURTEEN

ORGANIZING PRINCIPALS

Watkins Glen was an unlikely venue for a bold act that would spark an insurrection. A small, bucolic town in the Finger Lakes region of Upstate New York, Watkins Glen was both a resort destination for city dwellers seeking relief from gritty summer heat and a quaint base camp for tours of glorious fall foliage. Motorsports fans knew it as the spiritual home of American road racing. It was there, on the serpentine roads near Seneca Lake, that the first American sports car race after World War II had been held in 1948. And for many years, a permanent circuit in Watkins Glen would be the site of the United States Grand Prix.

Interest in exotic European sports cars had been percolating since the 1930s, when an elite clique of East Coast blue bloods led by the Collier brothers, Sam and Miles, formed the Automobile Racing Club of America. ARCA started running members-only sports car races on their own expansive properties in 1934. By 1940, the organization was influential enough to stage a large public event at the New York World's Fair—a Formula Libre race featuring entries ranging from contemporary Grand Prix cars to Briggs Cunningham's Bu-Merc Special, a mixed-breed hot rod that married a Mercedes-Benz SSK body with a Buick frame. But when war was declared, racing ceased, and that was the end of ARCA.

The Sports Car Club of America was founded in 1944. Although the SCCA sponsored a handful of low-key tours and road rallies, credit for putting together the first race belongs to Cornell University law student Cameron Argetsinger. A photo from the period shows him peering out of the open cockpit of a Bugatti Type 35 with wire-rim glasses and an expression of steely determination. (Magazine editor David E. Davis would later write that he "looks like the president of your home town Kiwanis Club."[1]) Argetsinger had been born to a family of wealth in Ohio and co-owned a Packard dealership there, but he'd vacationed as a child near Watkins Glen, and it was there that he decided to promote a road race. "It's been said, and it's not entirely wrong, that I did it because I had an MG TC and didn't have a place to race it," he once explained.[2] During the winter holiday in 1947, he sketched out a 6.6-mile circuit by laying out magazines on an Oriental rug on the floor of his living room. After months of lobbying, he convinced civic leaders that a European-style road race would stimulate tourism. The Watkins Glen Grand Prix was flagged off on Franklin Street on October 2, 1948. Frank Griswold won in an exquisite Alfa Romeo 8C 2900B. Cunningham was second in his Bu-Merc. Sam Collier was fourth, Miles fifth, and Argetsinger ninth, all in spunky MGs. Drivers who failed to qualify for the final included road race star-to-be John Fitch, celebrated automotive engineer Bill Milliken, and Charles Addams, whose macabre cartoons appeared regularly in *The New Yorker.*

The first Watkins Glen circuit was a true road course, and as such, it was both demanding and dangerous. Sure enough, Sam Collier died in 1950 when he went end over end while leading the race in Cunningham's Ferrari 166. Two years later, SCCA president Fred Wacker's Allard brushed up against a crowd of spectators hugging the road. A seven-year-old boy was killed and twelve people were injured. Although a new public road circuit was devised and approved, it was clear that a dedicated facility was needed. Milliken helped design the 2.3-mile racetrack, and Argetsinger was instrumental in forming the Watkins Glen Grand Prix Corporation. After the first two US Grands Prix bombed at Sebring in

1959 and Riverside in 1960, Argetsinger made a successful bid to bring the race to the Finger Lakes. Watkins Glen staged its first Formula 1 event in 1961, and it would remain the site of the US Grand Prix until 1980.

From the start, Watkins Glen was a popular stop on the F1 circuit. In fact, in 1965, the Grand Prix Drivers' Association voted it the best-run race of the season. But in early January of the following year, Argetsinger made an announcement that would reroute the course of Formula 1 history. Speaking at a well-attended press conference in the Time-Life Building in Midtown Manhattan, Argetsinger said the purse for the Grand Prix was being raised from $11,000—the prize money that had been guaranteed when the race was run a few months earlier—to $102,400 in 1966. This would make Watkins Glen the most lucrative road race in the world, with a payout exceeded only by the Indianapolis 500, the Daytona 500, and the World 600. "I only wish the purse was retroactive," 1965 race winner Graham Hill quipped.[3] Actually, the increase wasn't quite as big as it seemed to be at first glance. Yes, only $11,000 in prize money had been offered in 1965, but Watkins Glen also paid $52,400 in starting money, which was sometimes called appearance money or, in NASCAR parlance, deal money. This was cash that was guaranteed no matter how badly cars and drivers performed. Argetsinger's decision to get rid of starting money in favor of prize money that was awarded solely on the basis of performance represented a seismic break with the financial foundation of European racing.

In the United States, prize money was king. Okay, promoters were businessmen, and they understood that they might have to slip a few bucks under the table to get, say, David Pearson to show up at Tar Heel Speedway on Thanksgiving Day. But the general rule of thumb was to post a purse ahead of time based on anticipated ticket revenue and prizes offered by sponsors. (The purse often included contingency money, which was misleading, since these were prizes that were awarded only if the driver was using products sold by the sponsors, such as Goodyear tires or Champion spark plugs.) The prize-money model appealed to the American faith in merit-based compensation and rugged individualism, and it made sense because most of the racing in the States was run on an openly professional basis. Not everybody who pounded around ovals made a living from the sport. But if the promoters were earning money from ticket and concession sales, the drivers and car owners figured that they deserved a piece of the action.

Road racing developed along a different path. The SCCA was a strictly—and zealously—amateur organization. This was fine as long as the sport was the private preserve of prosperous playboys who were content to compete for bragging rights over cigars and glasses of sherry. But attitudes shifted as participation grew. Soon, SCCA fields featured a wider cross-section of enthusiasts in humdrum Healeys and 356s, while at the front of the grid, the cars got faster and more expensive, not to mention more difficult to drive. Pretty soon, wealthy owners were paying ringers—covertly—to race their brawny Ferraris and Maseratis. The best known interloper was Carroll Shelby, who liked to say, "I drove cars professionally in an amateur sport."[4] Out on the West Coast, Ken Miles led the independent California Sports Car Club in an open revolt against the SCCA and sham amateurism. When the SCCA refused to budge, professional sports car races were run under USAC sanction (with the SCCA threatening to excommunicate any nonbelievers). It wasn't until 1963 that the SCCA finally saw the light and created the professional US Road Racing Championship. The Can-Am and Trans-Am series would follow in 1966, and the SCCA eventually split into club racing and pro divisions.

In the States, as early as the 1920s and '30s, there were hundreds of oval tracks surrounded by grandstands where low-bucks racers could get paid for driving midgets, jalopies, and stock cars. In Europe, there was no broad opportunity for blue-collar types to get involved in the sport. Classes for cheap cars didn't exist, and since most races were contested on long public road circuits, promoters had trouble corralling paying customers to buy tickets. The motorsports ecosystem expanded dramatically after World War II, but there was no tradition of offering substantial sums of prize money to attract entrants. And prize money really wasn't what they were after. Here's why: Imagine you were a Formula 3 owner/driver who lived in the UK. You wanted to compete in the Coppa d'Oro Pasquale Amato in Caserta, Italy, just north of Naples. You were looking at a long, tiring, pricey tow. There was a better than fifty-fifty chance that your race car would break or that you would fail to qualify. If things went badly—not a crash, necessarily, just a mediocre finish—you wouldn't earn enough in prize money to cover your travel expenses.

So instead of offering substantial pots of prize money, promoters paid drivers starting money or appearance money—fees that were negotiated ahead of time and awarded simply for showing up. (Actually, money usually didn't change hands until the Monday after a race, which could be a problem if lousy ticket sales left the promoter with a shortfall.) Prize money was distributed as well, but not very much of it, and it wasn't something that racers counted on. As Bruce McLaren explained, "I can't just hope I'll finish highly enough to make enough money every time I run."[5]

Although this attitude was alien to American racers, it was commonplace in Europe. In 1966, when it was announced that prize money would be the sole form of compensation in the newly inaugurated Can-Am series, McLaren was dubious. "None of them [European drivers] will come unless they get appearance money," he predicted.[6] It turned out that his crystal ball was defective. Contrary to his expectations, Team McLaren not only competed in Can-Am, but it also earned far more in prize money than it ever would have received in starting money. Even so, this didn't change the European preference for getting a partial payment guaranteed rather than being paid solely on merit. So starting money remained baked into F1 contracts despite the example of Watkins Glen.

The transformative impact of Argetsinger's thunderclap in 1966 wasn't that it weaned Formula 1 from its addiction to starting money. It's that the purse offered at Watkins Glen confirmed what F1 drivers and constructors had long suspected but hadn't been able to prove—that there was gold in them thar hills. For years, Grand Prix promoters had pleaded poverty as an excuse for offering entrants subsistence wages. At the time, purses varied widely according to deals negotiated by the promoters. For a well-attended Grand Prix, the going rate, figured generously, might have been $50,000 in starting money and $25,000 in prize money. Now, amazingly, Watkins Glen was offering $102,400, *plus* paying $50,000 to ship the cars and a thousand pounds of spares, all insured for $750,000, on a BOAC jet freighter. First place alone in the US Grand Prix was worth $20,000. The car that finished twentieth would earn $2,800, which was $1,000 more than Jim Clark had received for *winning* the French Grand Prix the previous year. Something, clearly, was rotten in the state of Formula 1.

When road racing resumed after World War II, deals between promoters and entrants were negotiated on a one-on-one basis, leading to crazy-quilt arrangements that varied not only race by race but also team by team and driver by driver. Recognizing that there was strength in numbers, associations of Formula Junior and Formula 2 entrants were created in the early 1960s. Ditto for the GPDA, which made some noise about addressing safety but which was mostly concerned about money. Drivers who weren't eligible for membership in the GPDA either hammered out their own deals with promoters or hired companies that, for a fee, would do the haggling for them. Meanwhile, the so-called Paris Agreement signed in 1962 guaranteed two grid spots per constructor, but starting money and prize money remained fluid.

The first inkling that F1 drivers and entrants were being shortchanged came after the European invasion of Indianapolis began in earnest. In 1963, Clark and Team Lotus earned nearly as much for finishing second in the 500 as they had for winning seven Grands Prix and the world championship. This helped inspire the representatives of several constructors to meet at the Steering Wheel Club in London at the end of the year to draft a contract that could be used with all F1 race organizers. In January 1964, the Formula 1 Constructors' Association was created. The founding members were Brabham, BRM, Cooper, and Lotus. It was barely noticed at the time, meriting only a brief mention in *Autosport*'s "Pit and Paddock" section. Curiously, British Racing Partnership wasn't allowed to join because it wasn't a constructor, but privateer (and whiskey scion) Rob Walker was welcomed on an unofficial basis.

F1CA lobbied for additional starting money, more prize money, and travel expenses, especially for races outside Europe. It didn't make much progress. Politically, the constructors didn't have enough leverage to move the needle. Rather than serving as a neutral arbiter, the

Commission Sportive Internationale (CSI) reflexively supported the organizers, since the national clubs were members of the FIA. Although F1CA and the GPDA were usually on the same side, drivers were employees of the constructors, so their agendas sometimes diverged. It didn't help that F1CA couldn't present a unified front because Ferrari, the most powerful and influential constructor, refused to join. (Enzo Ferrari preferred to arrange his own deals according to what he jokingly called "the Gorgonzola Agreement."[7]) But the real problem was that the constructors were just that—constructors rather than businessmen. Okay, sure, they had to earn enough money to keep the doors open,

Lorenzo Bandini rockets into the lead of the US Grand Prix in 1966. The race is best remembered for Jim Clark, to Bandini's left, giving the troubled BRM H-16 engine its only win. But the more lasting impact of the event was that the then-astronomical amount of prize money being offered—a whopping $102,400—encouraged constructors to start demanding a bigger slice of the financial pie. *Revs Institute / Karl Ludvigsen Photograph Collection*

but their top priority was winning races, and success on the track didn't always translate into profitability beyond the paddock. Colin Chapman, who sold road-going Lotuses as well as race cars, was the only founder who fit the modern conception of an entrepreneur. As a result, most of the F1CA meetings were a waste of time. "I didn't say much in these things because I used to laugh so much," Walker said. "They were so funny. Always bickering and always out for their own team's interests."[8]

The next few years produced plenty of griping but very few accomplishments. By December 1967, F1CA was so frustrated by the intransigence of the organizers that it and the GPDA demanded a meeting with the CSI at a hotel in London. The result was the creation of a London Committee with Chapman (representing F1CA), Jo Bonnier (GPDA), Walker (private entrants), Brands Hatch chief executive John Webb (circuit owners), British Racing & Sports Car Club executive director Nick Syrett (organizers), and Fédération Française du Sport Automobile president Claude Bourillot. Despite the collective clout of its members, the committee didn't have the power to actually *do* anything. "Continuous approaches to the FIA during the past five months have resulted only in a series of evasions," the committee wrote peevishly. "It is evident that stronger measures are required, and the delegation is therefore suggesting to the London Committee members that a further international conference should be arranged in the near future with the object of organizing a World Motor Racing Association to represent more forcibly the majority view of all participants in the sport."[9] This suggestion died on the vine, and the London Committee itself withered away. No great loss, everybody agreed. Writing in *Automobile Year*, journalist José Rosinski likened the creation of the committee to "a repainting of the façade when a total reconstruction job was called for."[10]

During the late 1960s, money started flowing into the sport in the form of sponsorship, and teams were able to use this newfound capital to upgrade their operations. But the purses offered by continental promoters remained pathetically stingy. In 1971, the total payout at Monaco, the most prestigious race on the F1 calendar, was a mere $89,500. Meanwhile, the Questor Grand Prix at Ontario Motor Speedway near Los Angeles, which wasn't even a championship event, offered $278,000, including travel expenses. Further complicating matters, the affordability and widespread availability of the Cosworth DFV engine had allowed several upstarts to bootstrap their way into Formula 1. To make sure that the F1CA stalwarts didn't get shut out from any races, a new Geneva Agreement guaranteed seven grid spots for the number one drivers of the "established" constructors (Ferrari, Lotus, BRM, McLaren, Matra, March, and Brabham), plus three more for past world champions Graham Hill, John Surtees, and Jackie Stewart. The unseeded drivers would have to qualify for slots on the grid. This arrangement led to the chaotic Spanish Grand Prix at Jarama in 1970, where only sixteen cars were supposed to race. After frenetic back-and-forth negotiations, the organizers agreed to allow twenty cars to start. Come Sunday afternoon, twenty cars were lined up on the dummy grid. Then a CSI official announced that only sixteen cars could race after all. Chaos ensued. Drivers were physically barred from the grid, and punches were thrown. "Get out of the fucking way," Hill growled, fighting his way to his Brabham.[11] Eventually, four cars were removed from the grid, and the race proceeded without any more glitches. But the whole affair left a bad taste in everyone's mouth.

The bickering in Spain exposed the schizophrenia buried deep in the soul of F1CA. Was it a nuts-and-bolts trade association interested only in dollars and cents or was it an alliance of like-minded designers, engineers, and builders who wanted to make the sport a better place for their creations? BRM boss Louis Stanley staked out the former position. "After all, we're not Boy Scouts," he said. "We're in business. We're here to make money."[12] To which Bruce McLaren replied, "If we were only interested in making money we wouldn't be in this ridiculous game. It's a sport, isn't it?"[13] Walker, who was one of the last living links to a simpler, less commercial age, split the difference. As he put it, "I prefer to think of it as a sport with peripheral perks."[14]

But Walker was an anachronism who was on his way out. (He would shut down his race team at the end of the year.) Even as he was departing, F1 received some new blood in the form of March Engineering, which had been founded by four raging optimists who invested $6,000 apiece to fund the start-up. As it turned out, the team would have a checkered history in Formula 1 (and Indy cars, IMSA, and several other series). But long after the company closed its doors, one of its founders would continue to cast a long shadow over the sport. The "M" in March stood for Max Mosley, who would later serve as the president of the FIA. Mosley was a reasonably accomplished driver who'd competed in the F2 race at Hockenheim where Clark was killed. (He finished ninth.) He retired the next year after concluding that, first, he wasn't going to be a world champion, and second, he was probably going to be killed if he didn't quit. Though his formula car exploits weren't very memorable, Mosley was already a known figure, thanks to his father, the disgraced Sir Oswald Mosley, who'd been interned during World War II because of his Nazi sympathies. To escape from his father's shadow, Mosley earned a degree in physics at Oxford and later worked as a barrister, the wig-wearing British attorneys who argue cases in court. He brought his legal and business expertise with him when he was invited to attend his first F1CA meeting, and he was shocked by the bumbling he encountered. "So I'm sitting in this first meeting thinking, 'This is a major world sport. I can't believe what I [am] witnessing,'" he recalled. "I couldn't believe it was run like that. It just wasn't possible."[15]

Adding Mosley to the constructors' association gave it some additional credibility. Ferrari finally broke down and joined F1CA, and the CSI brokered a deal that raised the minimum purse at every Grand Prix to nearly $108,000. But these were baby steps when giant leaps were required. Mosley couldn't do it alone. He needed a partner in crime. He got one at the end of 1971, when the Brabham team was bought by a diminutive used-car dealer who'd spent years on the periphery of the F1 scene without ever becoming beholden to the powers that be: Bernard Charles Ecclestone. Universally known as Bernie, the press delighted in referring to him as racing's "F1 Supremo," a sobriquet that captured both his absolute power and his utter ruthlessness. "He was a dealmaker, a wheeler-dealer, and absolutely hard as nails, commercially," Doug Nye said. "Promoters had the upper hand until the 1970s. What happened was that they got 'Bernied.' He said things like, 'You're going to disagree with me, are you?' And he'd look at you and you'd think, 'I'm going to lose my kneecaps.' I mean, that's a flippant remark, but there's a sort of a truth to it. Bernie could be a very, very threatening power. He was very,

very manipulative, and he was a man with tremendous influence. And not all of that influence was benign."[16]

When Ecclestone attended *his* first F1CA meeting, Mosley gravitated to him like a magnet, two sharks in a school of tuna. Before long, they'd imbued the association with a more pugnacious attitude, and the other members were content to follow their lead. "I will better your lot," Ecclestone promised. "I will guarantee a better deal [with the organizers]."[17] McLaren team manager Phil Kerr, who'd been a core member of F1CA since it was formed (while he was at Brabham), recognized the possibilities created by Ecclestone's business acumen and negotiating chutzpah, and the two of them adopted a good cop/bad cop routine. When exasperated promoters appealed to Kerr, who'd been a soft touch for so many years, he would innocently, almost apologetically, turn the floor over to Ecclestone. "I had nothing to do with all these earlier negotiations," Ecclestone would say blithely. "This is a whole new world now, we are starting from scratch, and we just have to figure this out differently." Then, Ecclestone would slide in the knife and give it a quick twist: "You can be a part of this. But if you think this is too difficult, then that's okay, we can go find another circuit and save you the problems."[18]

Ecclestone started flexing his muscles in the spring of 1972. Plans already approved by the CSI called for a maximum of twenty cars to race in the Monaco Grand Prix. This would have left the cars of several F1CA members on the sidelines. Two weeks before the race, Ecclestone and Mosley—who were assuming the roles of Michael Corleone and Tom Hagen—met with Michel Boeri, the president of the Automobile Club de Monaco. Although the ACM was one of the most powerful clubs in Europe, Boeri was pressured into agreeing to allow twenty-five cars to race. But when the F1 circus reached Monaco, the constructors were informed that only twenty cars would be permitted after all. Testy negotiations devolved to the point that the local police were dispatched to lock all the race cars in the garage on Avenue Princess Grace, which served as the paddock. Ecclestone decided to end the standoff himself. "I stupidly got in my car and tried to drive out of the garage," he said.[19] "There happened to be a policeman standing in front of me with a different idea. I managed to not miss him, but not damage him, and get him to move." Ecclestone sat down with Boeri and made him an offer he couldn't refuse. "He was a bit difficult at first," Ecclestone acknowledged, "but in the end, he became sensible and realized that what we were doing was probably the right thing. And the race went on."[20]

By the summer of 1972, Ecclestone had finagled a look at documents showing how much race promoters were actually making. Armed with these figures, F1CA's freshly overhauled finance committee, which now consisted of—surprise, surprise—Ecclestone, Mosley, and Kerr, demanded that purses more than double to almost $250,000 per Grand

Small in stature but towering metaphorically over his contemporaries, Bernie Ecclestone was often identified in print as "F1 Supremo." Starting as Brabham team owner in 1971 and later as the head of the Formula One Constructors' Association, he ramrodded the transformation of Formula 1 from a glorified sport into a multibillion-dollar industry. Here, he looks on skeptically while his longtime collaborator, Max Mosley, meets the press. *Revs Institute / Ove Nielsen Photograph Collection*

Prix in 1973. Ecclestone also wanted F1CA to be in charge of distributing the money, which was part of his grand plan to shift control of F1 from the promoters to the constructors. After two decades of walking all over the carmakers, race organizers were understandably mortified by the threats posed by Ecclestone's bellicose leadership. In October, promoters representing Austria, Great Britan, Belgium, Brazil, Canada, France, Germany, Italy, Monaco, Holland, South Africa, Spain, Sweden, and the United States banded together into a cartel called Grand Prix International (GPI). Heading it was Henri Treu, the scion of a Dutch yacht fortune. Like Ecclestone, he was an ambitious and polarizing figure; only six months earlier, he'd been deposed as secretary general of the CSI. Treu immediately rejected F1CA's propositions. "Needless to say that both proposals were considered totally unrealistic by the members of Grand Prix International," he wrote in a long letter that read like a manifesto.[21] Treu argued that racetracks were already looking at huge expenditures to pay for safety upgrades for the drivers and better viewing facilities for the fans. Also, he said, only six driver/car combinations were famous enough to use for promotional purposes. Under the circumstances, he offered a bit more than $125,000 a race, or roughly half of what F1CA demanded. Then he set a deadline of December 14 for the constructors to take it or leave it.

The deadline came and went. "They want to have a multi-million-pound sport paid for at club-level prices," Kerr complained.[22] To ratchet up the pressure on the constructors, Treu got the CSI to agree to his plan to use Formula 2 and Formula 5000 cars if the F1 grid wasn't full. When this didn't work, he floated a never-gonna-happen scheme to import Indy cars as field fillers—a hobby horse that Dan Gurney had been flogging unsuccessfully for years. Instead of compromising with Treu, Ecclestone made an end run around him by negotiating separate contracts with non-European tracks where the proposed GPI fees wouldn't apply because large travel expenses had to be added to the purse. Before long, it became apparent that Treu was standing on a foundation made of sand, and every step he took further eroded his base. GPI didn't lose the war with F1CA so much is it simply sank into the battlefield until no trace of its existence was left. As Ecclestone summed up Treu's failed putsch, "He wanted to take over everything, including sponsorships," Ecclestone said. "We had to make sure it didn't happen."[23] Ecclestone had triumphed so comprehensively that Treu was reduced to the status of a nonperson.

For 1973, the constructors negotiated fifteen separate contracts with the fifteen Grand Prix promoters at rates significantly higher than the ones that had been offered by the now-moribund GPI. By 1975, the going rate for an F1 race was close to the pie-in-the-sky $250,000 purse F1CA had requested two years earlier. The *really* big money would come a few years later, when television rights turned several constructors into millionaires. But Ecclestone had embarked on the road to riches long before then. For him, the journey began in May 1974. When it looked like financial woes were going to sink the Belgian Grand Prix at Nivelles, Ecclestone proposed that F1CA step in and promote the race itself, sharing equally in the profits—or losses. The constructors weren't interested. "Colin [Chapman] and most of them had the attitude, 'We want to race, we don't want to be involved in selling tickets to the public or anything like that,'" Ecclestone recalled. "It was the last thing they wanted, so I had to do it personally."[24] About seventy thousand spectators showed up for the race, which generated enough revenue for him to pay his creditors and retain a healthy bonus for himself. But the money was merely icing on the cake. The most valuable takeaway from the experience was that it gave Ecclestone an inside look at the myriad ways race promoters can turn a profit in addition to selling tickets—through track signage, race programs, title sponsorship, hospitality, and so on. In years to come, he would have his fingers in all of those pies.

Thanks largely to Ecclestone's business acumen, Formula 1 would grow into a multibillion-dollar industry, and Ecclestone himself would emerge as one of the richest men in the United Kingdom. Looking back, it's tempting to think that he had an elaborate strategy for world domination—that he was playing three-dimensional chess while everybody else was playing checkers. The truth is probably more prosaic. "I think the evolution was more organic than that," said John Watson, who drove for Ecclestone (among others) before retiring from the cockpit and embarking on a long career as a broadcaster. "Everybody else in Formula 1 at that time was focused on racing. Bernie was focused on money. He realized that, if he could persuade the other teams to give him the autonomy to act on their behalf, he could do a better job for them than they could themselves. Eventually, they realized that their skill was running a team, not running a business. So it was a natural progression."[25]

There's an old adage in racing. Question: How fast do you want to go? Answer: How much money do you have? The constructors were making money faster than they ever had before. Naturally, some of it ended up in their pockets, and some of it was spent on snazzier uniforms and cooler graphics. But most of it was sunk back into the team to hire more mechanics, fund more development, buy more esoteric components, use more tires, freshen engines more often—anything to make the cars go faster. As the gaps between the haves and the have-nots narrowed, the competition got tighter, which motivated drivers to push that extra little bit harder. Another factor contributing to the general flattening of lap times from top to bottom was the ubiquity of the Cosworth DFV, which was not only the best engine on the market but was also the most cost-effective, at $15,300. Of the eleven teams that entered most of the F1 events in 1972, eight used Cosworths, and they won ten of the twelve races. Thanks in part to the DFVs, the grids were bigger, the cars were quicker, and they were running closer together than ever before. Accidents were a natural byproduct of this newfound financial prosperity. But nobody was sure what to do about them.

In 1972, a safety advocacy group called the Jim Clark Foundation commissioned a study of the 224 accidents that had occurred during Formula 1 race weekends and test sessions over the past seven years. The result was a sixty-four-page book titled *Grand Prix Accident Survey 1966–1972*. (There's something to be said for truth in advertising.) The text was written by five motorsports journalists working mostly from published reports. The data they collected was crunched by a Ford mainframe computer in an attempt—largely futile—to tease out some trends that might be useful in a big-picture sense. The book is riveting but also curiously unsatisfying—riveting because it features unadorned but richly detailed accounts of the most serious accidents, unsatisfying because the just-the-facts-ma'am approach means it's short on analysis and recommendations to improve safety in the future. Also, a lack of funding meant the book wasn't published until 1975, by which time F1 had moved a light-year away from the wingless, cigar-shaped, skinny-tired cars of the 1960s.

Still, the book offers some fascinating insights. Six drivers died in the seventy-nine world championship races contested from 1966 to 1972, which translates into one fatality every thirteen races. (Another driver was killed in a non-championship race, and an eighth died while testing.) By comparison, there's been only one death in nearly six hundred F1 races since 1994. It's also chilling to discover that 3.1 percent of the accidents between 1966 and 1972 resulted in a fatality. And most of the wrecks back then were the product not of driver error but of mechanical failures, from deflating tires to fractured uprights to locked-up transmissions to foot-to-the-floor brake failures. Not only are modern cars several orders of magnitude more reliable, but when they do break, they don't usually cause crashes. Another surprise was how many accidents occurred after drivers spun on oil, presumably dropped by engines that were leaking fluid or blowing up comprehensively—a failure scenario that's largely been eliminated.

By drilling down deeper into the data, it's easy to see how drivers continued to push their cars ever closer to the limit as the competition heated up. As the margin for error diminished, the number of accidents climbed inexorably. In 1966, there were fourteen accidents (four of them in the rain at Spa) in twelve race weekends (including non-championship races), or roughly one per event. By 1970, the numbers were up to thirty accidents in sixteen weekends, or roughly two per event. By 1972, there were sixty-four accidents in nineteen race weekends, or more than *three* per event. Thanks to better safety gear, safer cars, and fewer racetrack hazards, the outcomes weren't as severe. Still, the number of accidents reflects how much harder the drivers were trying. Another telling measure of the intensity of the competition was the growing number of car-to-car collisions. Wheel-to-wheel contact was virtually unheard of in Formula 1 in the 1950s, and it was still exceedingly rare in the 1960s. When Ickx banged wheels with Stewart en route to winning the Canadian Grand Prix in 1969, he apologized profusely for an optimistic but not-irrational lunge that modern race stewards would probably have investigated without taking action. Three years later, Ickx's mea culpa seemed almost quaint. During the 1972 season, there were no fewer than nine car-to-car collisions—not nose-to-tail, mind you, but side-to-side contact between drivers clashing over the same piece of real estate.

The fact that no drivers died in sixty-four F1 accidents in 1972 while two were killed in fourteen wrecks in 1966 was a testament to how much safety had improved in the intervening years. "Many of these changes were the result of lessons learned the hard way—sad incidents recorded in this report," the authors of the *Accident Survey* concluded. "Others arose through the activities of pressure groups within the sport—notably the Grand Prix Drivers' Association. A lot has been achieved in the critical years since 1966. But there is no room for complacency; in the field of safety there is always room for improvement."[26]

As it happened, 1973 would be one of the most fraught years in Grand Prix history. It would end with Stewart retiring immediately after his teammate, François Cevert, was killed at Watkins Glen, and the GPDA began its glide path to impotence. For many years, the safety movement lacked a leader with enough influence to advance the cause. Eventually, a pair of unlikely advocates would fill the void—none other than Bernie Ecclestone and Max Mosley. Not so surprising when you really think about it. In racing, after all, you finish the lap right where you started it.

DRIVING ALL THE WAY TO THE BANK

To call Jim McElreath a journeyman is to damn him with faint praise. The taciturn Texan won the inaugural California 500 at Ontario Motor Speedway, which paid $150,384—a huge payday back in 1970—and was later inducted into the Sprint Car Hall of Fame. From 1945 to 1992, he raced everything from clunky dirt track jalopies to cutting-edge ground effects Indy cars, and his five Indy car wins equal the totals of the more-celebrated Greg Moore and Barney Oldfield. "Not sure the general public knew much about Jim," said fellow Texan Johnny Rutherford, "but all the guys that raced with him knew how good he was."[27]

In 1960, Rutherford and McElreath agreed that they'd outgrown the rinky-dink Devil's Bowl Speedway in Dallas and decided to try their luck on the big-boy circuit in the Midwest. "We had a '51 Ford pickup with an Oldsmobile engine and a camper on the back," Rutherford recalled. "Man, we hit the road."[28] A handful of sprint car and midget wins earned McElreath a look-see at Indianapolis. Driving a five-year-old Kurtis roadster, he qualified seventh and finished sixth in 1962, earning Rookie of the Year honors.

But here's the thing: During the downtime at Indy that May, McElreath picked up some extra cash by working as a union bricklayer at a school eight blocks from the Speedway. He continued to moonlight as a bricklayer for the next few years, and in 1968, he went to the trouble of renewing his union license even though he was coming off a season when he recorded seven top-five finishes and placed seventh in the Champ Car standings. It may come as a surprise to learn that McElreath wasn't the only guy who had a "real" job in addition to racing in the 1960s. George Follmer was selling insurance when he won the US Road Racing Championship in 1965. When he first raced at Le Mans, David Hobbs still worked for his father's transmission company. And while Derek Bell was establishing his reputation in international Formula 3, he recalled, "I didn't get paid for it because my stepfather was paying the bills, and I was living off earning £20 [$48] a week as a farm manager."

Richard Childress's story was typical stock car fare. "I was working at a company called Douglas Battery at the time, and I went over there and told Mr. Douglas I wanted off to go to Daytona," Childress said. "He told me, 'Biggest mistake you'll ever make, son. You'd better stay here.' 'Mr. Douglas, I gotta go.' He said, 'Well, you don't need to come back.' I did everything I could to earn some money. I was a stunt driver. I run a garage on the weekend. I rebuilt wrecked cars and worked on other cars at night. That's how we had to make it back in the day."[29]

Well into the 1960s, except for those on the top tiers of the pyramid, racing was a hand-to-mouth vocation. That applied to car owners, drivers, and mechanics—especially mechanics, particularly the ones in the UK. When Jim Chapman got hired by the BRP Formula 1 team in 1961, he was paid the equivalent of thirty-three dollars a week. "I was so passionate about that sport that I didn't worry about how much they paid me as long as it was enough to just exist," he said.[30] Herbie Blash was in much the same predicament when was he hired at Lotus in 1968. "Now, you can make a *really* good living out of racing," he said. "When I got started, you had to give your right arm to go racing, right? You did it for the love of it. In my day, it was a passion, or you didn't do it."[31]

In 1971, Porsche dealer Vasek Polak campaigned a Porsche 917 PA in the prestigious Can-Am championship and managed to finish sixth with a team that consisted entirely of driver Milt Minter, mechanic Alwin Springer, a Chevrolet ramp truck, and a camper. "We would pull the car up with a winch, and, under the sides of the truck, we had the toolbox and the spare parts, and the tires were on top of the motor home," said Springer, who went on to run Porsche's North American motorsports operation. "I drove the Chevy and Milt drove the motor home. We cooked together, slept together, and traveled together for almost six months without going home."[32]

By the end of the decade and into the 1970s, the arrival of millions of dollars in sponsorship and television rights remade the financial structure of the sport. There was a lot of noise made about Jackie Stewart becoming the first road racer to achieve millionaire status, but several Indy car drivers had already beaten him to the punch. "In Formula 1, they were not doing well at all. I mean, it was basically starting money. It was nothing like what we were getting in Indy car, not even close," Mario Andretti said. "After I qualified on the pole [in the US Grand Prix] in 1968, Colin [Chapman] offered me a ride as the number one driver. But as much as I wanted to be in Formula 1, I could not afford to take it. It happened again a few years later with Enzo Ferrari. He wanted me to drive Formula 1 and sports cars. I thanked him profusely, but I could not take it. I had the responsibility of a young family, and if something happened to me, I didn't want Dee Ann and the kids to be on the street."[33]

Financially, open-wheel racing had always been more profitable in the States, largely because the sport was organized on a professional basis. Prize money grew proportionately as you moved up the pecking order from local midgets and sprint cars to regional and national shows. By the time you reached the Championship Trail, the purses were reasonably substantial, and they grew dramatically over the course of the 1960s. The total prize money awarded to the top ten finishers in the standings in 1960 was about $360,000. This rose to $552,000 in 1964, $804,000 in 1968, and $1.278 million in 1972, until the OPEC fuel embargo put a brake on further growth. The standard split was 40 percent for the driver—sometimes 50 percent for a win—and 10 percent for the mechanics, with the crew chief getting the biggest cut. "If you did good at Indianapolis, that was half a year's wages made right there," says Tom Bigelow, who scored the biggest payday of his career—$41,313—for finishing eighth at Indy in 1980 but who drove a milk truck to make ends meet when he was getting started.[34]

The onset of the tire wars was a gigantic windfall for drivers. Goodyear and Firestone lavished hundreds of thousands of dollars on Indy car luminaries like Andretti and A.J. Foyt, and even the spear carriers got deals worth $5,000 and $10,000. Team owners started to pay annual salaries to their drivers, a practice that had been unheard of in years past. Andy Granatelli got the ball rolling by giving Parnelli Jones a briefcase filled with $100,000—in cash!—to drive the STP Turbine in 1967. The retainers weren't huge—$25,000, $50,000, numbers in that range. Then again, most drivers also collected 40 percent of the prize money they won. And to guys who were accustomed to percentage-only deals, getting a salary seemed like manna from heaven.

One of the beneficiaries of the new economy was Tom Sneva, who managed to do eight Indy car races with three marginal teams in 1973 while holding down a full-time job as a high school math teacher. "At the end of the school year," he recalled, "the school district said, 'Hey, you're going to have to make a decision. We can't let you take a month off during the school year to go play with a race car.'"[35] He quit teaching and landed a full-time ride in 1974. The highlight of his season was qualifying eighth at Indy in an underfunded Eagle knockoff built by Grant King. This put him on the third row of the grid, next to a genuine AAR Eagle driven by Bobby Unser. Dan Gurney was thoroughly annoyed, but Roger Penske was so impressed that he invited Sneva to a meeting at the Speedway Motel when the year was over. "We'd like you to drive for us next year for $30,000," Penske said. Sneva gulped and told him, "Roger, I'd love to drive for you, but I don't have

$30,000."[36] A nonplussed Penske explained that he'd be paying Sneva, not the other way around.

That's not how business was transacted in the world of European road racing. "When I started, race drivers had an attitude completely different from today's; there wasn't nearly as much money involved, and we were racing the way that gentlemen amateurs played polo," said Masten Gregory, who spent his entire inheritance—and more—on racing. "People like Portago, and Taffy von Trips, Peter Collins, Mike Hawthorn, Carel de Beaufort, if they were still alive, I don't know how they'd fit in. They were all hedonists, they were doing it for fun first and money second, if at all."[37]

Stirling Moss was the first thoroughly modern professional driver. By the time his career ended in 1962, he commanded as much as $3,000 in starting money per race and was making about $150,000 a year. Because the prize money and starting money was so paltry in those days, modest retainers were common. But even astute businessman like Roy Salvadori, Graham Hill, and Tony Brooks would have been lucky to earn half as much as Moss, while drivers working their way up through the lower formulas faced a constant struggle to stay out of the red. There's a hugely entertaining subgenre of anecdotes detailing the picaresque escapades of diehards rambling around Europe with inadequate budgets and unsuitable tow vehicles to and from races that barely paid enough to cover travel expenses. Tim Schenken was one of the few who managed to turn a profit, thanks to sterling results and a factory Merlyn deal that provided him with a car and an engine builder. "Mind you," he said, "I was living in a one-bedroom apartment with four of us sleeping on four mattresses on the floor."[38] Two years later, he was racing in Formula 1.

The financial structure of European road racing underwent a drastic transformation during the 1960s. The overhaul began when drivers began venturing across the Atlantic Ocean to race at Indy and then in Can-Am and Formula 5000. The size of the purses in America dwarfed the meager amounts of prize money and appearance money doled out by European promoters. Jim Clark was one of the first big beneficiaries of Indy car largesse, and his plunder encouraged him to move to Paris to avoid the bite of the taxman. By mid-decade, Ford Motor Company

Graham Hill is interviewed after winning the Indianapolis 500 in 1966 while car owner John Mecom Jr. looks on. For this single victory, Hill earned $156,297—far more prize money than he took home for winning F1 world championships in 1962 and 1968. Even so, racing made so little financial sense at the time that Mecom lost money despite fielding cars that finished first, sixth, and fifteenth. *Revs Institute / Karl Ludvigsen Photograph Collection*

was paying drivers $1,000 and then $3,000 per endurance race. In F1, retainers climbed to $30,000, $40,000, $50,000. When numbers north of $100,000 were floated, Enzo Ferrari scoffed, "If Nuvolari came back to earth, I wouldn't give him that sort of contract!"[39] Yet by 1970, Ferrari reportedly was paying Jacky Ickx $112,000, and retainers for the acknowledged aces ranged from $75,000 to $150,000. Peter Revson made $300,000 in 1973 driving F1 and Indy cars as well as a few sports car races, and salaries would balloon even more over the the next few years.

Still, the days when drivers routinely commanded million-dollar retainers were decades away, and those who hadn't achieved superstar status had to hustle to earn a living. When Pedro Rodriguez was killed while leading an insignificant Interserie race at the Norisring in 1971, his colleagues were shocked. "It was unbelievable," said John Horsman, chief engineer of the Porsche 917s that Rodriguez drove for JW Engineering. "He never crashed."[40] But what was even more stunning than his accident was the fact that Rodriguez was doing a one-off race in a privateer Ferrari 512 S that had been converted to 512 M specifications. He agreed to race the car only after the organizers offered him $3,600 in starting money, and, as he told Horsman, "I need the money."[41] This despite the fact that Rodriguez had factory deals with Porsche in sports cars and BRM in F1 and had already done twenty-one races in 1971 through mid-July.

At the same time, a sizable portion of the F1 grids in the early 1970s got their rides by paying for them out of their own pocket or by bringing sponsorship to the team. At some races in 1971, for example, there were five Marches on the grid, but the only driver being paid by the factory was Ronnie Peterson, and he wasn't getting rich off his retainer. "Most successful drivers come from affluent backgrounds and have access to money—whether an inheritance like mine or simply the generosity of a sympathetic family—with which they finance their careers," Sam Posey wrote at the time. "I have spent a great deal of my own money, but other drivers have spent more, and in any case it is only a matter of degree. What made me so uniquely vulnerable to the 'rich kid' image was not the money I spent or how I spent it, but my candor in talking to the press about it."[42]

It was a period when the rules were still being written, and fortune favored the brave. In 1969, for instance, Posey got a call from Shelby

American team manager Lew Spencer. Revson, who usually drove one of the team's Trans-Am Mustangs, couldn't make the race at Lime Rock, so Spencer asked Posey how much he wanted to sub for him. When Posey impulsively asked for $5,000, Spencer asked him to hang on. Then Posey heard a voice with a distinctive Texas twang shout, "Who the fuck is Sam Posey?"[43] Evidently, Spencer provided the right answers, and Carroll Shelby agreed to hire Posey, who went on score the team's only victory of the year.

Brian Redman, on the other hand, wasn't audacious enough. In 1974, Penske decided to pull the all-conquering Porsche 917/30 out of mothballs for the Can-Am race at Mid-Ohio. Mark Donohue was retired at the time, so Penske asked Redman how much he'd like for a one-off drive. The previous year, Jim Hall and Carl Haas had paid him $5,000 a race, plus 45 percent of the prize money, to drive a Formula 5000 Lola T330. So Redman asked Penske for $5,000. Penske agreed quickly. Too quickly, Redman realized. "Brian," Penske said cheerfully, "you're the most reasonable racing driver I've ever met."[44]

The juxtaposition of modern race car and ancient building suggests that this image is a clever Photoshop mash-up. But, no, it's the real deal—Arturo Merzario driving the Ferrari 312 PB he shared with Sandro Munari en route to winning the Targa Florio in 1972. Meanwhile, Helmut Marko set the all-time lap record in a futile attempt to chase down the leader in his factory Alfa Romeo T33/TT/3. *Pete Lyons*

CHAPTER FIFTEEN

BOOM AND BUST

History, it's said, is written by the winners, and the losers are erased from approved narratives. Sometimes the disappearance is literal, like Leon Trotsky being airbrushed out of official Soviet photos. Usually, though, the fall from grace is more subtle. When the first stories are written, the soon-to-be forgotten figures are leaders, visionaries, the powers that be. A few years later, when the retrospectives and anniversary accounts are published, they're foils, footnotes, and cautionary tales. After a generation has passed and well-burnished anecdotes have hardened into "facts," the forgotten men are little more than the answers to trivia questions. Which is why almost nobody has heard of Larry LoPatin, who, within a few heady years, built the largest racetrack empire in the United States and briefly challenged the reign of Bill France.

Larry LoPatin was a prosperous Michigan-based real estate developer who had no particular interest in motorsports other than what he could get out of it. He hadn't been born into a racing family, wasn't a racer himself, and didn't know much about the sport. That was both the secret of his success and the source of his failure. To him, racing was a business, and he was a businessman. What could go wrong? Quite a lot, as it turned out. LoPatin was crippled partly by a run of bad luck so implausibly dire that it seemed to be the stuff of Greek tragedy. But he was also victimized by his own hubris, believing that, despite his inexperience, he could unseat France and take control of oval track racing. His meteoric rise and even more precipitous fall perfectly illustrate the time-honored dictum that if you take aim at the king, you'd best not miss.

In 1964, LoPatin put together a deal to build Windsor Raceway, a harness horse racing track in Ontario, Canada, just across the Ambassador Bridge from Detroit. The permit allowed for racing only during the winter. To maximize profits, LoPatin wanted to build a second track for cars to compete on in the summer. When this proposal was rejected, he began exploring other possibilities because he was convinced that motorsports were the next big thing—or, as he felicitously dubbed it, "the sport of the Seventies."[1]

The sport of the Seventies. As slogans went, it was genius—sibilant and alliterative, a snappy and satisfying turn of phrase that you might expect from a crack copywriter. It was so good, in fact, that other publicists applied it to skiing, tennis, professional basketball, Roller Derby, and hot-air ballooning. But LoPatin had a point. With tobacco companies prohibited from advertising on television, a substantial portion of their marketing budgets would be bestowed on racing. Television was bringing the sport to millions of viewers with no previous interest in it. Car manufacturers were sinking unprecedented amounts of money into race teams and engineering R&D. Professionalism was the order of the day. No longer would motorsports be confined to a blue-collar ghetto. The Louis Harris Poll showed that 10 percent of Americans considered racing their favorite sport, just behind basketball. *Business Week* ran a story about the sport's surging popularity. Then, to tie a bow around the trend, Richard Nixon invited more than one hundred racers, ranging alphabetically from Tony Adamowicz to Brock Yates, to the White House, where the whole gang congregated for a photo op around Richard Petty's electric-blue Hemi-powered Plymouth Road Runner. "Auto racing nearly burst its buttons," veteran motorsports reporter Shav Glick wrote in the *Los Angeles Times*. "In a manner of speaking, it came out of the closet, or the garage, into the living room of the family of sports."[2]

To be clear, the hoopla was more than empty hype. Racing was about to embark on the greatest racetrack-building boom in the sport's history. Between 1967 and 1971, the hit parade included more than a dozen state-of-the-art facilities, not only across the United States but also in France, Austria, Belgium, and Sweden. Ontario Motor Speedway, erected on the fringe of suburban LA was the most opulent and user-friendly racetrack ever built, full stop. Meanwhile, Circuit Paul Ricard, located in however you say "the middle of nowhere" in French, established the model for the soulless, ultrasafe racetracks that now dominate the Formula 1 schedule. And there were new drag strips as well as superspeedways and road courses. "This was the era when we went beyond airport runways," the NHRA's Steve Gibbs said. "Orange County International was a really nice track with a beautiful tower. Dallas International was a nice track. There were a lot of first-class racing facilities, and the sport took on a professional look. I mean, you actually felt like you belonged to the motorsports community and weren't just a bunch of greasy hot rodders running on the weekends."[3]

LoPatin saw an opportunity—a business opportunity. As he put it, "I'm profit-oriented, not just dealing in fun and games."[4] When his proposal to build a racetrack in Windsor was nixed, he formed American Raceways Incorporated (ARI) and began searching for alternatives. Ypsilanti was his first choice because it was only a hop, skip, and jump from Detroit and all the heavy hitters in the automobile industry. When he couldn't make that happen, he settled on the scenic and lightly populated Irish Hills of Michigan. He bought six parcels of farmland totaling 1,400 acres and hired Charlie Moneypenny, best known for laying out Daytona International. Moneypenny designed a moderately banked, two-mile D-shaped oval. Consultant Stirling Moss then used the oval as the foundation of a road course that he described as combining "the southern Michigan countryside with downtown Detroit."[5] Ground breaking commenced in September 1967. Somewhere between $4 million and $6 million was spent—a bunch of it in overtime pay—to finish construction in time for an Indy car race barely a year later. The track was named Michigan International Speedway (MIS). (The Canadian and American anthems were both sung before races.) Ronnie Bucknum won the inaugural 250 miler, taking home $20,088, which was good money in those days. Paid attendance was 55,108, also impressive. Better still, the crowd included none other than Bill France, who was central to LoPatin's blueprint for the future.

LoPatin wanted ARI to expand to twelve tracks, both new and existing. He'd already begun working on an $8 million project, which went way over budget, to build a carbon copy of MIS in College Station and name it Texas International Speedway. He was also negotiating to acquire a 48 percent stake in Riverside International Raceway and a controlling interest in Atlanta Motor Speedway. Hanford Motor Speedway in Central California was another track on his radar, though he eventually decided not to buy it. Of course, racetracks don't earn money sitting idle. LoPatin needed commitments for race dates. As he put it, "Dates are a very precious commodity in the racing industry. I want all the dates I can get."[6] Nobody had more dates to offer than NASCAR's Bill France. So LoPatin set about romancing him, and he did a hell of a job. "Larry was a salesman, maybe the best I ever knew," said longtime Riverside boss Les Richter, a one-time LoPatin ally who would become one of his worst nemeses. "He could sell refrigerators to Eskimos and make them think they had a hell of a deal."[7]

LoPatin pitched France with an attractive business proposal sweetened with some old-fashioned flattery. "He's like an old-line Southern politician," LoPatin said admiringly. "He's played Solomon down there for years, and he's a great administrator; he had to be to hold Chrysler and Ford in line and maintain good relations with General Motors at the same time. It's a miracle."[8] In a meeting the day after the first race at Michigan, France signed a deal promising LoPatin two annual NASCAR races at MIS for the next ten years. He also guaranteed that the prestigious Grand National finale would be staged at the track that ARI was planning to build in Texas. (Construction hadn't even begun yet.) Both parties walked away happy. France was thrilled to get access to two luxurious tracks in markets where NASCAR wanted to put down roots. With France on board, LoPatin persuaded Mark Donohue to sign on to a project to build a road course in Maryland. He also hired Richter, an immensely popular—and formidable—college and professional football star with a long track record in racing, as ARI vice president and head of competition. ARI company stock, which had once traded at five dollars a share, zoomed up to forty dollars a share. LoPatin went into 1969 thinking the sky was the limit. Instead, events conspired to rain on his parade—literally.

The first sign of impending doom was the failure of USAC and ARI to agree on the size of the purse to be offered for the expected Indy car race at Michigan, so it was pulled from the schedule. Instead, the MIS season opened with a Trans-Am weekend in May. It rained for three days before the weekend, and it was so unseasonably cold that sleet fell during qualifying. Early in the race, a Shelby American Mustang skated onto the slick grass and understeered into a pair of parked Javelins, killing AMC employee Derwood Fletcher. The first NASCAR race, the Motor State 500 a month later, was a solid success, drawing 46,278 fans and the approval of the stock car crowd. But during the summer, the Dixie 500 at Atlanta was delayed a week by rain, which depressed attendance to 14,300. (The spring race at Atlanta had drawn 85,000 fans.) Then, the Yankee 600 at MIS was red-flagged after 330 miles thanks to more miserable weather. But the real killer came the next week at the Alabama 500, which wasn't even an ARI race

Talladega Superspeedway was France's pride and joy. Also his biggest investment. So he had a huge personal stake in the success of what was going to be its first race. As advertised, Talladega proved to be the fastest track in the world, with drivers lapping at better than 199 miles per hour. Unfortunately, tires kept failing, prompting Firestone (but not Goodyear) to withdraw and virtually every top driver to boycott the race. France ignored the complaints and mulishly ran the event anyway, filling the depleted field with pony cars designed to run in the second-tier Grand American series. The race was won by little-known Richard Brickhouse, who broke the driver's strike. The episode was a black eye for France and the lowest point in his long tenure running NASCAR. Besides taking a huge financial hit, he'd alienated the tire manufacturers, the automakers, and his star drivers.

With France weakened, LoPatin saw a chance to muscle him out of the way. He mobilized a media offensive lambasting France for putting self-interest ahead of the good of the sport by breaking the rules to allow Grand American cars to run in a Grand National race. "That was the end of an era is stock car racing. The auto racing car can never again run without rules and regulations like it did at Talladega and be a major sport," he said.[9] "If France continues to fight with the drivers and, say, suspends them or declares their cars illegal, what can the rest of us promoters do? We need the Richard Pettys, Cale Yarboroughs and the like to put on any races. How many people would a Richard Brickhouse bring to my next race in Texas?"[10] But LoPatin wasn't content merely to kick France when he was down. He also wanted to neuter NASCAR—and other sanctioning bodies like USAC and the SCCA—and shift power to the track owners. He envisioned a sport structured like Major League Baseball or the National Basketball Association, with each track owner running a franchise within a larger organization. "I have lined up other track operators and promoters and I am talking to the racing companies—I have already talked to Ford—about finding a commissioner for our sport just as pro football has Pete Rozelle," he announced.[11]

The way most stock car racers figured it, they already had a Pete Rozelle, and his name was Bill France. Not that France was universally loved, and the Talladega fiasco had tarnished his reputation. But he'd been a racer and a promoter himself, and he'd accumulated three decades of goodwill to draw upon, and even those who didn't like him generally respected him. LoPatin, on the other hand, was a Yankee carpetbagger with no connection to the culture of the South or the sport of stock car racing. Nobody knew if he had the guts, grit, or grim determination to win a bar fight with France. When it became clear that they had to take sides, the racers lined up behind the devil they knew. Richter was the first to defect, leaving ARI in October. (He said he resigned; LoPatin said he was fired for "siding with France and siding with drivers."[12]) Jim Hunter, a PR institution at Atlanta, was next. Then France unleashed a counteroffensive. He unilaterally canceled ARI's year-end race at Texas, supposedly because the purse was too small. LoPatin scrambled to come up with additional money, and the race was reinstated, but he wasn't happy about France's high-handedness. At the Ford awards banquet in Dearborn at the end of the year, they squared off in a corner and angrily pointed fingers at each other until France stormed off during dinner. This was to be LoPatin's last victory.

The Texas 500 was a debacle. Three days of rain turned the infield into a quagmire, and fewer than twenty-four thousand fans showed up.

Then, when France negotiated NASCAR's first big TV deal—$1.365 million from ABC to televise nine races on *Wide World of Sports* in 1970—he made sure that none of the money would go to LoPatin. Cash-strapped, ARI ended the year with an operating loss of $1.2 million. LoPatin convened an emergency meeting at Riverside to install a new board of directors, which still included Richter. But Richter, who'd been the valedictorian of his class at the University of California, Berkeley, as well as an All-American, knew a little something about business and politics. He persuaded several other members to ditch the meeting, and without a quorum in attendance, LoPatin couldn't take any action.

In January, the scheduled groundbreaking for ARI's $3.5 million Chesapeake International Raceway was canceled. (The track was never built.) The SCCA declined to renew the Can-Am races at MIS and Texas. Then the USAC races at Texas and Riverside were axed due to money issues. The NASCAR events didn't fare much better. Rain forced the March race at Atlanta to be pushed back a week, to Easter Sunday, and attendance was understandably light. Scheduling conflicts prevented many of the Grand National drivers from making the June race at Riverside, and only 18,500 fans showed up. Then, a Goodyear strike forced the cancellation of the Lone Star 400 in Texas. "Michigan was making money, but LoPatin was milking money made there to pay the bills in other places," Richter said. "He was spreading himself too thin, especially considering the way the economy was turning around. When he couldn't make the payments to the contractor that built the Texas track, the whole thing began to fall apart."[13]

Four Boston-based mutual funds held $6 million in ARI notes. When LoPatin defaulted on a $100,000 interest payment, the creditors demanded a meeting in Detroit. After four days of legal wrangling, six board members—all LoPatin loyalists—were booted and Richter was named chief operating officer. LoPatin was out after thirty tumultuous months as what *Car and Driver* described as "the single most controversial figure in American automobile racing."[14] He remained defiant to the end. "I know my concept was right. The question is: Was Larry LoPatin's personality right for it?"[15] The answer, in NASCAR World, was a resounding, "Hell, no!" "His fall was long overdue," wrote Daytona Beach sportswriter Bernard Kahn, who had been one of the participants in the famous meeting in 1947 at the Streamline Hotel, where and when NASCAR was founded. "The Detroit promoter came in racing as a fast mouth looking for a fast buck."[16]

That seems a little harsh. Looking back, LoPatin's biggest mistake is one you'd think a real estate developer would have avoided—failing to recognize that racetracks are all about location, location, location. MIS would have fared better if it had been closer to Detroit, and while College Station was roughly equidistant to Houston, Dallas, and San Antonio, it was equally inconvenient to reach from any of them. Ultimately, though, ARI was a victim of forces beyond its control. Contrary to the hype, it turned out that racing *wasn't* the sport of the Seventies. Yes, all the elements were in place, but a lot of entrepreneurs got out over their skis before everything had a chance to coalesce and mature into a healthy ecosystem. Their crime, such as it was, was that they were ahead of their time. And nobody was punished more mercilessly than the group behind Ontario Motor Speedway.

Ontario wasn't just a racetrack. It was a palace of speed and a precursor to the lavish, sprawling, multiuse, publicly funded, no-expense-spared sports-entertainment complexes that now dominate the landscape. "We wanted to revolutionize the sport," said Dave Lockton, who shepherded the project to completion and ran the track during its first year. "We wanted the biggest, safest, most modern, and most unusual stadium ever built."[17] The Indianapolis Motor Speedway was the inspiration, but Ontario was designed to be mo' better—a lot mo' better. Although the dimensions of the circuits were identical—2.5-mile rectangles—Ontario was wider, to permit more passing, and the short chutes were slightly banked, so the lap speeds were higher. And while Indy had only an oval, Ontario also featured an NHRA-quality drag strip and a world-class road course designed by John Hugenholtz, the Dutchman responsible for laying out the Formula 1 tracks at Zandvoort, Jarama, and Suzuka. Ontario pioneered the concept of energy-absorbent walls, VIP suites, and garages so plush that they made Gasoline Alley look like a relic of the Dust Bowl. A public-address system powered by 28,000 watts (Cape Canaveral had only 20,000 watts) blasted through 450 speakers

The promotional blitz that preceded the inaugural event at Ontario Motor Speedway in 1970 generated a sell-out crowd of 180,000 for the California 500. Unfortunately, dust kicked up by the Santa Ana winds killed more than a dozen engines, and only eight of the thirty-three starters were running at the finish. Jim McElreath scored the biggest win of his career, and Dick Simon podiumed for the only time in his 183 Indy car races. *Wikimedia Commons*

placed strategically throughout the grounds. Antennas buried beneath the pavement sent signals to an IBM 1130 minicomputer to provide fans with—for the first time ever—live timing and scoring information that was beamed to the giant tower looming over the front straight. "The scoring system that we developed was quickly adopted by all automobile racing because it addressed one of the biggest problems the sport had at the time, which was that you couldn't tell who was ahead," Lockton said. "The scoreboards were ten laps behind, and the cars would get all jumbled up. How can you enjoy a sport when you're not sure who is where?"[18]

Everybody agreed that Los Angeles was fertile ground for a state-of-the-art racetrack. After all, it was a major metropolitan area with hospitable weather, lots of money, plenty of star power, and a deeply rooted car culture. Hot rodding had been born there. So had drag racing. Until the 1960s, most of the top Indy cars came out of shops in Southern California. That's where the Scarab and Eagle Formula 1 cars had been built. And there was a long list of racetracks that had operated in the region before World War II, from Gilmore Stadium and board tracks in Beverly Hills and Culver City, to the short ovals in Ascot, Gardena, Carrell, and Saugus and so on after the war. Since opening in 1957, Riverside International Raceway had hosted the most lucrative sports car races in the world and served as a West Coast outpost for NASCAR. But road racing was—and would always be—a tough sell in a country where spectators were accustomed to sitting in grandstand seats with a panoramic view of all the action on the track. So bringing a large oval to Southern California seemed not only obvious but predestined.

In fact, two groups had already made a run at building a new track in Ontario, a bedroom community thirty-five miles east of downtown Los Angeles and, crucially, twenty miles closer to LA than Riverside. For a variety of reasons, neither of the projects made it much past the starting line. Then, some of the research used by the would-be developers found its way into Lockton's hands. An Indianapolis native, Lockton was a bright and imaginative attorney who'd opened his own law firm when he was twenty-eight. One of the first potential clients to walk in his door was the supremely well-connected racing insider Chuck

Barnes, who'd run Firestone's public relations department. At the time, drivers were starting to earn real money from the tire companies and other sponsors, and they needed professional representation. Barnes and Lockton formed Sports Headliners to serve as their agents. They quickly signed Indy 500 winners Rodger Ward, Parnelli Jones, and A.J. Foyt before branching out to Grand Prix racing and snagging Jim Clark, Graham Hill, and Denny Hulme. Later, the roster expanded to include nonracers like O.J. Simpson, Evel Knievel, and Johnny Unitas. Besides working with his drivers/clients, Lockton served on the USAC board of directors, so he had a deep understanding of how the sport worked. "And when I finally sat down and read all the research [about Ontario]—it was about a foot tall—I saw that it painted a very glowing picture of the potential of a racetrack, which would seem to be obvious, considering the population base and the purported interest in racing," Lockton said.[19]

With the backing of the Wall Street firm Donaldson, Lufkin & Jenrette and several other high-powered investors, Lockton put together a complicated—and creative—business plan to develop Ontario Motor Speedway. A nonprofit corporation was formed to issue $25.5 million in tax-free bonds, while an independent for-profit entity was established to run the facility. This operating company, financed with $5 million in equity, was responsible for nearly $2 million in rent and annual interest payments. To cover this nut, the track was committed to running flagship events for each of the four major professional sanctioning bodies in America: USAC, NASCAR, NHRA, and the FIA. That meant building a facility unlike anything that had ever been seen before. Against all odds, Lockton delivered. "When we drove up into that infield, it was the most beautiful racetrack I think any of us had ever seen," said Buddy Baker, who would win a NASCAR five hundred miler there in 1975. "It was fast, we could pass, the garage and the facilities were second to none, and we'd have guys like Steve McQueen and Muhammad Ali walking up and down pit road."[20]

Still, there were plenty of skeptics who doubted that Ontario could attract enough paying customers to cover its operating costs and pay off its extraordinary debts. The naysayers pointed out that the track had to compete not only with illustrious Los Angeles sports franchises such as the Dodgers and the Lakers but also Riverside Raceway nearby. "Angelenos have so much to do in the way of leisure that they are blasé and extremely difficult to lure through turnstiles," Brock Yates wrote in *Car and Driver*.[21] From the beginning, there was plenty of tension between the two neighboring racetracks. Over time, it evolved into open hostility, and an acrimonious war of words played out in newspapers and magazines. Riverside loyalists included Yates, track manager Les Richter, and NASCAR's Bill France, so Ontario responded by creating a star-studded board of directors featuring racing heroes Parnelli Jones, J.C. Agajanian, Briggs Cunningham, and Roger Penske as well as actor Kirk Douglas and comedian (and Formula 5000 driver) Dick Smothers. The board then approved a PR campaign aggressively marketing Ontario as "the Indy of the West."

The charm offensive worked so well that tickets for the track's first race, USAC's inaugural California 500, were sold out two months before the event. Even so, Lockton had a bad case of opening night jitters when he woke up on Sunday morning, September 6, 1970. "When I got on the street, I didn't see a car or a bus," he recalled. "I knew these streets should have been mobbed, and I started to panic. I drove up to my private parking space outside the stadium, and there wasn't anybody there either. I started to hyperventilate. I burst into the suite. It was empty. There was nobody at the bar. Now, I was *really* getting paranoid. Then I looked out the front, and—Wow! The grandstands were completely full!" The official attendance figure was 180,000. California governor Ronald Reagan was there, along with what seemed to be half the celebrities in Hollywood. A one-thousand-voice choir sang "The Impossible Dream." The only sour note was smog thick enough to completely obscure the nearby San Gabriel Mountains. But shortly before the race, as if on cue, a Santa Ana wind blew in and swept away the haze. "The mountains were crystal clear, and it was like a miracle," Lockton remembered.[22]

Next up were the Supernationals, an event the NHRA had created for the new track. Mattel signed on as the title sponsor to promote its Hot Wheels models, and the $250,000 purse was the biggest offered by the NHRA that year. The weekend was a success, which meant that Ontario was on target to hit the attendance numbers it needed to

Team owner Roger Penske, left, and driver Mark Donohue, center, were renowned racing royalty, while Les Richter, right, was the low-profile power behind various motorsports thrones over the years. A member of both the college and pro football halls of fame, Richter served as the longtime president of Riverside International Raceway, helped orchestrate the downfall of upstart track owner Larry LoPatin, and later worked as a vice president at NASCAR. *Bill Warner*

meet its debt obligations. NASCAR came to Ontario a few months later. The $180,000 stock car purse was second only to Daytona's, and nearly eighty thousand spectators showed up for the Miller High Life 500. Although ticket sales were slightly lower than anticipated, the track was still in reasonably good financial shape going into its fourth event, which was slated to be a Formula 1 race. To sell the FIA on giving the country a second F1 event, Lockton lined up the support of Cameron Argetsinger, who ran the US Grand Prix at Watkins Glen. Then he and Douglas flew to the Monaco Grand Prix with a huge scale model of the track—it was the size of a pool table—and met with FIA executives at the Hotel de Paris. At the meeting, the FIA gave Ontario a date for a race. But when Lockton got back to California, he discovered, to his horror, that it wasn't for a world championship event. It was for a practice race to demonstrate that Ontario was worthy of the real thing. The Questor Grand Prix, as it was called, pitted F1 cars against Formula 5000 cars with stock-block American V-8s. Selling fans on a glorified exhibition was a promotional nightmare. About fifty-five thousand people turned out, which sounds impressive until you realize that fifty thousand had shown up at Ontario the previous month to watch Evel Knievel jump a motorcycle over nineteen parked cars. Lockton had projected ninety thousand to one hundred thousand fans for a bona fide F1 race. The shortfall left Ontario in a hole it was never able to dig out of. Lockton resigned as scheduled after the first season, and the track continued to slide slowly and erratically downhill, like a novice skier on a bunny slope.

Ontario never got an F1 date, and the road course was used for pro racing only one more time. In 1973, the operating company was sold in a valiant effort to save the patient, but this only slowed the bleeding. It turned out that the track was a more popular venue for raucous festival-style rock concerts—California Jam and California Jam II—than it was for motorsports. The last race staged at Ontario was NASCAR's Los Angeles Times 500 in November 1980. Paid attendance was a pitiful fifteen thousand. Later that year, Chevron foreclosed on the property, and Ontario was added to the long list of defunct Southern California racetracks. Conventional wisdom notwithstanding, building a better mousetrap isn't always a blueprint for success.

Several other racetracks that had been built around the same time suffered a similar fate, as the rosy economic predictions made in the late 1960s ran into the headwinds of recession and stagflation. Then came the tsunami known as the OPEC fuel embargo of 1973, which led to interminable lines at gas stations and nearly stopped racing in its tracks. NASCAR shortened the length of several of its races—the premier event of 1974 was the Daytona *450*—while the 12 Hours of Sebring and 24 Hours of Daytona were canceled altogether. The drag strip at Dallas International went bankrupt in 1973. Orange County International, originally called the Super Track, hung on through the 1970s while surviving several management takeovers before finally expiring in 1983. The superspeedway at College Station was renamed Texas World Speedway after ARI went bankrupt, but it, too, was the victim of diminishing returns. The final Indy car race there was held in 1979, and it last appeared on the Winston Cup schedule in 1981.

Another track that went on life support in the 1970s was Sears Point International Raceway, a lovely up-and-down road course nestled in Sonoma Valley, the picturesque home of Northern California's wine industry. It had been built in 1968 by a group of wealthy enthusiasts who quickly sold the track to Filmways, the production company behind television staples such as *The Beverly Hillbillies*, *The Addams Family*, and *Hollywood Squares*. (Filmways had also made an abortive run at building a speedway at Ontario before Lockton and company got involved.) In its first year of operation, Sears Point hosted a remarkable variety of cars and sanctioning bodies. The one common thread was that the races kept losing money. "A bunch of money," said Ken Clapp, former president and director of sales and marketing. "It was expensive to put on Indy car races and big NASCAR and SCCA and NHRA events. We had Trans-Am. We had Formula 5000. The only major event we never had was a Can-Am race. But we had no TV revenue, no big sponsorships, too many employees, and I'm the first to say it could have been better managed than it was being managed, even in my departments."[23]

Filmways executives quickly recognized that it was a lot tougher to turn a profit from racing than it was to bedazzle TV viewers with a talking horse on *Mister Ed*. In the summer of 1970, they dispatched Clapp to Indianapolis to find a buyer for their NorCal money pit. Clapp talked to Andy Granatelli. He pitched representatives of Schlitz Brewing and several other major corporations. He then sat down with Roger Penske, who was just starting to build his business empire. "We met in a room at the Speedway Motel, where I was staying, Roger in a suit and tie, me in a suit and tie," Clapp recalled. "We talked for ten minutes. He said, 'What are you looking at, money-wise?' I told him, 'Seven and a half million dollars.' He stood up, shook my hand, said, 'Have a great day. Good luck.' And he turned around and walked out."[24]

Pro racing disappeared from Sears Point for the next six years. After that, it was a regular stop on the IMSA, SCCA, and NASCAR's Winston West circuits. But the top-tier Winston Cup series didn't return until 1989 and Indy cars until 2005. So it's fair to say that Penske made the right call when he walked away from the deal in 1970. Three years later, though, he reached a different conclusion when Michigan International Speedway came up for sale. At the time, he was running the American Motors Corporation's racing program in Winston Cup, and AMC was committed to leasing the track for testing. After outmaneuvering fellow Indy car owner Pat Patrick, Penske bought MIS for about $2.7 million. The first race under Penske's ownership, NASCAR's Motor Trend 400, was only three weeks away, so gearing up for it was a thrash.

"Roger and I and Les Richter were out in front selling tickets, directing traffic and checking overnight campers for hideaway fans on Saturday night before the race," recalled Walt Czarnecki, who'd joined Penske after leaving AMC and later became one of his top lieutenants. "We had rolls of tickets with an apron to hold the money. About 3 a.m., a thunderstorm hit and drenched us to the skin. Worse, the money got soaked. Have you ever tried to pry apart paper money when it was wet? It's next to impossible. We didn't have an office then, so we went to an old farmhouse on the property to count the money. It was all stuck together. We really wondered if we'd made the right decision that night. I think we got about two hours' sleep and then had to get up and put on the race."[25] Turnout was good, and it got a lot better over Penske's next quarter century of ownership.

There was one largely unintended and wholly beneficial consequence to the boom in racetrack construction: Racing got significantly safer. Ontario, it's true, was designed with safety in mind, hence the precast concrete retaining walls and miles of fencing. Safety was also a paramount consideration in the design of Circuit Paul Ricard, with its expansive runoff areas. (No driver ever died at Ontario, and the first fatal race accident at Paul Ricard wasn't until 2013.) Although the other new tracks didn't explicitly focus on safety, they incorporated the latest safety advances. At the time, some road courses still featured trees and ditches, some dirt tracks still had wood guardrails, and some drag strips didn't have any guardrails at all. The designers of circuits laid out in the 1970s were able to draw on not only the lessons of the previous century but also on information that was being disseminated by the recently formed Motor Racing Safety Society.

The MRSS was the brainchild of industrious journalist and aspiring entrepreneur Karl Ludvigsen. A writer and editor who began contributing to car magazines in 1954—using his own byline and the nom de plume Eric Nielssen—Ludvigsen did a stint in public relations at GM before hanging out his shingle as a freelance writer in 1967. Technical subjects were a particular strength, so he had a keen interest in the emerging technology that was creating a new industry devoted to safety. Ludvigsen had already started a company named Formula 1 Enterprises to import racing accessories, most notably stylish Momo steering wheels. Now, he decided to get in on the ground floor of the growing safety space by selling various versions of the Freon-based fire suppression systems found on the Le Mans–winning Ford GT Mark IV. But at the same time, he wanted to do more to promote safety in the racing world.

"Jackie Stewart was very active in the field of safety, but I realized that he needed other people raising the issue," he explained. "I thought, 'Gee, there really ought to be a society that gathers information about new developments in motor racing safety and disseminates it to interested parties and, indeed, to other parties that that weren't aware of them.' We needed an institution that helped people compare notes and suggest solutions."[26]

The Motor Racing Safety Society was formed in Watkins Glen the Monday after the US Grand Prix in 1969. Ludvigsen was named president pro tem and Jo Bonnier vice president. Other organizing board members included prominent safety advocates such as Stewart, Louis Stanley, Bill Simpson, Snell Foundation founder Dr. George Snively, crack engineer Bill Milliken, driver-turned-safety-advocate John

Fitch, and Can-Am racer Oscar Kovaleski. Judy Stropus, famed for her timekeeping exploits, was designated as general secretary. The bylaws established standing committees to study subjects ranging from fire control and head protection to vehicle structures and course design.

The MRSS published a bimonthly newsletter called the *Racing Safety Journal*, which reproduced articles covering everything from advances in seat belt design to the deaths of spectators at tracks far from the beaten path. The society also got involved in driver training, made recommendations for "barrier principles," and issued an annual tally of fatal racing accidents. "The challenge to our abilities seems enormous, even overwhelming," Ludvigsen wrote. "As one MRSS member said to me, 'There seems to be little any individual can do.' That's why, of course, we have formed this Society. Together I am certain we can question more, discover more, and do more. Every 'unknown' that we can convert into a 'known' will mark a forward step for the sport we all love and the people in it we love even more."[27]

The sport was also moving forward in another direction, thanks to a little creative destruction. In 1969, John Bishop, who'd been instrumental in pushing the SCCA to get involved in pro racing, found himself on the losing end of a C-suite power struggle and was squeezed out of his position as executive director. Two weeks later, he got a call from Bill France. They'd been friends for nearly a decade. France invited him to Daytona to "drink some Scotch, do some fishin' and do some talkin'."[28] After sharing a few libations, they agreed to partner up to form the International Motor Sports Association as a new destination for professional road racing. "IMSA's tagline used to be 'Racing with a difference,'" said Bishop's son, Mitch Bishop, "and one of the differences was that at the end of a weekend, my mom [Peggy Bishop] would set up a table, and she would write the prize-money checks right there. And a lot of times the teams needed that money to get home."[29]

SCCA already had pro series for Can-Am, Trans-Am, and Formula 5000, so Bishop decided to cater to small-bore formula cars, and thanks to his ties to France and NASCAR, he figured oval tracks would be the way to go. The first race was for Formula Fords and Formula Vees at Pocono. The next month, IMSA was at Talladega. A growing collection of wrecked race cars convinced Bishop that running low-powered open-wheelers on big ovals was a lousy idea since it led to pack racing that encouraged huge accidents. In 1971, he shifted his emphasis to GT cars. Later that year he and his wife made a pilgrimage to R.J. Reynolds in Winston-Salem, and in 1972 the tobacco conglomerate became the title sponsor of the Camel GT Challenge. The new format proved to be so popular that at the season-ending Presidential 250 at Daytona fifty-five cars qualified on time and fifty-three more ran a consolation race to fill the last ten spots in the field.

Sanctioning the 12 Hours of Sebring in 1973 cemented IMSA's credibility, and the organization continued to grow over the next few years. But it wasn't until the end of the decade that LoPatin's vaunted sport of the seventies finally got its groove back. In 1979, Indy car racing received a much-needed shot in the arm when Championship Auto Racing Teams, better known as CART, split from USAC and formed its own highly successful breakaway series. That same year, a postrace brawl in the infield at Daytona between Cale Yarborough and the Allison brothers was broadcast live on CBS while much of the country was housebound after a blizzard—an episode that helped put NASCAR on the national map. (Later, Bill France Jr. was asked if he was going to fine the drivers. "*Fine them? Fine them*?" he said. "Boy, I might give them all a bonus."[30]) In 1980, the debut of the Grand Touring Prototype category allowed IMSA to spread its wings as it expanded beyond GT cars. And in 1981, the Concorde Agreement between warring factions gave Formula 1 the peace it needed to enjoy a period of unprecedented prosperity.

The sport of the Eighties was more like it.

COURSE CORRECTIONS

The story sounds too good to be true, and maybe it is. But sometimes there's more truth in the myth than there is in a bald recitation of the facts. So here goes.

Graham Hill was scheduled to race in the Targa Florio for the first time. When he arrived in Sicily, he hitched a ride to his hotel. It was a long drive on a narrow, bumpy road that snaked through breathtaking mountain passes, wound past stone structures in remote villages, and skirted along the crumbling edges of ravines and cliffs. "Beautiful scenery," Hill said. "Now where's the track?" To which his host replied, "We're driving on the track."[31]

By the 1970s, the Targa Florio consisted of eleven laps over the 44.7-mile Circuito Piccolo delle Madonie. Calling it a "circuit," implies that it was a racetrack. Not so. The race was run on public roads that were ideal for donkeys pulling carts. Yet in 1970, the entries included factory Ferrari 512 Ss, Porsche 908/3s, and Alfa Romeo T33/3s. (A Porsche 917K was entered but didn't compete.) In 1972, Helmut Marko repeatedly broke the lap record en route to finishing second in an

The Ferrari 250 GTO codriven by Innes Ireland and Tony Maggs in the 24 Hours of Le Mans in 1964 leans on its left-side suspension as the car drifts through Tertre Rouge before wailing down the Mulsanne Straight. Slapping white paint on the trunks of the unprotected poplars that lined this ultra-high-speed stretch of road was one of the only accommodations the organizers made to safety. *Revs Institute / Eric della Faille Photograph Collection*

Alfa. Two months later, a stone pierced his visor and destroyed his left eye during the French Grand Prix on the natural road circuit at Clermont-Ferrand. He later became a team owner and ran Red Bull's driver development program for twenty years. His performance in the Targa Florio was the pinnacle of his career as a driver. "Seventy-two kilometers on a tiny, twisty road through villages and so on with a sports prototype that was faster than Formula 1 cars at that time," he said. "It was crazy."[32]

When journalist Ted West first attended the Targa Florio in 1970, he thought he'd entered *The Twilight Zone*. "None of the regular rules apply," he wrote in *Road & Track*. "Huge clumps of people sit on the grass verge right outside the apexes of turns. Others sit on the guardrails themselves, their legs dangling over at mid-fender height, waiting to be sliced off. Everywhere you look there's a tree to be hit squarely, or a steep hill to roll off helplessly, or a private house to drive through the kitchen of. People walk right along the side of the course from the first and later they begin to encroach on even that sacrosanct territory until by the end there are several sections that are only two cars wide."[33]

Drivers never knew what they were going to encounter. In 1970, while practicing in his 908/3, Toine Hezemans—who would win the race the following year—hit a dog that ended up in his passenger seat. Five years earlier, driving a wildly unsuitable GT40, Bob Bondurant spun after clouting a giant piece of dislodged asphalt and nailed a kilometer marker. "I hit that thing so fucking hard that it broke the seat belt, shoved the front end in, and put me up on two wheels," he said. "I almost went over, but I was lucky enough that I didn't have that much speed, and the car came back down on four wheels. I walked back to town, found a bar, and sat down and had a beer."[34]

How the Targa Florio survived so long after the other epic road races were condemned to oblivion remains a mystery. The Carrera Panamericana lasted only from 1950 to 1954, by which time it had claimed the lives of so many drivers, codrivers, spectators, policemen, and stray animals that it could have kept a funeral home and a taxidermy shop busy for weeks. The Mille Miglia was canceled after the notorious crash in 1957 that killed Alfonso de Portago, codriver Ed Nelson, and nine spectators. The Targa Florio had much better luck, maybe because it was much tighter and, therefore, slower. But in 1973, after a driver and a spectator were killed and ten more spectators and a co-driver were injured, it was finally pulled from the international calendar.

Of course, back in the 1960s, virtually every road course was pretty sketchy, from the standpoint of safety. A few random comments:

- Longford Circuit, Tasmania: "People were shit-scared of it. In the end, it did get a lot of people. It was a brilliant place to drive on, but you were really happy when the day was over." —Frank Matich[35]
- Mosport Park, Canada: "Talk about dangerous. Fucking hell. Up that straight, there were drop-offs on both sides, trees and holes and shit everywhere, just a terrible, terrible place." —David Hobbs[36]
- Candlestick Park, California: "You looked at it, and you thought, 'Holy cow, I'd hate to be driving on that thing.' It had one curve with a ten-foot cube of concrete at the outside edge of the corner, and then it went down along a row of electric poles. It was a really nasty track." —Chuck Cantwell[37]
- Pukekohe Park Raceway, New Zealand: "If I had known how dangerous it was I wouldn't have come." —Mike Hailwood[38]

Many of the racecourses used in the 1960s and '70s dated back to the dawn of motorsports. In years past, drivers had accepted the risks these circuits posed as unpleasant but inescapable realities, like bad weather or rush hour traffic. But this was the change-or-die era of racetrack design. No road racing track escaped from the 1970s unscathed by demands of the safety lobby, and several of them were abandoned altogether—Candlestick Park in 1965, Longford in 1968, Langhorne in 1971, to name three.

The highest-profile casualty was Spa-Francorchamps, where the first Belgian Grand Prix had been won by Antonio Ascari, Alberto's father, in an Alfa Romeo P2 in 1925. Formula 1 drivers boycotted the track in 1969. In 1970, the organizers made a half-hearted effort to address safety concerns, spending $250,000 to erect Armco and insert a chicane before Malmedy to slow the entry to the Masta Kink, but the changes didn't satisfy the drivers, and they requested more upgrades after the Belgian Grand Prix was run at Spa in 1970. The organizers estimated that the changes would cost another $360,000, but the Belgian Public Works Ministry was willing to pay only $120,000. When the impasse couldn't be resolved, Spa was deleted from the F1 schedule. Prototype sports cars continued to race there until 1975 and touring cars longer than that. Four drivers and two marshals would die before the track was completely redesigned in 1979, and F1 didn't return to Spa until 1983.

The Nürburgring, which opened in 1927, underwent a more dramatic makeover—or maybe that should be "makeovers," plural. In 1967, a series of curves were added to slow the cars as they approached the pits, and additional changes costing a total of $300,000 were made over the next few years. But safety advocates weren't impressed, and the German Grand Prix moved in 1970 to Hockenheim, which had been lined with guardrails to prevent another accident like the one that had killed Jim Clark two years earlier. To entice F1 back to the Nürburgring, $1 million was spent recontouring and resurfacing the road, chopping down trees, blasting away rock outcroppings, bulldozing berms and hedges, and adding guardrails, catch fences, and runoff areas. "The redesign of the track in 1970, which widened the field of vision, gave me a bit of a fright," Derek Bell said. "Suddenly I could see where I would have ended up if I'd flown through the hedge."[39]

Despite further upgrades, the track remained a killer. In the German Grand Prix in 1974, both Mike Hailwood and Howden Ganley suffered injuries that ended their F1 careers. A GT driver was killed the next year, as were a Super Vee racer and a Formula 3 entrant the year after that. Niki Lauda's near-fatal crash in 1976 finally ended open-wheel racing at the Nordschleife, though it remains a popular venue for sports car events.

Few tracks have a more storied history—or a more appalling safety record—than the Autodromo Nazionale Monza. Carved out of a city park near Milan, it was the oldest purpose-built circuit in continental Europe. It opened in 1922, when Pietro Bordino won the Italian Grand Prix in a Fiat 804, and quickly established itself as a fan favorite. Outrageously fast and wide open, it was the site of epic slipstreaming battles. In 1969, the first four finishers were blanketed by 0.19 seconds.

Two years later, Peter Gethin won the Italian Grand Prix in a McLaren M14 at an average speed of 150.754 mph, an F1 record that would stand for thirty-two years. In 1972, a pair of chicanes were added to slow down the entries to the OMG! corners at Curva Grande and Ascari. It wasn't a perfect solution, but it was better than the alternative, which was abandoning the track altogether.

Open-wheel cars have been racing on the arcaded streets of Monte Carlo since 1929, and the event is so glamorous and such a commercial powerhouse that it remains a cornerstone of the F1 schedule even though the claustrophobic circuit is a patently absurd venue for modern race cars. The first safety upgrades arrived in 1964, when a few strands of Armco were erected. But many of the myriad obstacles were "protected" only by hay bales. After Lorenzo Bandini's death in 1967, the chicane where he was killed was tightened and miles of guardrails were installed. These proved to be a mixed blessing, as Clay Regazzoni found when he was nearly decapitated in a Formula 3 car. "I threw myself down into the cockpit and just managed to duck under in time," he said.[40] By 1972, the circuit was encircled almost entirely by Armco, and in 1973 it was thoroughly revised by lengthening the tunnel (and making it less intimidating) and adding the Swimming Pool complex that's still used in 2026.

Other racetracks were modified on a case-by-case basis as events (read: accidents) warranted. After Jody Scheckter's wayward McLaren M23 took out half the field at the British Grand Prix in 1973, a chicane was added to slow the entry to Woodcote. In Mexico City, the problem wasn't the circuit; it was crowd control. About 250,000 spectators swarmed the Autódromo Hermanos Rodriguez for the Mexican Grand Prix in 1970. They overran fences, ignored guardrails, encroached on corners, and showered the track with bottles. Unnerved drivers reluctantly agreed to race only because the promoters insisted that the crowd would riot if they didn't. "It was crazy," Emerson Fittipaldi recalled. "When I came out of the fourth corner, my rear wheel passed a half meter from the head of a guy who was lying on the [exit] curb taking pictures with a yellow Instamatic. I could not believe it! A half-lap later, when my engine blew, I said, 'Thank you, God.'"[41] F1 didn't return to Mexico City until 1986.

At Le Mans, virtually the only concession made to safety was to use white paint to coat the trunks of the poplar trees that lined the 3.7-mile-long Mulsanne Straight, technically known as the Ligne Droite des Hunaudières. This struck most drivers as a cruel joke rather than a practical benefit. As A.J. Foyt put it, "What I didn't like, to be honest, was the way they whitewashed the damn trees. You know that if you went off at 200 miles per hour, you was in a lot of trouble, and you probably wasn't coming back."[42]

Guardrails were interposed between the track and the trees in 1969, and by 1971, virtually the entire circuit was circumscribed by Armco barriers. In 1972, the widely feared Maison Blanche section was bypassed in favor of a new series of fast, technically challenging corners dubbed the Porsche Curves in honor of the company that had financed building them. (This was the same rationale behind the naming of the Ford Chicane before the pits in 1968.) The biggest alteration to the track came in 1990, when the Mulsanne Straight was trisected by a pair of chicanes. Although the chicanes have their critics, racers generally consider the Porsche Curves to be the most rewarding part of the track—proof that safety and driving pleasure don't have to be mutually exclusive. It was a lesson that racetrack designers would put to good use in the decades to come.

At the start of the 1973 Indy 500, Salt Walther ran over the wheel of Jerry Grant's Eagle and flew into the catch fence, dismembering his McLaren M16A and spewing fuel into the crowd. The mangled chassis landed upside down, on fire, with Walther's unprotected legs extending beyond the front edge of the tub. The eleven-car accident was a harbinger of even worse things to come when the rain-delayed race resumed two days later. *Indianapolis Motor Speedway*

CHAPTER SIXTEEN

THE WORST OF TIMES

Was the 1973 Indianapolis 500 snakebit from the start? Had the fates issued a collective thumbs-down even before the gates opened for practice? The men who lived through it likened it to trench warfare—days of quotidian misery punctuated by moments of terror. Indy wasn't like other races back then, with practice, qualifying, and racing over the course of single weekend. It was a month-long soap opera that cranky crewmen called "the year of May." Cars would practice and practice and practice and practice until teams ran out of engines, tires, drivers, patience, energy, or money. There were four days of qualifying over two weeks. Full days, by the way, because sixty-two cars were garaged in Gasoline Alley in 1973 and only thirty-three were going to make the race, so the event played out like a high-speed, no-limit version of musical chairs. "It was a horrific year," said mechanic Mike Lashmett, who was in the middle of the mayhem. "It was just really ugly."[1]

The cognoscenti were anticipating something special when the 1973 schedule reached the month of May. Turbocharged engines were making more than 1,000 horsepower. Colossal rear wings generated unprecedented levels of downforce. Wide, slick tires provided oodles of stick. And the volume was cranked up to eleven and beyond because no-quarter-asked-or-given wars were being fought between Ford and Offenhauser, Firestone and Goodyear, and McLaren and All American Racers. The previous month, on the high banks of Texas World Speedway, Bobby Unser had turned a qualifying lap at the pinch-me-I-must-be-dreaming speed of 212.766 miles per hour. With its flatter turns, the Indianapolis Motor Speedway wasn't quite that fast. But the railbirds were hoping that the 200 mph barrier would be breached for the first time. So there was a palpable sense of anticipation going into the month of May. At the same time, there was also trepidation. As recently as 1970, only three cars had gone faster than 170 mph. Now, it looked like it was going to take 190 mph just to make the show. Food for thought.

The weather in Indiana tends to be unpredictable in late spring. In 1973, it was consistent—consistently bad. Rain fell on at least half the days the track was ostensibly open, and when it wasn't wet, it was cool and windy. Speeds were slower than expected early in the month, partly due to the conditions but mostly for a more practical reason. Although it was possible to screw up the boost of the turbos—literally, you turned a screw—to make gobs of power, nobody wanted to pop a motor when it didn't really matter. During Goodyear tire tests in March, Gordon Johncock had been clocked at 199.4 mph, but prior to qualifying, he didn't bother going faster than 195 mph, and the quick time of the month had been run by his teammate, Swede Savage, at 197 mph and change.

On the Friday before Pole Day, Art Pollard went 193.9 mph in his Eagle-Offy. A forty-six-year-old grandfather and a favorite among his fellow drivers, he was best known for winning a Champ car race at Dover with a stock-block Plymouth and driving an STP turbine at Indy in 1968. In 1972, he qualified for the 500 but broke his leg in a crash during practice and couldn't take the green flag. On Saturday morning in 1973, during the practice session before qualifying, Pollard turned a lap at better than 192 mph. The next time around, he hit the outside wall a ton in Turn One, and the car burst into flames. Although he was quickly pried out of the burning car by the first-rate Indy safety team, Pollard was pronounced dead an hour later. Smoke inhalation was the official cause of death, but he also suffered head, neck, and chest injuries. He was the fiftieth driver or riding mechanic to die at Indianapolis since 1909.

ABC was there, of course. When Indy was first featured on *Wide World of Sports* back in 1961, it had been an experiment. The network knew that the sport was difficult to cover technically, and it wasn't clear how big the audience could be. For the next few years, it covered racing on a now-and-again basis, cherry-picking events that fit into its broadcast schedule, though Indy remained a staple of its programming. By the end of the decade, racing was starting to generate some buzz—the sport-of-the-Seventies thing. In 1970, ABC Sports announced it would cover four races on special Sunday programs in addition to *Wide World of Sports*. All told, the network planned to broadcast a dozen events: Indy, Monaco, Le Mans, two Can-Am races, and several NHRA and USAC dates. ABC signed a separate contract with NASCAR to televise nine races in 1970 for $1.365 million, with options for twenty-six races in 1971 and 1972. "Viewer interest in the sport confirms our belief that the time is ripe for automobile racing's expansion on television," ABC Sports president Roone Arledge declared.[2]

Sensing that there was money to be made, a few upstarts put together packages of their own. They didn't pan out. In 1969, the Television Sports Network (TVS), which had been focusing on college basketball, signed a two-year contract with USAC for live coverage of eight races a year—Indy excluded—for $500,000 the first year and $700,000 the second. Ratings were disappointing, and TVS backed out of the deal before it was completed. Another company, Triangle Program Sales, spent two years trying to make money producing Can-Am broadcasts. No go. "That was an economic disaster for us," said Charles Keller, director of film production. "With the TV rights fees, which had to be paid each track, and the high production costs—the ratio of film that had to be shot to produce a half-hour color show of an action event which is not predictable—we lost a ton of money."[3]

Looking for a new partner for Can-Am, the SCCA contracted with Anatoly Arutunoff of Tulsa. Today, Toly is one of the grand old men of road racing, and even then, he was an ebullient one-of-a-kind character who'd raced a Ferrari in the Targa Florio and would eventually build his own racetrack, the Hallett Motor Racing Circuit. What he hadn't done before, however, was anything remotely like producing a television broadcast. "I started the company with Bill Pryor, who was in media and advertising," Arutunoff recalled. "And we were good buddies with Andy Sidaris, who invented the 'honey shot' [a random image of an attractive woman in the crowd] for *Wide World of Sports*. He had all the connections. We televised the Mid-Ohio and Watkins Glen Can-Ams—live, with nine cameras, which they'd never used on a road course. We were getting set up to do some more live Can-Am telecasts the next year, but our agent didn't block out time with the networks soon enough. Then Nixon pulled his wage-and-price-freeze routine, and there was the oil embargo, and we lost about half our sponsors and, I don't know, twenty grand or something like that."[4] Arutunoff Enterprises was out of the racing business and Can-Am wasn't looking too healthy either.

Only ABC had unlocked the code for making money from racing on television. Its formula involved emphasizing its premier properties, with Indy at the top of its list. During the 1960s, the race had been broadcast on closed-circuit TV and shown in movie theaters by the Music Corporation of America. When MCA's contract expired in 1970, after years of break-even results, the company chose to exit the racing business. ABC seized the opportunity to double down on Indy, and it negotiated a $500,000 deal with the Speedway for a same-day broadcast of the race. There were internal discussions about carrying it live, which had already been done for a couple of shorter races, but this was thought to be too risky for something as long and complicated as Indy. (The interminable delays in 1973 no doubt convinced executives that they'd been right.) So instead of broadcasting the 500 a week after the fact on *Wide World of Sports*, ABC planned to run a quickly edited version the same night of the race in a two-hour slot in prime time. It was a bold and, frankly, risky proposition, but the network pulled it off in 1971, and it would continue to use the same format until switching to a live broadcast in 1985.

ABC's race coverage had come a long way since 1961. The broadcast team was still headed by Jim McKay, who'd become reasonably knowledgeable about racing over the years and had been valorized for his imperturbable work at the Olympic Games in 1972 after eleven Israeli athletes and coaches were taken hostage and murdered by terrorists. Chris Economaki continued to provide expert commentary and insider information from his post in Pit Lane, but he'd been replaced in the broadcast booth in 1973 by Jackie Stewart, who was taking advantage of a break in the Formula 1 schedule. Wearing a canary-yellow ABC blazer, fashionably wide tie, and meticulously coiffed long hair, the diminutive Stewart looked more like a student dressed for his high school prom than a world champion, but at least he knew what he was talking about. Despite the upgrades, ABC continued to go low whenever possible.

The previous year, during qualifying, Jim Malloy hit the wall in Turn Three nearly head-on and was transported to the hospital in critical condition. The wreck was shown several times in slow motion on *Wide World of Sports* while Malloy was still alive, and it was then replayed again and again during the race broadcast after he'd died. "There is a difference between objectively reporting a racing accident, even a fatal accident, and milking it for all it's worth in cheap emotional thrills," editor Mike Knepper wrote in *Autoweek*. "Writing this, I find it hard to transmit to you the total feeling of disgust the proceedings evoked in me. . . . After ABC's treatment of Bandini's fiery crash at Monaco a few years ago and the swarm of mail from an incensed public, I had assumed the network had learned that sensationalizing death is a philosophy best left to the *National Observer* or the *Police Gazette*."[5]

The 1973 edition of the Indy 500 gave ABC a chance to listen to its better angels—or the devil on its shoulder. On Monday, Memorial Day, rain delayed the start for four hours, but the network hung tough. When the green flag was finally waved, the race ended almost as soon as it began after Salt Walther, starting in the middle of the sixth row, touched wheels with Jerry Grant and was propelled into the outside wall just past the start-finish line. His McLaren climbed the wall into catch fencing secured with stout poles and steel cables. The cables sheared the nose off the car, which exploded into flames as it sprayed fuel and debris over fans sitting on the other side of the fence. The car flew for 120 feet and landed upside down on the front straight, gyrating like a blazing pinwheel. On the ABC broadcast, McKay couldn't hide his dismay. "This is what everyone has feared," he said. "This is why there's been such a terrible atmosphere of fear here all weekend long."[6]

Walther wasn't wearing an antisubmarine belt. This turned out to be a blessing in disguise because the roll bar bent back when it hit the ground, so Walther's skull probably would have been crushed if he hadn't slid down into the cockpit. The car came to rest with his legs protruding nakedly from the twisted wreckage. By the time the safety crew extricated him from the car, his fire suit was blackened. He suffered burns over 40 percent of his body. The damage to his left hand was so severe that his fingertips had to be amputated, and the fingers of his smashed right hand healed at odd angles. But he survived. And he would return the next year to make the race.

Seven spectators were taken to the hospital, and four more were treated at the track. Miraculously, none of them was seriously injured. Ten other cars were involved in the accident, some damaged extensively, but Walther was the only driver hurt. ABC's cameras followed him as he was loaded into an ambulance. Then it cut to a commercial. "Now comes Miller Time," came the upbeat voiceover.[7] It probably wasn't what Miller Brewing Company had in mind when it bought the advertising spot for "The Champagne of Beers."

The race was red-flagged after the accident. By the time everything was cleaned up, it was raining again, so the race was postponed until Tuesday. Although there was no consensus on the cause of Walther's accident, drivers privately slammed race officials for screwing up the start—again. (The previous year's start had been botched, and two years before that, the pace car had crashed.) Their cars were geared to run 200-plus mph, so trundling behind the pace car at 80 mph was not only ludicrous but also dangerous, especially since power delivery with the turbos was like a light switch. It didn't help that the late green flag meant the field had been bunched up like rush hour traffic. Disgruntlement over the perceived incompetence of USAC officials would be one of the major reasons that CART was formed in 1979.

More rain prevented the race from being resumed on Tuesday. Wednesday looked like it was going to be another washout until the sun emerged around midday. Scheduled to start at 9 a.m., the race didn't begin until 2:10 p.m. Bobby Unser led from the green flag, and the race settled into a rhythm, with cars lapping at around 185 mph to save fuel. When Unser pitted, Johncock moved in front, and when Johncock stopped, Savage took over, with Al Unser pestering him. Savage held him off for twelve laps before Unser slipped past. They were the first twelve laps Savage had ever led at the Speedway. Nobody expected them to be the last.

Like his mentor Dan Gurney, David "Swede" Savage was a handsome, easygoing Southern Californian who exuded the aura of a golden boy. Jacque Passino, who ran Ford's racing program, described him as "our next Freddy Lorenzen," referring to the personable stock car superstar of the 1960s.[8] A one-time motorcycle racer, Savage was hired young by All American Racers to go road racing, and he scored a somewhat fortunate oval track Indy car win at Phoenix in 1971 when the race leader ran out of fuel on the last lap. A few months later, Savage crashed hard when his throttle stuck at Ontario in the Questor Grand Prix. He was in a coma for four days and loopy for several months afterward. By the time he was ready to race again, there was no room for him at AAR. In 1972, still only twenty-five, he rejected an offer from Roger Penske and signed with Pat Patrick, who'd lined up sponsorship from STP. The 1972 season had been a bust, but things were looking up in 1973, now that he and Johncock were in a pair of matching Eagles.

Savage pitted from second place. He returned to the track with seventy-five gallons of methanol and a new right-rear tire. Bobby Unser, his former AAR teammate and current frenemy, was right behind him. On lap fifty-nine, Unser made a move in Turn Two but couldn't make it stick. He tucked in and was following Savage when the rear end of Swede's car twitched in Turn Four. "Louis Meyer, the three-time winner, was sitting up at his usual place inside Turn Four, by the big oak tree," longtime Patrick mechanic John Anderson said. "Swede got loose. We'd always told him, 'If you can't hold onto it, turn hard left and get on the brakes and spin it to the inside.' But he didn't. He turned right and tried to catch it. Louie could hear that Offy pulling hard. When the car got sideways, it hooked up and shot directly into the inside wall and exploded. And, of course, he was a dead man right there, even though he didn't die right away."[9]

Savage speared the inside barrier at almost a perfect ninety-degree angle. It's hard to describe—or even imagine—the ferociousness of the hit. "When Swede crashed, it was like an explosion went off. I mean, literally," said Lashmett, who was manning a sign board for Dick Simon.[10] On the ABC broadcast, Economaki murmured, almost privately, "What a crash. God Almighty."[11] McKay sounded shell-shocked as he tried to make sense of the images on his monitor. "That's the worst thing I've ever seen on a racecourse anywhere," he said in a subdued tone.[12] The Eagle disintegrated—there's no other way to describe it—after it drilled the wall. "One of the tires went straight up in the air, and it seemed to just hang there forever," Lashmett said.[13] The back half of the chassis, with the engine and transaxle, tumbled down the track, clawing divots in the pavement as it rolled. Savage, completely unprotected, remained in what was left of the cockpit, with his broken legs folded underneath him, fanning away the small flames that were licking at him. A properly suited firefighter was there almost immediately, but when he hit the cockpit with fire retardant, the methanol flames, which had hardly been visible up until that point, suddenly flared up into a full-fledged and completely uncontrolled inferno. Savage was trapped in the burning car for nearly a minute. As he struggled to get out of the cockpit, he looked ghoulishly like the cyborg emerging from a conflagration in *The Terminator.* Amazingly, Savage remained conscious throughout the entire ordeal. "Holy Christ, what a mess!" he radioed to his crew.[14] According to legend, he even asked the rescue guys for a cigarette.

On the television broadcast, the image jumped suddenly from a long shot of smoke enveloping the front straight to a shot in the pits of a motionless figure on the ground, with his limbs splayed out in the discombobulated pose of a thoughtlessly discarded rag doll. This, it turned out, was Armando Teran, a twenty-three-year-old sign board man who'd been nailed by an emergency vehicle racing the wrong way down Pit Lane and thrown at least fifty feet in the air. "This 500 has been jinxed from the start, Jim," Economaki said as the camera lingered on the scene for five, ten, fifteen seconds.[15] Then the broadcast shifted back to the nightmare in Turn Four. ABC showed a slow-motion replay of the crash, followed by an on-camera interview with driver Jerry Grant, who'd witnessed the accident. Next, there was a second replay before cutting to an obscenely cheerful commercial featuring a beaming Andy Granatelli leading a group of actors in a hokey jingle extolling the benefits of STP. Knowledgeable viewers knew that Granatelli was the major sponsor of

Dan Gurney, right, and his protégé, Swede Savage. Driving for All American Racers, Savage scored a couple of podiums in Trans-Am and won the Bobby Ball 150 Champ Car race at Phoenix in 1970. But serious head injuries suffered when he wrecked a privateer Eagle in the Questor Grand Prix early the next year derailed his career, and he achieved only modest success after recuperating. *Revs Institute / Albert R. Bochroch Photograph Collection*

Savage's now-demolished car, which had been festooned with STP decals and painted the company's signature Day-Glo red. Awkward.

Teran died of massive head and chest injuries. Savage was admitted to Methodist Hospital with burns, two broken legs, a fractured arm, and injuries to his lungs and kidney. His right hand was in particularly bad shape because his glove had flown off after he hit the wall. (That's why race gloves are now secured with Velcro straps.) Savage spent thirty-three days in intensive care before dying suddenly of kidney failure. Dr. Steve Olvey insisted that neither burns nor head injuries were to blame. The problem, he said, was an infusion of tainted plasma. "His death was the result of a colossal medical screw up," Olvey wrote.[16] The Savage family, on the other hand, contended that Savage died as the result of complications from his injuries, not human error. In big-picture terms, this was a distinction without a difference.

The race resumed after a seventy-one-minute red-flag delay. The action was desultory, as engines let go with monotonous regularity until barely a dozen cars were left running. Johncock was leading when rain forced another red flag—the fourth, officially—on lap 133. With the track wet and light fading, he was declared the winner. Nowadays, this race is often regarded as the Worst Indy Ever. In light of the Speedway's dismal track record, there's plenty of competition for this dubious title. Was 1973 worse than 1964, when Eddie Sachs and Dave MacDonald died in a fireball, or 1958, when Pat O'Connor was killed in a fifteen-car opening-lap crash, or 1933, when no fewer than three drivers and two riding mechanics lost their lives during the month of May? Or was this another distinction without a difference?

If the reviews in the general-interest press had been any more inflammatory, the paper they were written on would have combusted spontaneously. "The slaughter that marked the 1973 Indianapolis automobile race cannot be categorized as accidental deaths. What happened on the infamous speedway has come to be a routine form of homicide," the *New York Times* editorialized. "Such lethal circuses are in no sense justified by their morbid popularity. The prime issue is that of public safety and of public morality (concern for human life). But there are important secondary issues too, notably the wasteful consumption of fuel at a time of shortages which threaten to curtail the legitimate use of automobiles and aircraft. Such intolerable waste—along with the glorification of murderous speed—in the face of a worsening energy crisis is comparable to the public burning of food at a time of famine. The 1973 debacle at Indianapolis deserves to be turned into tombstone and epitaph of a savage aberration in the world of sport."[17]

What made 1973 especially notorious was that it was seen by tens of millions of TV viewers rather than the few thousand spectators who happened to be sitting near the accidents. In 1933, commercial television didn't exist. In 1958, it didn't cover racing. In 1964, same-day race footage was seen only by people who attended closed-circuit broadcasts. Until the 1970s, racing was the private domain of fans who understood and accepted the fatalism that was integral to the sport. But by showing Indy on network television, racing was suddenly accessible to a new universe of fair-weather fans and couch potatoes whose attention may have been attracted while channel surfing rather than any special interest in the subject. According to Nielsen ratings estimates, the race was seen by seventeen million viewers, many of whom had tuned in with the expectation of seeing some light entertainment, not death in living color.

Some members of the racing establishment reacted to the public outcry by circling the wagons and insisting—unconvincingly—that there was nothing to see here. "A race driver gets killed at Indy and they call for the banishment of the 500," editor and publisher Carl Hungness wrote in the 1973 edition of the *Indianapolis 500 Yearbook*. "A Blue Angel pilot falls out of the sky and they call his death unfortunate. Thus, being a race fan is a very difficult title to wear on occasion."[18] But even among the enthusiast press, there's wasn't much support for USAC and the Indianapolis Motor Speedway. "Without further dramatic preventive measures, Indianapolis can become a terminal cancer to the sport of motor racing," ran an unsigned editorial in *Autoweek*. "And if this in fact becomes the case *Autoweek* does not see it has any choice but to assist in every way in the cutting out of the malignancy."[19]

To their credit, USAC and IMS officials immediately authorized heroic measures to save the patient. In reaction to the Walther accident, the Speedway spent about $300,000 to raise the outer wall to a height of thirty-four inches all around the track and to eliminate the 140 box seats where fans had been showered with methanol and debris. Also, the concrete barrier that Savage (and MacDonald) had crashed into was modified. Meanwhile, USAC reduced fuel capacity to a maximum of forty gallons by closing off the right-side tank and ordering it filled with energy-absorbent material. A pop-off valve was mandated to limit turbo boost to eighty inches while the total fuel allowed for five-hundred-mile races was reduced from 375 gallons to 340 gallons. At the same time, the width of rear wings was trimmed from sixty-four inches to fifty-five inches. The changes went into effect in time for the Pocono 500 the following month, but the impact was minimal.

At Pocono, Al Unser crashed so hard that he punctured the boiler-plate-sheathed wall and suffered a concussion. At the end of the 1973 season, Bobby Unser destroyed his Eagle at Phoenix, and Al withdrew from the race to accompany his brother while he was airlifted to a hospital. The next driver to get bitten was Lee Kunzman, who'd resurrected his career after being disfigured in a sprint car fire that laid him up for a year. He was coming off several fine Indy car results in 1973 when he suffered a traumatic brain injury in a crash during a postseason tire test at Ontario, and he was out of racing for nearly a year and a half while he relearned how to walk and talk. (In his first race after returning to the cockpit, he finished fourth at the same track where he'd nearly been killed.) Kunzman's wreck ended the year on an appropriately apocalyptic note.

Road racers were careening down their own road to epiphany. In theory, fire shouldn't have been as deadly a scourge in Europe as it was in the United States because the racers over there generally didn't have to worry about hitting walls made of concrete—or boiler plate, as the case may be. Also, the fiery death of Jo Schlesser in the French Grand Prix in 1968 had highlighted questionable car design and inept emergency services, signposting the changes that needed to be made. Sad to report, the safety measures instituted by the FIA in response were feeble and ineffectual. Four-time Le Mans winner-to-be Henri Pescarolo was badly burned during the Le Mans Test Day in 1969. (He grew what was to become his signature beard to hide his scars.) And a first-lap collision that caused both Jackie Oliver's BRM P153 and Jacky Ickx's Ferrari 312B to catch fire in the Spanish Grand Prix early in 1970 illustrated the farcically incompetent firefighting facilities at Jarama.

Oliver, initially trapped by his steering wheel, escaped only after a superhuman effort to bend the steering column. Ickx, too, did most of the heavy lifting himself. "In Spain, clearly what saved me was the instinct of self-preservation," he said. "The problem was that my chassis was bent and I had difficulty reaching my seat belt. My helmet was completely burned. Then, when I was running away, I fell in the fuel that was going out of my car. But there were some heroes who had no fear to help me. There was a Spanish gardener from Seville, and he tried to stamp out the flames on my overalls, and he was badly burned."[20] Once the drivers were safe, a "comic opera" ensued as a lone firefighter sprayed the cars with foam from across the track.[21] Not only did this fail to extinguish the fire, but it also blinded the drivers trying to squeeze past, and the foam turned that portion of pavement into a stretch of slick track. Even though other firefighters eventually arrived, the Ferrari burned for twenty-five minutes; the BRM, for an hour.

The following month, during practice for the 1000 Kilometers at the Nürburgring, fire had more dire consequences. Hans Laine, a young Finn, hit a nasty bump on the fast Döttinger Höhe stretch. His Porsche 908/2 did a backflip, landed upside down, and burst into flames. There's some conjecture that he died instantly. What's known for sure is that the tiny fire extinguishers carried by the marshals couldn't suppress the inferno, and fifteen minutes passed before Laine was removed from the cockpit. The incident didn't receive much attention at the time, probably because it was one of nine fatal accidents—nine!—to occur at the 'Ring in a fifteen-month stretch. (That's just the race car accidents, by the way; two motorcyclists died there as well during the same period.) Granted, most of the drivers were club racers in plebeian equipment—touring cars, mostly, but also a Formula 2 car, a Formula Vee, and even a go-kart. Still, the regularity of the deaths at the manifestly unsafe Nordschleife called to mind the definition of insanity as repeating the same mistake over and over again while expecting a different result.

A month later, yet another fatal accident marred the Dutch Grand Prix at Zandvoort. Before the race, the drivers requested that guardrails be installed on the super-fast section on the back side of the circuit where Chris Lambert had been killed in a Formula 2 car two years earlier. Their request was rebuffed. During practice, Jack Brabham and Pedro Rodriguez had scary offs when their tires failed on precisely that stretch of road, but neither driver was hurt. Jochen Rindt qualified on the pole in the stunning new Lotus 72. On the inside of the fourth row was Piers Courage. The heir to the Courage Brewery Fortune, he obviously had a lot of money, but also plenty of talent. This was his second year in F1 driving for Frank Williams, who was then a small-time operator three decades, millions of pounds, and nine constructors' titles away from being knighted. Rather than racing cars of his own manufacture, Williams was campaigning a Cosworth-powered chassis built by Alejandro de Tomaso, a mercurial Argentine whose reach tended to exceed his resources. Courage and Williams had nicknamed the overweight car "the Tomato." Ninth on the grid at Zandvoort was their best qualifying result of the year, and Courage was running seventh when something broke.

Courage veered off the track at 150 mph and knocked down three poles precisely where the drivers had requested a guardrail. The car sped up a sand dune, somersaulted, and immediately ignited. Something—a tire, perhaps, or maybe one of the poles—wrenched the helmet off Courage's head and sent it rolling down the track. An improperly sited fire truck didn't arrive for a good twenty minutes. Meanwhile, firefighters tried to douse the flames with water, but in a demoralizing reprise of Schlesser's fatal accident at Rouen, this merely caused the magnesium in the chassis to flare up and burn more furiously. "The intensity of the fire was overwhelming, so much so that the crews didn't have enough foam to extinguish it and finally had to cover the entire car with a tarpaulin and then bury it in sand, just to cover it, with Piers still inside," Jackie Stewart, one of Courage's closest friends, wrote in his diary. "It wasn't until well after the race that they finally got him out, and even then, when they took the tarpaulin off to get to him, air got in and the fire started again. Both the chassis and the engine were melted."[22]

As usual, there was a great hue and cry about the inadequacy of the safety crew and the barbarity of the sport. And as usual, nothing changed. In fact, the following weekend, Derrick Williams died in a Formula 5000 race in Anderstop when his Lola T142K flipped and caught fire while he was trapped inside the cockpit. Even though a professional emergency crew arrived immediately and bravely fought the blaze—two firefighters were hospitalized with serious burns—Williams couldn't be rescued. After the race was stopped, a tarp was unceremoniously thrown over the blackened car, with Williams still inside, and then the race continued.

A crash at a lesser Formula 3 race on a makeshift airport circuit at Dijon would have more enduring ramifications. Up-and-coming Frenchman Jean-Pierre Cassegrain, then second in the French F3 championship, crashed his Brabham BT28 in the first turn. The car flipped and erupted into flames. Watching the race was a young Dijonnaise named Yves Morizot. "I was a baker, but I was fed up with bread, and I was crazy for racing," he said.[23] When the marshals dallied, he and a few other spectators leapt over the fence to drag Cassegrain out of the car. Although a fire suit protected Cassegrain's body, the fire burned through his leather gloves, and he lost two fingers. "I was obviously a nobody then. But deep inside, I knew I had to do something," Morizot wrote later. "From then on, I started thinking about safety."[24] Morizot was inspired to found Stand 21, which continues to set new benchmarks for the design and manufacture of helmets and fire-retardant gear.

Morizot didn't start selling fire-retardant uniforms—originally incorporating asbestos (!)—until 1972, when he was finally able to secure a large enough supply of Nomex. But another event, at the end of 1971, had an even greater impact on the sport. Back then, Formula 1 wasn't the rigidly structured sports-marketing machine it is today, and several events were run on an ad hoc basis by promoters looking to generate some extra revenue. In 1971, in addition to eleven Grands Prix counting toward the world championship, there were eight non-championship races. The last one, open to both F1 and F5000 cars, was the Victory Race at Brands Hatch. Jo Siffert, renowned for his exuberant driving style, qualified on the pole in his BRM P160. A love tap from Ronnie Peterson's March 711 nudged him back to tenth at the start, but he was fighting his way forward when, on lap sixteen, he angled left due to a mechanical failure of some sort. (The precise cause was never determined.) The BRM blasted up an earthen bank—no guardrails in sight—at more than 125 mph and hit a large stone that sliced through the fuel bladder like a laser. The car speared a sign board at Hawthorn Bend, turned turtle, and slid on its back before cartwheeling over a marshals' hut, landing upside down, and exploding. Although a firefighter wearing an aluminized suit was quickly on the scene, none of the three fire extinguishers at the corner station worked, and a fire truck didn't arrive for five minutes. At a subsequent inquiry, Grahame White, clerk of the course and general manager of the British Automobile Racing Club, testified that upgrading the firefighting operation "would be too costly and impractical to implement."[25] The investigation found

In the 1950s, most road racers wore street clothes. In the 1960s, driving uniforms became the norm. Awaiting the start of the 1972 Belgian Grand Prix, Ronnie Peterson is swaddled in a fire-retardant race suit, balaclava, and gloves, and his safety gear includes a full-face helmet and a Willans six-point harness. On the other hand, the crude-looking airbox appears to be secured with a bungee cord. *Bryant McMurray, courtesy of J. Murrey Atkins Library, UNC Charlotte*

that the only injury suffered by Siffert was a broken leg and that he died from asphyxia after the fire sucked all the oxygen out of the air. Siffert's loss seemed so senseless that Vatican Radio felt compelled to weigh in, decrying race car drivers as "kamikazes dedicated to death."[26]

Siffert was the first driver to be killed in a BRM since the marque began entering races in 1951. Team principal Louis Stanley was appalled by his death, which he described as being "entirely due to the shameful mishandling of the accident."[27] Stanley was by far the most vocal safety advocate not only among the constructors but also Formula 1's leadership writ large. For him, Siffert's preventable death was a bridge too far. "I am not apportioning degrees of blame—the coroner did that for me," he said. "Something had to be done."[28] Stanley established the Jo Siffert Advisory Council, drawing experts from civil aviation, the professional firefighting community, the Home Office (responsible for public safety), and the Ministry of Defence. He also tested—personally—garments to confirm that they provided fire protection for at least thirty seconds. The FIA was finally shamed into promulgating more stringent regulations regarding fuel cells and cockpit safety. Still, the timing was curious. Why act now and not after any one of the other dozen or so largely identical fire-related deaths? Stanley had a theory. "Public reaction was immediate," he wrote. "Reading about a driver being burned to death is acceptable; it is not visual and therefore impersonal. But when national newspapers splash photographs across front pages highlighting the moment of death, it offends every sensitivity."[29]

And it wasn't just the newspapers. The BBC had broadcast an edited version of the Victory Race, including Siffert's crash, on the afternoon of the race. British television had a hot-and-cold relationship with motorsports. Barely a month after it launched, the BBC showed footage of the antique car rally from London to Brighton, and in 1938 it was responsible for the world's first live broadcast of a motor race, the Imperial Trophy Race at Crystal Palace. The British Grand Prix was first aired in 1953, Monaco in 1955. Well into the 1960s, racing was featured occasionally on *Sportsview* and *Grandstand*, the BBC counterparts to *Wide World of Sports*. ITV, the Beeb's commercial rival, also showed racing on its own omnibus show, *World of Sport*. In those days, the voice of televised motorsports wasn't the perennially excited

Murray Walker but the dry, polished, authoritative Raymond Baxter, a World War II fighter pilot who exuded gravitas. Unlike ABC in the United States, the BBC shied away from sensationalism, and the network's prohibition against advertising put it in an awkward position as Formula 1 became ever more commercial. But by the early 1970s, F1 was too big and successful to ignore.

Fans were looking forward to a banner year in 1973. The F1 schedule had expanded to fifteen races, the most ever. Thanks to the availability of the Cosworth DFV and new sponsors, the grids often featured more than two dozen cars. On the safety front, no drivers had been killed in 1972—the first year without a fatal accident since 1965 and only the fourth since 1952. That almost changed at Kyalami, during the South African Grand Prix. After an early-race kerfuffle involving several cars, Clay Regazzoni T-boned Mike Hailwood's Surtees TS14A, and both cars ignited. Hailwood freed himself after punching the onboard fire extinguisher, but Regazzoni was knocked out by the collision. As flames flared around the BRM P160D, Hailwood hurried over and tried to pull Regazzoni out of cockpit. Unfortunately, Regazzoni was wedged inside the deformed chassis. Hailwood struggled valiantly to free him until his own gloves and one boot were burning like tiki torches. He sprinted across the track and hurled himself onto the grass, rolling around to smother the flames. Meanwhile, several marshals equipped with fire extinguishers courageously braved tremendous heat to knock down the fire, but they couldn't free Regazzoni. So Hailwood ran back and, with the help of another corner worker, wrenched him out of the cockpit. Regazzoni spent ten days in the hospital, and Hailwood was awarded the George Medal, second only to the Victoria Cross among British decorations for gallantry.

But profiles in courage don't always produce happy endings, as the Dutch Grand Prix would demonstrate with heartbreaking clarity. The two principals, both young, both British, both driving identical cars, had been born worlds apart, yet they're now linked forever by a macabre thread. Roger Williamson was the son of a garage owner and former speedway rider who'd climbed through the club racing and lower formula car ranks until attracting the patronage of Tom Wheatcroft. A construction magnate who'd amassed an unparalleled collection of vintage Grand Prix cars, Wheatcroft bought a March 731 for Williamson to race in F1. Williamson's first start, in the British Grand Prix, ended almost immediately when he was caught up in the nine-car pileup at the end of the opening lap. For his second race, at Zandvoort, he qualified eighteenth out of twenty-four cars. Lining up almost directly behind him was David Purley. The son of the founder of the LEC Refrigeration empire, Purley had seen combat as an army paratrooper before getting into racing. He rented a March 731 in 1973 and was poised to make his third F1 start.

Nobody was particularly happy to be at Zandvoort. Many of the mechanics were knackered after spending much of the previous two weeks repairing cars that had been wrecked during the crashfest at Silverstone. Also, bad memories lingered from Courage's fatal accident in 1970. In fact, the race had been removed from the F1 schedule in 1972 due to safety concerns, and it was reinstated this year only after a new promoter spent nearly $900,000 on resurfacing the track as well as adding 5.5 miles of Armco, three miles of spectator fencing, and two new corners to slow lap times. It rained on Friday, effectively washing out the practice sessions. Then, on Saturday, Emerson Fittipaldi crashed in the fast section on the back side of the circuit, and his Lotus 72 got tangled up in the catch fencing. He was lucky to get away with nothing worse than two badly bruised ankles. Although he was able to take the start, he was in so much pain that he retired after two laps.

Come race day, Peterson led from the pole, while Williamson and Purley squabbled for thirteenth. On the eighth lap, on the fastest part of the circuit, the left-front tire of Williamson's car burst. He left the track at the first of two fifth-gear corners and hit a guardrail that had been installed as part of Zandvoort's off-season safety upgrades. But the posts weren't secured into concrete footings, as conventional construction practices—not to mention common sense—would have suggested. Instead, they were simply sunk into the sand, which naturally gave way when the March cannoned into the Armco. The railing bent back to form a miniature ski ramp tilted up at a forty-degree angle. The fuel cell shredded as the car rode up the rail and corkscrewed off before landing upside down and catching fire. Purley slithered to a stop and jumped out of his cockpit. After finding a gap between cars streaming past, he sprinted across the track toward Williamson and his burning March. This was the prelude to one of the most disheartening and disturbing episodes in racing history.

Purley jumped over a sheared-off wheel and other debris from the wreck. As he tried to right Williamson's car by pushing on a rear tire, two marshals in civilian clothes hurried over to join him. The car didn't budge. At this point, the fire was reasonably small but growing ominously, so Purley ran across the track, then hustled back with a handheld fire extinguisher and a third marshal. Race cars continued to drive past, not going at full speed but not exactly crawling either. Purley circled the burning car, spraying it liberally with foam, then crouched down to hit the cockpit. He could hear Williamson shouting, "For God's sake, get me out of here!"[30] even as the flames intensified. Realizing that the single handheld fire extinguisher couldn't control the blaze, Purley waved the marshals over, begging them to help him push the car upright. They ignored his pleas. In their defense, they weren't wearing fire-retardant clothing, and the heat was fearsome. Exhausted, Purley bent over with his hands on his knees like a winded athlete. After catching his breath, he attacked the rear wheel again with manic vigor, and, after more desperate waves, the marshals briefly joined in. But the fire was too intense, and the car clearly wasn't going to budge. When one of the marshals finally pulled him away, Purley gave him a shove and took a half-hearted swipe before stumbling disconsolately across the track. Dejected, defeated, and disgusted, he shook his fist at the passing race cars, but none of the drivers paid any attention. Behind him, the fire continued to burn unabated, with Williamson still trapped inside the cockpit and the air thick with black smoke.

While all this was going on, police were threatening to arrest spectators who were trying to join in the effort to rescue Williamson. In retrospect, this was probably the right decision since it's not clear what the fans realistically could have done, and they might have caused more problems running across the track. But it wasn't a good look. And even if you ignore the unseemly spectacle of officials actively trying to prevent people from helping, there was plenty of blame to go around, starting with how the guardrail that Williamson struck had been improperly—and negligently—erected on a foundation of sand. The corner marshals were unconscionably unprepared to deal with the fire, and a fire truck didn't arrive until long after Williamson was beyond saving. (A second fire truck never moved.) The race wasn't red-flagged because there was a breakdown in communication between the corner station and Race Control. Of course, the drivers could have stopped on their own, but they chose not to. As Niki Lauda said—notoriously—after the race, "I am paid to race, not to stop."[31] Although that sounds callous, drivers in this era routinely sped past accidents. Some of them even saw yellow flags as an opportunity to gain an advantage over more scrupulous rivals. And in this particular case, several racers said later that they didn't realize that two drivers were involved. When they saw Purley standing on the side of the track, they assumed that he'd gotten safely out of the wrecked car, end of story, and they couldn't understand why he was waving at them. It wasn't until after the race was over that they learned, to their horror, that Williamson had been killed.

The mood in the pits was understandably somber. Wheatcroft, in particular, was devastated by Williamson's death. Normally gregarious and hard as carbon steel, he wandered forlornly around the paddock, dazed by the news, his cheeks slick with tears. Meanwhile, some drivers wrestled privately with the guilt they felt for failing to stop to help Purley. But beneath the pervasive gloom was an undercurrent of anger directed at the officials who'd mishandled the situation. During the race, Denny Hulme, who'd recently succeeded Stewart as president of the GPDA, had driven up to the edge of the pit wall and shaken his fist at the tower in an effort to persuade Race Control to throw a red flag. As it happened, nobody up there had any idea what was happening on the back side of the circuit. "We just don't learn . . . we just don't learn," Hulme wrote plaintively in *Autoweek*. "We get the most horrifying kinds of lessons and yet we simply do not learn from them."[32]

The organizers of the calamitous Paris–Madrid race, aka The Race to Death, deserve a pass because, until 1903, nobody understood just how deadly the newfangled sport of automobile racing could be. But nothing that transpired at Zandvoort should have come as a surprise to anybody with even the most superficial knowledge of the sport. Williamson's accident was almost a carbon copy of the wrecks that had killed Courage, Laine, and Siffert as well as Lorenzo Bandini at Monaco in 1967 and

Jo Schlesser at Rouen in 1968, not to mention countless other drivers who'd perished in fires in lower-profile events. The solution was as clear as a huge neon sign in an empty desert on a cloudless night—staffing corner stations with adequately equipped and properly trained corner workers augmented by fire trucks able to respond quickly to accidents.

After a sterling self-funded club-racing career, Roger Williamson came to the attention of construction magnate Tom Wheatcroft. Backed by Wheatcroft, Williamson dominated Formula 3 before graduating to F1. In only his second Grand Prix, he would become the first member of what writer David Tremayne called "The Lost Generation" of precocious British F1 drivers of the 1970s to die in an accident. *Revs Institute / Ove Nielsen Photograph Collection*

"To say it all again after Roger Williamson's fatal crash as the fire raged unchecked at Zandvoort seems almost futile," Hulme wrote.

Like Hailwood, Purley received the George Medal. His bravery, coupled with the needlessness of Williamson's death, made the incident a national story, one that displayed racing in the worst possible light. Several newspapers ran ghastly photos of the charred corpse. Even more horrifying were the images beamed into living rooms on tens of thousands of British televisions "during the placidity of afternoon tea," as one critic put it in a newspaper column titled "When taste and news value clash." As he wrote, "Was its showing justified at an hour when so many children were bound to see it?"[33] But the larger issue, according to another columnist, wasn't propriety. It was the barbarity that seemed to be an acceptable part of the sport. "Those who watch it or take part in it know the risks," he wrote. "And undoubtedly the attitude of the racing driver is, 'Don't mourn me when I'm gone'—in other words, the show must go on. Fair enough. If people want to watch motor racing or drive racing cars, let them get on with it. They're doing me no harm. I just hope the sport will realise more has to be done to put its house in order."[34]

Many viewers were equally revolted. Some blamed the television networks, like a letter writer quoted in *Autoweek,* complaining about a clip broadcast repeatedly by ABC: "It then became quite obvious that the real reason for the report was to show the viewer, in gory detail, the fatal crash of Roger Williamson and the anguish of those who tried to rescue him. Once again, *Wide World of Sports* had exploited motor racing in an irresponsible attempt to increase the show's ratings."[35] But others put the blame squarely where it belonged—on a motorsports culture that allowed such tragedies to occur again and again and again. "For the third time I have just witnessed on my television set the sickening spectacle of a young man being burnt to death in a Grand Prix car, with people standing around apparently unable to help," a reader wrote to *Motor Sport*. "I would have thought Bandini's accident at Monaco would have been sufficient to stir organisers into providing something along these lines [grappling hooks on long chains]. But to allow Siffert, and now Williamson to die in exactly the same way is surely unforgivable."[36]

A Grand Prix season that began with great promise had mutated into a nightmare. In addition to Williamson's fatal accident at Zandvoort and Regazzoni's near-death experience at Kyalami, John Watson broke his leg and had to be cut out of his car at Brands Hatch. Ditto for Andrea de Adamich at Silverstone. (The crash effectively ended his driving career.) Lauda broke his wrist at the Nürburgring. Then, Arturo Merzario suffered a concussion at Mosport during practice for a Canadian Grand Prix marked by the first deployment of a safety car in F1 history. Next, it was on to Watkins Glen, where more tragedy awaited.

THE HARD CELL

Like millions of Americans, S. Harry Robertson watched the *Wide World of Sports* telecast of the Indianapolis 500 in 1973. And like millions of Americans, he was horrified by the fiery crashes that killed Swede Savage and maimed Salt Walther. But unlike just about anybody else in the country, he knew how to prevent them from happening again.

A former drag racer who flew B-47s in the US Air Force, Robertson had several friends and crew members who'd died in fires that erupted after otherwise survivable aviation crashes. When he left the military, he began studying what caused the fuel tanks to fail. During the 1960s, he oversaw the crash tests of forty-four full-size aircraft and hundreds of fuel tanks. His conclusion? "There's no reason for someone to survive a crash—and then die in a fire," he said.[37]

The problem was particularly acute in helicopters flying combat missions in the Vietnam War, where 40 percent of the fatalities were the result of postcrash fires. Drawing on his aviation knowledge and failure-analysis expertise, Robertson designed and built the Robertson Crashworthy Fuel System, which immediately went into service on the workhorse Bell UH-1 Huey. Nicknamed the "Robbie Tank," the system virtually eliminated postcrash fires. The US Army later estimated that it saved eight thousand lives over the next three decades.

Robertson thought that a variation on the technology used in the Robbie Tank would work in Indy cars. Coincidentally, USAC technical director Frankie DelRoy had precisely the same idea. So even as a letter written by Robertson was on its way to the USAC office in Indianapolis, DelRoy was on an airplane to Arizona to see Robertson.

DelRoy was old enough to have sat on the pole at Indy as a riding mechanic way back in 1937, and he'd been the chief mechanic on the car that Mike Nazaruk, a US Marine who survived the brutal jungle warfare on Iwo Jima only to die in a sprint car at Langhorne, drove to a second-place finish in the 500 in 1951. When USAC was formed in 1955, DelRoy was one of its first hires. He'd overseen the implementation of the first-generation Firestone and Goodyear fuel cells after the Sachs-MacDonald conflagration in 1964. Now, he knew, it was time for an upgrade. He and Robertson talked for two days. In December, Robertson released a thirty-four-page design manual describing the upgraded fuel system that he and DelRoy had discussed.

The most obvious difference was that the new fuel cell was much thicker and sturdier than the old one. The bladders from the '60s were like balloons, which made them more pliable and, therefore, easier to work with. The Robertson-designed bladders were so stout that they wouldn't deform even if someone stood on them. This made them ten times more resistant to cuts and shredding but also an ordeal to install. "The joke was that it was like wrestling a black bear," said longtime crew chief Mike Devin, who would eventually hold DelRoy's position as USAC technical director. "It would take everybody in the shop with hammers and two-by-fours beating in the corners, and it was a fistfight because they were so stiff."[38]

To protect the bladder, it was cocooned in a thick sock made of felt (later Kevlar) and all the hoses were sheathed in steel-wire sleeves. But even as the cell was being strengthened, Robertson shaped it with a smooth contour so that, in the event of a major accident, it would come loose as a single unit rather than getting snagged and ripping. Toward that end, the main fuel line and all the attachment points were fitted with aerospace-spec breakaway valves that sealed automatically when they were damaged. The idea was that, as long as the bladder remained intact, no methanol could escape to fuel a fire.

Meanwhile, independently, work was being done to make the act of refueling safer. Well into the 1960s most fuel filler necks were sealed with flip-top caps that latched shut. (In the road-racing world, they

Soldiers with the 1st Cavalry Division dismount from a Bell UH-1D helicopter, popularly known as a Huey, prior to intense fighting near Hue in 1966. S. Harry Robertson developed an innovative fuel system to prevent the postcrash fires that accounted for 40 percent of all helicopter fatalities during the Vietnam War. The lifesaving technology in his so-called Robbie Tank was later adapted for Indy cars and other forms of racing. *US Army*

were known as Monza caps, and they were a popular boy-racer accessory on streetable sports cars.) As you might imagine, these caps weren't ideal if the car flipped over, and they were known to fly open on rare occasions even if they were right-side up.

Carroll Shelby, who was running Mustangs for Ford in the Trans-Am series, had an idea that would make refueling safer. In 1969, he walked into the Redondo Beach shop of David Ayres, an American Airlines pilot who did custom machine work on the side. Shelby wanted to replace the Monza cap with a dry-break fitting to prevent fuel spillage during pit stops—and on the track, if something went wrong. By the time Ayres created a prototype, Shelby had quit racing. But George Bignotti, the winningest crew chief in Indy history, fitted one of Ayres's new dry-break valves to the Johnny Lightning Special that Al Unser drove to victory in 1970. By 1973, Ayres's RedHeads were found on thirty-one of the thirty-three cars racing at the Speedway. Dry-break refueling "buckeyes" are still used in 2026.

Robertson was too busy with military work to supply fuel tanks for racing, so Goodyear and Firestone built fuel cells to his specifications. In 1976, they became standard equipment in Indy car racing. Although up to three tanks were permitted, the demands for clean underwings in ground-effects cars of the 1980s prompted everybody to go to a single cell between the driver and the engine. This, too, remains the accepted practice.

In terms of fire, refueling is still the most fraught period of any race. In 1981, there were three serious pit fires during a two-month stretch. Rick Mears underwent plastic surgery on his nose after a nasty episode at Indy, and fourteen people were injured in a huge blaze at Michigan. Methanol burns invisibly, which makes pit fires especially tricky to contain, and they still occur now and then. But crash-related fires are largely a relic of the bad old days. "There's always an oddball chance that something could happen," Devin said. "But modern fuel cells pretty much solved the problem of catastrophic fires from a total rupture."[39]

Helicopter pilots aren't the only ones who owe a debt to S. Harry Robertson, the Father of the Crashworthy Fuel Tank.

Handsome, talented, and charismatic, François Cevert was on the cusp of stardom when he crashed fatally at Watkins Glen in 1973 during practice for the US Grand Prix. His death prompted the immediate retirement of his teammate and mentor Jackie Stewart. But for the rest of the F1 circus, nothing changed. Another generation would pass before fatal accidents were largely eradicated from Formula 1. *Revs Institute / Bill Oursler Photograph Collection*

CODA

A CHANGE IS GONNA COME

François Cevert was a charming and glamorous Frenchman with eyes so crystalline blue that he could be identified even with his helmet on. The son of a Parisian jeweler, he was a classically trained pianist and a member of an exclusive fraternity of talented countrymen who would find their way to Formula 1, from his brother-in-law, Jean-Pierre Beltoise, to Patrick Depailler, who eventually took his place on the Tyrrell team. He'd been hired to back up Jackie Stewart when Johnny Servoz-Gavin retired unexpectedly in the middle of the 1970 season. (Tyrrell needed a Gallic driver on the team because Elf, the French oil conglomerate, was a major sponsor.) Stewart and Cevert had a sensei-and-student relationship, and the younger man dutifully followed in his elder's wheel tracks for most of the next three years. Cevert scored a fine win at the US Grand Prix in 1971—outrunning Stewart—and finished second to his teammate on six occasions. By 1973, he was roughly Stewart's equal on qualifying pace, if not race results.

In the fall of '73, two weeks after the Canadian Grand Prix, the Formula 1 carnival reconvened in Watkins Glen for the final race of the F1 season. Stewart had already clinched the world championship, and even though Tyrrell and Lotus were still dueling for the constructors' title, there was a relaxed end-of-term atmosphere in the paddock. On Friday night, Cevert played "The Mexican Hat Dance" on the piano at the rustic Seneca Lounge in honor of mechanic Jo Ramirez. The big "news" was a story that hadn't broken yet: JYS intended to retire after this, his one hundredth Grand Prix. The secret was so closely guarded that even Stewart's wife, Helen, didn't know about it. For business reasons, Ken Tyrrell had been informed, and he'd already decided to elevate Cevert to team leader in 1974.

On Saturday, during a break in the second qualifying session, the Tyrrell teammates discussed how to approach the high-speed Esses up the hill. Stewart preferred the stability of fourth gear while Cevert thought the top of third was faster, though it required more work. Sure enough, Cevert was a few tenths quicker. With six minutes remaining in the session, officially classified as fourth fastest, he hit a dip in the Esses, and his Tyrrell 006 wiggled at about 130 miles per hour. He was able to catch it but not before brushing the Armco on the right. This sent him spinning back across the track into the guardrail on the left—hard. As had been the case in both Williamson's and Rindt's accidents, the Armco had been sited perfectly but installed improperly.

"Okay, so they put up Armco barriers," Herbie Blash said. "But back then, people never thought about how the Armco was installed. It was, 'Oh, well, there's a barrier.' Armco was a brilliant invention that saved many, many lives and prevented many, many serious injuries. But unfortunately, in those early days, it wasn't always assembled correctly."[1] Today, guardrails are supported by posts sunk into a solid footing every three feet. In 1973, the posts were six, or eight, or even ten feet apart. Many drivers were badly hurt and, in several cases, decapitated when their cars slid under or through the guardrails. "They were not rigid enough," Beltoise explained. "They were too flexible."[2]

When Cevert slammed into the Armco, the bottom strand of metal gave way. It sliced off part of the chassis as the Tyrrell burrowed underneath it until hitting a post and flipping on top of the guardrail. After the fiasco in Zandvoort, drivers no longer trusted safety crews to handle an emergency, so cars started stopping at the scene of the accident. Jody Scheckter was the first to reach the wrecked Tyrrell. He undid Cevert's belts before realizing that nothing more could be done. (The scene was so traumatic that he can't remember what he saw.) When Stewart stopped, Scheckter told him, "Don't go there. You don't want to see."[3] Stewart ignored his well-meaning advice. Back in the pits, angry and upset, he flung his helmet into his car.

Stewart didn't take the start for what was supposed to be his final race. Instead, Tyrrell withdrew his car as well as a third entry that had been entrusted to Chris Amon to help in the fight for the constructors' championship. But for the rest of the teams, it was business as usual. "It affected me as a young person, seeing somebody killed like that for the first time," Scheckter said. "But the thing I remember is that everybody just carried on like it was before."[4] In the Brabham pit, Bernie Ecclestone heard the news, processed it, and immediately moved on. "My attitude was, 'Well, practice is going to start in an hour. So better get ready,'" he recalled. "It was a pity that he got killed, and everyone was upset because he was such a nice guy. But don't forget, we used to lose a couple of drivers a year, and there wasn't much anyone could do about it. The guys died, and that was it."[5]

Although this sounds tone-deaf to contemporary ears, it was still the prevailing attitude in the paddock, even as late as 1973. It seems likely that, if another driver had lost his life at the Glen, Cevert wouldn't have hesitated to return to the track for the next qualifying session. "Racing is the most dangerous job you can find. But you must choose. The choice is either to not race and live what for me would be a sad and dull life or choose to live with racing," he told an interviewer not long before he was killed. "But I would certainly like to see the day come when a driver is not automatically dead if he loses the car or has a mechanical failure at 200 mph."[6]

And it was that second statement—the belief that the penalty for making a mistake shouldn't be fatal—that represented the way forward. Cevert had been born in 1944, during World War II but too late to have absorbed its mindset. He was part of a fresh cohort of drivers who came of age with an expectation of safety. They'd barely known an era without Nomex and guardrails, fuel cells and full-face helmets. The Targa Florio was gone, the original Spa was history, and the Nordschliefe's days were numbered. Drivers would still die on occasion, and Formula

1, in particular, suffered more than its share of tragedies in the 1970s. But no longer would it be acceptable to, as Ecclestone put it, "lose a couple of drivers a year."

"In the '70s, we started seeing a new generation of young drivers who had a different perspective," said John Watson, who was himself born in 1946 and who would race into an era when race cars were built around carbon fiber safety cells. "They wanted to have a career in racing. They didn't want that career to end prematurely because they had an injury. They certainly didn't want to be a statistic. I blame the governing body of motorsport because the [officials in their] blue blazers didn't do enough. It was like the bullfighting mentality. They sat back and thought, 'Well, if a driver dies, a driver dies. So what?' That was part of the sport. Well, Jackie Stewart didn't want to die. So he railed against that philosophy, and he made himself unpopular in certain circles. But gradually, gradually, changes were made."[7]

The changes came from without, but also from within. Increasingly, drivers rejected the stereotypes that had been promoted by journalists and embraced by fans for decades. They saw themselves as modern athletes trying to make a living, not knights-errant observing an antiquated code of chivalry. They were clear-eyed about the risks they ran, and they understood that "motor racing is dangerous," as it says on the release of liability form signed by every participant in the sport, from the lowliest club race to the Indy 500. But they ridiculed the notion that drivers had to conquer their fear of death to be true champions. "Complete bollocks," said Jackie Oliver, who flirted with death on a few occasions but didn't consider that to be the defining attribute of his career. "There is as much fear involved in making the last putt to win the Masters as there is in the last lap to win a motor race. The participants aren't concerned about death. They're concerned about losing."[8]

The incessant drumbeat of fatalities had a cumulative effect on everybody involved in the sport. Stewart's career lasted only eleven years, yet during that relatively brief period, he often recounted, no fewer than fifty-seven of his colleagues were killed. Among them were four of his closest friends—Cevert, Jim Clark, Piers Courage, and Jochen Rindt. Team owner John Mecom Jr. walked away from the sport after buying the New Orleans Saints in part because of the emotional toll exacted by racing. "I'd gotten really close to all of the drivers," he said. "That was part of what I enjoyed about it. I still have more friends in motor racing than I ever had in professional football. But it got to the point when I looked forward to the end of the race more than the beginning. I just couldn't handle it."[9]

Fans, too, began looking at the sport in a different way. Partly, this was because attitudes about safety were changing across the board, from mandatory seat belt use to public safety campaigns aimed at preventing kids from getting trapped in empty refrigerators. But the attitudes were also different because the fans were different. Television had brought millions of newcomers to the sport who weren't nostalgic about Juan Manuel Fangio wheeling an Alfetta through the sun-dappled roads near Bern or Rex Mays slinging a Kurtis-Winfield around the Milwaukee Mile. Simon Taylor, who was the editor in chief of *Autosport* during this era, remembered meeting one of these newbies. "He told me, 'Motor racing is my favorite sport. I never miss a race,'" he recalled. "I said, 'Well, what was the last race you were at?' 'Oh, no, I've never been to a race. I watch every one on television.' So I said to him, 'Look, you're not a real racing fan until you sit on top of an earth bank at Snetterton in the rain when it's twenty-eight degrees Fahrenheit.' But, of course, he didn't know what I was talking about."[10]

One of the favorite tropes that critics love to trot out when trashing the sport is that fans watch races because they want to see the crashes. And to be fair, most people *do* perk up when they see a wreck, the bigger, the better. But being fascinated by crashes isn't the same thing as rooting for a tragedy. When Dave Lockton was building Ontario Motor Speedway, he commissioned a marketing study that found that there were only fifty thousand hardcore racing fans in the area. Even if he got every one of them to attend his races, he knew that Ontario wouldn't make a single penny. So he commissioned a second study aimed at figuring out how to attract spectators who weren't already obsessed by racing. "One of the questions was, why don't you go to the races?" Lockton said. "And at the top of the list of answers was, 'I don't want to see somebody hurt or killed.' People were afraid that they would see something unpleasant."[11]

Lockton realized that he needed to do something to address safety. Sponsors were reaching the same conclusion. This wasn't a consideration

This evocative photo printed from a glass negative showcases an era before organizers worried about the safety of drivers, much less the fans in harm's way. Rounding "Death Curve"—yes, that was the official name of the corner—Mercedes hero Ralph DePalma is about to thunder past William Carlson's Duesenberg on the streets of Santa Monica while winning the Vanderbilt Cup race in 1914. *Library of Congress*

when the major players were carmakers, tire companies, and the manufacturers of automotive accessories because they were selling performance. But by the 1970s, the roster of advertisers ranged from Coca-Cola to Mattel, Samsonite to Durex condoms. These companies were selling a lifestyle, and death and destruction wasn't the message they wanted to send to potential customers. "You want to celebrate the brand," Mario Andretti said. "You bring in people to showcase your involvement in racing, be part of a championship, or whatever, and all of a sudden, you're going to a funeral? You don't want to do that."[12]

Safety was the entry point that lured Philip Morris into European racing. Patrick Duffeler, who played a critical role in making Marlboro a major sponsor in F1, met with Circuit Paul Ricard track manager Jean-Pierre Paoli shortly before the brand-new circuit was about to host the French Grand Prix in 1971. Paoli admitted that he was running short of money, and he told Duffeler he needed $100,000 to pay for safety equipment. "Okay, $100,000 is well above what the company would consider for one race," Duffeler said. "But if you were to put 'Marlboro' on all the safety equipment and Marlboro signs all around the track as part of a ten-year contract, I think I could sell that idea to the board."[13] Paoli agreed, and Duffeler made good on his promise. And when Paul Ricard staged its inaugural GP, pole sitter Jackie Stewart's hammerhead Tyrrell led the field under a red-and-white Marlboro sign cantilevered prominently over the track on the run down to Turn One.

So there was a commercial case as well as a moral imperative to be made for promoting safety. Still, the safety movement didn't really take off until it found an unlikely ally in Bernie Ecclestone. During his years racing cars and motorcycles himself, his attitude about safety couldn't have been more indifferent. "I would hope that the people in front of me would have an accident," he admitted.[14] Even the deaths of two of the drivers he managed—Lewis Stuart-Evans, from burns suffered in the Moroccan Grand Prix in 1958, and Jochen Rindt, at Monza, in 1970—had no appreciable effect on his attitude. Buying the Brabham team in 1971 and being around F1 on a daily basis changed his perspective. Besides Cevert, the death toll on his watch included Jo Siffert in 1971, Roger Williamson in 1973, Peter Revson and Helmut Koinigg in 1974, Mark Donohue in 1975, and Tom Pryce in 1977, and that was just in F1. "A lot of the guys who got killed were good friends, so it hurt me a lot more than it did promoters and people like that," he said.[15] As the president of the Formula One Constructors' Association, now known as FOCA rather than F1CA, Ecclestone was also acutely sensitive to commercial considerations, and he knew that watching drivers die on television was bad for business.

In May 1978, Ecclestone hired Dr. Sid Watkins as the chief surgeon for Grand Prix racing. At Hockenheim for the German Grand Prix, Watkins was mortified to discover that there was no permanent medical facility. Making matters worse, the medical team was denied entry to Race Control. When Watkins complained to Ecclestone, Bernie informed the promoters that he'd pull the drivers off the grid if they didn't shape up. "If you do that, what are we going to do with this huge crowd of German people waiting to watch the race?" they demanded.[16] After suggesting that they perform an anatomically impossible act, Ecclestone told Watkins, "I'll go down and stand in front of the grid. If things are OK, put your thumb up. If not, I'll get the drivers out of the cars."[17]

The promoters backed down, the medical team got access to Race Control, and the race went off as planned. Several other promoters would get Bernied in similar fashion over the next few years as Ecclestone bulldozed them into upgrading circuit safety. "I made myself a little bit unpopular in lots of ways because I insisted with Professor Watkins that they make all these changes," he said. "Obviously, it cost the promoters money to do that. And so they thought, 'Well, we never had to do it before. Why should we do it now? Accidents happen, and that's that.' But we said that, unless they complied with these various restrictions, they wouldn't get a Formula 1 race. So they decided that they'd better do all the things that needed to be done."[18]

Ecclestone promoted safety with the zeal of a fresh convert. There was no mistaking the impact of his crusade. Only two drivers—Gilles Villeneuve and Riccardo Paletti—died during F1 weekends in the 1980s. (Patrick Depailler and Elio de Angelis were killed in private tests.) But the real paradigm shift didn't materialize until 1994, when Roland Ratzenberger was killed during qualifying and Ayrton Senna in the race at the ill-fated San Marino Grand Prix at Imola. In the United States, the safety epiphany arrived a few years later, after Dale Earnhardt's death at Daytona in 2001. These accidents prompted a flurry of soul-searching along with an exhaustive rethinking of car design, track design, and the fundamental meaning and purpose of racing. Today, virtually every form of racing has a zero-tolerance attitude regarding death, and no avenues are left unexplored in the effort to eradicate risk.

There are those who say that the demand for safety at all costs and in all circumstances has sucked the romance out of the sport. While no serious person disagrees with Cevert's belief that the penalty for making a mistake or suffering a mechanical failure shouldn't be fatal, some observers—including more than a few of the drivers who survived life-threatening wrecks of their own—argue that the pendulum has swung too far in the other direction, that every runoff area shouldn't stretch to infinity, and that the safety car shouldn't be deployed every time a front wing endplate winds up on the track. You don't have to take a position on the merits of the case to acknowledge the indisputable fact that it was exponentially more daunting to race on a circuit that was bumpy and crowned, with blind high-speed corners bordered by trees and ditches, than it is on a modern circuit explicitly designed to minimize danger.

Niki Lauda would have died at the Norsdschleife in 1976 if Arturo Merzario and Brett Lunger hadn't stopped and pulled him out of his flaming Ferrari. Yet despite suffering disfiguring burns, he remained a fan of the track. "Still, I have only positive things to say about the Nürburgring," he insisted. "For a racing driver it represents the ultimate challenge, in terms of taking risks, driving ability and many other obstacles that must be overcome. This is true today and has been for the last 90 years for everyone who competed there, back in the '30s for Caracciola and company, in the '50s for Fangio, Moss and their contemporaries, depending on the vehicle and the current state of the track."[19]

To critics who say that modern racing is nothing more than a three-dimensional video game, contemporary racers say, "WTF?" Anybody who's seen the video of Romain Grosjean's miraculous escape from his blazing Haas after spearing through a guardrail during the Bahrain Grand Prix in 2020 realizes that, despite all the safety upgrades, racing is still a potentially lethal proposition. At any rate, nobody slams baseball players or golfers because they don't brave death every time they compete. Sport is about excellence, not some bogus ideal of grace under fire. Never has the racing been more competitive than it is today. Never have drivers consistently come closer to the limit. Never has less been left on the table. Modern drivers are no less committed than their predecessors were because they never whistled through Maison Blanche or white-knuckled it through Puke Hollow.

Then again, let's not forgot how we got here, and let's not overlook all the men who gave their lives so that racing should no longer be a blood sport. To modern racers and their fans, the 1960s and '70s seem like an incomprehensibly homicidal age. But at the same time, this was the period when safety first became a serious concern, and it's possible to draw a straight line from Jackie Stewart to the halo in Formula 1 and the aeroscreen in IndyCar. It was the best of times, it was the worst of times, it was the age of wisdom, it was the age of foolishness. . . .

I remember these times, and I remember the debates over safety—not as a participant but as a teenage fan, following the sport from afar.

On the first lap of the 2024 Indianapolis 500, rookie Tom Blomqvist lost the rear end of his Dallara DW12 and collected Marcus Ericsson, who plowed nose-first into the wall. Sixty years earlier, both cars would have exploded, and who knows how the drivers would have fared. But modern fans expect drivers to walk away from even the most violent crashes, and that's exactly what Blomqvist and Ericsson did. *Indianapolis Motor Speedway*

None of my friends or family were interested in racing, and I didn't live near any racetracks, so I learned about and followed the sport through books and magazines. Two of my early primers were *The Racing Driver* by Denis Jenkinson and *Grand Prix Year* by Ted Simon—books, I now realize, that offered clashing views of motorsports. Jenkinson was an enthusiast first and a journalist second, and his writing reflected his admiration for the drivers who were willing to explore the limit, even at the risk of their own lives. Simon was a journalist first, and I don't know if he was an enthusiast at all. His book was a detailed and incisive account of the troubled 1970 Formula 1 season, which was marked by unprecedented political upheaval and the deaths of Courage and Rindt. To Jenkinson, great drivers were demigods; to Simon, they were human beings with fears and foibles.

In 1973, while I was a college freshman, I wrote an English paper trashing ABC-TV for its sensationalistic coverage of the tragic Indianapolis 500 where Armando Teran was killed and Swede Savage suffered the injuries that eventually led to his death. It's probably just as well that I can't find the paper, and the fact that I got credit for it says less about the quality of my writing than the standards of a liberal arts education back then. But after all these years, I still remember the kicker of my piece: "Racing isn't barbaric, but the television coverage of it is." At the time, I thought it was a great line. Now, I'm not so sure.

In retrospect, I realize that I was shooting the messenger. Without consciously understanding it, I'd bought into Jenkinson's belief system and accepted fatal accidents as the unfortunate but inevitable byproduct of racing. It never occurred to me that the sport could be safer, much less that it *should* be safer. I was a passionate fan, and I was also part of the problem. It was easier for me to blame television for rubbing my nose in racing's fundamental inhumanity than it was to question my willingness to glorify the deaths of young men who weren't engaged in the heroic act of saving lives or preserving democracy but who were simply trying to go a few tenths faster than the other guy.

Is racing better today than it was fifty years ago? That's a loaded question. First, you have to define "better." And even then, your mileage may vary. But if racing hadn't changed, I suspect it would have gone the way of bullfighting and gladiatorial combat. If it had somehow managed to survive in something like its original form, it would be as a fringe sport, like wingsuit flying, free soloing, or big wave surfing, with hardly any participants and a passionate but minuscule fan base. Instead, racing is more popular and profitable than it's ever been. It's also safer than ever before. Coincidence? I don't think so. If there's a lesson to be learned from the deadliest decade, it's that others don't have to die so that we can be entertained.

ACKNOWLEDGMENTS

I always experience mixed emotions whenever I sit down to write acknowledgments—relief and satisfaction that I've finally finished the manuscript, anxiety and regret because I wonder if I could have done a better job. One of the blessings that come with writing about the 1960s and '70s is that those were the glory days of print media, which means that I had plenty of great material to start with. Also, a lot of wonderful books have been published since then. Readers who want more details about the subjects I've covered should look closely at the extensive bibliography that follows.

As a writer, I have a special affinity for the printed word. But as a fan of the sport, I have to confess that the most rewarding aspect of this project was getting to talk to so many of the people who were active during this era—drivers, mechanics, engineers, owners, executives, writers, and so on. Their recollections and insights are the lifeblood of this book, and I owe each one a profound debt of gratitude. Sadly, many of them have died since they shared their memories with me. But I'd like to thank all of them:

Andrea de Adamich, Cary Agajanian, Donnie Allison, Chris Amon, John Anderson, Mario Andretti, Toly Arutunoff, Richard Attwood, Roger Bailey, Buddy Baker, Skip Barber, Richie Barsz, Patrick Bedard, Derek Bell, Tom Bigelow, Mitch Bishop, Herbie Blash, Bob Bondurant, Peter Brock, Chuck Cantwell, Pancho Carter, Joe Cavaglieri, Jim Chapman, Steve Chassey, Richard Childress, Luigi Chinetti Jr.,

Ken Clapp, Jim Cook, Will Cronkrite, Chuck Daigh, Mike Devin, Jim Dilamarter, Patrick Duffeler, Bernie Ecclestone, John Fenning, Emerson Fittipaldi, Helmut Flegl, George Follmer, Greg Foust, A.J. Foyt, Joe Freitas, Howden Ganley, Don Garlits, Steve Gibbs, Paul Goldsmith, Stu Grant, Dan and Evi Gurney, Leroy Hales, Jim Hall, Trevor Harris, Michael Henderson, Phil Henny, Phil Hill, David Hobbs, John Horsman, Hal Horton, Mike Hull, Carl Hungness, Jacky Ickx, Tommy Ivo, Gordon Johncock, Parnelli Jones, Jim Kinsler, Gerard Larrousse, Mike Lashmett, Philippe de Lespinay, Dave Lockton, Karl Ludvigsen, Dan Luginbuhl, Pete and Lorna Lyons, Jim McGee, Herschel McGriff, John Mahoney, Terry Malone, Dave Marcis, Helmut Marko, Andrew Marriott, Rick Mears, John Mecom Jr., Yves Morizot, John Morton, Bob Muravez, Doug Nye, Jackie Oliver, Steve Olvey, Carl Olson, Wally Pankratz, Johnny Parsons, Wally Peat, Roger Penske, Richard Petty, Ed Pink, Sam Posey, Don Prudhomme, Larry Rathgeb, Brian Redman, Phil Remington, Bob Riley, Roland Roy, Johnny Rutherford, Joe Scalzo, Jody Scheckter, Tim Schenken, Hugh Scully, Carroll Shelby, Dave Sims, Roman Slobodynskyj, Tom Sneva, Alwin Springer, Jackie Stewart, Simon Taylor, Kenny Troutt, Bobby Unser, John Watson, Ted West, Humpy Wheeler, Waddell Wilson, Leonard Wood, Woody Woodard, and Alex Xydias.

I'd also like to thank those who generously offered suggestions, made corrections, shared contacts, and generally went *way* beyond the call of duty, friendship, and professional courtesy: Mike Allen, Derek Bowers, Don Capps, Tim Coffeen, Frank Honsowetz, Jon Ingram, Michael Jordan, Ed Justice, George Levy, Matt McFadden, Mark Raffauf, Phil Reilly, Gary Schroeder, Steve Shunck, Dan Simone, Doug Stokes, Tony Thacker, and Bill Warner.

I couldn't have written this book without the help provided by the patient, knowledgeable, and unfailingly cooperative staff members at four tremendous American institutions devoted to the study and preservation of racing history: Scott George, Arthur Carlson, and Paul Kierstein at the Revs Institute in Naples, Florida; Jim Hahn (and Laura Fisher before him) at the Petersen Automotive Museum in Los Angeles; Duke Argetsinger at the International Motor Racing Research Center in Watkins Glen, New York; and Joe Skibinski at the Indianapolis

Motor Speedway Museum. If you're a fan of motorsports, you owe these institutions your support and patronage.

I owe special thanks to Lee Klancher, Faith Garcia, Tom Heffron, and the rest of the talented gang at Octane Press, not only for indulging my desire to write this book and doing such a fabulous job editing and producing it, but also for their unwavering commitment to motorsports journalism. Books about racing have never been gigantic sellers, and there are those who insist that print is a dying medium. Yet Octane manages to keep the doors open while publishing high-quality books that continue to celebrate the sport. I'm proud to be part of the team.

I'd also like to express my gratitude for the editors I've worked with over the years, from my earliest days in daily newspapers, then as a freelancer writing for magazines, and more recently as a book author. We didn't always see eye to eye, and there was some gnashing of the teeth on both sides of the equation. But my copy has been improved by their probing questions, thoughtful suggestions, and necessary trims. That said, no editor has ever done more for my writing—or for me, personally—than my longtime companion, Emily Young. Without her unflagging support and inestimable editing, I'm not sure I ever would have finished this project.

ENDNOTES

INTRODUCTION

1. Bill Libby, *The Coaches* (Regnery, 1972).
2. Mike Devin, interview by author.

CHAPTER ONE

1. Robert Edelstein, *Full Throttle: The Life and Fast Times of NASCAR Legend Curtis Turner* (Abrams Books, 2006).
2. Kim Chapin, *Fast as White Lightning: The Story of Stock Car Racing* (Three Rivers Press, 1998).
3. Chapin, *White Lightning.*
4. Chapin, *White Lightning.*
5. Chapin, *White Lightning.*
6. Edelstein, *Full Throttle.*
7. Smokey Yunick, *Best Damn Garage in Town : My Life & Adventures* (Carbon Press, 2004).
8. *Sports Illustrated*, February 26, 1968.
9. Yunick, *Best Damn Garage.*
10. H.A. Branham, *Big Bill: The Life and Times of NASCAR Founder Bill France, Sr.* (Fenn-M & S, 2015).
11. Sylvia Wilkinson, *Dirt Tracks to Glory: The Early Days of Stock Car Racing as Told by the Participants* (Algonquin Books, 1983).
12. Wilkinson, *Dirt Tracks.*
13. Neal Thompson, *Driving with the Devil: Southern Moonshine, Detroit Wheels, and the Birth of NASCAR* (Crown Publishers, 2006).
14. Daniel S. Pierce, *Real NASCAR: White Lightning, Red Clay, and Big Bill France* (The University of North Carolina Press, 2010).
15. Thompson, *Driving with the Devil.*
16. Pierce, *Real NASCAR.*
17. Thompson, *Driving with the Devil.*
18. Wilkinson, *Dirt Tracks.*
19. Betty Boles Ellison, *The Early Laps of Stock Car Racing: A History of the Sport and Business through 1974* (McFarland & Company, 2014).

20. Wilkinson, *Dirt Tracks*.
21. Chapin, *White Lightning*.
22. Greg Fielden, *Forty Years of Stock Car Racing, Volume 2: The Superspeedway Boom, 1959–1964* (Galfield Press, 1989).
23. "Joe Weatherly," Historic Racing, http://www.historicracing.com/driverDetail.cfm?driverID=2318&otd=on.
24. *Los Angeles Times*, January 20, 1964.
25. *Los Angeles Times*, January 20, 1964.
26. Peter Golenbock, *American Zoom* (Macmillan, 1993).
27. Tom Madigan, *Boss: The Bill Stroppe Story* (Darwin Publications, 1984).
28. Chapin, *White Lightning*.

CHAPTER TWO

1. Charles Jarrott, *Ten Years of Motors and Motor Racing* (Foulis, 1956).
2. Jarrott, *Ten Years of Motors and Motor Racing*.
3. *Motor Sport*, October 2011.
4. Michael Cannell, *The Limit: Life and Death on the 1961 Grand Prix Circuit* (Twelve, 2011).
5. Smokey Yunick, *Best Damn Garage in Town: My Life & Adventures* (Carbon Press, 2004).
6. *Autoweek*, May 12, 1973.
7. Joe Scalzo, *The American Dirt Track Racer* (MBI, 2001).
8. *Chicago Tribune*, June 2, 1971.
9. *Los Angeles Times*, January 29, 1966.
10. *Road & Track*, October 1964.
11. John Mecom Jr., interview by author.
12. *Autoweek*, June 17, 1967.
13. *Motor Sport*, August 1970.
14. Emerson Fittipaldi, interview by author.
15. Emerson Fittipaldi, interview by author.
16. David Craft and Johnny Rutherford, *Lone Star J.R.: The Autobiography of Racing Legend Johnny Rutherford* (Triumph Books, 2000).
17. Clint Brawner and Joe Scalzo, *Indy 500 Mechanic* (Chilton Book Company, 1975).
18. Bob Riley, interview by author.
19. David Hobbs, interview by author.
20. Brian Redman with Jim Mullen, *Brian Redman: Daring Drivers, Deadly Tracks* (Evro Publishing, 2016).
21. Brian Redman, interview by author.
22. Brian Redman, interview by author.
23. Mario Andretti, interview by author.
24. Phil Hill, interview by author.
25. *Car and Driver*, January 1973.
26. Steve Chassey, interview by author.
27. Patrick Bedard, interview by author.
28. Skip Barber, interview by author.
29. Wally Pankratz, interview by author.
30. Wally Pankratz, interview by author.
31. Redman and Mullen, *Brian Redman*.
32. Mike Lawrence, *The Story of March* (Aston, 1989).
33. Phil Shirley, *Deadly Obsessions: Life and Death in Motor Racing* (HarperCollins, 2000).
34. *Automobile Year: Number 6, 1958–59* (Hanover House, 1958).

35. Ken Purdy, *Ken Purdy's Wonderful World of the Automobile* (Crowell, 1963).
36. Denis Jenkinson, *The Racing Driver: The Theory and Practice of Fast Driving* (Robert Bentley, 1959).
37. Purdy, *Ken Purdy's World of Automobiles.*
38. Bill Libby, *Parnelli: A Story of Auto Racing* (Dutton, 1969).
39. Michael J. Cox, *Masten Gregory: Totally Fearless; Two Decades of Motorsport Through the Spectacles of the Kansas City Flash* (MTCA Creations, 2004).
40. *The Independent* (UK), July 18, 1995.
41. Peter Manso, *Vroom: Conversations with the Grand Prix Champions* (Pitman, 1970).
42. Jackie Stewart and Peter Manso, *Faster! A Racer's Diary* (Farrar, Straus and Giroux, 1972).
43. *Motor Sport*, June 1969.
44. Doug Nye, interview by author.
45. "BUCKLING UP WITH ROVER," Simanaitis Says, https://simanaitissays.com/2017/09/04/buckling-up-with-rover/.
46. *The Nation*, April 11, 1959.
47. *The Nation*, October 1963.
48. "A Moment in Time: Highway Safety Breakthrough," FHWA News 2021, https://highways.dot.gov/highway-history/general-highway-history/moment-time-highway-safety-breakthrough.
49. *Sports Car Graphic*, September 1969.
50. *Autoweek.*
51. *Car and Driver*, March 1969.
52. Mario Andretti, interview by author.
53. Mario Andretti, interview by author.
54. Brawner and Scalzo, *Indy 500 Mechanic.*
55. "DRS. STEPHEN OLVEY AND TERRY TRAMMELL IN MOTORSPORTS HALL OF FAME OF AMERICA'S CLASS OF 2023," Road Racing Drivers Club, https://rrdc.org/2023/02/28/drs-stephen-olvey-and-terry-trammell-in-motorsports-hall-of-fame-of-americas-class-of-2023/.
56. Dr. Stephen Olvey, *Rapid Response: My Inside Story as a Motor Racing Life-Saver* (Evro Publishing, 2019).
57. Hugh Scully, interview by author.
58. Hugh Scully, interview by author.
59. Sid Watkins, *Life at the Limit: Triumph and Tragedy in Formula One* (Motorbooks International, 1996).
60. Louis Stanley, *Grand Prix 10* (David McKay, 1969).
61. Howden Ganley, *The Road to Monaco: My Life in Motor Racing* (Denley Publications, 2015).
62. Leroy Hales, interview by author.
63. Leroy Hales, interview by author.
64. Leroy Hales, interview by author.

CHAPTER THREE

1. Mike Devin, interview by author.
2. Don Prudhomme, interview by author.
3. Dave Marcis, interview by author.
4. Dave Marcis, interview by author, entire exchange.
5. Richard Childress, interview by author.
6. Phil Hill, interview by author.
7. Richie Barsz, interview by author.

8. Mario Andretti, interview by author.
9. Max Mosley, *Max Mosley: Formula One and Beyond; The Autobiography* (Simon & Schuster, 2015).
10. Rob Kauffman, interview by author.
11. Mario Andretti, interview by author.
12. Richie Barsz, interview by author.
13. Helmut Marko, interview by author.
14. Alan Henry, *Jochen Rindt* (Hazelton, 1990).
15. Helmut Marko, interview by author.
16. *Autosport*, February 25, 1966.
17. *Autosport*, August 12, 1966.
18. Hartmut Lehbring, *90 Years Nürburgring: The History of the Famous "Nordschleife"* (Delius Klasing Verlag, 2016).
19. David Hobbs, interview by author.
20. Tony Rudlin, *Mr. Monaco: Graham Hill Remembered* (Patrick Stephens, 1983).
21. Dr. Stephen Olvey, *Rapid Response: My Inside Story as a Motor Racing Life-Saver* (Evro Publishing, 2019).
22. *Autoweek*, June 20, 1972.
23. *Car and Driver*, July 1968.
24. Jim Hall, interview by author.
25. Joe Scalzo, interview by author.
26. Bobby Unser, interview by author.
27. Paul Goldsmith, interview by author.
28. Parnelli Jones, interview by author.
29. Mario Andretti, interview by author.
30. A.J. Foyt, interview by author.
31. Brian Redman, interview by author.
32. Brian Redman with Jim Mullen, *Brian Redman: Daring Drivers, Deadly Tracks* (Evro Publishing, 2016).
33. Redman with Mullen, *Brian Redman*.
34. Ted Simon, *Grand Prix Year* (Coward, McCann & Geoghegan, 1971).
35. *Autoweek*, August 31, 1968.
36. David Hobbs, interview by author.
37. *Car and Driver*, September 1967.
38. Sam Posey, interview by author.
39. John Matthews, *Grand Prix: The Killer Years* (Arena Sport, 2016).
40. Louis Stanley, *Grand Prix 10* (David McKay, 1969).
41. Terry Malone, interview by author.
42. Art Bagnall, *Roy Richter: Striving for Excellence* (Art Bagnall Publishing, 1990).
43. Tim Considine, *American Grand Prix Racing: A Century of Drivers & Cars* (Motorbooks International, 1997).
44. Bagnall, *Roy Richter*.
45. *Baltimore Sun*, May 26, 1994.
46. *Sports Car Illustrated*, July 1957.
47. *Motor Sport*, January 2001.
48. Evi Gurney, interview by author.
49. Tom Bigelow, interview by author.
50. Steve Chassey, interview by author.
51. Brian Redman, interview by author.
52. Bagnall, *Roy Richter*.

CHAPTER FOUR

1. Johnny Rutherford, interview by author.
2. Johnny Rutherford, interview by author.
3. Bill Libby, *Parnelli: A Story of Auto Racing* (Dutton, 1969).
4. Doug Nye, *Theme Lotus* (Motor Racing Publications, 1978).
5. Josh Wilker and G.S. Prentzas, *A.J. Foyt* (Chelsea House Publishers, 2007).
6. Joe Freitas, interview by author.
7. Joe Freitas, interview by author.
8. Wally Peat, interview by author.
9. Johnny Rutherford, interview by author.
10. Jack Brabham and Elizabeth Hayward, *When the Flag Drops* (Coward, McCann & Geoghegan, 1971).
11. Bob Gates, *Hurtubise* (Witness Productions, 1995).
12. Gates, *Hurtubise.*
13. Gates, *Hurtubise.*
14. Gates, *Hurtubise.*
15. Godwin Kelly, *Fireball: An Unauthorized Biography* (Carbon Press, 2005).
16. Kelly, *Fireball.*
17. Greg Fielden, *Forty Years of Stock Car Racing, Volume 2: The Superspeedway Boom, 1959–1964* (Galfield Press, 1989).
18. Bill Simpson and Bones Bourcier, *Racing Safely, Living Dangerously: The Hard Life and Fast Times of a Motorsports Mogul* (Performance Media, 2001).
19. Kim Chapin, *Fast as White Lightning: The Story of Stock Car Racing* (Three Rivers Press, 1998).
20. Vic Elford, *Vic Elford: Reflections on a Golden Era in Motorsports* (David Bull, 2006).
21. Steve Lehto, *Dodge Daytona & Plymouth Superbird: Design, Development, Production and Competition* (CarTech, 2020).
22. *Virginian-Pilot,* August 2, 1994.
23. Mike Lashmett, interview by author.
24. Peter Bryant, *Can-Am Challenger: The Cockney F1 Mechanic Who Designed and Built America's Best Can-Am Cars* (David Bull Publishing, 2007).
25. Howden Ganley, interview by author.
26. Mel Kenyon, interview by author.
27. Mel Kenyon, interview by author.
28. "Poly-meta-phenylene isophthalamides," Google Patents, https://patents.google.com/patent/US3287324A/en.
29. *Car and Driver,* March 1966.
30. *Autoweek,* April 15, 1967.
31. *Autoweek,* April 29, 1967.
32. *The Sporting News,* June 17, 1970.
33. *The Sporting News,* June 17, 1970.
34. Tom Bigelow, interview by author.
35. Bill Simpson, interview by author.
36. Mario Andretti, interview by author.
37. Rick Mears, interview by author.
38. Unnamed Source, interview by author.
39. Philippe de Lespinay, interview by author.
40. Bill Simpson, interview by author.
41. John Morton, interview by author.
42. Bill Simpson, interview by author.

43. Bill Simpson, interview by author.
44. Bill Simpson, interview by author.
45. Bill Simpson, interview by author.
46. Bill Simpson, interview by author.
47. Bill Simpson, interview by author.
48. Simpson and Bourcier, *Racing Safely, Living Dangerously.*
49. Parnelli Jones, interview by author.

CHAPTER FIVE

1. Bert Sugar, *"The Thrill of Victory": The Inside Story of ABC Sports* (Hawthorn Books, 1978).
2. Roone Arledge, *Roone: A Memoir* (HarperCollins, 2003).
3. Arledge, *Roone.*
4. Arledge, *Roone.*
5. Chris Economaki, *Let 'Em All Go: The Story of Auto Racing by the Man Who Was There* (Books by Dave Argabright, 2006).
6. Dick Wallen and Michael Jordan, *Roar from the Sixties: American Championship Racing* (Ben Franklin Press, 1997).
7. Monaco Grand Prix Library, "25th GrandPrix – 1967," http://monaco-grandsprix.org/pagesE/1967.html.
8. David Phipps, *Autocourse 1966–67* (Haymarket Press, 1967).
9. *Road & Track*, August 1967.
10. Michael Cooper-Evans, *Risk Life, Risk Limb* (Pelham Books, 1968).
11. *New York Times*, May 22, 1967.
12. Sam Posey, interview by author.
13. oldSCCAguy yah, "USAC National Championship at Riverside, 1968," YouTube, https://www.youtube.com/watch?v=ljmflhrSRdA.
14. *New York Times*, May 22, 1967.
15. *Car and Driver*, March 1969.
16. *Autoweek*, April 5, 1969.
17. *Car and Driver*, July 1970.
18. *Car and Driver*, July 1967.
19. *Road & Track*, September 1965.
20. *Esquire*, March 1965.
21. *Road & Track*, August 1966.
22. Pauline Kael, *Kiss Kiss, Bang Bang* (Bantam Books, 1969).
23. *New York Times*, June 24, 1971.
24. "Racing at the Movies, Part 2," *Motor Sport.*
25. Sam Posey, interview by author.
26. Sam Posey, interview by author.
27. Sam Posey, interview by author.

CHAPTER SIX

1. Phil Remington, interview by author.
2. Richard Attwood, interview by author.
3. Peter Bryant, *Can-Am Challenger: The Cockney F1 Mechanic Who Designed and Built America's Best Can-Am Cars* (David Bull Publishing, 2007).
4. Gordon Kirby, *Unser: An American Family Portrait* (Anlon Press, 1988).
5. *Car and Driver*, November 1967.
6. Jim Chapman, interview by author.

7. *Autosport*, February 3, 1967.
8. *Road & Track*, June 1968.
9. Michael Henderson, interview by author.
10. Michael Henderson, interview by author.
11. *The Independent* (UK), September 15, 2004.
12. *The Independent* (UK), September 15, 2004.
13. John Fenning, interview by author.
14. Michael Henderson, interview by author.
15. Derek Bell, interview by author.
16. Dave Sims, interview by author.
17. *Car and Driver*, July 1968.
18. Eoin Young, *Forza Amon! A Biography of Chris Amon* (HarperSports, 2003).
19. Michael Henderson, interview by author.
20. John Fenning, interview by author.
21. John Fenning, interview by author.
22. John Fenning, interview by author.
23. Michael Henderson, interview by author.
24. Dave Sims, interview by author.
25. Michael Henderson, interview by author.
26. Concept Cars, "1968 Pininfarina Sigma GP," https://web.archive.org/web/20110929120221/http:/www.conceptcars.it/martin/sigmagp.htm.
27. Concept Cars, "1968 Pininfarina Sigma GP."
28. *Autoweek*, April 12, 1969.

CHAPTER SEVEN

1. *Motor Sport*, December 1967.
2. *Autosport*, February 2, 1968.
3. Jabby Crombac, *Colin Chapman: The Man and His Cars* (Haynes, 2001).
4. *Motor Sport*, October 1965.
5. Andrew Marriott, interview by author.
6. *Road & Track*, October 1968.
7. *Autosport*, December 22, 1967.
8. Patrick Duffeler, interview by author.
9. David Tremayne, *The Science of Safety: The Battle Against Unacceptable Risks in Motor Racing* (Haynes, 2000).
10. Michael Oliver, *Lotus 72: Formula One Icon* (Coterie Press Limited, 2003).
11. Mike Kettlewell, *Autocourse: International Motor Racing and Rallying 1972–73* (Haymarket Publishing, 1973).
12. *Motor Sport*, February 1973.
13. Patrick Duffeler, interview by author.
14. Louis Stanley, *Grand Prix: The Legendary Years; The Personal Memories of Louis Stanley* (Queen Anne Press, 1994).
15. Mark Yost, *The 200-MPH Billboard: The Inside Story of How Big Money Changed NASCAR* (MBI Publishing, 2007).
16. *Car and Driver*, May 1971.
17. Humpy Wheeler, interview by author.
18. "Tobacco Roar," *Our State*, February 27, 2023, https://www.ourstate.com/tobacco-roar/.
19. Dave Marcis, interview by author.
20. Ken Clapp, interview by author.
21. Donnie Allison, interview by author.

22. Kenny Troutt, interview by author.
23. Yost, *The 200-MPH Billboard.*
24. *Autoweek*, August 15, 1970.
25. Cary Agajanian, interview by author.
26. "Richard Petty," STP, https://stp.com/about-us/racing/richard-petty/.
27. *Car and Driver*, May 1972.
28. George Levy, *Can-Am 50th Anniversary: Flat Out with North America's Greatest Race Series 1966–74* (Motorbooks, 2016).
29. *Autoweek*, May 26, 1973.
30. *Car and Driver*, June 1972.
31. Roger Penske, interview by author.
32. Guy Edwards, *Sponsorship and the World of Motor Racing* (Hazelton, 1992).
33. LJK Setright, *The Grand Prix, 1906 to 1972* (W.W. Norton, 1973).
34. Setright, *The Grand Prix.*
35. Carl Hungness, interview by author.
36. Tim Schenken, interview by author.
37. The Chaparral Files, "Collectors stuff," https://thechaparralfiles.com/collectors_stuff.php.
38. Richard Falconer and Doug Nye, *Chaparral* (Motorbooks International, 1992).
39. Tom Madigan, *Snake vs. Mongoose: How a Rivalry Changed Drag Racing Forever* (Motorbooks, 2009).
40. Steve Gibbs, interview by author.
41. Jim Cook, interview by author.
42. Jim Cook, interview by author.

CHAPTER EIGHT

1. Chuck Daigh, interview by author.
2. *Road & Track*, September 1966.
3. Jackie Stewart, *Winning is Not Enough* (Headline, 2007).
4. Stewart, *Winning is Not Enough.*
5. Stewart, *Winning is Not Enough.*
6. José Rosinski, *Formula 1 Racing: The Modern Era* (Madison Square Press, 1973).
7. Richard Jenkins, *Tyrrell: The Story of the Tyrrell Racing Organisation* (Evro Publishing, 2023).
8. *Motor Sport*, August 1972.
9. *Autoweek*, August 31, 1968.
10. *Autoweek*, March 24, 1973.
11. David Phipps, *Autocourse: International Motor Racing and Rallying 1968-69* (Haymarket Press, 1969).
12. Denis Jenkinson, *The Racing Driver: The Theory and Practice of Fast Driving* (Robert Bentley, 1959).
13. *Motor Sport*, May 1969.
14. Howden Ganley, interview by author.
15. Peter Manso, *Vroom: Conversations with the Grand Prix Champions* (Pitman, 1970).
16. Manso, *Vroom.*
17. Manso, *Vroom.*
18. *National Speed Sport News*, July 15, 1970.
19. *Motor Sport*, July 1972.
20. *Motor Sport*, May 1971.
21. *Motor Sport*, August 1970.
22. *Motor Sport*, July 1970.

23. George Levy, *Can-Am 50th Anniversary: Flat Out with North America's Greatest Race Series 1966–74* (Motorbooks, 2016).
24. Pete Lyons, *Can-Am* (Motorbooks International, 1995).
25. *Autoweek*, September 11, 1971.
26. David Hobbs, interview by author.
27. David Hobbs, interview by author.
28. Levy, *Can-Am 50th Anniversary.*
29. David Hobbs, interview by author.
30. Levy, *Can-Am 50th Anniversary.*
31. Levy, *Can-Am 50th Anniversary.*
32. *Motor Sport*, August 1972.
33. Richard Attwood, interview by author.
34. *Autoweek*, February 3, 1973.
35. Jacky Ickx, interview by author.
36. Jacky Ickx, interview by author.
37. Jacky Ickx, interview by author.
38. Jacky Ickx, interview by author.
39. Jacky Ickx, interview by author.

CHAPTER NINE

1. *Motor Sport*, August 1956.
2. Richard Attwood, interview by author.
3. John Morton, interview by author.
4. Sam Posey, interview by author.
5. Jim Hall, interview by author.
6. Jim Hall, interview by author.
7. Andy Green, interview by author.
8. Jim Hall, interview by author.
9. Jim Hall, interview by author.
10. J.E. Hall et al., Aerodynamic Spoiler for Automotive Vehicles, US Patent 3,455,594.
11. Phil Hill, interview by author.
12. Alan Henry, *Ferrari: The Grand Prix Cars* (Hazelton, 1989).
13. Herbie Blash, interview by author.
14. Jackie Oliver, interview by author.
15. Jackie Oliver, interview by author.
16. Dave Sims, interview by author.
17. Dave Sims, interview by author.
18. *Autosport*, May 23, 1969.
19. *Road & Track*, February 1970.
20. Frank Moriarty, *Supercars: The Story of the Dodge Charger Daytona and Plymouth Superbird* (Howell Press, 1995).
21. Moriarty, *Supercars.*
22. Moriarty, *Supercars.*
23. Moriarity, *Supercars.*
24. Larry Rathgeb, interview by author.
25. Larry Rathgeb, interview by author.
26. Buddy Baker, interview by author.
27. RACER, "RETRO: Dan's magic bullet . . . The story of the Gurney Flap," https://racer.com/2022/04/08/retro-dans-magic-bullet-the-story-of-the-gurney-flap.
28. RACER, "RETRO: Dan's magic bullet . . ."

29. Mike Devin, interview by author.
30. Roman Slobodynskyj, interview by author.
31. Roman Slobodynskyj, interview by author.
32. Mike Lashmett, interview by author.
33. Johnny Rutherford, interview by author.
34. Roger Bailey, interview by author.
35. Joe Scalzo, *Indianapolis Roadsters, 1952–1964* (MBI, 1999).
36. John Anderson, interview by author.
37. Roger Bailey, interview by author.
38. Roger Bailey, interview by author.
39. Helmut Flegl, interview by author.
40. Roger Penske, interview by author.
41. Woody Woodard, interview by author.
42. Porsche Archives.
43. *Motor Trend*, March 1972.

CHAPTER TEN

1. Motorsports Hall of Fame of America, "Clint Brawner," https://www.mshf.com/hall-of-fame/inductees/clint-brawner.html.
2. Clint Brawner and Joe Scalzo, *Indy 500 Mechanic* (Chilton Book Company, 1975).
3. Mario Andretti, interview by author.
4. *Car and Driver*, February 1970.
5. Parnelli Jones, interview by author.
6. *Car and Driver*, January 1965.
7. Parnelli Jones, interview by author.
8. Johnny Rutherford, interview by author.
9. Leon Mandel and Peter Revson: *Speed with Style: The Autobiography of Peter Revson* (Doubleday, 1974).
10. Joe Scalzo, *Stand on the Gas! Sprint Car Racing in America* (Prentice Hall, 1974).
11. Scalzo, *Stand on the Gas!*.
12. Mario Andretti, interview by author.
13. Parnelli Jones, interview by author.
14. Scalzo, *Stand on the Gas!*.
15. *Car and Driver*, December 1973.
16. Tom Bigelow, interview by author.
17. *National Speed Sport News*.
18. Steve Chassey, interview by author.
19. Steve Chassey, interview by author.
20. Dan Gurney, interview by author.
21. Mitch Bishop, interview by author.
22. *Road & Track*, December 1966.
23. George Levy, *Can-Am 50th Anniversary: Flat Out with North America's Greatest Race Series 1966–74* (Motorbooks, 2016).
24. Karl Ludvigsen, *Group 7: The World's Most Powerful Road Racing Cars* (World Publishing Company, 1971).
25. Jim Hall, interview by author.
26. Jim Hall, interview by author.
27. Levy, *Can-Am 50th Anniversary*.

CHAPTER ELEVEN

1. Mike Devin, interview by author.
2. Mike Devin, interview by author.
3. Jack Brabham and Elizabeth Hayward, *When the Flag Drops* (Coward, McCann & Geoghegan, 1971).
4. *Road & Track*, April 1967.
5. Jeffrey Rodengen, *The Legend of Goodyear: The First 100 Years* (Write Stuff Syndicate, 1997).
6. Rodengen, *The Legend of Goodyear.*
7. Dave Friedman, *Remembering the Shelby Years—1962–1969* (Carroll Shelby Children's Foundation, 1998).
8. Gordon Johncock, interview by author.
9. Jim Cook, interview by author.
10. Dave Lockton, interview by author.
11. Greg Foust, interview by author.
12. Rodengen, *The Legend of Goodyear.*
13. Humpy Wheeler, interview by author.
14. Greg Foust, interview by author.
15. Hal Horton, interview by author.
16. John Anderson, interview by author.
17. Mike Lashmett, interview by author.
18. Rich Taylor, *Indy: Seventy-Five Years of Racing's Greatest Spectacle* (St. Martin's Press, 1991).
19. John Watson, interview by author.
20. John Watson, interview by author.
21. Greg Fielden, *Forty Years of Stock Car Racing, Volume 2: The Superspeedway Boom, 1959–1964* (Galfield Press, 1989).
22. Fielden, *Forty Years.*
23. Humpy Wheeler, interview by author.
24. Greg Foust, interview by author.
25. Alan Henry, *Brabham: The Grand Prix Cars* (Hazelton, 1985).
26. José Rosinski, *Formula 1 Racing: The Modern Era* (Madison Square Press, 1973).
27. *Motor Sport*, September 1970.
28. Javier Del Arco, *40 Years of Motor Racing History at the Park Circuit of Montjuïc* (RACC Club, 2000).
29. Howden Ganley, interview by author.
30. John Watson, interview by author.
31. Graham Robson, *Cosworth: The Search for Power* (Patrick Stephens, 1995).
32. Robson, *Cosworth.*
33. *Motorsport News*, January 10, 2001.
34. Robson, *Cosworth.*

CHAPTER TWELVE

1. Greg Fielden, *Forty Years of Stock Car Racing, Volume 2: The Superspeedway Boom, 1959–1964* (Galfield Press, 1989).
2. Fielden, *Forty Years, Volume 2.*
3. Fielden, *Forty Years, Volume 2.*
4. *Atlanta Journal-Constitution*, November 6, 1977.
5. Fielden, *Forty Years, Volume 2.*
6. Humpy Wheeler, interview by author.

7. *Car and Driver*, May 1968.
8. *Car and Driver*, May 1968.
9. Donnie Allison, interview by author.
10. Donnie Allison, interview by author.
11. *Autoweek*, September 13, 1969.
12. Greg Fielden, *Forty Years of Stock Car Racing, Volume 3: Big Bucks and Boycotts, 1965–1971* (Galfield Press, 1989).
13. *Car and Driver*, November 1969.
14. *Car and Driver*, November 1969.
15. Humpy Wheeler, interview by author.
16. *Aniston Star* (Alabama), September 13, 1969.
17. *Autoweek*, October 4, 1969.
18. *Associated Press*, September 14, 1969.
19. Richard Childress, interview by author.
20. Donnie Allison, interview by author.
21. Fielden, *Forty Years of Stock Car Racing, Volume 3*.
22. *Kingsport Times* (Tennessee), January 6, 1970.
23. Richard Childress, interview by author.
24. Greg Fielden, *Forty Years of Stock Car Racing, Volume 4: The Modern Era, 1972–1989* (Galfield Press, 1990).
25. Fielden, *Forty Years of Stock Car Racing, Volume 4*.
26. *Autoweek*, May 15, 1971.
27. *Motor Trend*, February 1972.
28. NHRA, "Indy 1971: 'The Great Burndown,'" https://www.nhra.com/news/2021/indy-1971-great-burndown.
29. Don Garlits, interview by author.
30. *Autoweek*, July 1, 1972.
31. Don Garlits, interview by author.
32. *Autoweek*, June 17, 1967.
33. *Autosport* December 29, 1967.
34. Jackie Stewart, *Winning Is Not Enough* (Headline, 2007).
35. David Phipps, *Autocourse: International Motor Racing and Rallying 1968–69* (Haymarket Press, 1969).
36. *Motor Sport*, July 1970.
37. *The Times* (UK), June 11, 1968.
38. Stewart, *Winning Is Not Enough*.
39. *Autoweek*, January 27, 1968.
40. *Motor Sport*, July 1971.
41. *Motor Sport*, July 1973.
42. *Autosport*, May 31, 1973.
43. *Autosport*, May 31, 1973.
44. *Road & Track*, August 1966.
45. Doug Nye, interview by author.
46. *Motor Sport*, June 1975.
47. *Southern Exposure* 7, No. 3.
48. *Southern Exposure* 7, No. 3.
49. "Independent 250" racing poster, https://grandnationaleast.com/Features/Indepdendent%20250/Poster.jpg.
50. *Burlington Daily Times-News* (North Carolina), November 14, 1973.
51. *Southern Exposure*.

52. Dave Marcis, interview by author.
53. *Southern Exposure.*
54. *Southern Exposure.*

CHAPTER THIRTEEN

1. Don Prudhomme, interview by author.
2. *Racin' Today*, September 30, 2009.
3. Robert C. Post, *High Performance: The Culture and Technology of Drag Racing, 1950–2000* (Johns Hopkins University Press, 2001).
4. *Hot Rod*, January 1980.
5. NHRA, "NHRA History," https://www.nhra.com/nhra-101/nhra-history.
6. Steve Gibbs, interview by author.
7. We Did It For Love, "Great Drag Racing Quotes," https://wediditforlove.com/techtalk16.html.
8. NHRA, "NHRA History," https://www.nhra.com/nhra-101/nhra-history.
9. Don Garlits, interview by author.
10. Don Garlits and Brock Yates, *King of the Dragsters: The Story of Big Daddy "Don" Garlits* (Chilton Book Company, 1970).
11. Bob Muravez, interview by author.
12. Carl Olson, interview by author.
13. Bill Simpson and Bones Bourcier, *Racing Safely, Living Dangerously: The Hard Life and Fast times of a Motorsports Mogul* (Performance Media, 2001).
14. Don Garlits, interview by author.
15. *Hot Rod*, January 1973.
16. Post, *High Performance.*
17. Don Prudhomme, interview by author.
18. Tommy Ivo, interview by author.
19. Tommy Ivo, interview by author.
20. Tommy Ivo, interview by author.
21. Leroy Hales, interview by author.
22. Carl Olson, interview by author.
23. Post, *High Performance.*
24. Post, *High Performance.*
25. Carl Olson, interview by author.
26. NHRA, "Don Prudhomme says 'I Quit' vs. Jim Nicoll in 1970," YouTube, https://.www.youtube.com/watch?v=wAhsQvDscK4.
27. Don Garlits, interview by author.
28. Don Garlits, interview by author.
29. Post, *High Performance.*
30. Carl Olson, interview by author.
31. Don Garlits, interview by author.
32. *Autoweek*, May 5, 1973.
33. Don Prudhomme, interview by author.
34. Steve Gibbs, interview by author.
35. Doc Hales, interview by author.
36. Carl Olson, interview by author.
37. *Autoweek*, June 3, 2009.
38. "Maximum bite" advertisement, https://www.jalopyjournal.com/forum/attachments/scan-jpg.3379257/.
39. Post, *High Performance.*

40. Post, *High Performance.*
41. Don Prudhomme, interview by author.
42. Stu Grant, interview by author.
43. *Autoweek*, April 4, 1968.
44. Steve Gibbs, interview by author.
45. Stu Grant, interview by author.
46. Don Prudhomme, interview by author.

CHAPTER FOURTEEN

1. *Car and Driver*, March 1966.
2. *New York Times*, April 27, 2008.
3. *The Chronicle-Express* (Penn Yan, New York), January 13, 1966.
4. Carroll Shelby, interview by author.
5. *Autoweek*, July 23, 1966.
6. *Autoweek*, July 23, 1966.
7. *Motor Sport*, June 1970.
8 Timothy Collings, *The Piranha Club* (Virgin, 2001).
9. *Autosport*, May 3, 1968.
10. José Rosinski, *Automobile Year 1973/74* (Edita Lausanne, 1974).
11. Ted Simon, *Grand Prix Year* (Coward, McCann & Geoghegan, 1971).
12. Simon, *Grand Prix Year.*
13. Simon, *Grand Prix Year.*
14. Simon, *Grand Prix Year.*
15. Mike Lawrence, *The Story of March* (Aston, 1989).
16. Doug Nye, interview by author.
17. Terry Lovell, *Bernie's Game: Inside the Formula One World of Bernie Ecclestone* (Metro, 2003).
18. Phil Kerr, *To Finish First* (MRP, 2008).
19. Bernie Ecclestone, interview by author.
20. Bernie Ecclestone, interview by author.
21. *Autosport*, December 14, 1972.
22. Kerr, *To Finish First.*
23. Bernie Ecclestone, interview by author.
24 Adam Cooper, "When Ecclestone Realised Where The Real Money in F1 Is," *Motorsport*, May 12, 2023, https://www.motorsport.com/f1/news/ecclestone-real-money-belgium-1974/4792168/.
25. John Watson, interview by author.
26. Adrian Ball, *Grand Prix Accident Survey, 1966–1972* (Jim Clark Foundation, 1975).
27. RACER, "Jim McElreath, 1928–2017," https://racer.com/2017/05/18/jim-mcelreath-1928-2017.
28. National Sprint Car Hall of Fame & Museum, "Jim McElreath," https://www.sprintcarhof.com/helper_pages/FileGet.aspx?id=65.
29. Richard Childress, interview by author.
30. Jim Chapman, interview by author.
31. Herbie Blash, interview by author.
32. Alwin Springer, interview by author.
33. Mario Andretti, interview by author.
34. Tom Bigelow, interview by author.
35. Tom Sneva, interview by author.

36. Tom Sneva, interview by author.
37. Ken Purdy, *Ken Purdy's Wonderful World of the Automobile* (Crowell, 1963).
38. Tim Schenken, interview by author.
39. *Road & Track*, March 1969.
40. John Horsman, *Racing in the Rain: My Years with Brilliant Drivers, Legendary Sports Cars, and a Dedicated Team* (David Bull Publishing, 2006).
41. Horsman, *Racing in the Rain.*
42. Sam Posey, *Mudge Pond Express* (Putnam, 1976).
43. Sam Posey, interview by author.
44. Brian Redman, interview by author.

CHAPTER FIFTEEN

1. *Road & Track*, October 1970.
2. *Los Angeles Times*, December 25, 1980.
3. Steve Gibbs, interview by author.
4. Race Fans Forever, "50 Years of NASCAR Racing: Larry Lopatin and American Raceways (Post 24)," https://racefansforever2014.weebly.com/50-years-of-nascar-racing--larry-lopatin-and-american-raceways-post-24.html.
5. *Sports Illustrated*, October 21, 1968.
6. Race Fans Forever, "50 Years of NASCAR Racing."
7. *Los Angeles Times*, August 10, 1993.
8. *Car and Driver*, August 1971.
9. Greg Fielden, *Forty Years of Stock Car Racing, Volume 3: Big Bucks and Boycotts, 1965–1971* (Galfield Press, 1989).
10. *Charlotte News*, September 17, 1969.
11. *Charlotte News*, September 17, 1969.
12. Racers Reunion, "Racing History Minute For November 29th," https://racersreunion.com/community/forum/stock-car-racing-history/29209.
13. *Los Angeles Times*, August 10, 1993.
14. *Car and Driver*, August 1971.
15. *National Speed Sport News*, August 5, 1970.
16. Fielden, *Forty Years of Stock Car Racing, Volume 3.*
17. Dave Lockton, interview by author.
18. Dave Lockton, interview by author.
19. Dave Lockton, interview by author.
20. *Los Angeles Times*, February 28, 1971.
21. *Car and Driver*, April 1969.
22. Dave Lockton, interview by author.
23. Ken Clapp, interview by author.
24. Ken Clapp, interview by author.
25. *Los Angeles Times*, August 10, 1993.
26. Karl Ludvigsen, interview by author.
27. *Racing Safety Journal* 1, No. 4 (1970).
28. John Starkey, *Racing with a Difference: The History of IMSA* (Gryfon Publishers, 2001).
29. Mitch Bishop, interview by author.
30. Al Pearce, "How a Brawl Made the 1979 Daytona 500 NASCAR's Greatest Show on TV," *Autoweek*, February 18, 2023, https://www.autoweek.com/racing/nascar/a42957471/.
31. *Autoweek,* May 9, 1970.

32. Helmut Marko, interview by author.
33. *Road & Track*, August 1970.
34. Bob Bondurant, interview by author.
35. Tony Davis, *Jack Brabham: The Untold Story of Formula One* (HarperCollins, 2019).
36. David Hobbs, interview by author.
37. Chuck Cantwell, interview by author.
38. Howden Ganley, *The Road to Monaco: My Life in Motor Racing* (Denley Publications, 2015).
39. Hartmut Lehbrink, *90 Years of Nürburgring: The History of the Famous "Nordschleife"* (Delius Klasing Verlag, 2016).
40. David Tremayne, *The Science of Safety: The Battle Against Unacceptable Risks in Motor Racing* (Haynes, 2000).
41. Emerson Fittipaldi, interview by author.
42. A.J. Foyt, interview by author.

CHAPTER SIXTEEN

1. Mike Lashmett, interview by author.
2. *Autoweek*, January 24, 1970.
3. *Autoweek*, June 5, 1971.
4. Toly Arutunoff, interview by author.
5. *Autoweek*, June 10, 1972.
6. Indianapolis Motor Speedway, "Full Race Broadcast: 1973 Indianapolis 500," YouTube, https://www.youtube.com/watch?v=2udvMANVZeQ.
7. Indianapolis Motor Speedway, "Full Race Broadcast: 1973 Indianapolis 500."
8. *Autosport*, February 14, 1969.
9. John Anderson, interview by author.
10. Mike Lashmett, interview by author.
11. Indianapolis Motor Speedway, "Full Race Broadcast: 1973 Indianapolis 500."
12. Indianapolis Motor Speedway, "Full Race Broadcast: 1973 Indianapolis 500."
13. Mike Lashmett, interview by author.
14. Carl Hungness, *The 1973 Indianapolis 500 Yearbook* (Indy Publications, 1973).
15. Indianapolis Motor Speedway, "Full Race Broadcast: 1973 Indianapolis 500."
16. Dr. Stephen Olvey, *Rapid Response: My Inside Story as a Motor Racing Life-Saver* (Evro Publishing, 2019).
17. *New York Times*, June 1, 1973.
18. Hungness, *The 1973 Indianapolis 500 Yearbook*.
19. *Autoweek*, July 7, 1973.
20. Jacky Ickx, interview by author.
21. *Road & Track*, July 1970.
22. Jackie Stewart and Peter Manso, *Faster! A Racer's Diary* (Farrar, Straus and Giroux, 1972).
23. Yves Morizot, interview by author.
24. Yves Morizot, *Stand 21 50 Anniversary* (pub. by author).
25. *Autoweek*, December 25, 1971.
26. *Autoweek*, November 20, 1971.
27. Louis Stanley, *Grand Prix: The Legendary Years; The Personal Memories of Louis Stanley* (Queen Anne Press, 1994).
28. Stanley, *Grand Prix*.
29. Stanley, *Grand Prix*.
30. David Tremayne, *The Lost Generation: The Battle Against Unacceptable Risks in Motor Racing* (Haynes, 2000).

31. Tremayne, *The Lost Generation.*
32. *Autoweek*, September 8, 1973.
33. *The Scotsman* (UK), August 4, 1973.
34. *Wolverhampton Express & Star* (UK), July 30, 1973.
35. *Autoweek*, October 20, 1973.
36. *Motor Sport*, September 1973.
37. *Lift: The Alumni Magazine of Embry-Riddle Aeronautical University*, Fall 2009.
38. Mike Devin, interview by author.
39. Mike Devin, interview by author.

CODA

1. Herbie Blash, interview by author.
2. John L. Matthews, *Grand Prix: The Killer Years* (Arena Sport, 2016).
3. Jody Scheckter, interview by author.
4. Jody Scheckter, interview by author.
5. Bernie Ecclestone, interview by author.
6. Michael Argetsinger, *Formula One at Watkins Glen: 20 Years of the United States Grand Prix, 1961–1980* (David Bull Publishing, 2011).
7. John Watson, interview by author.
8. Jackie Oliver, interview by author.
9. John Mecom Jr., interview by author.
10. Simon Taylor, interview by author.
11. Dave Lockton, interview by author.
12. Mario Andretti, interview by author.
13. Patrick Duffeler, interview by author.
14. Bernie Ecclestone, interview by author.
15. Bernie Ecclestone, interview by author.
16. Sid Watkins, *Life at the Limit: Triumph and Tragedy in Formula One* (Motorbooks International, 1996).
17. Watkins, *Life at the Limit.*
18. Bernie Ecclestone, interview by author.
19. Hartmut Lehbrink, *90 Years Nürburgring: The History of the Famous "Nordschleife"* (Delius Klasing Verlag, 2016).

BIBLIOGRAPHY

Andretti, Mario, with Bob Collins. *What's It Like Out There?* Henry Regnery Company, 1970.

Argetsinger, Michael. *An American Racer: Bobby Marshman and the Indianapolis 500.* Racemaker Press, 2019.

Argetsinger, Michael. *Formula One at Watkins Glen: 20 Years of the United States Grand Prix, 1961–1980.* David Bull Publishing, 2011.

Argetsinger, Michael. *Mark Donohue: Technical Excellence at Speed.* David Bull, 2009.

Arledge, Roone. *Roone: A Memoir*, HarperCollins, 2003.

Arneson, Erik. *Mickey Thompson: The Fast Life and Tragic Death of a Racing Legend.* MBI, 2008.

Automobile Year: Number 6, 1958–59. Hanover House, 1958.

Bagnall, Art. *Roy Richter: Striving for Excellence.* Art Bagnall Publishing, 1990.

Ball, Adrian. *Grand Prix Accident Survey, 1966–1972.* Jim Clark Foundation, 1975.

Bamsey, Ian. *Lola T70: V8 Coupes; A Technical Appraisal.* Haynes, 1990.

Bell, Derek, with Alan Henry. *Derek Bell: My Racing Life.* Patrick Stephens, 1988.

Berger, Phil, and Larry Borstein. *The Boys of Indy.* Corwin Books, 1977.

Bishop, Mitch, and Mark Raffauf. *IMSA 1969–1989: The Inside Story of How John Bishop Built the World's Greatest Sports Car Racing Series.* Octane Press, 2019.

Boyce, Doug. *Drag Racing's Rebels: How the AHRA Changed Quarter-Mile Competition.* CarTech, 2023.

Brabham, Jack, with Elizabeth Hayward. *When the Flag Drops.* Coward, McCann & Geoghegan, 1971.

Branham, H.A. *Big Bill: The Life and Times of NASCAR Founder Bill France, Sr.* Fenn-M & S, 2015.

Brawner, Clint, with Joe Scalzo. *Indy 500 Mechanic.* Chilton Book Company, 1975.

Bryant, Peter. *Can-Am Challenger: The Cockney F1 Mechanic Who Designed and Built America's Best Can-Am Cars.* David Bull Publishing, 2007.

Cannell, Michael. *The Limit: Life and Death on the 1961 Grand Prix Circuit.* Twelve, 2011.

Chapin, Kim. *Fast as White Lightning: The Story of Stock Car Racing.* Three Rivers Press, 1998.

Chini, Jim. *Tow Money: The History of the United Racing Club.* Rose Racing Publications, 2007.

Cimarosti, Adriano. *The Complete History of Grand Prix Motor Racing.* Crescent Books, 1990.

Clapp, Ken, with Bones Bourcier. *Sea to Shining Sea: Racing from the Wild West to Daytona.* Coastal 181, 2022.

Collings, Timothy. *The Piranha Club.* Virgin, 2001.

Considine, Tim. *American Grand Prix Racing: A Century of Drivers & Cars.* Motorbooks International, 1997.

Cooper-Evans, Michael. *Risk Life, Risk Limb.* Pelham Books, 1968.

Cooper-Evans, Michael. *Rob Walker.* Hazelton Publishing, 1993.

Cox, Michael J. *Masten Gregory: Totally Fearless; Two Decades of Motorsport Through the Spectacles of the Kansas City Flash.* MTCA Creations, 2004.

Crombac, Gérard. *Colin Chapman: The Man and His Cars.* Haynes, 2001.

Daley, Robert. *The Cruel Sport: Grand Prix Racing, 1959–1967.* Motorbooks, 2005.

Davidson, Donald, and Rick Shaffer. *Autocourse Official History of the Indianapolis 500.* Icon Publishing, 2013.

Davis, Tony. *Brabham: The Untold Story of Formula One.* HarperCollins, 2019.

Del Arco, Javier. *40 Years of Motor Racing History at the Park Circuit of Montjuïc.* RACC Club, 2000.

Deschenaux, Jacques. *Jo Siffert.* W. Kimber, 1972.

Donohue, Mark, with Paul Van Valkenburgh. *The Unfair Advantage.* Bentley Publishers, 2000.

Dymock, Eric. *Jim Clark: Racing Legend.* MBI, 2003.

Edelstein, Robert. *Full Throttle: The Life and Fast Times of NASCAR Legend Curtis Turner.* Abrams Books, 2006.

Edwards, Guy. *Sponsorship and the World of Motor Racing.* Hazelton, 1992.

Elford, Vic. *Vic Elford: Reflections on a Golden Era in Motorsports.* David Bull Publishing, 2006.

Ellison, Betty Boles. *The Early Laps of Stock Car Racing: A History of the Sport and Business through 1974.* McFarland & Company, 2014.

Falconer, Richard, and Doug Nye. *Chaparral.* Motorbooks International, 1992.

Ferguson, Andrew. *Team Lotus: The Indianapolis Years.* Patrick Stephens, 1996.

Fetherston, David. *Heroes of Hot Rodding.* Motorbooks International, 1992.

Fielden, Greg. *Forty Years of Stock Car Racing, Volume 2: The Superspeedway Boom, 1959–1964.* Galfield Press, 1989.

Fielden, Greg. *Forty Years of Stock Car Racing, Volume 3: Big Bucks and Boycotts, 1965–1971.* Galfield Press, 1989.

Fielden, Greg. *Forty Years of Stock Car Racing, Volume 4: The Modern Era, 1972–1989.* Galfield Press, 1990.

Fittipaldi, Emerson, with Elizabeth Hayward. *Flying on the Ground.* W. Kimber, 1973.

Foyt, A.J., with William Neely. *A.J.: The Life of America's Greatest Race Car Driver.* Times Books, 1983.

Fox, Jack C. *The Illustrated History of the Indianapolis 500.* Carl Hungness Publishing, 1967.

Fox, Jack C. *The Illustrated History of Sprint Car Racing.* Carl Hungness Publishing, 1985.

Friedman, Dave. *Remembering the Shelby Years—1962–1969.* Carroll Shelby Children's Foundation, 1998.

Gabbard, Alex. *Indy's Wildest Decade: Innovation and Revolution at the Brickyard.* CarTech, 2004.

Ganley, Howden. *The Road to Monaco: My Life in Motor Racing.* Denley Publications, 2015.

Garlits, Don, with Brock Yates. *King of the Dragsters: The Story of Big Daddy "Don" Garlits.* Chilton Book Company, 1970.

Garner, Art. *A.J. Foyt: Survivor, Champion, Legend.* Octane Press, 2024.

Garner, Art. *Black Noon: The Year They Stopped the Indy 500.* Thomas Dunne Books, 2014.

Garrett, Richard. *Fast and Furious: The Story of the World Championship of Drivers.* Arco Publishing, 1968.

Gates, Bob. *Hurtubise.* Witness Productions, 1995.

Girdler, Allan. *Stock Car Racers: The History and Folklore of NASCAR's Premier Series: Tail Straight Out and Belly to the Ground* . Motorbooks International, 1988.

Granatelli, Anthony. *They Call Me Mr. 500.* Copp, Clark, 1969.

Hallé, Jean Claude. *François Cevert: A Contract with Death.* W. Kimber, 1975.

Hamilton, Maurice. *British Grand Prix.* Crowood Press, 1989.

Hamilton, Maurice. *Frank Williams.* Macmillan, 1998.

Henderson, Michael. *Motor Racing in Safety: The Human Factors.* Patrick Stephens, 1968.

Henny, Phil. *Dan Gurney: Nostalgie.* Editions Cotty, 2018.

Henry, Alan. *Brabham: The Grand Prix Cars.* Hazelton, 1985.

Henry, Alan. *Ferrari: The Grand Prix Cars.* Hazelton, 1989.

Henry, Alan. *Jochen Rindt.* Hazelton, 1990.

Henry, Alan. *March: The Grand Prix & Indy Cars.* Hazelton, 1989.

Henry, Alan. *Niki Lauda.* Hazelton, 1989.

Henry, Alan. *The Power Brokers: The Inside Track on the Controllers of Formula 1.* Haynes, 2003.

Henry, Alan. *Ronnie Peterson: Grand Prix Racing Driver; The Story of a Search for Perfection.* Foulis, 1975.

Henry, Alan. *Williams: The Business of Grand Prix Racing.* Patrick Stephens, 1992.

Hobbs, David, and Andrew Marriott. *Hobbo: Motor Racer, Motor Mouth; The Autobiography of David Hobbs.* Evro Publishing, 2018.

Horsman, John. *Racing in the Rain: My Years with Brilliant Drivers, Legendary Sports Cars, and a Dedicated Team.* David Bull Publishing, 2006.

Hungness, Carl. *The 1973 Indianapolis 500 Yearbook.* Indy Publications, 1973.

Huntington, Roger. *Design & Development of the Indy Car.* H.P. Books, 1981.

Jarrott, Charles. *Ten Years of Motors and Motor Racing.* Foulis, 1956.

Jenkins, Richard. *Tyrrell: The Story of the Tyrrell Racing Organisation.* Evro Publishing, 2023.

Jenkinson, Denis. *The Racing Driver: The Theory and Practice of Fast Driving.* Robert Bentley, 1959.

Kael, Pauline. *Kiss Kiss, Bang Bang.* Bantam Books, 1969.

Kelly, Godwin. *Fireball: An Unauthorized Biography.* Carbon Press, 2005.

Kerr, Phil. *To Finish First.* MRP, 2008.

Kettlewell, Mike. *Autocourse: International Motor Racing and Rallying 1972–73.* Haymarket Publishing, 1973.

Kettlewell, Mike. *Autocourse: International Motor Racing and Rallying 1973–74.* Haymarket Publishing, 1974.

Keyser, Michael. *The Speed Merchants.* Prentice-Hall, 1973.

Kirby, Gordon. *Boost! Roger Bailey's Extraordinary Motor Racing Career.* Racemaker Press, 2022.

Kirby, Gordon. *Jim McGee: Crew Chief of Champions.* Racemaker Press, 2014.

Kirby, Gordon. *Mario Andretti: A Driving Passion.* David Bull Publishing, 2001.

Kirby, Gordon. *Unser: An American Family Portrait.* Anlon Press, 1988.

Lang, Mike. *Grand Prix! Volume 2: 1966–1973.* Haynes, 1992.

Lauda, Niki. *Niki Lauda, Meine Story*. Orac, 1985.
Lawrence, Mike. *The Story of March*. Aston, 1989.
Lehbrink, Hartmut. *90 Years Nürburgring: The History of the Famous "Nordschleife."* Delius Klasing Verlag, 2016.
Lehto, Steve. *Dodge Daytona & Plymouth Superbird: Design, Development, Production and Competition*. CarTech, 2020.
Lerner, Preston. *Ford GT: How Ford Silenced the Critics, Humbled Ferrari and Conquered Le Mans*. Motorbooks, 2015.
Lerner, Preston. *Scarab: Race Log of the All-American Specials, 1957–1965*. Motorbooks International, 1991.
Lerner, Preston. *Shelby American: The Renegades Who Built the Cars, Won the Races, and Lived the Legend*. Octane Press, 2020.
Levine, Leo. *Ford: The Dust and the Glory; A Racing History*. Macmillan, 1968.
Levy, George. *Can-Am 50th Anniversary: Flat Out with North America's Greatest Race Series 1966–74*. Motorbooks, 2016.
Levy, George. *Texas Legend: Jim Hall and His Chaparrals*. Evro Publishing, 2024.
Libby, Bill. *The Coaches*. Regnery, 1972.
Libby, Bill. *Parnelli: A Story of Auto Racing*. Dutton, 1969.
Lovell, Terry. *Bernie's Game: Inside the Formula One World of Bernie Ecclestone*. Metro, 2003.
Ludvigsen, Karl. *Group 7: The World's Most Powerful Road Racing Cars*. World Publishing Company, 1971.
Ludvigsen, Karl. *Gurney's Eagles: The Exciting Story of the AAR Racing Cars*. Motorbooks International, 1976.
Ludvigsen, Karl. *Indy Cars of the 1960s*. Iconografix, 2001.
Ludvigsen, Karl. *Indy Cars of the 1970s*. Iconografix, 2003.
Lyons, Pete. *Can-Am*. Motorbooks International, 1995.
Lyons, Pete. *Shadow: The Magnificent Machines of a Man of Mystery; Can-Am, Formula 1, F5000*. Evro, 2020.
Madigan, Tom. *Boss: The Bill Stroppe Story*. Darwin Publications, 1984.
Madigan, Tom. *Follmer: American Wheel Man*. Ejje Publishing Group, 2013.
Madigan, Tom. *Snake vs. Mongoose: How a Rivalry Changed Drag Racing Forever*. Motorbooks, 2009.
Mandel, Leon, and Peter Revson. *Speed With Style: The Autobiography of Peter Revson*. Doubleday, 1974.
Manso, Peter. *Vroom: Conversations with the Grand Prix Champions*. Pitman, 1970.
Matthews, John L. *Grand Prix: The Killer Years*. Arena Sport, 2016.
Miller, Denny: *Eddie Sachs, the Crown Prince of Racing: The Life and Times of the World's Greatest Race Driver*. AuthorHouse, 2005.
Moriarty, Frank. *Supercars: The Story of the Dodge Charger Daytona and Plymouth Superbird*. Howell Press, 1995.
Morizot, Yves. *Stand 21 50 Anniversary*. Published by the author.
Morton, John. *Inside Shelby American: Wrenching and Racing with Carroll Shelby in the 1960s*. Motorbooks, 2013.
Mosley, Max. *Formula One and Beyond: The Autobiography*. Simon & Schuster, 2015.
Moss, Stirling, with Ken Purdy. *All But My Life*. W. Kimber, 1963.
Neely, William. *Tire Wars: Racing With Goodyear*. Aztex Corporation, 1993.
Nye, Doug. *The Autocourse History of the Grand Prix Car 1945–65*. Hazelton, 1993.
Nye, Doug. *The Autocourse History of the Grand Prix Car 1966–85*. Hazelton, 1986.
Nye, Doug. *Cooper Cars*. Osprey, 1983.
Nye, Doug. *McLaren: The Grand Prix, Can-Am and Indy Cars*. Hazelton, 1984.

Nye, Doug. *Theme Lotus*. Motor Racing Publications, 1978.
Oliver, Michael. *Lotus 49: The Story of a Legend*. Veloce, 1999.
Oliver, Michael. *Lotus 72: Formula One Icon*. Coterie Press Limited, 2003.
Olvey, Dr. Stephen. *Rapid Response: My Inside Story as a Motor Racing Life-Saver*. Evro Publishing, 2019.
O'Reilly, Maurice. *The Goodyear Story*. Benjamin Company, 1983.
Petty, Richard, with Bill Libby. *"King Richard": The Richard Petty Story*. Doubleday, 1977.
Petty, Richard, with William Neely. *Grand National: The Autobiography of Richard Petty as Told to Bill Neely*. Regnery, 1971.
Pierce, Daniel S. *Real NASCAR: White Lightning, Red Clay, and Big Bill France*. The University of North Carolina Press, 2010.
Phipps, David. *Autocourse: International Motor Racing and Rallying 1968–69*. Haymarket Press, 1969.
Phipps, David. *Autocourse: International Motor Racing and Rallying 1969–70*. Haymarket Press, 1970.
Phipps, David. *Autocourse: International Motor Racing and Rallying 1970–71*. Haymarket Press, 1971.
Phipps, David. *Autocourse: International Motor Racing and Rallying 1971–72*. Haymarket Press, 1972.
Phipps, David. *Autocourse Review of International Motor Sport, 1966–67*. Haymarket Press, 1967.
Phipps, David. *Autocourse Review of International Motor Sport, 1967–68*. Haymarket Press, 1967.
Posey, Sam. *Where the Writer Meets the Road: A Collection of Articles, Broadcast Intros, and Profiles*. Phoenix: David Bull Publishing, 2015.
Posey, Sam. *The Mudge Pond Express*. Putnam, 1976.
Posey, Sam. *Sam's Scrapbook: My Motorsports Memories*. Evro Publishing, 2021.
Post, Robert C. *High Performance: The Culture and Technology of Drag Racing, 1950–2000*. Johns Hopkins University Press, 2001.
Prudhomme, Don, with Elana Scherr. *Don The Snake Prudhomme: My Life Beyond the 1320*. CarTech, 2020.
Purdy, Ken W. *Ken Purdy's Wonderful World of the Automobile*. Crowell, 1963.
Redman, Brian, with Jim Mullen. *Brian Redman: Daring Drivers, Deadly Tracks*. Evro Publishing, 2016.
Rendall, Ivan. *The Power Game: The History of Formula 1 and the World Championship*. Cassell & Company, 2000.
Robson, Graham. *Cosworth*. Patrick Stephens, 1995.
Rodengen, Jeffrey L. *The Legend of Goodyear: The First 100 Years*. Write Stuff Syndicate, 1997.
Rose, Buzz. *California Hot Shoes: CRA Sprint Cars 1955–1970—Volume 1*. Rose Racing Publications, 2003.
Rosinski, José. *Automobile Year 1973/74*. Edita Lausanne, 1974.
Rosinski, José. *Formula 1 Racing: The Modern Era*. Madison Square Press, 1973.
Rudd, Tony. *It Was Fun! My Fifty Years of High Performance*. Haynes, 2000.
Rudlin, Tony. *Mr. Monaco: Graham Hill Remembered*. Patrick Stephens, 1983.
Rutherford, Johnny, with David Craft. *Lone Star J.R.: The Autobiography of Racing Legend Johnny Rutherford*. Triumph Books, 2000.
Scalzo, Joe. *The American Dirt Track Racer*. MBI, 2001.
Scalzo, Joe. *Indianapolis Roadsters, 1952–1964*. MBI, 1999.
Scalzo, Joe. *Stand On the Gas! Sprint Car Racing in America*. Prentice-Hall, 1974.

Scheckter, Jody. *Jody: An Autobiography*. Keartland, 1976.
Setright, LJK. *The Grand Prix, 1906 to 1972*. Norton, 1973.
Shirley, Phil. *Deadly Obsessions: Life and Death in Motor Racing*. HarperCollins, 2000.
Simon, Ted. *Grand Prix Year*. Coward, McCann & Geoghegan, 1971.
Simpson, Bill, with Bones Bourcier. *Racing Safely, Living Dangerously: The Hard Life and Fast Times of a Motorsports Mogul*. Performance Media, 2001.
Stanley, Louis. *Grand Prix: The Legendary Years: The Personal Memories of Louis Stanley*. Queen Anne Press, 1994.
Stanley, Louis. *Grand Prix 10*. David McKay, 1969.
Stanley, Louis. *Strictly Off the Record: Grand Prix Controversy and Intrigue*. Salamander, 1999.
Starkey, John. *Racing with a Difference: The History of IMSA*. Gryfon Publishers, 2001.
Stewart. Jackie. *Winning Is Not Enough*. Headline, 2007.
Stewart, Jackie, with Peter Manso *Faster! A Racer's Diary*. Farrar, Straus and Giroux, 1972.
Sugar, Bert. *"The Thrill of Victory": The Inside Story of ABC Sports*. Hawthorn Books, 1978.
Surtees, John. *John Surtees, World Champion*. Hazelton, 1991.
Thompson, Neal. *Driving with the Devil: Southern Moonshine, Detroit Wheels, and the Birth of NASCAR*. Crown Publishers, 2006.
Tipler, John. *Ronnie Peterson Formula One: Super Swede*. Coterie Press, 2003.
Tremayne, David. *The Lost Generation: The Brilliant but Tragic Lives of Rising British F1 Stars Roger Williamson, Tony Brise and Tom Pryce*. Haynes, 2009.
Tremayne, David. *The Science of Safety: The Battle Against Unacceptable Risks in Motor Racing*. Haynes, 2000.
Van Valkenburgh, Paul. *Chevrolet = Racing? Fourteen Years of Raucous Silence!* Walter R. Haessner and Associates, 1972.
Vollstedt, Rolla, Chris Economaki, and Ralph Zbarsky. *Vollstedt: From Track Roadster to Indy Cars; The Rolla Vollstedt Story*. Vancouver, ZED Engineering, 2003.
Wagstaff, Ian. *Formula 1's Unsung Pioneers: The Story of the British Racing Partnership and How It Launched . . . Motorsport into the Modern Era*. Evro Publishing, 2022.
Wallen, Dick, and Michael Jordan. *Roar from the Sixties: American Championship Racing*. Ben Franklin Press, 1997.
Wallen, Dick, and Michael Jordan *Seventies Championship Revolution: American Racing Championships*. Dick Wallen Productions, 2003.
Watkins, Sid. *Life at the Limit: Triumph and Tragedy in Formula One*. Motorbooks International, 1996.
Watkins, Susan. *Bernie: The Biography of Bernie Ecclestone*. Haynes, 2011.
Wheeler, Humpy, with Peter Golenbock. *Growing Up NASCAR: Racing's Most Outrageous Promoter Tells All*. MBI, 2010.
White, Gordon Eliot. *Offenhauser*. Motorbooks International, 1996.
Wilker, Josh, and G. S. Prentzas. *A.J. Foyt*. Chelsea House Publishers, 2007.
Wilkinson, Sylvia. *Dirt Tracks to Glory: The Early Days of Stock Car Racing As Told by the Participants*. Algonquin Books, 1983.
Wilkinson, Sylvia. *The Stainless Steel Carrot: An Auto Racing Odyssey—Revisited*. Carrara Media, 2021.
Woerner, Ted. *Savage Angel: Death and Rebirth at the Indianapolis 500*. Savage42, 2021.
Yost, Mark. *The 200-MPH Billboard: The Inside Story of How Big Money Changed NASCAR*. MBI, 2007.
Young, Eoin S. *Forza Amon! A Biography of Chris Amon*. HarperSports, 2003.
Young, Eoin S. *It Beats Working: My 35 Years Inside Motor Racing*. Patrick Stephens, 1996.

Young, Eoin S. *McLaren! The Man, the Cars & the Team*. Bond, Parkhurst Publications, 1971.
Yunick, Smokey. *Best Damn Garage in Town: My Life & Adventures*. Carbon Press 2004.

There are hundreds, if not thousands, of websites devoted to various aspects of racing. So much fine work is being done by so many people that I hesitate to call out a few of them for fear of inadvertently leaving out others worthy of attention. But these websites were particularly helpful to me in providing historical data that would have taken months, if not years, to find by using tools such as books and magazines.

- Motorsportmemorial.org
- F1.fandom.com
- Racingsportscars.com
- Racing-reference.info
- Ultimateracinghistory.com
- Oldracingcars.com
- NHRA.com (Phil Burgess)
- Forums.autosport.com (The Nostalgia Forum)
- Jalopyjournal.com (The Hokey Ass Message Board, aka H.A.M.B.)
- 8w.forix.com
- Doctorindy.com

INDEX

Page references in italics indicate images.

ARTURO MERZARIO
SANDRO MUNARI
3
KONI
FERODO